**COLLECTIVE CLIENTELISM**
**The Lomé Conventions and North-South Relations**

The Political Economy of International Change
John Gerard Ruggie, General Editor

ACP COUNTRIES

LOMÉ CONVENTION

TUNISIA

MOROCCO

CANARY IS.

WESTERN
SAHARA

ALGERIA

LIBYA

EGYPT

CAPE
VERDE

MAURITANIA

MALI

NIGER

CHAD

SUDAN

DJIBOUTI

SENEGAL
GAMBIA

GUINEA
BISSAU

GUINEA

NIGERIA

CENTRAL AFRICAN
REP.

ETHIOPIA

SIERRA
LEONE

LIBERIA

IVORY
COAST

UPPER
VOLTA

GHANA

BENIN

TOGO

SAO TOME
PRINCIPÉ

EQUATORIAL
GUINEA

CAMEROON

GABON

CONGO

ZAÏRE

UGANDA
KENYA

SOMALIA

SEYCHELLES

RWANDA
BURUNDI

MALAWI

TANZANIA

COMOROS

ANGOLA

ZAMBIA

MOZAMBIQUE

MADAGASCAR

NAMIBIA

REP. OF
SOUTH
AFRICA

ZIMBABWE

SWAZILAND

BOTSWANA

LESOTHO

MAURI-
TIUS

BAHAMAS

BELIZE

JAMAICA

• Antigua and
  Barbuda
• Dominica
• St Lucia
• Barbados
• Grenada
• St Vincent and
  Grenadines
• Trinidad and
  Tobago

GUYANA

SURINAM

SOLOMON ISLANDS

KIRIBATI

TUVALU

PAPUA
NEW
GUINEA

VANUATU

WESTERN
SAMOA

FIJI

TONGA

# COLLECTIVE CLIENTELISM
## The Lomé Conventions and North-South Relations

*John Ravenhill*

Columbia University Press
New York   1985

Library of Congress Cataloging in Publication Data

Ravenhill, John.
  Collective clientelism.

  (The Political economy of international change)
  Includes bibliographical references and index.
    1. European Economic Community—Developing
countries.   2. Lomé Convention (1975)   3. Lomé Conven-
tion (1979)   I. Title.   II. Series.
HC241.25.D44R38   1985      337.40172′4   84-17674
ISBN 0-231-05804-7 (alk. paper)


Columbia University Press
New York   Guildford, Surrey
Copyright © 1985 Columbia University Press
All rights reserved

Printed in the United States of America


Clothbound editions of Columbia University Press Books are Smyth-sewn
and printed on permanent and durable acid-free paper.


Book design by Ken Venezio.

*For M.S.W.*

# Contents

# Figures

# Tables

# List of Abbreviations

| | |
|---|---|
| AASM | Associated African and Malagasy States |
| ACP | African, Caribbean and Pacific signatories to the Lomé Convention |
| BSC | British Sugar Corporation |
| BTN | Brussels Tariff Nomenclature |
| CAP | Common Agricultural Policy |
| CARICOM | Caribbean Common Market |
| CCCN | Customs Cooperation Council Nomenclature (formerly the BTN) |
| CET | Common External Tariff |
| CFA | African Financial Community (formerly the French African Colonies) |
| CID | Centre for Industrial Development |
| COREPER | Committee of Permanent Representatives |
| CSA | Commonwealth Sugar Agreement |
| DAC | Development Assistance Committee (OECD) |
| DOM | Overseas Departments (France) |
| EAMA | Associated African and Malagasy States |
| ECA | (U.N.) Economic Commission for Africa |
| ECOWAS | Economic Community of West African States |
| EEC | European Economic Community |

| EDF | European Development Fund |
| EFTA | European Free Trade Area |
| EIB | European Investment Bank |
| FED | European Development Fund |
| FEOGA | Agricultural Guarantee and Guidance Fund |
| GATT | General Agreement on Tariffs and Trade |
| G77 | Group of 77 |
| GSP | Generalized System of Preferences |
| IBRD | World Bank |
| IDA | International Development Association |
| ISA | International Sugar Agreement |
| LDC | Less Developed Country |
| LLIC | Least Developed, Landlocked and Island Countries |
| MFA | Multifibre Arrangement |
| MFN | Most Favored Nation |
| MUA | Million Units of Account (see UA) |
| NICs | Newly Industrializing Countries |
| NIEO | New International Economic Order |
| OAU | Organization of African Unity |
| ODA | Overseas Development Assistance |
| ODI | Overseas Development Institute (London) |
| OECD | Organisation for Economic Cooperation and Development |
| OPEC | Organisation of Petroleum Exporting Countries |
| SADCC | Southern African Development Coordination Conference |
| SITC | Standard International Trade Classification |

STABEX    System for the Stabilization of Export Earnings

SYSMIN    System for the Promotion of Mineral Production and Exports

TNC       Transnational Corporation

ua        Unit of account. Until 1977 the unit of account was the monetary unit of the EEC budget, equal to 0.889 grams of gold ($1 U.S. in the Bretton Woods period). From 1978 to 1980 the budgetary unit was the European Unit of Account (EUA) whose value was determined by a basket of currencies of the EEC member states. In January 1981 the EUA was replaced by the European Currency Unit (ECU) based on a basket of national currencies whose composition and weight was the same as the EUA. Since for accounting purposes the EEC holds 1 ua to be equal to 1 EUA = 1 ECU, the single abbreviation, ua, is used throughout this study to avoid unnecessary complication.

UNCTAD    United Nations Conference on Trade and Development

# Preface

Strategies less developed countries might pursue in their efforts to reduce their vulnerabilities in international economic relations have long held a major interest for international relations scholars. Attention in the 1970s was focused primarily on two new developments: the success of the Group of 77 in elevating proposals for a New International Economic Order to a position of prominence on the agendas of international organizations; and the emergence of a group of Newly Industrializing Countries [NICs] which has acquired not only the manufacturing capacity to penetrate the markets of the industrialized world, but also the bureaucratic capacity to bargain effectively in bilateral and multilateral negotiations. While the NICs have continued to enjoy impressive rates of economic growth despite the New Protectionism, the results of the global dialogue on restructuring the international economic order have been disappointing. Even before the stalemate in global negotiations became obvious, it was evident that few of the proposed reforms of international economic regimes would hold much interest for the poorest of the developing countries.

Unable to take effective unilateral action to reduce their vulnerabilities, and unlikely to be significant beneficiaries of reforms at the global level, least developed countries sought other means of increasing the benefits from their external economic relations. This book examines one such strategy (which I term "collective clientelism"): the attempt by a group of African, Caribbean, and Pacific countries to capitalize on their traditional links with the European Community to establish a relationship that would provide them with exclusive benefits. This they hoped to achieve through the Lomé Conventions, the first of which was signed in 1975. At the time of its signature, the first Convention generated considerable interest as the most comprehensive international agreement between groups of developed and developing countries; its more enthusiastic proponents proclaimed it to be a model for the new international economic order. A principal objective of this book is to examine why the Convention has failed to live up to the high expectations that many held for it.

This book had its origins in a doctoral dissertation for the University of California at Berkeley. I was particularly fortunate in having a dissertation committee—Ernst B. Haas, Bent Hansen, Robert M. Price, and Carl G. Rosberg—who have not only been invaluable advisers but good friends also. I could not have hoped for a more supportive chairman than Ernie Haas, whose prompt, constructive comments on successive drafts were much appreciated. Significant changes were made in revising the dissertation for publication. New introductory and concluding chapters were written and chapters 3 through 8 were substantially revised to incorporate more recent data. In revising the manuscript I have greatly benefited from comments on draft chapters by Andrew W. Axline, Thomas M. Callaghy, Graeme Gill, Stephan Haggard, Gerald K. Helleiner, Miles Kahler, Peter J. Katzenstein, Stephen D. Krasner, Donald Rothchild, John Gerard Ruggie, and Fred Teiwes. Responsibility for any errors of interpretation or fact remains mine alone.

Generous financial support from the University of California, Berkeley, and the Institute for the Study of World Politics, New York, enabled me to make research trips to Brussels in 1979 and 1980. Revision of the manuscript was facilitated by a University Research Grant from the University of Sydney. William Forwood of the Canberra Delegation of the Commission of the European Communities kindly arranged a visit to the European Commission in January 1984. Barbara Sloan of the Commission delegation in Washington, and Peter Juhler and his staff in the Canberra delegation, went to extraordinary lengths to obtain often obscure documents for me. Research assistance was provided by David Church, Fitzgerald Sarramegna, Sue Jackson, Joseph Kechichian, Peter McEvoy, and Paul Veazey. Ravi Thomas made an invaluable contribution to the computations performed for chapter 5. This chapter is a product of fruitful collaboration with Professor Joanna Moss of San Francisco State University. Nancy van Duren, Debbie Hurd, and Martha Rucker typed some of the tables. Most of the other typing was my own. Rita Devine and Judith Scholfield of the Word-Processing Office at the University of Sydney produced the final version of the manuscript.

Numerous officials of the ACP Group, the European Commission, the Council of Ministers, and countries participating in the Convention kindly made themselves available for interview and shared a number of unpublished documents with me. The necessity for anonymity precludes a general listing of names; I would like to acknowledge, however, the particular contribution made by Edwin Carrington, Deputy Secretary-General of the ACP Secretariat, who went out of his way to encourage me and make me feel at home in the sometimes hostile environment of Brussels. Kaye Whiteman and Pierre Cros of the Press and Information Service of the Commission's Development Directorate provided me with desk space during my 1979 visit.

Any study of an ongoing relationship is a potential victim of the time that it takes for international organizations to publish statistical data. In finalizing revisions to the manuscript in early 1984, I was able to include data for 1981 and, also in some instances, for 1982. The patterns of trade and aid relations under the Convention are now well established and unlikely to change in other than a marginal way by the time the book appears in print. I follow the preference of the EEC itself in referring to it as the European Community. Since the analysis is generally for the period before the accession of Greece to the Community, I use EEC, member states, and the "Nine" interchangably. Enlargement of the Community in this study thus refers to the first enlargement when Denmark, Ireland, and the United Kingdom joined the original six member states. Since the principal sources for the study are documented extensively in the footnotes, an additional bibliography appeared superfluous.

A first book is an appropriate occasion to acknowledge all those who have encouraged and supported the early stages of my academic career. First, my parents, who sacrificed much to give me the opportunity for further education. Lena and Norman King, L. H. Nichols, J. M. Jones, David Rubinstein, Tim Shaw, John and Joanne Lovell, Jeanne Wilson and Rocky Shwedel, Bernie Morris, Dick Stryker, and Ken Jowitt all contributed in one way or another to this enterprise. Special thanks go to my former colleagues at the University of Virginia and their spouses— Larry and Lesley Rose, Larry Sabato, Paul Light and Margo Hauk, and Bob and Debbie Roberts. Finally, Stefa, to whom this book is dedicated, participated in this work at all of its stages and at times neglected her own dissertation in order to assist me with mine.

John Ravenhill

Sydney, January 1985

**COLLECTIVE CLIENTELISM**
**The Lomé Conventions and North-South Relations**

# Introduction

"A major turning point in the history of international economic relations in the second half of the twentieth century—in fact, in history itself"; "one of the greatest achievements of the Commission in Brussels"; "an agreement unique in history and unique in the world"; "revolutionary".[1] Such was the acclamation that greeted the signature of the Lomé Convention in 1975. The Convention, a multilateral treaty negotiated originally between the nine members of the European Community and 46 developing countries from Africa, the Caribbean, and the Pacific (the ACP Group), includes provisions for cooperation in the fields of trade, aid, investment, industry, and the stabilization of ACP earnings from commodity exports.[2] In short, the Convention deals, on a regional basis, with many of the principal issues in the North-South dialogue. Its signature at a time when little progress was evident in the global dialogue prompted claims that it served "to establish a new model for relations between developed and developing states, compatible with the aspirations of the international community towards a more just and more balanced economic order."[3] In a similar vein, Richard Falk wrote that Lomé represented "the most ambitious North-South experiment in international economic cooperation yet to be made."[4]

Within four years, however, the Lomé relationship had become little less than acrimonious; it would have been difficult indeed to find a representative from either the Community or the ACP Group that continued to regard the Convention as a model for a new economic order. While some of the sentiments expressed above can be attributed to the euphoria that surrounded the successful conclusion of the agreement, there can be few arguments with the proposition that the Convention aroused high expectations that subsequently have not been fulfilled. One of the aims of this book is to explain why this was the case.

On one matter, the quotations above are undoubtedly correct. Lomé is unique. Its coverage of a wide range of issue areas differentiates it from narrow functional arrangements such as the Generalized Systems of Preferences or the Multifiber Arrangement; on the other hand, its "regional" nature distinguishes it from the various North-South arrangements conducted within the universal framework of the United Nations and its subsidiary organizations. This sui generis nature of Lomé is what makes it of particular interest and yet, at the same time, peculiarly difficult to conceptualize.

Typically, Lomé has been viewed within the framework of dependency theory, which over the last decade has become the dominant metaphor in the discussion of North-South relations.[5] While this perspective has provided a useful reminder of the structural constraints that the international system places on its weaker members, I have not found it particularly useful in explaining some of the more interesting issues that arise in a study of the Convention, in particular the reasons why the ACP Group entered the relationship, the type of arrangements they sought, and why they have failed to achieve their aspirations. Writers in the dependency tradition have criticized the Convention as neocolonial for its promotion of European interests and for its failure to transform the economies of the ACP states. That the European Community would use the Convention to attempt to preserve and promote its interests in ACP countries is hardly a significant revelation and need not necessarily preclude advantage to the ACP themselves. The very composition of the ACP Group makes Lomé a "neocolonial" arrangement in the sense that the vast majority of the ACP Group are former colonies of one or more EEC member state. Similarly, little insight is gained by criticizing the Convention for failing to bring about a radical transformation of the economies of the ACP states. Lomé, but one of many factors weighing on ACP economies, cannot itself magically engineer interdependence between such unequal parties in a short period of time; change, at best, will occur in an incremental fashion. As Green has argued cogently, writings on the Convention from a dependency perspective too often mistake cause and effect: Lomé largely reflects the inequalities of the international economic system rather than being a significant cause of them.[6]

Among the principal weaknesses of the dependency approach are its tendency to treat less developed countries (LDCs) in an undifferentiated manner, ignoring the great disparities that exist between their capacities for taking advantage of opportunities arising from the evolution of the global economy; an inordinate emphasis on structural constraints, which causes insufficient attention to be paid to the opportunities for constructive action in support of change;[7] and a discounting of the prospects for mutual gain from relations with the industrialized world. An alternative approach is suggested in chapter 1: to conceive of Lomé as a form of clientelist relationship—an attempt by weak states to construct a particularistic arrangement that would preserve their position in the EEC market and provide insurance against the insecurities of the marketplace. Weakness constrains choice. ACP countries, among the weakest in the world, have few viable options available to them in their efforts to overcome the constraints imposed by their economic weakness. Collaboration with their most important economic partner, the EEC, was a rational response to their predicament. "Collective clientelism" thus represents a type of associative strategy—but one which differs on some significant dimensions from "associated dependent development."

The concept of collective clientelism developed in chapter 1 is primarily a heuristic device whose value will be determined by its descriptive and explanatory power. I shall suggest that the concept facilitates an understanding of why Commonwealth states that had long been hostile to the EEC opted for the Lomé relationship, the particular issues covered by the Convention itself, the types of demand that the ACP made for its improvement, and ultimately, the inherent contradictions in the strategy that caused its failure to realize the anticipated benefits.

A major advantage to the clientelist literature is its demonstration, contrary to the assertions of some dependency writers, that vertical ties between unequal parties are not inevitably exploitative. Clientelism involves the exchange of noncomparable resources, e.g., votes for economic favors, such that the weaker party may be the principal beneficiary from the exchange of *economic* resources in the relationship. This was certainly the aspiration of the ACP Group in entering the Lomé partnership: they sought a variety of material benefits and expected to provide little by way of reciprocity. A major part of this book examines what success the ACP Group enjoyed in pursuing this strategy. The approach adopted views the relationship from the bottom up, the perspective of the clients in the Convention.

Whereas EEC and ACP interests coincided in their desire to reach an agreement, they diverged on the form an agreement should take. For the ACP the essence of collective clientelism was to reach an agreement that would guarantee their position by placing constraints on the autonomy of European policymaking on issues of vital interest to them. Community member states on the contrary sought an agreement that would enable them to preserve their position in ACP states at low cost—in terms of resources transferred, damage to domestic interests, and constraints on foreign economic policy decision-making. Inevitably, to satisfy both parties, the Convention contained numerous ambiguities regarding their respective responsibilities. And equally inevitably, this produced divergent interpretations of the Convention.

In 1975 the ACP Group believed that its strategy of collective clientelism had been successful in constructing an equal partnership whose contractual nature guaranteed their position in the European market and that the EEC in its role of patron would safeguard their interests where these were not specifically protected by provisions in the Convention. In reality, as chapters 3 through 8 (which discuss the principal provisions of the Convention—commodities earnings stabilization, cooperation in the fields of trade, industry, and aid) demonstrate, the contract the ACP had negotiated was riddled with loopholes. These had the effect of removing the constraints on the autonomy of EEC action that the ACP believed had been successfully negotiated. Nothing in the relationship proved to be guaranteed. Accordingly, the benefits that the Convention produced fell far short of expectations. And inevitably, given the lack of reciprocity and different vulnerabilities of the parties, the much-vaunted equality of the partnership proved illusory.

Chapter 9 discusses why the Lomé Convention fell far short of expectations. Here the concept of collective clientelism is particularly useful in understanding why the very nature of the relationship itself inhibited attempts by the ACP Group to bargain effectively with its partner and why the particular type of relationship to which the Group aspired was unacceptable to the EEC. Lomé may survive—since it continues to produce tangible benefits for many of its parties—but in a form far removed from the model of a new economic order that the ACP had in mind in 1975.

# 1

# Collective Clientelism

With the delinking of the dollar from gold in August 1971, the international economic system entered a new era of turbulence.[1] Less developed countries (LDCs) were simultaneously the principal beneficiaries and principal victims of the new international economic disorder: beneficiaries in that the weakening of prevailing rules and norms of international economic relations enabled them to challenge the existing distribution of gains from international economic intercourse; victims in that the selective exceptions to the liberal trade order imposed by industrialized countries occurred primarily at their expense.

Growing instability and complexity in the international economic order offered a variety of new opportunities to LDCs. These arose from the manner in which international economic relations had become politicized. The "two-track" system whereby trade issues had been largely kept off the political agenda in the postwar years was disrupted, first as a result of the growing U.S. trade deficit, second, as the more advanced LDCs increasingly penetrated the domestic markets of traditional sectors in the industrialized world. Politicization of international economic relations was the outcome of governments' attempts to minimize the costs of the growing sensitivity of economic exchange. As the need for a major overhaul of international economic institutions became increasingly obvious and uncertainty prevailed, the way was open for governments to try to link often diverse issues in order to maximize their bargaining power. For LDCs the new fluidity in the system offered an unprecedented opportunity to press their case for a significant redistribution of the benefits from international transactions.

While the governments of the industrialized world were increasingly inclined to intervene in economic matters, it was also the case that new forms of transnational economic relations had largely escaped their control: the scope of governmental authority had simply failed to keep pace with the evolution of markets. Nowhere was this more obvious than in the mushrooming Eurodollar market. Again, these developments offered new opportunities to LDCs to diversify their economic links. A growth in the number of transnational corporations—some of which were willing to offer turnkey plants with no ongoing commitment for the purchaser—improved the bargaining position of developing countries. Meanwhile the Eurodollar market provided a new source of (apparently unconditional) finance capital to those countries deemed credit-worthy.[2]

These developments also highlighted the growing differentiation of the Third World. Clearly, not all LDCs were equally well placed to take advantage of the new opportunities available in the international economic system. Academic writing has been slow to acknowledge this. For the past two decades the study of the political economy of the Third World, and of North-South relations, has been dominated by the metaphor of "dependency." While providing a useful reminder of how international structures and class relations have constrained and conditioned the choices available to Third World governments, and of the advantages to developing countries of a diversification of their economic ties, much of the writing in the dependency tradition has tended to treat Third World countries as a passive, undifferentiated group. Even the more sophisticated writings from this perspective have used an image of a universal world system dichotomized between countries experiencing "situations" of dependency and others (whose characteristics are seldom defined and can only be assumed, by default, to enjoy "autonomy" in their choice of economic path).[3]

This dichotomy has little utility in the contemporary international system. In an era of increasing market integration among developed capitalist economies, even the least vulnerable countries find their economic development conditioned by events elsewhere in the world capitalist system. It would be difficult to argue that the economies of Western Europe were not "conditioned" by the policies pursued by the United States in the period of postwar reconstruction. The old adage that when the United States sneezes, Europe catches a cold is a reflection of popular perceptions of continuing "conditioning." Similarly, to treat Third World countries as an undifferentiated group ignores these societies' rich variety of precolonial histories and the variations in the colonial experience that were to have a profound effect on the opportunities for indigenous accumulation and thus on the prospects for local capitalism in the postindependence period.[4] By emphasizing the continuity between the colonial period and "neocolonialism," dependency approaches have also underestimated the flexibility and increased bargaining power former colonies gained when they achieved their political sovereignty.

While the international system constrains the choices available to all states, particularly its weaker members, none are entirely passive entities. Even the most penetrated state enjoys some decision-making autonomy. Ghana and the Ivory Coast, for instance, have pursued markedly different development strategies in the postindependence period with predictably divergent results. This is not, of course, to assert that all Third World countries are equally well equipped to take advantage of developing opportunities in the international system. Internal capacity is critical to the ability of states to capitalize on changes in the international division of labor. One of the unfortunate characteristics of dependency approaches is that in rejecting the ahistorical and static analyses of conventional development economics, they have underemphasized the importance of internal characteristics of economies and of political systems that together are the principal determinants of LDCs' potential for industrialization, their attractiveness to multinational capital, and their ability to bargain with external actors.[5]

Relations between transnational and local actors—the central focus of dependency analysis—cannot be understood except with reference to the structural characteristics of the domestic system as a whole, as well as to those of the international system. For the student of international political economy, what is of principal interest are changes in both systems and the interrelationships between them. Not all countries of the periphery are potential candidates for "associated dependent development." This is explicitly acknowledged by Evans in his attempt to place the Brazilian case in comparative perspective. He employs Wallerstein's concept of the "semi-periphery" to differentiate a group of countries that have the potential to follow the Brazilian path. And the principal characteristic he uses to assess the potential of Third World countries is one central to "conventional" writing on economic development—"sheer scale" in terms of size of GNP: "Most of the countries of the third world are poor and tiny. As long as there is a periphery they are likely to be in it."[6]

Evans' use of the concept of semiperiphery is clearly preferable to the simplistic dichotomy of "dependent" states and "others" characteristic of much of the writing in the field. But this intermediate category does not take us very far toward a comprehensive typology. "Dependency" is a multidimensional phenomenon. A Third World country's capacity to pursue successful counterdependency strategies will be determined by a number of internal and external factors and the interactions between them. Among the most important internal characteristics are the mobilizable economic resources of the country, which Evans emphasizes. But this is only the beginning in constructing a typology of relevant factors. In addition, it is necessary to consider political and social variables such as the skills (and thus bargaining capability of the domestic bureaucracy) and the ability of the state to impose unpopular domestic policies on relevant domestic sectors who must bear the costs involved in capital accumulation (which would involve *inter alia* a consideration of the coercive capacity of the domestic government, its legitimacy, and its ability to mobilize the necessary constellation of class forces).

Relevant external factors might be considered in terms of the opportunities offered by the international system that constrain or support domestic diversification strategies; here the important variables would include the degree of openness of the international trade system, the role of transnational corporations in fostering a new international division of labor, and the availability of capital and foreign exchange through public or private sources. Structural characteristics thus condition the range of alternative strategies a country may pursue; a consideration of the potential alternatives available to a country provides a useful indication of its autonomy and freedom of maneuver vis-à-vis external actors. One problem with much of the dependency literature is that such counterfactuals are not considered except in terms of a utopian socialist alternative.

Writers in the dependency tradition have perceived the Lomé Convention as merely a further extension of existing dependency relations: a higher stage of neocolonialism. From this perspective little credence is given to the possibility of mutual benefits arising from the relationship. Nor is sufficient attention paid to the reasons why the relationship evolved in its present form; it is frequently assumed, for example, that this was the inevitable product of "comprador" elites having been bribed/duped/coerced into selling out the interests of their countries. Writings in this vein are frequently guilty of a new paternalism that asserts that Third World elites are either incapable of identifying the national interest or are incapable of pursuing or unwilling to pursue it since it conflicts with class interests that inevitably coincide with those of metropolitan elites and transnational capital. This chapter proposes an alternative approach: to perceive the Lomé relationship as a logical response to the constrained range of choices that face the governments of countries that are among the weakest in the world.

ACP states are the embodiment of economic weakness. Although there are significant differences between ACP countries with regard to geographical area, population, resource endowment, etc., their similar economic structures relative to middle-income developing countries and their export dependency on raw materials and agricultural products allow generalization without imparting great distortion. If some countries are in a more favorable position than others, this is frequently a matter of which primary products they export—essentially the luck of the geological draw. Nigeria, for instance, which Evans identifies as a possible candidate for semiperipheral status, has an economic structure much more reminiscent of those of its neighbors in West Africa than of Brazil or Taiwan.

Table 1.1 provides details of the structural characteristics of ACP economies at the time that they negotiated the Convention. Most ACP countries are essentially monoexport economies: for 33 of the 50 ACP countries for which data are available, a single export accounted for more than 50 percent of their total export earnings in trade with the European Economic Community (EEC) in 1975. There are three principal sources of foreign exchange: production of tropical agricultural products for export; exploitation of mineral products (and, in some cases, their processing, which has given rise to small enclave industrial sectors); and tourism—which again has produced an enclave "modern" sector. A predominant characteristic of all ACP states is a lack of economic flexibility—in Kindleberger's terminology the absence of a "capacity to transform"[7]—that renders them extremely vulnerable to both internal and external shocks caused by natural and manmade disasters.

Within the ACP Group are many of the world's poorest states—at the time the Lomé Convention was renegotiated in 1978–79, twenty-one of the thirty-one countries designated as "least developed" by the United Nations were ACP states. For the purposes of the Convention, 35 countries are included in a "least developed" category: in 1976 these had an average per capita income of only $176. Most ACP countries have incomes far below those prevailing in other LDCs—the exceptions being found primarily among the Caribbean states. Economic weakness in fact was a *prerequisite* for membership in the ACP Group. When Britain originally applied for membership in the EEC, the Six were emphatic that

**TABLE 1.1.**
ACP Structural Characteristics

| Country Name | Population (millions) | Geographical Area (sq. miles) | GNP (U.S.m) | GNP per capita (U.S. $) | Debt Service as % Exports ($) | EEC Share in | | | | Share of Principal Product in Exports to EEC (%) | Share of Manuf. in GDP (%) |
|---|---|---|---|---|---|---|---|---|---|---|---|
| | | | | | | EX (%) | IM (%) | Net ODA (%) | Net Private Flow (%) | | |
| Bahamas | 0.20 | 5,380 | 443 | 2,184 | n.a. | n.a. | n.a. | 15.7 | 36.9 | 80.0 | n.a. |
| Barbados | 0.24 | 166 | 368 | 1,500 | 4.3 | 29.4 | 29.5 | 27.3 | 99.9 | 81.0 | 10.6 |
| Benin | 3.11 | 43,483 | 506 | 170 | 6.7 | 49.5 | 59.9 | 60.5 | 100.0 | 16.0 | 8.6 |
| Botswana | 0.69 | 231,804 | 286 | 414 | n.a. | n.a. | n.a. | 24.6 | 100.0 | 57.0 | 7.2 |
| Burundi | 3.93 | 10,747 | 433 | 110 | n.a. | 58.3 | 58.9 | 76.9 | 100.0 | 65.0 | 9.8 |
| Cameroon | 7.53 | 183,568 | 2,736 | 363 | 7.0 | 63.7 | 71.0 | 62.0 | 100.2 | 36.0 | 12.7 |
| Cape Verde | 0.30 | 1,557 | 40 | 138 | n.a. | n.a. | n.a. | 35.2 | 100.0 | n.a. | 3.4* |
| Central African Republic | 1.79 | 240,534 | 357 | 200 | 11.8 | 70.1 | 76.1 | 84.6 | 38.4 | 62.0 | 8.7 |
| Chad | 4.03 | 495,752 | 483 | 120 | 10.6 | 6.1 | 58.4 | 65.0 | 114.2 | 91.0 | 9.1 |
| Comoros | 0.30 | 863 | 60 | 180 | n.a. | n.a. | n.a. | 98.6 | 100.0 | n.a. | 7.6* |
| Congo | 1.35 | 132,046 | 688 | 509 | 14.3 | 64.9 | 69.1 | 73.1 | 111.2 | 47.0 | 9.5 |
| Djibouti | 0.11 | 8,800 | 220 | 2,040 | n.a. | n.a. | n.a. | n.a. | n.a. | 26.0 | 10.1* |
| Dominica | 0.08 | 18,816 | 26 | 343 | n.a. | n.a. | n.a. | n.a. | n.a. | n.a. | 4.0 |
| Equatorial Guinea | 0.32 | 10,830 | 95 | 294 | n.a. | n.a. | n.a. | 1.0 | 100.0 | 72.0 | 5.3* |
| Ethiopia | 27.47 | 471,799 | 2,776 | 97 | 0.9 | 21.9 | 39.6 | 29.4 | 92.9 | 51.0 | 11.2 |
| Fiji | 0.57 | 7,055 | 656 | 1,151 | 0.7 | 60.2 | 16.9 | 48.6 | 1.2 | 81.0 | 10.5^b |
| Gabon | 0.52 | 103,346 | 1,466 | 2,813 | 7.0 | 58.3 | 82.0 | 78.2 | 79.5 | 54.0 | 9.4* |
| Gambia | 0.52 | 4,361 | 93 | 178 | 0.7 | 81.7 | 46.1 | 41.0 | 26.9 | 94.0 | 1.6 |
| Ghana | 9.87 | 92,099 | 3,715 | 372 | 6.3 | 41.2 | 37.9 | 51.3 | 125.0 | 71.0 | 9.2* |
| Grenada | 0.10 | 133 | 44 | 379 | n.a. | n.a. | n.a. | 38.3 | n.a. | 24.0 | 2.8 |
| Guinea | 4.42 | 94,925 | 762 | 162 | n.a. | n.a. | n.a. | 4.9 | −1,294.1 | 63.0 | 9.4* |

| | | | | | | | | | | | |
|---|---|---|---|---|---|---|---|---|---|---|---|
| Guinea-Bissau | 0.53 | 13,948 | 130[d] | 140[d] | n.a. | n.a. | n.a. | 25.6 | 100.0 | 66.0 | 1.3* |
| Guyana | 0.78 | 83,000 | 400 | 512 | 5.0 | 37.1 | 30.2 | 6.3 | 2,044.5 | 50.0 | 12.0 |
| Ivory Coast | 6.71 | 124,503 | 4,176 | 617 | 10.7 | 57.5 | 58.2 | 83.2 | 83.6 | 42.0 | 11.8 |
| Jamaica | 2.04 | 4,232 | 2,713 | 1,328 | 9.8 | 23.4 | 19.9 | 22.2 | 36.1 | 38.0 | 16.8 |
| Kenya | 13.40 | 224,960 | 3,411 | 252 | 5.9 | 34.6 | 39.9 | 47.0 | 81.6 | 56.0 | 12.4 |
| Kiribati | 0.06 | 264 | 39 | 649 | n.a. | n.a. | n.a. | n.a. | n.a. | n.a. | n.a. |
| Lesotho | 1.19 | 11,720 | 242 | 203 | 35.68 | 62.8 | n.a. | 38.4 | 100.0 | 36.0 | 4.1 |
| Liberia | 1.57 | 43,000 | 540 | 343 | n.a. | 39.2 | 30.2 | 9.8 | 57.2 | 70.0 | 5.4 |
| Madagascar | 7.68 | 226,657 | 1,664 | 217 | 4.1 | 59.3 | 57.4 | 62.8 | 309.0 | 46.0 | 13.7 |
| Malawi | 5.04 | 45,747 | 704 | 134 | 12.1 | 22.3 | 35.2 | 54.9 | 100.3 | 42.0 | 12.5 |
| Mali | 5.81 | 478,764 | 548 | 94 | 4.0 | n.a. | 47.6 | 57.9 | 100.0 | 56.0 | 11.1 |
| Mauritania | 1.42 | 397,953 | 350 | 247 | 23.4 | 86.1 | n.a. | 38.7 | 96.6 | 93.0 | 10.2 |
| Mauritius | 0.86 | 790 | 488 | 552 | 2.0 | 66.6 | 37.1 | 51.0 | 68.8 | 71.0 | 18.3 |
| Niger | 4.60 | 489,189 | 670 | 146 | 5.8 | 46.3 | 43.8 | 61.1 | −21.8 | 59.0 | 16.4 |
| Nigeria | 65.66 | 356,667 | 30,934 | 412 | 3.0 | 37.6 | 59.9 | 39.9 | 46.6 | 86.0 | 7.4 |
| Papua New Guinea | 2.76 | 178,260 | 1,228 | 452 | 4.5 | n.a. | 8.1 | 00.2 | −0.7 | 35.0 | 8.2 |
| Rwanda | 4.20 | 10,169 | 601 | 146 | 1.4 | 23.8 | 48.0 | 69.4 | 114.2 | 59.0 | 3.6 |
| St. Lucia | 0.11 | 238 | 56 | 508 | n.a. | n.a. | n.a. | n.a. | n.a. | n.a. | n.a. |
| St. Vincent & Grenadines | 0.09 | n.a. | 30[e] | 320 | n.a. | 75.2 | 30.0 | n.a. | n.a. | n.a. | 8.8 |
| Sao Tome & Principe | 0.08 | 372 | 31 | 395 | n.a. | n.a. | n.a. | 9.1 | 9.1** | 97.0 | 9.2* |
| Senegal | 4.98 | 75,750 | 1,716 | 345 | 7.9 | 63.4 | 57.2 | 62.6 | 71.7 | 58.0 | 12.3 |
| Seychelles | 0.06 | 107 | 33 | 572 | n.a. | n.a. | n.a. | 98.0 | 80.8 | n.a. | 3.9* |
| Sierra Leone | 3.05 | 27,699 | 607 | 199 | 12.0 | 82.4 | 41.7[c] | 27.4 | 67.4 | 71.0 | 5.8 |
| Solomon Isl. | 0.19 | 10,983 | 57 | 302 | n.a. | n.a. | n.a. | n.a. | n.a. | n.a. | 1.4[a] |
| Somalia | 3.17 | 246,199 | 391 | 112 | 4.4 | 8.0 | 46.9 | 30.5 | 100.0 | 77.0 | 9.6 |
| Sudan | 15.73 | 967,494 | 4,744 | 296 | 32.1 | 41.0 | 41.2 | 19.4 | 89.9 | 46.0 | 9.7 |
| Surinam | 0.36 | 63,036 | 548 | 1,297 | n.a. | n.a. | n.a. | 97.3 | 99.6 | 40.0 | 7.1 |
| Swaziland | 0.49 | 6,703 | 221 | 457 | n.a. | n.a. | n.a. | 44.0 | 100.0 | 53.0 | 23.5* |
| Tanzania | 15.31 | 364,898 | 2,705 | 176 | 7.1 | 36.8 | 36.4 | 28.4 | 70.5 | 49.0 | 10.4 |
| Togo | 2.23 | 21,622 | 415 | 187 | 11.8 | 89.7 | 70.6 | 73.7 | 104.8 | 49.0 | 10.1 |

**TABLE 1.1. (Continued)**

| Country Name | Population (millions) | Geographical Area (sq. miles) | GNP (U.S.m) | GNP per capita (U.S. $) | Debt Service as % Exports ($) | EEC Share in EX (%) | IM (%) | Net ODA (%) | Net Private Flow (%) | Share of Principal Product in Exports to EEC (%) | Share of Manuf. in GNP (%) |
|---|---|---|---|---|---|---|---|---|---|---|---|
| Tonga | 0.10 | 270 | 38 | 391 | n.a. | n.a. | n.a. | 21.2 | n.a. | 88.0 | 3.2[c] |
| Trinidad & Tobago | 1.08 | 1,980 | 2,286 | 2,113 | 1.4 | 6.4 | 12.4 | 19.9 | 49.8 | 57.0 | 14.1 |
| Tuvalu | 0.006 | 10 | 52 | 968 | n.a. | n.a. | n.a. | n.a. | n.a. | n.a. | n.a. |
| Uganda | 11.55 | 91,133 | 3,327 | 294 | 3.0 | 37.8 | 55.5 | 15.5 | 95.4 | 87.0 | 6.9 |
| Upper Volta | 6.07 | 105,869 | 622 | 117 | 7.1 | 38.3 | 56.8 | 73.4 | −232.3 | 49.0 | 13.8 |
| Western Samoa | 0.15 | 1,097 | 46 | 300 | n.a. | 53.8 | 7.9 | 3.7 | 33.3 | 75.0 | 3.4[a] |
| Zaire | 24.90 | 905,562 | 5,144 | 212 | 18.1 | 51.0 | 51.5 | 80.5 | 64.8 | 41.0 | 9.9 |
| Zambia | 4.98 | 290,584 | 2,178 | 453 | 10.9 | 62.0 | 38.5 | 41.3 | 91.3 | 92.0 | 17.1 |

Sources:

Columns 1, 3, 4, 5, 6, 7, 8, and 12 *ACP: Statistical Yearbook 1972–78*, (Luxembourg: Eurostat, 1980).

Column 10 from *Analysis of Trade Between the European Community and the ACP States. Series: Trade Flows* (Luxembourg: Eurostat, 1979)

Column 2 from *Political Handbook of the World, 1978*, Arthus S. Banks, ed. (New York: McGraw-Hill, 1978)

Columns 8 and 9 from *ACP: Statistical Yearbook 1970–76*, (Luxembourg: Eurostat, 1977)

Note: All figures are for 1975, except for columns 8, 9, and 10. Columns 8 and 9 are for the mean 1973–75 (o/o); and column 10 figures are for 1977 (share of principal export product for each ACP in total EEC imports from that country, 1977—concentration o/o)

[a] Data are for 1972.
[b] Data are for 1973.
[c] Data are for 1974.
[d] Data are for 1976.
[e] Data are for 1977.

n.a. Data not available.

*The last column, Share of Manufacturing in GNP in 1975, also includes electricity, gas, and water when followed by an *.

**For Sao Tome and Principe, column 10, Net Private Flow, the figure includes the net official and private resource flow.

special trading arrangements would be made available only to countries of "comparable structure" to the Yaoundé Associates; the more developed states of the Asian Commonwealth were excluded.

Economic weakness is compounded by fragile sociopolitical structures. Increasingly it has been acknowledged that one of the principal reasons for the success of the newly industrializing countries has been the strength and effectiveness of their state apparatuses. ACP countries on the other hand are characterized by extremely weak states, typically reflected in a lack of extractive, executive, and enforcement capabilities;[8] a severe shortage of skilled personnel; ethnic subnationalism; and the consequent absence of an ethic that supports rational bureaucratic norms.[9] Caribbean and Pacific states are better placed than their African partners in this regard, but they suffer particularly from the economic consequences of small size.[10]

Weak states coupled with weak economies limit the opportunities for effective unilateral action in support of counterdependency strategies. Shortages of skilled personnel have handicapped ACP states in their bargaining with external actors: in many cases ACP governments simply do not have access to the detailed economic and technical information necessary to effectively defend and promote their own interests.[11] Few ACP states possess resources of such scarcity that they tip the bargaining scales in their favor. Of necessity, they must adopt a short time horizon: in most cases the urgent need for funds requires a quick agreement with external actors or the marketing of a product at the earliest opportunity, regardless of whether this provides a suboptimal return.[12] Although some ACP states have succeeded in borrowing from the Eurodollar market, few have been regarded as good credit risks—often with good reason. They have not been able, therefore, to rely on private overseas sources for a significant contribution to their capital needs. Whereas most ACP states in the postindependence period have enjoyed some success in diversifying their markets, their sources of supply, and the composition of their exports (and thus have reduced their vulnerability to economic pressure from any one external partner—normally the former colonial power), little progress has been made in transforming the structures of their economies. In Nigeria, for instance, according to the World Bank, manufacturing accounted for only 6 percent of GDP in 1980, merely 1 percent above the figure for 1960.

National self-reliance, a strategy that offers an opportunity for unilateral action in support of dependency reduction, has not proved to be a particularly attractive policy alternative. The reason is quite straightforward: given the economic structures inherited by LDCs at independence, continuing trading and investment ties with industrial countries are critical to development prospects. By reducing the role of the external sector, the share of foreign aid in domestic capital projects, etc., an effective self-reliant strategy would impose a heavy burden on the domestic population in terms of the need for increased domestic capital formation. Leontief calculated that a self-reliant development strategy would require savings amounting to between 30 and 40 percent of GNP, a performance that would demand either extraordinary self-discipline on the part of a population, or a state with effective extractive and repressive capabilities.[13] Self-reliance might be an attractive long-run strategy but is of little practical feasibility given existing economic and political constraints.

ACP states, by virtue of their structural characteristics, have been unable for the most part to take effective unilateral action to transform their external economic relations. Accordingly, they have sought the help of others in attempting to achieve these objectives. As Haas has argued cogently, "collaboration is an unanticipated consequence of failure."[14] It was in large part because of widespread perceptions of the ineffectiveness of national attempts to increase the share of benefits from international exchange that collaboration became the distinguishing feature of LDC strategies in the 1970s. Collaboration is a particularly attractive strategy for those countries whose domestic economic, political, and social structures afford them little flexibility in their choice of foreign economic policies. Collaboration with other states can occur on two dimensions: horizontally, that is, acting in concert with other countries that share common objectives, perceptions, or resources; or vertically, which, for weak states, typically takes the form of a clientelistic relationship that attempts to extract particularistic benefits from a more powerful partner.

## HORIZONTAL COLLABORATION

Horizontal collaboration, by offering the opportunity to act in concert with other developing countries to reduce dependency on the industrialized world, has particular ideological attraction to the Group of 77. Collaboration along the horizontal dimension has taken three principal forms:

universal "southern" coalitions in multilateral organizations, regional groupings aimed at promoting self-reliance and improving bargaining relations with external actors, and producer associations for various commodities.

Global fora have been the principal locus for horizontal collaboration among LDCs since they offer the greatest potential for capitalizing on numerical strength. Developing countries have tried to use their control over agendas to change the rules of the game, thereby aspiring to achieve more than would be possible through bargaining with industrialized countries on a bilateral basis.[15] Their demands for a New International Economic Order (NIEO), which figured so prominently on international agenda in the 1970s, were not so much novel proposals but a reformulation and synthesis of calls for reform that had, in many cases, been voiced for at least twenty years. The origins and underlying economic justification of the proposed reforms in many cases can be traced to the work of the Economic Commission for Latin America under Raoul Prebisch. As early as 1955, the Bandung Conference of Asian-African states had passed resolutions favoring increasing aid flows, commodity price stabilization, diversification of exports through raw materials processing, collective action against international shipping lines, and the promotion of Third World cooperation through joint ventures and the provision of technical assistance.[16] By the time of the Cairo Conference on the Problems of Economic Development in July 1962, the core principles of the NIEO had already been articulated and were subsequently elaborated at the first two sessions of the United Nations Conference on Trade and Development (UNCTAD).

Disappointment with postindependence growth rates (which although in many cases were high by historical standards nevertheless fell short of what was necessary to keep pace with a growing population's inflated expectations), when coupled with the failure of the developed world to provide anticipated assistance, led to a growing disillusionment with the distribution of gains from existing economic regimes.[17] No longer was there faith that market mechanisms or industrial countries of their own volition would supply the resources necessary to enable economic growth to take place at the desired rate. Rather than viewing the liberal economic order established by Bretton Woods as a collective good, it was increasingly perceived as a "bad" that had served particularistic interests rather than the universal benefit. Markets had concentrated wealth and power and had reinforced dependency relationships between weak and strong.[18] And with the growing acceptance of a dependency perspective, institutionalized through fora such as UNCTAD, came the search for means by which the vulnerability of the South could be reduced and demands for a change in the rules of the game.

Whereas earlier Third World meetings had been content to express concern that the interests of developing countries should be safeguarded in any reform of the international trade and monetary systems and had passed resolutions such as that at UNCTAD I, which recommended an increase in the participation of nationals of developing countries in the process of policy formulation through the employment of qualified experts on the senior staff of international financial and monetary institutions, the distinguishing characteristic of Third World demands in the 1970s was a call for *joint management* of the international economic system.[19] Long-standing economic proposals were supplemented by demands for a redistribution of decision-making power; LDCs tried to use their "metapower" (control over agendas)[20] to force through these changes in the rules of the game.

By the mid-1960s, LDCs enjoyed majorities in those multilateral institutions where voting was based on the principle of equal representation for each sovereign state. But this alone was insufficient to elevate the demands for a New International Economic Order to a central place on international agenda—in fact the late 1960s proved to be an era of further disillusionment for the Third World as the issues in which they were interested appeared to languish in peripheral organs of the UN system, most notably UNCTAD, where stalemate prevailed. Two additional factors were necessary before LDCs could capitalize on their metapower: the increasing politicization of international economic relations and the advent of oil power. Increasing politicization of international economic relations was the necessary prerequisite for LDCs to be able to exercise their control over agendas; the success of the OPEC oil embargo and the subsequent failure of Western attempts to delink energy from other issues of concern to LDCs permitted the elevation of the NIEO to a central place on the international agenda.[21]

Yet the importance of Third World metapower can easily be exaggerated. What became obvious very quickly was the disparity between LDCs' control over agendas on the one hand and both their lack of control over outcomes and their inability to enforce Western compliance with the ambitious nominal targets on which agreement had supposedly been reached. And while, as Krasner argues,[22] the Third World has benefited from the inclination of hegemonic states to create international organizations in which voting power is equally shared in order to enhance legitimacy, hegemonic powers also reserve most of the important decision-making powers for themselves either through the creation of exclusive organizations, such as the Security Council, or through weighted voting in universal organizations. This is not to belittle Third World advances in voting power in institutions such as the IMF where a veto power is now enjoyed.[23] But veto power is very far removed from a control over outcomes, and LDCs— with the partial exception of major oil exporters—remain very junior partners. Substantive progress has lagged far behind advance on procedural issues.

One response of industrialized countries to what Tucker terms the "new egalitarianism" pursued by the Group of 77 has been to reserve decision-making on issues of international economic reform for fora in which voting is weighted or where LDCs are not represented at all. Universal organizations where the principle of one state, one vote applies have been employed as an arena in which representatives of the industrialized countries engage in a strategy of "talking the Third World's reform proposals to death" while substantive issues are discussed among themselves elsewhere. Even when LDCs are in attendance they may be bypassed at critical junctures.[24] And lack of expertise in technical matters may prevent LDCs from exercising influence in proportion to their numbers— Ibrahim notes, for example, that few of the LDCs represented in the Tokyo Round talks participated actively in the negotiations.[25]

For most of the issues in the NIEO package no consensus has arisen regarding the means by which goals might be pursued, even in those cases (and these are relatively few) where some agreement exists about the proper ends at which policy should be aimed. As Haas argues, successful negotiations for institutionalizing international collaboration depend on both a congruence of interests and a consensus on the relevant knowledge to be applied in the policymaking process. Neither of these conditions is present in most of the discussion over the NIEO.[26]

The very process of negotiation in global fora tends to hamper the development of consensus. In order to maintain the fragile Third World coalition the UNCTAD Secretariat and other spokesmen of the Group of 77 have been compelled to negotiate in terms of general principles.

Conflict within their own constituencies is risked when divergent interests are exposed in the context of more specific proposals. Third World coalitions have been reinforced by a shared acceptance of dependency approaches to international political economy in which primary emphasis is placed on the negative effects of the existing international economic order. But, as Rothstein noted in the context of arguments over the Common Fund, it is very difficult to negotiate when the legitimacy of the system itself is questioned by one of the parties.[27] Since debates in global fora are also important opportunities for satisfying domestic audiences, rhetoric tends toward the extremes, further complicating the task of building a new consensus. The end product in many global North-South negotiations has been a futile group-versus-group confrontation that quickly assumed a ritualistic form.[28]

Even where some consensus exists as regards ends, there has been little agreement on the relevant technical knowledge and the means that might be employed. On the one hand, the South's approach is grounded in perceptions of international economic relations as predominantly conflictual, where bargaining at best occurs in situations of bilateral monopoly. But from the perspective of the most important Northern actors, little fault is to be found in existing market mechanisms: Southern aspirations might best be fulfilled by the North's better respecting its own rules of the game. Even among experts there has been a marked intolerance toward alternative opinions; a dialogue of the deaf has ensued in which opponents are contemptuously dismissed and little effort made to identify points of mutual interest.[29]

In principle, horizontal collaboration in global fora appears to offer LDCs the highest potential payoffs by enabling them to capitalize on their numerical superiority to change the rules of international economic intercourse. Even in the early 1970s, however, LDCs had sufficient experience of negotiations in global fora to know that the conversion of metapower into control over outcomes was unlikely. This perception was reinforced when it became evident that while OPEC was ready to engage in the politics of issue linkage to support the demands of less fortunate LDCs, it had too much at stake to force the hand of the industrialized world in matters that were not central to its own income.

Even before the stalemate in global fora over the NIEO became obvious, few of the proposals appeared to offer great potential for most ACP states, catering instead primarily to the interests of middle-income developing countries. Many countries in the group depend for their export earnings on commodities not amenable to buffer stocking; consequently although the Second Window of the Common Fund is of interest to them, they would not benefit from the Fund to the same extent as many middle-income producers of the "core" commodities. Debt rescheduling was of minor interest to most ACP countries given their inability to borrow heavily on the Eurodollar market. GSP schemes offered little prospect for benefit since most ACP states were unable to compete on equal terms with their more developed brethren, and, in the EEC case, actually threatened to reduce existing advantages. Given the large number of landlocked countries among the ACP Group, a package deal in the Law of the Sea negotiations that took account of their interests certainly promised much more than they might expect to achieve through unilateral action—however, promises here have also gone unfulfilled.

Some of the difficulties with horizontal collaboration in universal coalitions appeared to be avoidable if cooperation was undertaken on a regional basis. As opposed to joint action in global fora, it might reasonably be assumed that the politics of coalition maintenance are less complex at the regional level, given the partners' agreement on central goals, the means through which they might be achieved, the ability of the LDCs themselves to take action in support of the goals, and the relative lack of diversity between actors within a region in comparison to the Group of 77 as a whole. Yet the actual experience of Third World integrative schemes belies such facile assumptions. Their problems have been documented at great length and warrant only brief consideration here.[30]

Regional integration among LDCs has typically taken the form of free trade areas or customs unions. These grandiose designs in most cases have become highly politicized before major gains from regional cooperation have been realized. Principal among the problems are the "backwash" (or "polarization") effects associated with laissez-faire arrangements that cause gains from regional cooperation to accrue predominantly to the most developed country within a region. In the absence of effective compensatory mechanisms, less developed states may find themselves actually to be worse off than they would have been in the absence of the regional scheme. Disparities in gains may be exaggerated in situations (e.g., the East African Community) where ideological diversity prevails within the region, making some states more attractive than others to potential foreign investors and precluding effective action at the regional level to equalize gains. Where partner states are relatively equal in their levels of development (or poverty), it is difficult for those countries benefiting disproportionately from regional cooperation to make the side payments necessary to maintain the interest of their less favored partners in the scheme. Coalition maintenance may in fact be more difficult in the absence of a regional hegemonic power and in situations where the small number of states restricts both the size of the overall "package" for negotiation and the opportunities for trade-offs.[31]

Monetary compensation alone has usually proved to be insufficient to satisfy those countries that have been the victims of polarization effects in customs unions. A satisfactory solution to the problems arising from the uneven distribution of benefits from regional cooperation would inevitably seem to necessitate industrial planning on a regional scale. Where this is undertaken, the instruments employed may be consciously manipulated to improve the bargaining position of the regional partners vis-à-vis external actors. To date, only the Andean Pact among Third World integrative systems has consciously fashioned its investment laws in this manner. Its recent history has underlined the central difficulty with the strategy; that is, few LDC governments are willing to countenance the constraints a regional policy of this type inevitably places on the autonomy of their national economic decision-making.

While customs unions and free trade areas for these reasons appear to have little potential as a counterdependency strategy, their experience should not lead to an offhand dismissal of the opportunities for profitable regional cooperation among LDCs. Increasingly there has been recognition among Third World governments that gains may be realized from carefully controlled cooperation with their neighbors in the absence of a more grandiose regional design. Cooperation along functional lines in, for example, provision of common services, joint ownership of industries requiring inputs from more than one state, and in organized trade which takes advantage of local surpluses and deficits, offers considerable scope for mutual gain, even if it lacks the potential for automatic spillover to new areas of cooperation. Movement in this direction has taken place in two regional arrangements involving ACP states: the Caribbean Community (CARICOM) (especially the program for food self-sufficiency) and most prominently in the Southern African Development Coordination Conference (SADCC).[32]

Limited functional cooperation of this type represents the most practical horizontal collaboration that has taken place toward realizing Southern aspirations for collective self-reliance. Generally, however, this has remained little more than a political slogan whose frequent repetition has not hidden the failure of LDCs to implement the necessary policy measures to translate rhetoric into reality. Although increased economic interactions between Southern countries offer the potential to reduce their dependence on markets, technology, and finance from OECD members, the mere fact that the countries involved are "Southern" does not remove the inherent possibilities for conflict. Collective self-reliance can be realized only if policy measures are implemented that are based on intra-South bargaining that recognizes that a real divergence of interests exists among Southern states. To date, it has been easier to maintain Southern unity by mouthing the slogan of collective self-reliance than to undertake the diplomatic, institutional, and financial efforts necessary for an implementation of the strategy.[33]

By far the most successful example of horizontal collaboration among southern states is OPEC. Yet, despite many attempts at replicating the OPEC experience, oil remains very much the exception and, with hindsight, a limited one at best.[34] Producer organizations, like regional cooperation schemes, are attractive to LDCs in that they offer the potential for Southern states to act by themselves to improve their bargaining power. But there are few commodities with market structures suitable for this type of action, and the experience of producers of copper, for instance, has shown that while there may be agreement on ultimate ends, there is frequent disagreement among potential partners on the measures necessary to realize these ends. Other commodities lack a dominant producer that can reproduce the role of Saudi Arabia as the organization's manager. Some gains have been sustained by producers of bauxite, phosphates, and, to a lesser extent, coffee, but the principal lesson from the experience of recent years appears to be that other producer organizations have little chance of being effective unless they receive the support of Northern producers and/or consumers and even then that such gains will be limited unless there is sustained intercartel cooperation. So this again leads back to the question of the potential effectiveness of cooperation between Southern states in the face of a diversity of interests.

ACP states as the weakest of the weak had few policy alternatives available to them. Their scope for unilateral action in pursuit of counter-dependency objectives was extremely circumscribed. Nor did the various forms of horizontal collaboration offer significant hope for an improvement in the returns from external economic relations in the short term. Unable to compete effectively on equal terms in world markets with many of their more developed colleagues in the Group of 77, most ACP states relied heavily on their preferential links with their former colonial powers. The new turbulence in international economic relations threatened these traditional ties. Some of the more developed Third World countries, already more efficient producers of agricultural commodities of interest to the ACP, were attempting to increase their share of the market in industrialized countries as a means of earning foreign exchange to promote their industrialization efforts. Brazil, for instance, had significantly increased its exports of soya beans, Malaysia had raised its production of palm oil by more than 20 percent per annum since 1961, and Indonesia and Malaysia were rapidly increasing their production and exports of coffee and cocoa respectively. These developments threatened the export earnings of the ACP not only in third-country markets but in the EEC also; since the newly industrializing countries offered a significant and expanding market for the exports of the EEC, they were well placed to negotiate the reduction or elimination of tariffs that discriminated against their exports in favor of those from ACP states. Vertical collaboration with the EEC—a strategy that will be termed "collective clientelism"—appeared to offer the best available strategy for the ACP to defend their position in their principal market and a useful supplement to collaboration along the horizontal dimension.

## COLLECTIVE CLIENTELISM

A strategy of collective clientelism refers to a relationship in which a group of weak states combine in an effort to exploit the special ties that link them to a more powerful state or group of states. Through this means they hope to construct an exclusive regime under which they exert a claim on the stronger party in order to preserve or gain particularistic advantages not available to nonassociated states. Vertical collaboration thereby inevitably undercuts horizontal collaboration, with obvious implications in this case for South-South relations: the objective of the ACP was to obtain a privileged relationship not available to other countries of their general status. For the weaker party, the intention in pursuing a strategy of vertical collaboration is to take advantage of a dialectic of dependency:

to exploit their present dependence and special ties in order to gain resources that facilitate a future lessening of dependency. In Hirschman's words:

In general, trade and investment relations between countries A and B may lead initially to dependence of B on A, for reason of the various asymmetries, but to the extent that economic intercourse increases the resources at B's command it becomes possible for B to pursue, by diversification and other means, a policy of lessening dependence, be it at the cost of some of the welfare gains.[35]

Clientelship offers the weaker parties the opportunity to claim special advantages in the relationship on account of their weakness, which can also be used to ridicule the idea that their activities might pose a threat to the stronger parties. Their expectation is that their strategy will provide them both with additional resources and with some security—that in the event of a conflict of interest the stronger will not always wish to employ their strength in order to prevail.

Like all forms of clientelism, the collective variant typified by the ACP strategy in the Lomé Convention has its origins in scarcity and insecurity: the struggle of the weak to survive in an unpredictable world in which they are unable to compete on equal terms.[36] Effective global arrangements to provide for the economic security of the least developed have failed to emerge in the postwar period. This was seen initially in the rejection of the International Trade Organization, more recently in UNCTAD's lack of success in transforming the rules of the international trade regime to provide greater benefits for the Group of 77. Despite the supposed universalism of the principles of the General Agreement on Tariffs and Trade (GATT), its method of operation has failed to provide a global institutional framework in which weaker parties can seek security. Tariff levels—and concessions—continue to be set by national governments; these thereby increase the discretionary resources available to the major trading powers as potential patrons in the international system. Particularism continues to be the norm in many aspects of North-South economic relations. This was seen, for example, in the failure to introduce a universal generalized system of preferences—there emerging, instead, a variety of national schemes that discriminated among not only the products to be included but also among the states that might become beneficiaries. Selective protectionism, "voluntary" export restraints, and a failure to reach agreement on rules for the application of safeguard clauses have further undermined the universalistic norms of GATT.

As Eisenstadt and Roniger note, "it is the combination of potentially open access to the market, with continuous semi-institutionalized attempts to limit free access that is the crux of the clientelist model."[37] This is as true of the collective variant as of traditional patron-client relations. In an increasingly fragmented and politicized international trade regime it pays to have a patron. This is the case not only in order to attempt to gain access to particularistic concessions but also—in a manner akin to the "protection" provided by the Mafia—to be spared the irresponsible behavior of one's own patron. In general, the EEC has been one of the worst offenders in transgressing the universalistic norms of GATT—this being part cause and part effect of the special relations that Europe has provided to its former colonies. Collective clientelism thereby tends to become self-reinforcing and self-perpetuating; if successful the strategy would contribute to the undermining of universalistic norms and the growth of neomercantile trading blocs.

In times of difficulty, it is natural for weaker parties to turn to those with whom they are most familiar in their search for patrons. And, like all examples of patron-client relations, Lomé came about because of the lack of effective choice faced by the ACP. Hirschman's argument, originally published in 1945, remains relevant in the 1980s:

We do not have a complementarity between broad types of economies, the one agricultural and the other manufacturing, so that a given agricultural country can be considered as complementary to *any one* of the manufacturing countries. World trade is built, rather, in large proportion upon the reliance of the export products of one particular country upon the prosperity and tastes of one other individual country. New Zealand butter, Philippine sugar, and Bulgarian tobacco were not, in general, marketed in "industrial countries," but they were very specifically marketed in England, the United States, and Germany, respectively; possibilities of diversion from one of these countries to another hardly existed to any relevant extent.[38]

There is no need to belabor the relevance of these remarks for the relationships established between the European powers and their colonies. Even for competitive producers, as in the case of New Zealand and Australian lamb and butter, alternative markets were difficult to find when they were excluded from the enlarged EEC. In that the Community was now the world's largest trading bloc, it would have been impossible for ACP states to find alternative markets that would absorb significant quantities of their exports on terms that approximated those received from

**TABLE 1.2.**

Share (%) of EEC in OECD Imports of Selected Commodities 1975

|  | EEC | Canada | U.S.A. | Japan | Australia | Other OECD |
|---|---|---|---|---|---|---|
| Petroleum | 45.4 | 3.6 | 20.2 | 20.9 | 0.5 | 9.5 |
| Petroleum derivatives | 47.9 | 0.9 | 25.2 | 6.2 | 1.5 | 18.3 |
| Cocoa | 56.7 | 2.2 | 22.9 | 4.8 | 18.6 | 11.6 |
| Coffee | 40.8 | 3.6 | 36.2 | 4.0 | 0.6 | 14.8 |
| Copper | 70.7 | 1.2 | 8.5 | 6.0 | 0.2 | 13.4 |
| Tea | 64.8 | 5.5 | 14.7 | 5.1 | 5.6 | 4.3 |
| Iron | 38.9 | 2.1 | 15.1 | 38.6 | 0.0 | 5.2 |
| Aluminum | 57.5 | 3.2 | 13.4 | 10.8 | 0.4 | 14.7 |
| Bananas | 52.4 | 4.6 | 19.9 | 14.1 | 0.0 | 14.6 |
| Groundnut oil | 85.1 | 1.9 | 0.1 | 0.0 | 0.9 | 11.9 |
| Groundnuts | 63.6 | 9.0 | 0.1 | 8.9 | 0.4 | 18.0 |

Source: Calculated from data in *Trade by Commodities: Market Summaries: Imports*, OECD Statistics of Foreign Trade, Series C, Jan.–Dec. 1975, vol. 1 and 2. (Paris: OECD, 1977).

the EEC. Although most ACP states diversified their trading partners in the years following their independence, the EEC remains by far their most important market, accounting for an average of approximately 45 percent of total ACP exports.[39] For many of their most important exports, the EEC is the single largest importer in the world (see table 1.2). In the case of groundnut oil, for instance, the Community consumes close to 85 percent of total OECD imports of that product, and ACP countries supply close to 85 percent of Community imports. For most commodities the situation of the ACP was even more dire in that they were high-cost producers, unable to compete on equal terms outside the protected market offered by the former colonial power.

Lomé did not, of course, arise *ex nihilo* but succeeded existing arrangements that granted former European colonies preferential margins in the European market through the Yaoundé Conventions or the Commonwealth Preferences Agreement (which are examined in detail in the next chapter). Although the trade provisions of the Yaoundé Conventions had not led to the Associates' increasing their share of the European market, it is probable that their position would have been much worse in the absence of the preferential arrangements. Following British entry into the

EEC in 1973, Commonwealth countries faced possible discrimination in their traditional market if they failed to reach a successful agreement with the Community: it was almost certain that a successor to the Yaoundé Conventions would have been signed by the enlarged Community with the Francophone countries, which would not only have maintained their privileged position on the markets of the Six but also have given them a preferential margin in the British market, where Commonwealth countries had previously been the beneficiaries of protective tariffs. Britain had already signaled quite clearly during its earlier applications for Community membership where its loyalties would lie if the developing Commonwealth should attempt to force it to choose between the Six and its former colonies. Commonwealth sugar producers were particularly vulnerable; their guaranteed access to the British market under the Commonwealth sugar scheme would inevitably be terminated since sugar was one of the commodities included within the Community's Common Agricultural Policy. Their traditional market could be safeguarded only by negotiating with the Community as a whole. During the 1960s a number of Commonwealth countries had already demonstrated their fear of discrimination in the EEC market by reversing their original position, which was critical of the Community and its association arrangements, and seeking a preferential trade agreement. As is true of most clientelist relationships, the minimal goal of the weaker parties was defensive: to protect themselves from a further deterioration in their position.

ACP states were also relatively privileged recipients of EEC aid.[40] For the fifty-two ACP countries for which data are available, the EEC contributed an average of 44.8 percent of total receipts of overseas development assistance in the years 1973–75.[41] As was the case with trade, the prospects of finding alternative partners were not promising: in the same period the EEC provided on average 43.3 percent of the total aid given by members of the OECD's Development Assistance Committee and a mean of 31.8 percent of total world development assistance. In the provision of foreign capital the Community figured even more prominently: in the years 1973–75 ACP states on average received close to 87 percent of their foreign investment from EEC member states.

A further powerful incentive to ACP states to reach agreement with the Community was the fear that a failure to do so might well spill over to affect bilateral relations between the former metropole and ex-colony. In many instances this relationship was at least as important for the ACP state as the multilateral arrangement was with the Community. If Guinea's experience in 1958 was indicative, a disruption of relations might have painful consequences. Former colonial powers also continued to play the role of broker for their ex-colonies. They served as champions of their clients in international negotiations—within the EEC this was seen in Dutch promotion of Surinam, Belgium's of Zaire, Italy's of Somalia, as well as the more frequent French intervention in support of their former colonies. This brokership role was not confined to the EEC but was seen also in other multilateral negotiations, e.g., in Belgium taking a leading role in the rescheduling of Zaire's debts. The former metropoles, especially France, also played the role of lender of last resort.[42] And, in the French case in particular, there was always the possibility of military assistance if the local regime should encounter internal or external difficulties.

One of the principal roles played by landlords in traditional patron-client relations is to provide their tenants with social insurance against the vicissitudes of the market.[43] The EEC as patron had failed to provide this subsistence guarantee to the Associated states under the Yaoundé Conventions. As will be discussed in chapter 2, the price Germany and the Netherlands had extracted for the association agreement between the Community and French colonies under the Treaty of Rome was the phasing out of the French system of price supports for the commodity exports of associated states, a system that had guaranteed them at least a minimal subsistence income. Lacking their traditional insurance mechanisms, associated states were exposed for the first time to the full rigors of the international market in a manner similar to that experienced by peasant producers in Asia following colonization. Fifteen years of experience under the Treaty of Rome and the Yaoundé Conventions had shown that tariff advantages alone offered little protection to associated states against fluctuations in their earnings from the export of primary products. None of the provisions to assist primary producers in the Yaoundé Conventions provided an effective scheme of social insurance for the associates.

By publishing its proposals for a compensatory financing scheme for the export earnings of associated countries (known by the acronym STABEX) some months before the negotiations for the Lomé Convention began in earnest, the Commission of the European Communities offered an additional incentive to the potential clients to join the relationship. STA-

BEX, discussed in chapter 3, appeared to provide an effective mechanism to protect the income of the clients from fluctuations arising both from domestic mishaps and from the workings of the international marketplace. Through this scheme the Community promised to play the role of the traditional patron in providing social insurance—indeed, it even referred to the scheme in its own publications as a means of providing sickness and unemployment insurance. In that the margin of subsistence for many ACP states was frequently under threat, this promised to be a significant potential benefit. Lomé appeared to provide two of the principal advantages sought by the weaker parties in clientelist relations: a privileged access to markets and protection against the exigencies both of the international market and of nature.

Finally, an obvious advantage to a strategy of *collective* clientelism was that it strengthened the bargaining power of the states concerned; if LDCs generally have an interest in capitalizing on their strength in numbers in order to attempt to alter rules of the game, as Krasner argues, then the ACP as the weakest of the weak have a particular interest in attempting to achieve through collective action what is impossible for them to attain on a bilateral bargaining basis. As a group the ACP were far more valuable to the EEC than as individual states. For African countries a joint approach to the Lomé negotiations would mark a major step toward the symbolic goal of African unity. A joint approach also increased the opportunities for engaging in tactical linking of issues. And, as in the global North-South dialogue, collaboration in the pursuit of a collective clientelist strategy was itself a response to previous failure—in this case of clientelist strategies undertaken with individual European patrons. As chapter 2 will show, Francophone countries had become increasingly disillusioned with the ability and willingness of their traditional French government patron to act effectively to protect their interests in the course of the Yaoundé Conventions. Similarly, British behavior during the successive rounds of negotiation for Community membership had convinced Commonwealth states that the U.K. government could not be counted on as a reliable patron and, furthermore, could not by itself guarantee the access to the Community market that was becoming of increasing importance to their exports.

Collective clientelism from the perspective of the ACP states was primarily a defensive strategy—an effort to achieve, vis-à-vis what for most ACP countries is their single most important economic partner, many of the objectives that the Group of 77 have pursued under the banner of the New International Economic Order. While few may have anticipated that the Convention would make a decisive difference in terms of their development needs and could at best provide a partial solution on a regional basis to what were often global problems, the relationship would at least provide a partial insurance policy against matters' becoming worse. There was also the expectation that Lomé would indeed provide a model other industrialized countries subsequently would emulate.

A principal ACP objective was to negotiate a convention with minimum opportunity costs, one that provided assistance without strings and that would minimize the ways in which policy alternatives would be restricted. This was essential in order to accommodate the diverse economic development strategies pursued by various members that, in Rothchild and Curry's terminology, ranged from "accommodation" through "reorganization" to "transformation." Collective clientelism thus is not synonymous with a strategy of "associated dependent development." The latter refers to a development policy based on encouraging investment by transnational corporations (TNCs) and exploiting the technological, financial, organizational, and market connections TNCs can provide, to take advantage of changes in the international division of labor.[44] While collective clientelism, as represented by the Lomé relationship, might have been expected to facilitate a strategy of this type (and undoubtedly the EEC hoped that the Convention would *encourage* this—at least as regards European TNCs), this strategy was attractive to only a small minority of the more developed ACP states, e.g., Ivory Coast, Kenya, and Mauritius; the majority were more interested in an insurance arrangement that would not *oblige* them to pursue any particular foreign economic policy. In this objective the ACP states believed themselves to have been successful: as Green notes, "Lomé is apparently perceived as at least tactically consistent with remarkably different domestic strategies, power structures, income distributions, emphasis on exports, and other external economic links and political economic ideologies."[45]

So far, I have used the term "collective clientelism" to describe the ACP strategy in entering the Lomé negotiations and have asserted it is a special form of patron-client relationship. To justify this usage, it is necessary to link the concept to the conventional use of clientelism and to provide evidence that the ACP themselves perceived the relationship in this manner. Since the concept of patron-client relations originated in anthropologists' studies of small-scale peasant societies, any application of clientelism to the international system is vulnerable to accusations of conceptual stretching and a potential "levels of analysis" problem.[46] Owing to the larger number of actors involved and the diversity of ties between them, clientelism at the international level inevitably manifests characteristics that differ on various dimensions from those found in microrelationships. Crucial to the utility of collective clientelism as a concept is the question of whether the macrorelationship shares key structural attributes with patron-client relations in other settings.

An answer to this depends on how strict a definition is adopted: if it is a matter of possessing absolute attributes, then collective clientelism would be ruled illegitimate; if, instead, it is a matter of logic based not on absolutes but on "more or less," then "a good case can be made for ethnic groups, religious minorities, interest groups, *and even nations* standing as clients in relation to some more powerful entity."[47] Collective clientelism certainly manifests many of the characteristics of the more "classical" form of clientelism: moreover, identifying the characteristics that distinguish it from orthodox clientelist relations helps to provide an explanation of why the strategy has been so difficult to sustain and has not brought the benefits that the ACP Group anticipated.

Landlord-peasant relations in precolonial societies should be regarded, not as the only form of clientelism worthy of the name, but as an ideal type against which other forms of clientelism can be measured. A starting point for evaluating the ACP strategy as a variant of clientelism is the frequently quoted definition of political clientelism provided by Lemarchand and Legg: "a more or less personalized, affective and reciprocal relationship between actors, or sets of actors, commanding unequal resources and involving mutually beneficial transactions that have political ramifications beyond the immediate sphere of dyadic relationships."[48]

One of the easiest attributes to deal with is the question of asymmetry: the principle that patron-client relations can exist only between actors possessing unequal resources whether these be derived from political, economic, or status attributes. Decolonization in the postwar period has produced a tremendous increase in inequalities in the international system: it is commonplace now to observe that differences in wealth and power between nations are frequently greater than those that exist within nations. These inequalities are particularly marked within the Lomé relationship: the Federal Republic of Germany has a GNP that is more than 1600 times that of Tonga and a population six hundred times as large; only ten ACP states have a GNP that exceeds that of tiny Luxembourg, the smallest of the Community member states.[49] Lomé certainly meets this first necessary condition for clientelism.

More problematic is the matter of affectivity. Frequently this is seen in the literature on patron-client relations as a product of the personalized "face-to-face" nature of the relationship. Affective ties are contrasted with the instrumental dealings of the marketplace and are perceived as giving rise to diffuse mutual obligations and to a certain element of unconditionality in the relationship. Patron-client relations have thus been described as a special combination of specific exchange with what sociologists and anthropologists term "generalized exchange."[50] Generalized exchange—which in traditional societies typically took the form of gift-giving and the provision of hospitality—provides the basis for relations based on trust and solidarity that inevitably take on affective overtones: honor and obligation are important concepts in clientelist relations.

Macrorelationships such as Lomé offer much less scope for the development of personalized ties. All patron-client relationships, however, are not based exclusively on affective ties but on a combination of these and instrumental relations. As Legg points out, affectivity can arise from factors other than face-to-face contact; in the Lomé context affectivity is the product of language and historical ties reinforced through such organizations as the Commonwealth, and the Francophone Community.[51] Familial analogies are frequent in the descriptions of the relationship both by spokesmen for the ACP and those from the Community (although the parent-child metaphor of the colonial days has been replaced by references to spouses, siblings, or cousins). Whereas relations between the states of the European Community and their former colonies manifested a greater element of generalized exchange in the years prior to Lomé, the Convention itself is not confined to the specific exchange of the marketplace but includes, for instance, provisions for cultural cooperation and exchange. And Lomé is not alone in the relative decline of personalized relations and of the concept of unconditionality. Modernization has led to new forms of clientelism: deference toward the personal characteristics of the patron and affectivity are less marked in relationships where traditional notables have been superseded by machine politicians; the greater choice available to clients has improved their ability to bargain with potential patrons but has lessened the elements of mutual respect and unconditionality in the relationship.[52]

The ACP Group's perception of a generalized obligation on the part of the Community to promote their interests, I would assert, is the key element that distinguishes their strategy as a variant of clientelism. Lomé was perceived as being more than just a trade and aid agreement: the whole was more than the sum of its parts. In response to a journalist's inquiry about whether the new Convention was just a package deal of specific items, one of the principal ACP negotiators, P. J. Patterson, Jamaican Minister for Industry, Commerce, and Tourism, responded "No, I think it is something wider than the mere specific items which it contains."[53] ACP states have frequently made reference to what they perceive as the Community's obligations arising from the "spirit" of Lomé. Certainly, however, there has been a tension in the relationship between the idea of the Community's generalized obligation and its contractual obligations under the Convention; as succeeding chapters will show, as the ACP became increasingly disillusioned with what it perceived to be the Community's failure to live up to the "spirit" of the agreement, so it attempted to strengthen the contractual element.

Reciprocity is the third major element common to all definitions of clientelism. In this context, reciprocity refers to the exchange of non-comparable resources, usually effected by means of a package deal. For both parties the objective is to obtain resources that they perceive as being valuable and that would not otherwise be readily available to them. Emphasis is placed on the notion of noncomparability since this is the basis for the unequal exchange characterizing the relationship. Frequently the literature on patron-client relations assumes that the balance of exchange inevitably favors the patron, the stronger party in the relationship. Here it comes closest to the cruder types of dependency writings, which assume that the weak are inevitably the victims of exploitation in an asymmetrical relationship.

As Legg cogently argues, there is little evidence to suggest that the client is inevitably the loser in the exchange.[54] Often it is the client who receives material benefits in exchange for political, symbolic, or affective resources (which the client can make available at minimal or no personal expense). There are no a priori grounds on which the costs and benefits of the exchange to the two parties can be judged. For their part, clients

have the advantage of being able to exert moral pressure on the patron—
the principal resource of the weak. Patrons may be unwilling to exercise
their full bargaining resources in the relationship for fear of being labeled
as exploiters by the wider community—in other words, patrons may be
the victims of their own power.[55] Ultimately, the terms of exchange are
a matter of bargaining between the parties, with the result partially a matter
of the parties' respective urgency of need for the resources offered by the
others. Clientelism therefore allows—and this is a major advantage of this
perspective over most dependency writings—for the possibility not only
of the generation of mutual benefits but also of a relationship in which
clients may be perceived to be the principal beneficiaries of material exchange. Whether a relationship with this type of imbalance will be durable is, however, open to question.

Lomé certainly represents the type of package deal characteristic of a
clientelist relationship. Its comprehensiveness—comprising provisions for
trade; agricultural, industrial, financial, and technical cooperation; commodities earnings stabilization; and the promotion of mining and energy
development—stands in marked contrast to most agreements in North-
South relations, which tend to be issue-specific, an excellent example being
the various generalized systems of preferences. Lomé does contain elements of reciprocity, although the one-for-one exchange typified by the
reverse preferences of the Yaoundé Conventions has been replaced by a
more unequal exchange—material resources from the EEC in return for
largely symbolic resources from the ACP. Indeed, one can reasonably
argue that the principal commodity provided by the ACP in the Convention was their participation: their very "being there" brought symbolic
rewards to the European Community, which was able to claim Lomé as
the showpiece of its development policy.

There was one norm in the new relationship on which the ACP Group
insisted that runs counter to orthodox clientelist relations: recognition of
the equality of the partners. Conscious that the previous Association arrangements under the Treaty of Rome and Yaoundé Conventions had
been "neocolonial"—the important decisions being taken by the member
states and then handed down in imperial fashion to the Associates—the
ACP Group insisted that the new Convention should formally recognize
the equality of the partnership. Even if the Group was to be the client
in the relationship, there would be none of the deference typical of some
traditional clientelist relations—and, indeed, at times of the former atti-

tude of the Francophones toward France. Accordingly the terminology of the past relationship—the title of Associated State with its connotation of less than full membership in the agreement—was discarded. A norm of equality, however, is an uneasy companion to the norm of nonreciprocity on which the ACP were equally insistent; this conflict will be explored later at greater length.

One other element of clientelism warrants discussion at this stage. Patron-client relations are usually perceived as typically particularistic and are frequently described as extralegal, being juxtaposed with contractual relations. For this reason, some commentators deny that landlord-serf ties under feudalism can be characterized as a form of clientelist relationship. In Gellner's words, patronage "always belongs to some *pays réel* which is ambivalently conscious of not being the *pays légal.*"[56] As noted before, the very essence of the ACP Group's strategy of collective clientelism is its particularism: the granting of special benefits ("private goods") to a group of clients that are not available to the wider international community. These grounds have formed the basis for an attack on Lomé by other members of the Group of 77. This particularism has also cast doubt on the legality of Lomé given the universalistic norms of the international trade regime codified in GATT. Certainly, Lomé's predecessors— the Yaoundé Conventions—were manifestly illegal under GATT terms as that organization frequently pointed out (see chapter 2). Lomé's own status in relation to GATT is somewhat more ambiguous. But even though the Convention is an international treaty and its contractual nature is frequently emphasized by the parties, this is undermined by a wide variety of safeguard clauses and other loopholes that, as succeeding chapters will demonstrate, provide the patron in the relationship with considerable scope for discretionary administration.

## EUROPEAN INTERESTS

For a clientelist relationship to develop successfully there must be mutual interest in collaboration. Often, as Legg points out, clientelist relationships are initiated by potential patrons since they are the ones with specific resources to offer.[57] In the Lomé case, while it is difficult to disentangle the course of events in the negotiations to make a categorical statement regarding which party took the initiative, there is no doubt that the EEC and its member states played an active role in promoting the successful negotiation of the Convention. This occurred directly, e.g., through the Commission's proposals for the STABEX scheme and indirectly through third parties such as the Commonwealth. By no means was the EEC a reluctant suitor. As in most clientelist relations, the motivations of the potential patron were a mixture of psychological, political, and material factors.

In the psychological realm, there was undoubtedly a continuing element of noblesse oblige in the attitude of the European powers toward their former colonies; a certain psychological satisfaction was gained from providing development assistance to the ACP states, especially since the group contained a large number of the world's least developed countries. In the former colonial powers there were strong domestic lobbies in support of maintaining historical ties (even in Germany with respect to Tanzania, Cameroon, and Papua New Guinea). The British Government, in particular, was under pressure not to "sell out" the developing Commonwealth in its haste to gain admission to the European Community.

On the political side, a relationship with the ACP states constituted an integral part of the Community's elaborately constructed "fresco" of policies toward the developing world and appeared to represent the realization of the long-standing dream of EurAfrica. Early theorists of this concept had noted the "natural" complementarity between the two continents:

The African soil is too poor for Africa to be able to do without Europe. The African sub-soil is too rich for Europe to be able to do without Africa. Thus it must be admitted that Africa is an indispensable complement to Europe.[58]

These sentiments had in recent years been echoed in the EEC, albeit in the less colorful terminology of interdependence. To reach an agreement with virtually all the independent states of sub-Saharan Africa was prized highly by the Community—it was no accident that Commissioner for Development Claude Cheysson apparently overlooked the Pacific and Caribbean countries in exclaiming that "It is the first time in history that an entire continent has undertaken a collective commitment"; and "This kind of convention—[involving] the participation of the whole [*sic*] of independent black Africa—is unique in the history of the world."[59] A failure to have successfully negotiated a successor to the Yaoundé Conventions—the centerpiece of Community development policy since the Treaty of Rome—would have been an embarrassment for the member states and hardly a propitious beginning for the Community in its attempts to widen the scope of its relations with LDCs.

Important bureaucratic interests were also involved on the European side. A failure of the negotiations would have cast doubt on the *raison d'être* of Directorate-General (DG) VIII of the Commission of the European Communities, whose responsibilities were limited to relations with Associated states, and which was in competition with DG I, the Directorate responsible for other external affairs. On the other hand, enlargement of the relationship to include most of the developing Commonwealth, plus some previously nonassociated African states, would represent not only a major coup but also a significant extension of its bureaucratic mandate. There is no doubt that the Commission at least (some member states might not have shared its enthusiasm) envisaged a carving out of a sphere of influence in which the EEC would be the dominant economic partner—in his preface to a Community publication on interdependence, Cheysson foresaw a time when the European unit of account would be the reference currency not only for Europeans "but also for their principal clients and suppliers in the Third World."[60] Bureaucratic interests, then, were important in motivating the Commission to play a prominent and innovative role in the negotiations. Indeed in this instance the Commission appeared to escape from the straitjacket that had been imposed on most of its activities with the triumph of intergovernmentalism in the Community in the mid-1960s: the Commission's role in taking the initiative in the negotiations and in arbitrating disputes was akin to that anticipated by neofunctionalist theorists of integration.

For two of the member states, an agreement carried special significance for their own international standing. Maintenance of the Francophone Community and of the Commonwealth reinforced one of the remaining claims that France and Britain had to Great Power status and certainly gave them an influence in the world disproportionate to their economic strength. Whether the two groupings would have disappeared in the absence of the Lomé agreement is perhaps dubious; certainly the Commonwealth would have come under considerable strain if no arrangements had been made for continued access of its developing members to their traditional market in Britain. Although bilateral ties remained important—particularly in the case of France whose defense pacts with African countries provided Paris with an opportunity to flex its military muscles and offered a testing ground for its *forces d'intervention*—the multilateralization of economic ties under Lomé gave relations with the former colonies less of a neocolonial overtone than would otherwise have been the case.

ACP countries were also important hosts of European investment, particularly in the fields of minerals and energy. For France, Britain, and Belgium, their shares in total foreign direct investment (FDI) in Africa exceeded their average shares in total FDI in all Third World countries.[61] At their independence, ten Francophone African states had signed detailed covenants with Paris under which France was given prior claim to petroleum, uranium, and rare-earth elements and a veto power over exports to third countries if France determined that the minerals were needed for defense purposes.[62] In many cases, corporations from the former metropole enjoyed monopolies in the exploitation of the mineral wealth of the former colonies. In Francophone states, the French government was often a major partner; for instance, it owned 70 percent of the capital of the Equatorial Africa Oil Company (SPAFE), which exploited deposits in the Congo and Gabon, and the French Atomic Energy Commission had a one-third interest in the Air Mines Company (SOMAIR) created in 1967 to exploit Niger's uranium deposits.[63] The French government was also involved in mining bauxite in the Cameroon, manganese in Gabon, and potash in the Congo.

Inevitably in the asymmetrical clientelist relationship, the material resources of the client are relatively small in comparison to those that the patron can make available. This is not to suggest, however, that they are always insignificant. Certainly the ACP offered a relatively small market to the EEC. Although the Third World in aggregate had become the Community's principal customer by the early 1970s and provided approximately two-thirds of Europe's surplus in trade in manufactures,[64] the ACP countries as a whole accounted for only 7 percent of Europe's exports—a share smaller than that of Eastern Europe and one that had declined in recent years. Even for France the *chasse gardée* was, in aggregate terms, no longer of significance. For particular sectors of European business, however, the former colonies remained important clients. This was especially true of mercantile capital in France—the old trading houses. Long-established patterns of trade were also of some considerable significance in maintaining local employment, e.g., the refining of cane sugar imported from developing Commonwealth countries in certain English

**TABLE 1.3.**

Composition of EEC Exports to the ACP, 1975

| SITC | | % |
|---|---|---|
| 0 | Food products and live animals | 8.0 |
| 1 | Beverages, tobacco | 1.9 |
| 2 | Raw materials, inedibles | 0.8 |
| 3 | Mineral fuels | 2.2 |
| 4 | Animal and vegetable oils | 0.4 |
| 5 | Chemical products | 11.5 |
| 6 | Manufactured goods | 20.2 |
| 7 | Machinery, transport equipment | 47.8 |
| 8 | Other manufactures | 6.2 |

Source: Commission, Dossier Sur L'Interdépendance Europe—Tiers-Monde, p. 112.

port cities. And there is some evidence to suggest that traditional patterns of trade, facilitated by arrangements such as the franc zone, enables some member states to export to ACP states manufactures that are noncompetitive in open markets.[65] As a whole the Community earns a significant surplus in trade in manufactures from its relationship with ACP states (table 1.3 shows the commodity composition of EEC exports to the ACP).

In terms of the evolution of the collective clientelist relationship, the multilateralization of trade and investment relationships between the Community and ACP states is of especial interest. France's most rapidly growing markets in Black Africa were not her ex-colonies but Nigeria and Zaire. And during the Yaoundé Conventions, Germany and the Netherlands in particular had been successful in penetrating Associates' markets that had previously been monopolized by the colonial power (see chapter 2). Participating in the role of collective patron therefore offered resources—in the form of a guarantee of nondiscrimination in the clients' treatment of European imports and investments—that the smaller European states in particular probably would not have been able to obtain if they had been negotiating on a bilateral basis. Proposals for industrial cooperation with the ACP states—which took the form of a Centre for Industrial Development serving as a broker between ACP clients and European businesses (see chapter 7)—afforded the opportunity for a significant multilateralization of contacts and was again of particular significance for the smaller European states, which lacked their own organizations for this purpose.

Table 1.4 shows the importance of the ACP as suppliers of various commodities to the Community. While few of these appeared amenable to effective cartelization, either solely among the ACP or in conjunction with other Third World producers, and the ACP lacked other markets to which they could divert production, undoubtedly there was concern in the Community at the time of the negotiations regarding its ability to maintain and ensure in the future a diversity of suppliers. Europe, owing to its greater dependence on imported minerals than the United States (figure 1.1 shows this to approach the situation of Japan for many of the key commodities), was already inclined to be more conciliatory than Washington toward the Third World. Community concern regarding future security of supplies was heightened by the commodities boom of the early 1970s and also reinforced during the negotiations for Lomé by

**TABLE 1.4.**

ACP Share in EEC Imports of Raw Materials (1976) (in percentage of extra-EEC imports)

| | |
|---|---|
| 95–100 | Uranium |
| 90–95 | |
| 85–90 | Pineapples, palm nuts, & kernels |
| 80–85 | Groundnut oil |
| 75–80 | |
| 70–75 | |
| 65–70 | |
| 60–65 | |
| 55–60 | Groundnuts, raw sugar, sisal, wood, aluminum ore |
| 50–55 | Copper ores and concentrates, alumina |
| 45–50 | Groundnut cake |
| 40–45 | Coffee |
| 35–40 | Refined copper |
| 30–35 | Manganese |
| 25–30 | Tea, tin |
| 20–25 | |
| 15–20 | Beef, bananas, palm oil, raw cotton, phosphates, iron ore |
| 10–15 | Rice, rubber (natural), skins, diamonds |
| <10 | Copra, raw tobacco, unrefined aluminum, zinc, chrome, wolfram, crude petroleum |

Source: Commission des Communautés Européennes, Direction Générale de L'Information, *Dossier sur L'Interdépendance Europe—Tiers-Monde*, (Paris, 28 Août 1978) p. 68.

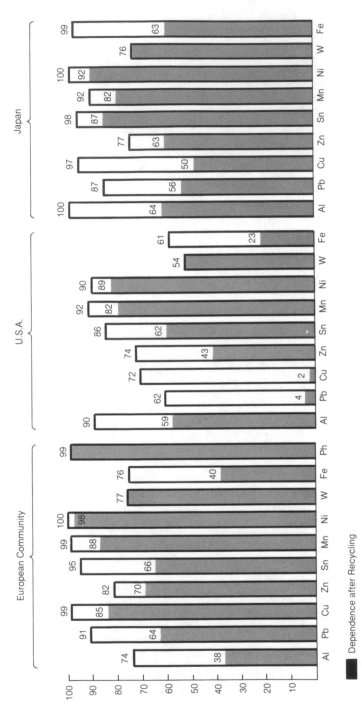

**FIGURE 1.1.**
Degree of Dependence in Respect of Certain Minerals of the EEC, USA and Japan (% of net imports in relation to 1975 consumption)

Al...Aluminum; Pb...Lead; Cu...Copper; Zn...Zinc; Sn...Tin; Mn...Manganese; Ni...Nickel; W...Tungsten; Fe...Iron; Ph...Phosphates.

 Dependence after Recycling

OPEC's revolutionary success. The ACP, in part because of the local dominance of Community corporations, were seen as playing an important role in the future. ACP states supplied approximately 10 percent of the Community's total imports of agricultural products and raw materials.

Again, a collective relationship with the ACP appeared to offer the potential patrons more than might be obtained solely on a bilateral basis. Germany, for instance, which had few historical ties with Africa, was becoming particularly interested in the continent's mineral wealth and troubled by the political instability that had led to a falling off in mining investments. STABEX appeared to offer not only a form of social insurance for the ACP but also an insurance policy for the patron by helping to increase the security of future supply of raw materials. Since STABEX in most cases would apply only to ACP exports to the Community, the intention was that it would ensure not only continued production by ACP states but also export to the European market and thus continuity of Community supplies.

Playing the role of collective patron offered the European Community the opportunity, in an era of increasing uncertainty, to reinforce the preferential relations enjoyed by the Community member states and their corporations with a large group of countries, some of which either were, or had the potential to become, significant suppliers of raw materials. As the chief ACP negotiator, Wenike Briggs, noted:

It is most unlikely that Europe would say "No" to Africa, its raw materials and its markets. . . . It is not easy for her to turn to another region and have ready replacements.[66]

Saying "Yes" to the ACP was made easier by the clients' economic weakness: collectively they appeared to pose little threat to Community economic interests. While the Convention itself might not produce significant material benefits in the short term for the larger member states, the advantages appeared to be sufficient to warrant ratification so long as the costs of patronage could be kept within reasonable bounds. Playing the role of patron in a collective clientelist relationship appeared to be a relatively low-cost strategy that offered the potential to realize some significant long-term benefits.

This is not to argue that the member states of the Community had identical perspectives on the type of relationship that should be pursued with the ACP nor that they shared the ACP's perception of the responsibilities that the Community as patron should undertake in the relationship. As chapter 2 illustrates, discussion of Community policy toward LDCs had always been marked by a split between "globalists" and "regionalists": respectively those countries that favored a universal policy toward the Third World (most notably Germany and the Netherlands) and those that gave priority to a special relationship on a regional basis with former colonies (France and, to a lesser extent, Belgium). Although France had held the upper hand in bargaining at the time of the Treaty of Rome, the globalists had succeeded in gradually eroding the advantages enjoyed by the Associates. In their efforts, the globalists had been assisted by the opposition of the international community, and especially the United States, to the neomercantile nature of the closed trading bloc established with the Associates. Britain's entry into the Community was expected to strengthen their position.

On the other hand, Britain perceived an obligation toward the Commonwealth associables that certainly strengthened their hand in the negotiation of the Lomé Convention. To the extent that they were willing to sign the Convention with its provision of exclusive special benefits for the ACP, all member states may be perceived to have accepted—at least nominally—the role of collective patron. For some, however, this was primarily a *tactical* move regarded as essential for attracting the ACP into a relationship all believed was important for the evolution of Community development policy. Their perceptions of their obligations as patrons in the relationship, however, differed significantly from those of the ACP. For the latter, although aware they had not realized all their objectives in the negotiations (see chapter 2), Lomé constituted a useful foundation, with the expectation that where its provisions fell short of their aspirations, the Community would accept its generalized obligations toward the promotion of ACP interests in the "spirit" of the agreement. For the globalists in the Community, however, Lomé was less of a first step than a final destination for the particularistic relationship. Hence the contractual obligations of the Convention were emphasized. Once negotiation of the Convention had been successfully achieved, attention could be turned toward improving relations with other developing countries—which inevitably would involve a whittling away of the particularistic advantages enjoyed by the ACP.

## SUMMARY AND CONCLUSIONS

The concept of collective clientelism provides a useful explanation of the type of relationship the ACP Group aspired to construct with the EEC through the Lomé Convention. Like all forms of clientelism, it aimed to build on the affective ties existing between the groups to achieve a particularistic relationship that would provide exclusive benefits. By accepting the role of patron in the "spirit" of Lomé, ACP states hoped that the Community would safeguard their interests even where there was no contractual obligation to do so; this notion of a generalized obligation made Lomé more than merely another trade and aid pact. And, like all forms of clientelism, the ACP strategy was primarily defensive, a response of the weak to the uncertainties of a politicized market system: the ACP sought a guarantee of security and of their subsistence needs through the Convention.

Collective clientelism is useful also in explaining the evolution of the relationship. This was subject not only to the factors typical of all clientelist relations but also to the special dynamics and internal contradictions resulting from the collective nature of the strategy and from the ACP insistence on the norms of equality and nonreciprocity.

By virtue of its collective nature, the ACP strategy had an inherent tendency toward instability. All clientelist relations are characterized by a predominance of vertical over horizontal ties. Normally this presents no significant problem—except where the clients wish to act together to improve their bargaining position with the patron. This was, of course, the very essence of collective clientelism. Although ACP states had shown surprising unity in negotiating the Convention (see chapter 2), the Group was almost completely lacking in institutionalization at the time the Convention came into force. To play an effective collective role in the relationship the Group had to become more than a loose-knit organization whose only role was to negotiate every five years with the Community.

If *collective* clientelism was to succeed, then the ACP Group qua group needed to install itself as the principal intermediary between individual ACP states and the European Community both as a whole (represented by the Commission) and its member states. Given the problems of forging a united front for more than fifty developing countries with diverse interests, this was no easy task. It was made all the more difficult by the structure of the relationship, which allowed little institutionalized role for the ACP Group in the day-to-day implementation of the Convention, and, second, by the fact that clientelism operated on several levels simultaneously. Figure 1.2b presents a sketch of how an idealized collective clientelist relationship would have operated in the Lomé framework: the reality is much closer to that represented by figure 1.2c, in which there are multiple relationships that sometimes overlap with each other. ACP states in many cases maintained their close ties with their former metropole, e.g., Zaire-Belgium, Surinam-the Netherlands, while subgroupings, e.g., the Francophones, looked collectively (but at a sub-ACP level) to their traditional patrons. For individual ACP states, the danger of the collective approach was that their traditional patron would feel less of an obligation toward safeguarding their interests once the obligations of the patron had been diluted by being collectivized to the Community as a whole. Accordingly, ACP states continued to attempt to exploit their traditional bilateral ties with individual Community member states to obtain particularistic concessions for themselves. Collective clientelism had to prove its efficacy by bringing benefits to the whole group; in the absence of obvious success in the short run, there would be an inevitable tendency on the part of ACP states to a regression toward bilateral clientelist relationships. Naturally this would facilitate a Community strategy of *divide et impera*.

A further source of instability in the relationship was that it looked to the past—in the sense of ties created during the colonial period—in order to safeguard particularistic advantages in the future. Here the ACP hoped to take advantage of the inertia effects of international regimes. Like international organizations, regimes tend to take on a life of their own that sometimes causes a lag between changes in the distribution of power and interest that underlie the regime and changes in the rules and norms of the regime itself.[67] ACP states fully realized they were becoming relatively less important economic partners for the Community. Yet if the particularistic advantages they enjoyed were to be sustained, the EEC would have to accept that its hands were tied with respect to certain aspects of its policies toward other LDCs. They hoped the Convention would achieve this. Here the impetus for a neomercantilist relationship came primarily from the weaker party, which obviously perceived it would obtain more benefits from vertical collaboration than from cooperation on the horizontal dimension with nonparticipant LDCs. An attempt to maintain the particularistic advantages conferred by the Convention,

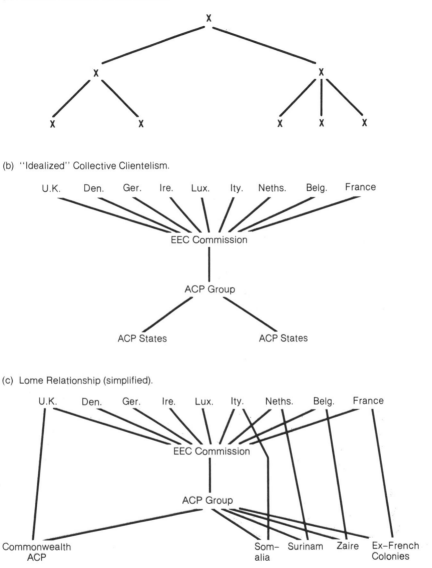

(a) Traditional Patron–Client Network.

(b) "Idealized" Collective Clientelism.

U.K.  Den.  Ger.  Ire.  Lux.  Ity.  Neths.  Belg.  France

EEC Commission

ACP Group

ACP States        ACP States

(c) Lome Relationship (simplified).

U.K.  Den.  Ger.  Ire.  Lux.  Ity.  Neths.  Belg.  France

EEC Commission

ACP Group

Commonwealth        Som–  Surinam  Zaire  Ex–French
ACP                      alia                  Colonies

**FIGURE 1.2.**
A Comparison of Clientelist Structures

however, placed the ACP in the incongruous position of undermining one of the objectives of the Group of 77. As the Nigerian Ambassador to the EEC noted:

The ACP states had hardly finished signing the Convention when they had to do battle to prevent erosion of their gains from multilateral trade negotiations. The (ACP) programme expressly seeks protection against such erosion. Furthermore the ACP states are placed in the dubious position of having to stand on the same side of the fence with a group of industrialised states "against" the group of 77 in this area.[68]

ACP unwillingness to grant more than token reciprocity in the Lomé relationship encouraged the Community's perceptions of the Group's growing irrelevance and further undermined its attempts to preserve its particularistic advantages. There was an inherent contradiction between the ACP Group's demand to be treated as an equal in the relationship and its unwillingness to provide reciprocity. A similar contradiction and tension underlay demands for equality and for a contractual relationship on the one hand and the expectation the EEC would play the role of a conventional patron on the other. ACP states aspired to the material benefits of clientelism while refusing to accept the status of clients or to appear subordinate in the relationship. When the EEC behaved in the manner of a typical patron in unilaterally defining the nature of the relationship and administering it in a paternalistic fashion, the ACP attempted to curtail this behavior by emphasizing the contractual obligations of the Community under the Convention. On the other hand, the ACP expected the Community to go beyond the terms of the Convention in meeting its generalized obligation to its client in the "spirit" of Lomé: in this instance, it was often the Community that fell back on the contractual nature of the Convention as a means of delimiting its obligations.

These tensions and contradictions in the strategy of collective clientelism are brought out in chapters 3 through 8, which discuss the implementation of the principal provisions of the Convention, and are examined in greater detail in chapter 9. Chapter 2 places the Convention in historical perspective by examining its predecessors and the negotiations that led up to its signature.

# 2

## From Rome to Lomé

Collective clientelism had its origins in the association bestowed on selected colonies of the six original EEC member states at the signature of
the Treaty of Rome. If Britain had been successful in its first application
for membership of the Community in 1961, these arrangements would
also have been imposed on the Commonwealth states of Africa, regardless of whether their governments desired this or not. This element of
coercion and the complete disregard for the sensitivites of the newly independent African states on matters concerning sovereignty were principal factors in the initial opposition of Commonwealth Africa to any relationship with the Community. In the period of a few years, however,
some of the most vociferous Commonwealth critics of the Rome and
Yaoundé treaties performed a *volte-face* and sought association agreements with the Community. Their reasons for doing so are examined in
the second part of this chapter.

Europe's relationship with the ACP under the Lomé Convention represents not so much a radical break but continuity with policies previously pursued toward African states under the Yaoundé Conventions, albeit a continuity that was adjusted for changes in the international
economic environment and to allow for the accession of Britain to the
Treaty of Rome. An examination of the relationship between the Community and the associated states (EAMA) under the Yaoundé Conventions highlights many of the problems that were not only to become significant issues at the time of the negotiation of the first Lomé Convention
but that also, in many cases, have remained unresolved (or, more precisely, not resolved to the satisfaction of the ACP). Given the continuity
of the arrangements, the results of cooperation between the parties under
the Treaty of Rome and Yaoundé Conventions serve as reasonable pre-
dictors of the likely effects of the Lomé provisions on the economies of
the ACP states.

## FROM ROME TO YAOUNDÉ

Future arrangments for French colonies were one of the last points to be agreed before the signature of the Treaty of Rome. France had not raised the issue of the future status of its colonies until the Venice conference of foreign ministers held in May 1956. There had been no reference to the problem in the Spaak Report; it had generally been assumed that the Treaty would not bring colonial and trust territories into the Communities but that each member would continue to carry out its own responsibilities for the dependent territories and, if so desired, to give preferential treatment within existing limits to imports from the dependencies. France's move was shrewdly timed: by making a satisfactory agreement on provisions for its dependencies a sine qua non for its signature of the Treaty, French bargaining power was maximized.

Foremost among the arguments of the French government was that sole responsibility for the development of its colonies placed an unfair burden on the French Treasury and on French industry (which was required to pay prices above those prevailing on the world market for raw material imports from the dependencies). French economic policy toward its dependencies had created a mercantilist system with dear trade in both directions. Tariff preferences introduced in 1928 had marked the foundation of the franc zone and subsequently were supplemented by discriminatory quantitative restrictions. In the conditions of the extreme dollar shortage in the immediate postwar years trade with the colonies was perceived as a means of overcoming payments difficulties: colonies were encouraged to export raw materials to dollar markets while their imports from third countries were strictly controlled. In the period following the Korean crisis a buyer's market replaced the shortage of primary commodities that had been experienced since the war and world prices slumped. Overproduction occurred in many French colonies, however, as a result of the *surprix* system, which guaranteed prices to colonial producers considerably above those prevailing on the world market (from 15 percent for cotton to 60 percent for coffee).

French importers were obliged to purchase at high prices from the colonies by the operation of an import licensing system (*Jumelage*) that guaranteed licences for imports from third countries only if a certain proportion of overall supplies were purchased from the franc zone. A similar form of import licensing required colonies to purchase the products of

French industry—again often at prices above those prevailing on the world market (local processing and manufacturing industries being discouraged). In many cases, the franc zone accounted for the majority of total exports of some French industries, suggesting these were not competitive on the open market. In the mid-1950s, in fact, French exports to the franc zone exceeded those to her future EEC partners (33 percent in contrast to 25 percent of total exports). African colonies, however, accounted for only one-third of franc zone trade.[1]

In addition to price supports, France provided a substantial part of the government revenue of the colonies—in 1958 the French contribution to current government expenditure ranged from 9.8 percent of the total in Madagascar to 12.1 percent in West Africa, and 16.1 percent in Equatorial Africa. In all territories at least half of the capital expenditure was defrayed by France, and in Equatorial Africa the metropole's contribution was as high as 94.4 percent.[2] Inflows of French public funds were also largely offset by outflows of private funds. Much of the capital expenditure financed public works contracts awarded to metropolitan firms, while current expenditure paid the salaries of expatriate officials, both types of aid resulting in a considerable repatriation of funds. But French aid to the colonies did place a considerable burden on the French Treasury—from 1956–59 French government grants and loans to LDCs (the majority of which went to the franc zone) totaled $3.1 billion compared with aid figures of $0.9 billion for the United Kingdom and $0.7 billion for West Germany.[3] Besides easing the direct burden on the economy, France also looked to the EEC as a means of securing new protected markets for the dependencies' products. The *surprix* system had encouraged overproduction to such an extent that the French market alone was no longer able to absorb the colonies' total output. Full membership of the Community for the colonies was not a practicable solution: their nascent industries could not have survived the competition from Western Europe that would have followed the lowering of tariffs.

France's future partners were reluctant to agree to share the burden of providing assistance to the dependencies. They did not relish the prospect of being tainted with allegations of pursuing a collective colonialism and had no desire to be perceived as contributing, however indirectly, to the capacity of the French treasury to sustain colonial wars. Both Germany and the Netherlands had extensive trading links with other Third World areas, purchasing most of their primary products from them rather than from Africa. Having recently extricated itself from the traumas of Indonesian independence, the Dutch government had no desire for further colonial involvement (and did not propose association of its dependencies of Surinam and the Netherlands Antilles under the Treaty of Rome). Italy was responsible for one trust territory—Italian Somaliland—but apart from its role as principal supplier of the Italian banana market this territory held little economic interest for the Rome government. Even the Belgian government, responsible for Congo (Kinshasa) and the Trust territories of Rwanda-Burundi, although sympathetic to French Eur-African aspirations, expressed little enthusiasm for the type of preferential trading arrangement envisaged by France. The three territories under Belgian administration had always applied nondiscriminatory tariffs as a result of the Congo Basin Treaties of 1883, and the Congo itself, by virtue of its mineral deposits, enjoyed unusually diversified trading links.

But in a situation where her potential partners urgently desired French signature of the Treaty, France held the upper hand in bargaining. Although the Dutch and German governments were able to win concessions on matters of detail—an initial limit of five years on the association, an aid budget lower than the French had requested and subject to stricter Community control, and multilateralization of preferences previously enjoyed by France—the principle of association and the creation of preferential access to Community markets for the Associates proved to be nonnegotiable. Accordingly, the Treaty of Rome's Part IV provided for association with the Six of the "non-European Countries and territories which have special relations with Belgium, France, Italy and the Netherlands," the stated objectives of which were to "promote the economic and social development of the countries and territories and to establish close economic relations between them and the Community as a whole."[4]

A single free trade area was to be progressively established between the Community and all Associates. Exports from the Associates (with the exception of certain "sensitive" products) would eventually receive duty-free access to the Community market around which a common external tariff (CET) would be constructed, thereby discriminating against imports from third countries. In order to justify the arrangements under GATT requirements for free trade areas, Associated territories were required to reciprocate by abolishing customs duties on imports from the Community and from each other at the same rate as prescribed for intra-Community trade. Associates could, however, "levy customs duties which correspond to the needs of their development and the requirements of their industrialization or which, being of a fiscal nature, have the object of contributing to their budgets" (Article 133). Those Associates bound by prior international obligations to maintain nondiscriminatory tariffs (Belgian Congo, Rwanda-Burundi, and French Equatorial Africa by virtue of the Congo Basin Treaties of 1883, and the U.N. Trust territories of Cameroon, Italian Somaliland, and Togo) were not required to reduce tariffs on imports from the Community. Those countries heavily dependent on tariffs for revenue were allowed to compensate for the elimination of tariffs by the imposition of fiscal charges *erga omnes*.

Quantitative restrictions had been as important as preferential tariffs in closing markets both in metropoles and their colonies to third party trade. The Treaty of Rome established a twelve- to fifteen-year timetable for the elimination of discriminatory quotas in Eur-African trade; quotas applied by Associates to trade other than with the metropole were to be made global and applied without discrimination between the member states and were to be enlarged each year in accordance with the provisions of Articles 32 and 33 of the Treaty. Liberalization of quantitative restrictions was a prerequisite if France's partners were to gain access to the market of Francophone Associates: the expansion of imports by these territories from member states other than France in the first two years following the signature of the Treaty attests both to the previous restrictive impact of the quotas and to the relative success in moving toward their eventual removal. Multilateralization of the benefits formerly enjoyed exclusively by France was sought also in the area of rights of establishment. Details of these arrangements were not finalized by the Six for two years, and it was not until April 1968 that the last discriminatory arrangements were removed (by Mali).[5] France's partners in the Community remained at a disadvantage in the markets of Francophone countries by virtue of the continued discriminatory monetary arrangements of the franc zone; this problem was never seriously addressed during the association period.

A principal innovation of the Treaty of Rome was the creation of the European Development Fund (EDF), for which the associated colonies and territories were designated as sole beneficiaries. A total capital of 581.25 million units of account (mua, at that time 1 ua was equivalent to $1.00) was subscribed for the five-year period of the Convention. The Fund was to be administered by the European Commission. Annual allocations from the Fund would be approximately equal to 50 percent of the annual average French investment in the Associates in the previous decade.[6]

It soon became clear that the provisions of the Treaty did not solve the problem of noncompetitive production in Associated states. Since they continued to produce at costs above the levels of world market prices (during the six years of the association period under the Treaty the French Associates received $325 million in price supports from France), their exports benefited little from the 40 percent reduction in tariffs in the markets of the other five members. In fact, they had exchanged a higher French tariff wall for a lower degree of preference in a larger preferential market. Not only was the tariff advantage reduced—from a weighted average on preference items of 8.7 percent under the pre-1958 French tariff to 5.1 percent under the CET, but the number of products (and hence the percentage of total exports) that enjoyed a tariff preference also declined.[7] And, for two of their major products, special dispensations in the Treaty allowed for duty-free import quotas from third countries (for bananas by Germany and for coffee by the Benelux countries and Italy). Competing African states (Angola, Ghana, Nigeria, Kenya, Tanzania, and Uganda) actually increased their share of the EEC market in the 1959–1964 period.[8]

What was to be done for the Associates' agricultural products remained the major dispute throughout the association period, one on which Dutch and German preference for open markets and a global development policy opposed the mercantilist conceptions of regional managed markets favored by France and the Associates. All tropical agricultural products had been included under the Treaty of Rome in a list of agricultural products to which "managed marketing" could apply. This was seized upon by the French government as a possible legal basis for providing a Community-wide protected market and price supports for the colonies. But the German and Dutch administrations perceived the problem not as one of finding a legal basis for increased protection but of assisting the Associated states to produce efficiently so that they would be able to compete effectively on the world market. Both the Dutch and German governments were admanatly opposed to increased discrimination against their traditional suppliers of tropical products and, indeed, were unwilling to agree to the maintenance of the existing free trade area with the Associates.

With the successful establishment of the Community the distribution of bargaining power among the members on the association issue changed, French leverage over the other member states being reduced. It was France's partners that now could threaten a veto—in this case, over the renewal of the association arrangements; this tactic was employed in order to impose their desire for a more open trading relationship in which the trade diversion costs of the arrangements would be minimized. In the pursuit of this objective they were aided by pressure from the international trading community—both from within GATT, where persistent criticisms of the association policies were voiced, and from the British government, which saw a reduction in the CET for tropical products as an alternative to Association status for the developing countries of the Commonwealth.[9] The first major test of strength on the issue came with the negotiations for a successor to the association arrangements of the Treaty, which expired in 1962.

On the one hand, the French (and the Belgians, less enthusiastically) supported the Associates' demands for the maintenance and strengthening of their existing preferences: on the other, the Dutch and Germans emphasized the need to consider the position of competing nonassociates and proposed a lowering of the CET on tropical products. The European Commission managed to bridge the gap by supporting the latter position on tariff reductions and on the phasing out of French price supports (as had previously been agreed) but favored the accelerated imposition of the CET and argued that the new (Yaoundé I) Convention should offer compensation to the Associates for lower preferences through Community aid. This would be designed to help Associates diversify and improve their productive structures and provide support for local price stabilization schemes.[10]

Despite the fact that the Francophone Associates had attained their independence in 1960, and in that year gained direct representation at the EEC for the first time, the principal negotiations took place among the Community member states.[11] The resolution was not far removed in its principles from the Commission's proposals. A free trade area between the Community and each Associate was to be maintained; the Eighteen were to benefit from an acceleration in the reduction of customs duties on their products—but the CET on certain tropical products (including coffee, cocoa, and pineapples) was to be reduced by margins ranging from 15 percent to 50 percent. Special dispensations in the Treaty granted to Italy and Benelux for the import of coffee were to disappear, but the earlier regime governing German banana imports was maintained. French price supports were to be phased out, but the Community would provide a total of $230 million in aid for production and diversification. The second EDF would also provide a further $500 million in aid of which $46 million would be in the form of special loans and $64 million in subsidized loans from the European Investment Bank (EIB), an innovation, for the EIB had not been permitted to provide funds for the Associates during the Rome Treaty.

As the Associates were now politically sovereign, the Convention provided for the Eighteen to determine their own commercial relations with each other and with third parties and allowed for customs unions among the Associates and between them and third parties "insofar as they neither are nor prove to be incompatible with the principles and provisions" of the Convention. Joint institutions were created to administer the Convention: an Association Council (to be assisted by an Association Committee), a Parliamentary Conference, and a Court of Arbitration.

Despite breaking off the negotiations in July 1962 after declaring that the financial aid package was inadequate, the Associates failed to achieve their principal demands. In a manner that was to be repeated in the negotiations for Lomé II, the Community juggled the financial aid figures to effect a marginal improvement in the total offer, although this was derived primarily from an increase in loan funds. The final offer accepted by the Associates was barely two-thirds of the amount proposed by the Commission to the Council in its initial memorandum. Since French price supports were to be ended in the new package, the total aid in monetary terms to be received was less than that obtained under the Treaty. The aid for production/diversification fell far short of the Associates' aspirations for price stabilization for their principal products. Nor did the Associates succeed in realizing another Commission proposal—the abolition of consumption taxes on their tropical products.[12]

Dissatisfaction that their preferential advantages had been diminished in negotiations from which they had been excluded led to the Associates' demanding joint management and participation in all decisions affecting them, including the setting of quotas for exports from competing non-Associates. These were rebuffed by the member states—the Convention providing merely that on matters of commercial policy "the Contracting Parties agree to keep each other informed and, should one of them so request, to consult together for the purpose of giving good effect to this

Convention" (Article 12). A further blow to the Associates' desire to preserve their exclusive relationship with the Community was struck by the Dutch government, following the French veto in January 1963 of Britain's application for membership in the Community. Maintaining their position that association should be opened to other African countries, the Dutch refused to sign the new Convention until a public assurance was given on this matter. A "Declaration of Intentions" to this effect was eventually agreed in the Council meeting of 2 April 1963 and distributed at the time of the signature of the Convention in mid-July.

A similar pattern occurred at the time of the renegotiation of the Yaoundé Convention in 1968–69. According to the Associates, the phasing out of the *surprix* system during the Convention had been a major factor contributing to the deterioration in their economic position since 1962. Not only had their exports to the EEC grown at a slower rate than those of other LDCs but also their terms of trade had deteriorated.[13] Accordingly, the Associates argued, a "policy based solely on tariff advantages is insufficient to promote commercial exchange profitable to the African and Malagasy states." Their principal spokesman, Diori Hamani, complained that the EEC offered only tariff advantages to the Associates whereas they had previously enjoyed price and outlet garantees for their primary products.[14]

Supported by the French government, the Associates pressed for organized markets for their products modeled on the Community's Common Agricultural Policy. Noting the relatively slow growth of their exports to the Community, and their inability to penetrate certain markets, e.g., that for bananas in Germany, the Associates argued that the Community had made a commitment to increasing their exports that was presently unfulfilled and could be realized only through guaranteed market shares. As evidence of a Community commitment, they pointed to Annex VII of Yaoundé I, which stated "The Member States will study ways and means to promote increased consumption of goods originating in the Associated states."

None of France's partners perceived this, however, as a commitment to a system of guaranteed markets. The Dutch and German governments continued to press for an opening of Community markets to nonassociated LDCs and in the negotiations called for the abolition of reverse preferences and a further lowering of the CET. Nor would the "globalists" among the Six countenance a return to the *surprix* system.[15] The only concession that the Community made toward Associates" aspirations for secure prices was a provision that 80 mua of the third EDF could be employed to support Associates who faced "special and extraordinary difficulties creating an exceptional situation, having serious repercussions on their economic potential, and resulting either from a fall in world prices or from calamities such as famine or floods."[16] This was a belated response to the Commission's 1961 proposal that the Community contribute to local price stabilization schemes.

As the Commission had envisaged in its proposals to the Council on renegotiation, the eventual agreement reached was unchanged in its principles from the initial Yaoundé Convention.[17] The Dutch and German governments were successful in their demands that the CET on three products of interest to nonassociates—coffee, cocoa, and palm oil—be lowered. Nor did the new Convention satisfy the Associates in their demand that their interests be reflected in a liberalization of the Community's Common Agricultural Policy (CAP). Exports of certain agricultural products had been threatened by the gradual implementation of the CAP during the first Convention. For example, the two sugar exporters among the Associates, Congo (Brazzaville) and Madagascar, lost their privileged access to the French market with the introduction of the common organization of the Community market in July 1968 and were required to pay the full CAP levy on sugar imports. Yaoundé II provided no reassurance to the concerns of producers in the Associated African and Malagasy States (EAMA): the Community refused to consider a general commitment to trade liberalization in CAP products. Protocol No. 1 of the Convention stated that the Community would determine on a case-by-case basis, after consultation with the Association Council, the treatment to be accorded to competing agricultural products. Associates were assured that the provisions for their products would be "more favorable than the general treatment applied to like products originating in third countries." These arrangements confirmed the Community's perceptions of the role of the Associates as suppliers of the residual market that Community producers could not fill and at best provided them with a slight advantage over third countries.[18]

After a lengthy dispute among the Six the 3rd EDF was set at $1 billion, an increase of 25 percent over its predecessor. For the first time the EIB was to be permitted to contribute to the formation of risk capital in the Associated states. The Convention also went further than its predecessors in promoting regional cooperation among Associated states and their neighbors—Article 25 provided that Community funds would be made available to regional or interstate bodies. But the principal concern of the Associates—the safeguarding of their export revenue—went largely unanswered.

## IMPACT OF THE ASSOCIATION

### Trade

Any attempt to isolate the impact of the tariff preferences granted under the Treaty of Rome and Yaoundé Conventions on trade between the Community and the Associates faces formidable difficulties. Full implementation of the provisions of the Treaty did not occur for some years after its signature—only in 1964 was the installation of the CET completed for the principal products of the Associates; the last quantitative restrictions on imports from the Community members were not removed by the Associates until June 1968, so that 1969 was the first full year in which the Six were accorded equal treatment. Temporal factors were important also in determining the response of the Associates to the opportunities provided by the Treaties in that none of the principal agricultural products that received preferential treatment were annual crops. There is a delay of five to eight years, for example, before newly planted coffee or cocoa bears fruit. Short-term elasticities of supply and export for many EAMA products consequently were of low magnitude. No data are available for these elasticities; indeed, for the early years of the Treaty, trade data are not even available for the individual Associates.

Community imports from the Associates were of a relatively small magnitude, which renders the data vulnerable to sizeable fluctuations arising from extraneous factors, for example, the exploitation of a new mineral source (as was the case with Mauritanian iron ore). The small absolute size of the trade flows also tends to distort the findings where studies rely on calculations of the comparative rates of growth of trade— which has been true of a number of the attempts to measure the impact of the preferences. Since virtually all of the Associates' exports were primary products, trade flows were upset by the vagaries of climate and subject also to the other natural and occasional political disasters with which the Associates were afflicted. Although substantial homogeneity might be expected for primary products even if derived from different sources, and thus the possibility of considerable substitutability among alternative sources of supply, this was by no means the case for some of the Associates' products. Associates' coffee, for example, was predominantly of the robusta variety, which was not in great demand outside France, other European consumers preferring the higher quality arabica variety. Similarly, there was a significant difference in taste between the bananas produced by the Associates and those from Central America preferred by German consumers, which, according to the Community's first Commissioner for Development, were "insipide, mais de bonne conservation."[19]

Some primary products were the subject of international commodity agreements that imposed limits on the Associates' exports and thus reduced the potential trade-expanding influence of preferential tariffs. Statistics on the value of trade were also affected by variations in the exchange rates of the Associates, particularly those that were members of the franc zone—the devaluation of the French franc in December 1958 and consequent devaluation of the CFA franc (originally franc des colonies Francaises d'Afrique) reduced the dollar value of the exports of French colonies and increased the competitiveness and share of French exports in the markets of franc zone Associates vis-à-vis exports from other Community member states.

A number of predictions can be made on an a priori basis regarding the expected impact of the tariff preferences on trade between the Community and the Associates. Since the two groups of countries produced essentially complementary rather than competitive products, except for certain agricultural products that were included within the Community's CAP (and thus excluded from the free trade regime of Yaoundé), trade diversion rather than trade creation would be expected. In particular, the most probable outcome of the preferences would be a shift in the Community's sources of supply of primary products away from other LDCs in favor of the Associates. Yet even in this sphere the effects might be expected to be of limited consequence. The new agreement brought fourteen of the eighteen Associates a wider preferential market at the cost of lower preferential margins than they had enjoyed under the French tariff, fewer preferential items, and, of course, the eventual phasing out of price supports. Whereas under the pre-1958 French tariff more than 55 percent by value of the exports of French colonies enjoyed preferential access to the French market, less than one-third of their exports enjoyed a preference in the Community market.[20] Preferential margins were lower and were reduced even further during the association period (table 2.1). Benefits from the tariff preferences were also highly concentrated: Robson calculated that only Senegal, Ivory Coast, Togo, Dahomey, Cameroon, Central African Republic, Zaire, and Madagascar enjoyed preferences in excess of 1 percent of the value of their total exports to all destinations in 1963.[21]

Aggregate data that compare EEC trade with the Associates and with other developing countries show that the Associates's exports to the Community grew at a slower rate than those of other developing countries and that, consequently, their share of the European market declined

**TABLE 2.1.**

The Common External Tariff on Principal EAMA exports

|  | *French Tariff* | *1958* | *1973* |
|---|---|---|---|
| Bananas (6) | 20 | 20 | 20 |
| Coffee, unroasted (3) | 20 | 16 | 7 |
| Palm oil (11) | 18 | 9 | 6 |
| Groundnut oil (7) | 18 | 10 | 10 |
| Cocoa (4) | 25 | 9 | 4 |
| Wood in rough (2) | 10 | 5 | 0 |
| Sawn timber | 15 | 10 | 0 |
| Alumina |  | 11 | 8.8 |
| Aluminum (13) |  | 10 | 7 |

A zero tariff was applied in 1958 to the following products:

| | |
|---|---|
| Calcium phosphate (15) | Ores [including iron ore (8), other metals (10)] |
| Cobalt | Rubber |
| Copper (1) | Sisal |
| Cotton (9) | Seeds and oleaginous fruits [including groundnuts (5)] |
| Gum arabic | Tea |
| Hides and skins | Tin (14) |
| Oil (crude) | Wood |

Sources: CET from European Community *Bulletin Supplement* 1/73: French tariff from R. Lawrence, "Primary Products, Preferences and Economic Welfare: the EEC and Africa," in P. Robson, ed. *International Economic Integration*, p. 366.

Note: Figures in parentheses refer to the relative importance of the commodity in total EAMA exports to the Community in the period 1963–67.

**TABLE 2.2.**
EEC-6 Trade with Africa (MUA*)

| | EEC-6 Imports | | EEC-6 Exports | |
|---|---|---|---|---|
| Year | From EAMA | From Nonassociated Developing Countries | To EAMA | To Nonassociated Developing Countries |
| 1958 | 915 | 979 | 714 | 1,517 |
| 1971 | 1,640 | 4,225 | 1,403 | 2,560 |
| 1972 | 1,717 | 4,009 | 1,461 | 2,889 |
| 1973 | 2,217 | 4,785 | 1,669 | 3,634 |
| 1974 | 3,327 | 10,086 | 2,178 | 5,843 |
| 1958–74 | | | | |
| Change | 2,412 | 9,107 | 1,464 | 4,326 |
| Percent | +264 | +930 | +205 | +285 |
| Annual growth rate (in percent) | 8.4 | 15.7 | 7.2 | 8.8 |
| 1958–73 | | | | |
| Change | 1,302 | 3,806 | 955 | 2,117 |
| Percent | +142 | +389 | +134 | +140 |
| Annual growth rate (in percent) | 6.1 | 11.2 | 5.8 | 6.0 |

Source: Eurostat. *Monthly Statistics, special number 1958–74* (Luxembourg, Statistical Office of the European Communities), pp. 24–25.
  *Unit of account of the EEC = 0.888671 gram of fine gold.

over the years 1957–74 (tables 2.2 and 2.3). In itself, however, this tells us little about the effects of the preferences since aggregate data reflect exports of products not competitive with those from the Associates, e.g., increasing European imports of petroleum and of manufactures from other LDCs. A number of attempts have been made to measure the effects of the preferences, employing a variety of statistical techniques, all of which involve some fairly heroic assumptions given the nature of the available data. Here it is sufficient to note that there is a consensus among the various studies that despite their preferential advantages, the share of the Associates in the European market declined in a statistically significant manner over the period of association; at best the preferences enabled the Associates to expand their exports to the Community at a more rapid

**TABLE 2.3.**
EEC-6 Trade with EAMA Compared to Total Developing Areas
(MUA)

|  | *1958* | *1973* | *1974* |
|---|---|---|---|
| Imports from: |  |  |  |
| EAMA | 915 | 2,217 | 3,327 |
| Developing countries | 6,827 | 23,805 | 44,841 |
| EAMA as a percent of developing countries | 13.4 | 9.3 | 7.4 |
| Exports to: |  |  |  |
| EAMA | 714 | 1,669 | 2,178 |
| Developing countries | 6,175 | 16,911 | 26,080 |
| EAMA as a percent of developing countries | 11.6 | 9.9 | 8.4 |

Source: Eurostat. *Monthly Statistics, special number 1958–74* (Luxembourg, Statistical Office of the European Communities), pp. 23–24.

rate than those to other industrialized countries and possibly helped to protect their share of the Community market for certain tropical products.[22] In their twelve most valuable exports, the Associates increased their share of the Community market in the years 1957–74 in only three products (tropical woods, calcium phosphate, and cocoa—the latter largely as a result of declining production in Ghana and Nigeria); in four products (coffee, petroleum, iron ore, and palm oil) their market share was unchanged; while declines were registered for their share of imports of copper, groundnut oil, groundnuts, and bananas.[23]

On the other hand, the share of the Associates in Community exports did not decline as rapidly as their share in Community imports. Exports from the five member states that previously did not enjoy preferential access to the Associates' markets grew at a more rapid rate to countries offering reverse preferences than their exports to other Associates and to other non-oil-exporting LDCs.[24] This appears to attest to the significance of the provisions for reverse preferences in the Conventions. Preferential margins offered to Community member states were not insubstantial. Kreinen estimated that these averaged 21.2 percent for the Central African Customs Union, 12.7 percent for the West African Union, and 13.8 percent for Madagascar.[25]

Again, an exact measurement of the effects of the reverse preferences is impossible. Young calculated that their cost to the Associates amounted to approximately 2 percent of their import bill, but the assumptions that underlie his calculations are so heroic that the figure quoted may be far removed from the true cost.[26] Kreinen found that the French export prices to the Associated states were generally more expensive than those charged in other markets and higher than those of alternative suppliers.[27] Hewitt cites calculations by the Cameroon government that reverse preferences cost the country CFA francs 39 billion in foregone revenue to 1975, which was not far short of the total EDF aid received in the same period (CFA francs 43.7 billion). Since 1975, when the Cameroon government imposed customs duties for the first time on imports from the EEC, revenue from these duties averaged CFA francs 5.5 billion p.a., which substantially exceeded the average aid received from the EDF (CFA francs 3.6 billion p.a.).[28]

Reverse preferences may also have hindered the efforts of the Associates to establish their own industries. Article 3, 2 of the first Yaoundé Convention permitted Associated states to retain or introduce customs duties and quantitative restrictions for revenue or development needs. Nominally, these appeared to be generous escape clauses, but in practice Community interpretation of them was less than liberal. Restrictions on imports from the Community in order to promote local development were subject to prior consultation with the Community in the Association Council. The annual reports of the Association Council show, first, that the number of cases on which the Associates requested authority to apply restrictions was small (table 2.4) and, secondly, that there was a marked reluctance on the part of the Community to agree to these actions.

Although the Association Council was required to respond within two months to requests to impose quantitative restrictions, action frequently took much longer as a result of Community demands for further information from the Associates. For instance, on 1 June 1967 Senegal requested authority to impose restrictions on imports of certain types of building materials. This was not granted until 18 December 1968—in the meantime the Community had expressed its desire that a quota of 5 percent of local consumption be reserved for the exports of the member states.[29] Similarly, the Community would not agree to restrictions on the import of trucks over three tonnes by Senegal until member states had been granted a quota of a minimum of 10 percent of the local market in 1966 to rise to 16.6 percent in 1967.[30]

**TABLE 2.4.**

Requests by the EAMA for Authority To Introduce Import Restrictions Presented to the Association Council

| | |
|---|---|
| 1964–65 | Ivory Coast: paints, matches, and detergents. |
| 1965–66 | Senegal: trucks over three tons. |
| | Ivory Coast: petroleum products. |
| | Madagascar: TV tubes. |
| 1966–67 | Senegal: trucks over three tons. |
| 1967–68 | Senegal: building materials, washing powders. |
| | Central African Republic: shoes. |
| | Dahomey: cycles and motorcycles. |
| 1968–69 | Senegal: building materials and washing powders. |
| | Cameroon: cement. |
| | Congo (D.R.): medicines |
| | Dahomey: cycles, motorcycles. |

Source: Compiled from *Rapport Annuel D'Activité du Conseil D'Association à la Conférence Parlementaire de l'Association (1965–72)*.

During the renegotiation of the Yaoundé Convention a group of experts was appointed at the request of the Community to study Associates' use of quantitative restrictions in imports. The Community used this opportunity to remind the Associates that any quantitative restrictions or measures of equivalent effect should be degressive in their operation.[31] By February 1972, the committee of experts had not completed its report and continued to demand further information from some Associates. A measure of the Associates' frustration with the Community attitude on this subject is seen in the eighth annual report of the Activities of the Association Council, which notes:

The Representatives of some of the Associated States emphasized the minor importance of these questions in comparison with the essential point, which was the general impact of the measures on imports and on the development of local industry. Furthermore, they considered that the consequences of a few minor breaches in procedure were minimal, whilst the measures adopted by the Community could have dire consequences on the economy of one or more Associated States. The Associated States . . . expressed the wish that only really important questions should be raised at the Association Committee level.[32]

A similar mean-spirited attitude was displayed by the Community over the rules to be applied to determine originating status for exports from the Associates. Protocol 3 of the first Yaoundé Convention stipulated that the Association Council, within seven months of the entry into force of the Convention, was responsible for drawing up rules of origin, on the basis of a draft to be prepared by the Commission. But the draft that the Commission initially submitted to the member states was considered to be too favorable to the Associates. Two years of deadlock ensued as each member state held out for special protective provisions for industries of particular national interest. Agreement was eventually reached in October 1968. The rules were considerably more restrictive than the African countries had desired, especially for products like textiles, which the Community regarded as sensitive; in many cases the rules required a higher local value added than was normally demanded in international trade.[33] This issue continued to be contentious during the Lomé relationship (see chapter 4).

As important as the economic impact of the reverse preferences on the Associates was their more general effect on relations between Africa and the Community and on the evolution of the international trading system. Parties to the Yaoundé Conventions were in essence locked into the support of an anachronism since reverse preferences were perceived as the principal guarantee of the continuation of the exclusive relationship between the Associates and the Community. Thus it is no surprise that the main advocates of reverse preferences were the Associates themselves, despite the potentially adverse effects that such arrangements might have had on their economic development. While some states argued that reverse preferences were necessary if Africa was to maintain its dignity, and also to preserve the "equality" of the relationship, the real reason for supporting the preferences more probably lay in African fears that their abolition would open the Community market to nonassociates. That their fears were not ungrounded was seen in the proposal by the Dutch and German governments for the abolition of reverse preferences as part of a package that would have lowered the CET and introduced a generalized system of preferences. Only France among the Community members was a strong advocate of reverse preferences—again the motivation was to preserve the exclusive position of the Associates.

Since reverse preferences were an aspect of Association other African states found most objectionable, it was the Associates who insisted they be required from other states that applied for preferential trading arrangements with the Community. They thus helped to perpetuate the division of the African continent, particularly since the obligation to grant preferences would have been incompatible with Associate countries' membership in regional customs unions or free trade areas that included other LDCs.[34] In that they contravened the norm of nondiscrimination, reverse preferences also had a negative impact on the wider international trading regime. Community policies set a dangerous precedent that encouraged the creation of exclusive regional trading blocs. As a result of the Yaoundé preferential system, Latin American states demanded they be accorded similar preferential treatment in North American markets.[35] On a number of occasions the U.S. government expressed sympathy with these sentiments and hinted that an American trade zone might be created in retaliation.[36] Washington also used the reverse preferences issue as a reason for delaying the introduction of its generalized preferences scheme.

### Financial and Technical Cooperation

In contrast to the disappointing results of trade cooperation under the Yaoundé Conventions, the Associates could find some compensation in the successive European Development Funds of which they were exclusive beneficiaries. When the first EDF was established, it was stipulated that national contributions to the Community's aid budget would be in addition to existing bilateral aid and that the latter would be continued at least at the previous levels.[37] Table 2.5 suggests this did in fact occur: only in the case of Belgium did the EAMA share in the bilateral aid of member states fall significantly over the association period. There was a tendency, however, for their share in the bilateral aid of other OECD states to decline, perhaps a reflection of their being perceived as primarily the "responsibility" of the Community.

Funds provided by the EDF were made available on exceptionally soft

**TABLE 2.5.**
Share of EAMA in Bilateral Aid 1962–72 (in percentages)

|  | 1962 | 1968 | 1969 | 1970 | 1971 | 1972 |
|---|---|---|---|---|---|---|
| Belgium | 76 | 69 | 57 | 61 | 56 | 53 |
| France | 29 | 31 | 30 | 28 | 27 | 27 |
| Germany | 2 | 3 | 6 | 6 | 5 | 4 |
| Italy | 11 | 7 | 10 | 6 | 9 | 9 |
| Netherlands | 0 | 0 | 0 | 1 | 2 | 1 |
| United States | 3 | 1 | 1 | 1 | 1 | 1 |
| All DAC bilateral aid | 9 | 6 | 7 | 7 | 7 | 7 |

Source: Calculated from data in F.E.D., 1:325; and OECD *Development Assistance* (annual).

terms: under the second Yaoundé Convention, for instances, 81 percent of total aid came in the form of grants, 9 percent in subsidized loans, and 10 percent from the European Investment Bank at commercial rates. These terms compared favorably with those for bilateral aid from the member states, where the grant element fell substantially over the association period. Fully 44 percent of total EEC bilateral aid took the form of technical assistance, mainly in the form of salary payments for expatriate officials, whose benefit to the recipients was questionable. Aid was untied within the EEC and the EAMA, and under the provisions of the second Yaoundé Convention the Community could grant a preference of up to 15 percent to EAMA companies on supply contracts. A further advantage of EDF aid was the provision for cofinancing, on which the Community had an excellent record. EDF aid grew more rapidly than bilateral aid receipts from the Community during the period of association; additional aid from the EDF helped to raise the Associates per capita receipts for the period 1969–71 to more than 84 percent above the level received by their future partners in the ACP Group.[38]

On the other hand, although grants and subsidized loans under the EDF were increased from 581.25 mua under the Rome Treaty to 730 mua in Yaoundé I, and 900 mua in Yaoundé II, this was insufficient to maintain the real per capita value of the EDF over the period owing to inflation and population growth in the Associates.[39] Community aid performance was even more disappointing if contributions are considered in relationship to the growth of member states' GNPs in this period—in other words, in the context of what might be termed the Community's capacity to give. The value of the aid to the Associates was also reduced by the long delays in disbursement for which the EDF became notorious: only 13 percent of the first Fund had been disbursed by the expiration of the Rome arrangements; for the second and third EDFs, only one-third of the funds were disbursed by the expiration of the respective Conventions. Some of the allocation for the first Fund, made in 1957, remained unspent by the expiration of the second Yaoundé Convention in January 1975. In part these delays were caused by the cumbersome procedures adopted by the Commission in order to satisfy member states that their nationals benefited from a reasonable share of awarded contracts. Projects that required coordination between the EDF and the EIB (located in Luxembourg) were typically subject to further delays. Again these problems were to continue in the Lomé relationship (see chapter 8).

Two other aspects of the EDF experience gave rise to considerable criticism: the country and sectoral allocations of the aid. Community procedures for distributing aid between recipients are quite extraordinary: for none of the EDFs has the Commission made public on an *ex ante* basis its country allocations. Nor has it been willing to provide a detailed explanation of the criteria used in the decision-making process. In practice, the distribution was heavily biased in favor of higher income countries: for the first three EDFs there was a positive correlation at high levels of statistical significance between per capita GNP in the Associates and per capita EDF allocations.[40] As table 2.6 shows, Gabon—with the

**TABLE 2.6.**

Country Allocations of EDF (in ua per capita)

| Country | 1972 GNP per capita | EDF I | EDF II | EDF III | Total EDF | % Total EAMA Pop. | % Total EDF | % Total IBRD/ IDA |
|---|---|---|---|---|---|---|---|---|
| Burundi | 67 | 2.41 | 5.89 | 8.19 | 15.49 | 4.5 | 3.04 | 1.04 |
| Cameroon | 202 | 11.17 | 9.36 | 9.51 | 27.95 | 7.2 | 8.83 | 13.43 |
| Cen. Afr. Rep. | 157 | 16.19 | 17.17 | 18.31 | 46.70 | 2.0 | 4.06 | 1.02 |
| Congo (B) | 295 | 30.62 | 17.95 | 18.31 | 58.08 | 1.4 | 3.58 | 5.66 |
| Ivory Coast | 340 | 16.02 | 10.94 | 10.00 | 29.62 | 6.5 | 8.48 | 10.66 |
| Dahomey | 106 | 12.80 | 8.59 | 8.09 | 24.12 | 3.5 | 3.65 | 2.18 |
| Gabon | 810 | 43.75 | 41.63 | 51.14 | 128.20 | 0.6 | 3.46 | 3.84 |
| Upper Volta | 72 | 9.12 | 5.64 | 7.85 | 18.85 | 6.8 | 5.64 | 2.52 |
| Madagascar | 140 | 11.65 | 9.73 | 8.35 | 25.99 | 9.0 | 10.20 | 9.55 |
| Mali | 74 | 11.62 | 6.45 | 9.76 | 24.47 | 6.4 | 6.86 | 4.84 |
| Mauritania | 178 | 25.05 | 15.60 | 21.93 | 50.50 | 1.5 | 3.28 | 7.32 |
| Niger | 69 | 13.32 | 7.50 | 10.75 | 26.01 | 5.1 | 5.83 | 1.81 |
| Rwanda | 64 | 2.19 | 5.92 | 7.66 | 14.90 | 4.7 | 3.06 | 1.84 |
| Senegal | 262 | 19.22 | 15.31 | 16.00 | 41.97 | 5.0 | 9.20 | 6.99 |
| Somalia | 79 | 3.38 | 9.35 | 11.76 | 24.49 | 3.6 | 3.89 | 4.30 |
| Chad | 84 | 10.94 | 9.02 | 7.64 | 24.31 | 4.6 | 4.90 | 1.99 |
| Togo | 159 | 14.38 | 9.87 | 13.15 | 30.89 | 2.5 | 3.41 | 1.51 |
| Zaire | 101 | 1.41 | 3.93 | 3.14 | 8.00 | 24.1 | 8.54 | 15.76 |
| Mean | 182 | 14.18 | 11.66 | 13.42 | 34.47 | | | |

Sources: Country Distribution of EDF from FED I, p. 182; GNP per capita from FED II, annex C-1; Population figure from FED I, p. 13; IBRD/IDA figures from FED II, annex C-1.

Note: Reported EDF totals per capita do not necessarily equal the sum of the figures for the three funds since the total per capita figure employs 1972 population data whereas figures for each fund utilize data for country populations at the beginning of each fund. This does not, however, affect the relative shares of each country.

highest per capita income among Associated states—received by far the highest per capita allocation of EDF aid. Cameroon, Ivory Coast, Mauritania, and Senegal similarly benefited from the bias in favor of the higher income countries, while Burundi, Dahomey, Upper Volta, Mali, Rwanda, and Somalia—the least developed of the Associates—received a disproportionately small share of EDF assistance. Table 2.6 also shows, however, that the EDF record in this regard was little worse than that of the World Bank (IBRD) and its soft-loan affiliate, the International Development Association (IDA), in the same period.[41]

A striking characteristic of the sectoral distribution of EDF commitments was the small share allocated to industrial projects. As table 2.7 shows, these accounted for less than 5 percent of total EDF funding. Even this figure somewhat overstates funding in this sector since it includes projects for energy production and distribution. In the course of the seven years of the association period a total of only twenty-seven plants were assisted, including three hydroelectric power facilities.[42]

This comparative underrepresentation of the industrial sector in EDF commitments was the consequence of a deliberate and explicit Community bias: according to the European Commission "as a general rule it is not in the nature of the EDF to act as an industrialist."[43] Not only would the European Commission itself not play the role of industrialist, but its spokesmen made clear that it expected this role to be played by the private sector, preferably European firms. Finance for industrialization was to be primarily the responsibility of the EIB, although the EDF frequently contributed by way of subsidizing interest rates. Contributions from the EIB were limited, however, to not more than 25 percent of the total capital of a project. Although EIB resources could be supplemented in that the EDF was allowed to contribute to the formation of risk capital by acquiring a temporary minority shareholding in projects in the Associates, this option was rarely exercised: Commission reports make reference to only two such interventions—in favor of a sugar refinery in the Cameroon and a textile plant in the Ivory Coast.

As a result of the small share of industrialization projects in the EDF allocations, Community aid had only a limited impact on the creation of directly productive projects in the Associates. By way of contrast is the dominant position of infrastructure in Community aid programs. A number of factors explain this: first was the tendency of the EDF in its early days to continue the pattern of aid practiced by colonial donors in which in-

**TABLE 2.7.**

Sectoral Distribution of EDF Commitments (in 000 ua) (position at 1 January 1975)

| Sectors | EDF I | % | EDF II | % | EDF III | % | Total | % |
|---|---|---|---|---|---|---|---|---|
| Industrialization | 4,175 | 0.73 | 42,288 | 5.61 | 49,489 | 7.15 | 95,952 | 4.61 |
| Tourism | — | — | 24 | — | 2,033 | 0.26 | 2,057 | 0.10 |
| Rural Production | 94,108 | 16.49 | 268,056 | 37.19 | 220,515 | 29.63 | 582,679 | 27.98 |
| Commercial Promotion | — | — | 1,445 | 0.21 | 7,142 | 1.04 | 8,587 | 0.41 |
| Transport, Communication | 248,390 | 43.51 | 233,642 | 32.30 | 289,665 | 37.45 | 771,697 | 37.05 |
| Education | 111,043 | 19.45 | 69,706 | 9.77 | 91,755 | 10.40 | 272,504 | 13.08 |
| Health | 50,028 | 8.76 | 28,830 | 4.08 | 23,447 | 0.92 | 102,305 | 4.91 |
| Water, Housing | 48,429 | 8.48 | 49,633 | 6.94 | 42,548 | 4.74 | 140,610 | 6.75 |
| Exceptional Aid | — | — | 475 | 0.07 | 29,594 | 4.66 | 30,069 | 1.44 |
| Others | 14,729 | 2.58 | 27,246 | 3.83 | 34,228 | 3.75 | 76,203 | 3.66 |
| TOTAL COMMITMENTS | 570,902 | 100 | 721,345 | 100 | 790,416 | 100 | 2,082,663 | 100 |
| Reserve (1) | 1,028 | | 14,078 | | 1,039 | | | |
| Not Yet Committed | 304 | | 4,626 | | 115,162 | | | |
| GRAND TOTAL (2) | 572,234 | | 740,049 | | 906,617 | | | |

(1) Provision for overspending.

(2) 1st EDF: 9,016,000 ua were transferred to the 2nd EDF; 2nd EDF includes 1,033,000 ua combined repayments and interest on special loans from the EIB; 3rd EDF includes 1,617,000 ua combined repayments and interest on special loans from the EIB, and a 5,000,000 ua supplement on the occasion of the accession of Mauritius to the Yaounde Convention (1 June 1973).

Source: FED Vol. 1 p. 66.

frastructure projects figured prominently. Second, the type of aid offered by the Community was ideally suited to projects where no visible
commercial return was derived; Associates looked to Community grants
rather than World Bank loans to finance projects not directly productive.
Large-scale infrastructural projects were not only prestigious for both donor
and recipient but also relatively easy for Commission officials to administer and attractive to Community contractors. Finally, many Associates
at independence had a need for improvements in communications to foster not merely economic development but political integration as well.

In later years the continuing prominent share of EDF resources devoted to infrastructural projects was increasingly criticized. Commission
officials were accused of having bureaucratic interests in the continuation
of such projects despite evidence of duplication of facilities, and European contractors were accused of promoting them for personal gain. An
assessment of these claims would require a case-by-case examination of
the projects financed. One survey of EDF infrastructural projects in the
railroad sector in Cameroon suggests they were undertaken on the basis
of overly optimistic assessments of future usage, that political critieria (at
least in one case where a major commitment was made) were more important than economic, that once committed the EDF continued to pour
scarce funds into a project incurring substantial cost overruns, and that
further costs were brought about by accepting the reasoning that the existing project could function successfully only if adjacent infrastructure
was upgraded.[44] Determination of which projects would be financed was
solely a European responsibility.

Next to infrastructure, rural production was the second most important beneficiary of Community aid. Only a minority of the Community's
aid, however, supported the production of food for local or regional consumption, the remainder being devoted to the production of crops (often
on plantations) for processing and/or export. Some idea of the relative
weight of the two sectors can be seen in the number of projects financed:
over the three EDFs, eight projects relating exclusively to food production were sponsored, seven "polyculture" projects that included both food
production and commercial agriculture, and seventy-three projects devoted exclusively to commercial agriculture. In terms of the acreage involved in the projects, approximately 40 percent was used for the production of food crops.[45] That the imbalance between food and commercial
crop production was perceived as problematic is suggested by the fact

that the Commission itself notes that during the first and second EDFs "agricultural projects had the tendency to favor commercial cultivation (palms, cotton, tea, pyrethrum)" but that "a certain evolution has led, in recent times especially, to place increasing emphasis . . . on food production."[46]

The most serious problem faced by the Associates that was unsatisfactorily resolved in the course of the Association period—a problem that had a significant adverse impact on the rural sector—was the instability of export earnings from the production of primary products. The Six succeeded in reaching agreement only on negative action—the phasing out of the French system of price supports. It is worth quoting at length the Commission's pessimistic conclusions on this matter:

The objective foreseen (the adaptation to returns on the world market) generally has been attained but at the price of important sacrifices as much for the public finances of the states concerned as for the producers. The danger of a lowering of the price paid to the latter is that they will lose interest in cultivation when the growth of production or of productivity is insufficient to compensate for a fall in unit price or to assure the producer a revenue at least equivalent to that of previous years.

Citing the example of groundnut production in Niger, the Commission opined: "only a very significant increase in productivity would permit adaptation to the world market without excessive sacrifices for the producer and the state—except in the case of a complete upheaval in the primary products market."[47]

Aid for production and diversification under the Yaoundé Conventions had a minimal impact, less than half of the funds available being used by the Associates. With the phasing out of French price supports, Associates received assistance only in the form of Community advances to local stabilization funds. In the second EDF 11 mua were committed for advances to five funds: cocoa in the Cameroon; groundnuts in Senegal; coffee in Burundi; cotton in Chad; and to l'Accord sucrier africain et malgache for sugar. Under the second Yaoundé Convention up to 80 mua of EDF resources could be employed in this manner, but the Commission records only one commitment—of 5.5 mua for Somalian bananas.[48] The limited impact of this program was subsequently acknowledged by the Commission: funds were not always used for the product to which they were nominally committed but were employed as budgetary supports; conditions for their award (temporary fluctuations in world prices) were too restrictive; and the stipulated period in which the transfers were to be reimbursed (after three years) did not take any account of the circumstances of the Associates, which were not necessarily more favorable at the time of reimbursement than when the transfers were received.[49]

Phasing out of French price supports left agricultural producers in the Associates in a more precarious position than what had prevailed at the beginning of the Association period. In the intervening years the Community failed to devise a program that effectively shielded them from the full force of fluctuations in world market prices. Since the overwhelming majority of the Associates' population were engaged in agricultural production, this failure to provide for their most immediate need was a critical gap in the Community's aid program. STABEX was the Commission's innovative response to this problem.

## COMMONWEALTH AFRICA AND THE COMMUNITY

Commonwealth Africa's colonial experience had been markedly different from that of its Francophone neighbors. A more open trading relationship and the absence of a policy of assimilation contributed to a widely shared belief that they enjoyed a greater degree of sovereignty than Francophone Africa. They were suspicious of the continuing close ties of the Francophones with the former metropole after independence, seen in the support for France in the General Assembly of the UN, continued membership in the franc zone, and the dominance of French civil servants in the postindependence administrations. Treatment of their former colonies by the Community reinforced Commonwealth suspicions of the motives of the Six: France's termination of assistance to Guinea following the latter's "no" vote in the De Gaulle referendum and its subsequent exclusion from the Rome Association; French disdain for African opinion, shown in its explosion of an atomic device in the Sahara, an action that caused Nigeria to break off diplomatic relations with France; Belgium's behavior in the Congo in the postindependence turmoil; Germany's invoking of the Hallstein Doctrine in threatening to cut off EEC aid to Mali if it should recognize the German Democratic Republic—all these actions suggested the Community had little respect for the newly won sovereignty of the Associates.

Community behavior toward Guinea and Mali was of particular importance given these states' close relationship with Nkrumah's Ghana and their role in the Casablanca group of radical African states. Association with the European Community thus became entangled with the larger question of the forging of African unity, the Associates providing the nucleus of the rival Brazzaville group. For the Casablanca group, the notion of Eur-Africa was divisive, Association being perceived as a barrier to continental unity and the attainment of true sovereignty. Nkrumah was the most articulate representative of this viewpoint, arguing that the Rome Treaty served the same purposes for neocolonialism as the Treaty of Berlin for colonialism: the European Community represented "a new system of collective colonialism which will be stronger and more dangerous than the old evils we are striving to liquidate."[50] Addressing the Ghanaian Parliament following the rejection of Association status at the Commonwealth Prime Ministers' Conference, he stated: "the Common Market is an imperialist device for the collective exploitation of the less developed countries of Africa by the protagonists of neo-colonialism. It must be avoided like the plague."[51]

Britain's handling of negotiations on the future status of the Commonwealth during its first application for membership in the Community was particularly inept. Neither the independent states nor remaining colonies of Commonwealth Africa were consulted during the negotiations. Britain demanded that Association be made available for Commonwealth Africa and the Caribbean and Pacific islands but conceded that this status was unfeasible, as far as its future partners were concerned, for the more economically advanced countries of Commonwealth Asia.[52] Showing total disregard for the sensitivities of states that were in the process of gaining their independence, the Commonwealth "associables" were informed that "it had been agreed that Association would be a suitable solution," a solution that was offered essentially on a take-it-or-leave-it basis.

British behavior during the negotiations did nothing to allay Commonwealth Africa's fears that the European Community was a means of exercising a collective neocolonialism in which no attention was paid to the wishes of African governments. Rejection of the proposed Association status at the September 1962 Commonwealth Prime Ministers' Conference by all independent African states except Sierra Leone was primarily the result of perceptions of the *political* connotations of Association rather than calculations of the economic costs/benefits of the proposed relationship—indeed, as Nye and Zartman make clear, most states came to the meeting with little idea of the likely effects of Association on their economies.[53]

Given the near unanimity with which the Commonwealth had rejected Association status in September 1962, the appearance of representatives from four Anglophone states in Brussels within the next nine months to negotiate special arrangements with the EEC appeared to signal a major *volte-face*. This was simply the reflection of a move from a focus on the political to the economic consequences of non-Association: Commonwealth Africa began to perceive the need to reach an accommodation with the Community in order to defend its access to the Community market, one growing more rapidly than that of its traditional colonial patron. Failure of the British application to the Community had removed the possibility that Commonwealth Africa might enjoy equivalent benefits to the Associates without the political strings. Although the CET was lowered on several items of interest to them as part of the Yaoundé package, tariffs remained at significant levels and discriminated in particular against processed products.[54]

Concern about the political connotations of Association had diminished for several reasons: French veto of the British membership application left Commonwealth Africa free to negotiate its own arrangements—sovereignty therefore was not impugned—and the East Africans discovered it was in fact the *Associates* that had demanded joint political institutions to govern the operation of the Convention, rather than their being part of a neocolonialist ploy by the Community, as the East Africans had originally suspected.[55] That Yaoundé allowed for the conclusion by the Associates of customs unions with other states was regarded as encouraging, particularly by the East African states, which were hoping to expand their common market. The Declaration of Intentions was similarly perceived as signaling a new openness on the part of the Community. Finally, the conclusion of preferential trading agreements with the Six by Greece and Turkey offered an alternative model to the Rome Association, an alternative that did not carry the same pejorative connotations—in Okigbo's words: "it began to emerge that the concept of association was sufficiently elastic to permit a relationship that was neither neo-colonialist nor subordinate."[56]

Three options were offered to Commonwealth Africa by the Declaration of Intentions: (1) accession to the Yaoundé Convention; (2) conclusion of sui generis conventions of association based on Article 238 of the Treaty of Rome to include reciprocal rights and obligations; and (3) conclusion of a nondiscriminatory trade agreement. Ideally, option three would have been preferred by Commonwealth African states since their motivation was to obtain the same treatment for their principal exports to the EEC as that enjoyed by their main competitors; at that time they were not seeking access to Community aid funds. But an agreement whereby the Community would remove its tariffs on tropical product imports was out of the question given the French commitment to protect the privileged position of the Associates. Both Nigeria and the member states of the East African Community—the four Commonwealth countries that displayed an immediate interest in the Community after the veto of Britain's application—consequently sought an agreement under Article 238 of the Rome Treaty.

The principal drawback of this type of agreement was the obligation to provide reciprocal concessions to the EEC. Commonwealth African countries typically employed a single-column nondiscriminatory tariff: although privileged access was enjoyed to other Commonwealth markets under the Commonwealth Preferences Scheme, African states were not obligated to provide reciprocal preferences. Other than token compliance with Community expectations of reverse preferences would thus be a retrograde step, moving away from the existing nondiscriminatory tariff regime. Commonwealth Africa was also concerned at possible repercussions of discrimination against Britain and other significant trading partners, most notably the United States. Commonwealth Africa's position was succinctly stated by P. N. C. Okigbo, Nigeria's chief negotiator in the talks with the EEC:

Nigeria's dilemma was how to obtain concessions like those from which her main competitors in the association benefitted, while having what appeared to be less significant concessions to offer the Community and yet retain, to the exclusion of the associated states, her Commonwealth preferences in Britain. Success in this endeavor would have obtained for Nigeria the best of both worlds at a minimum of sacrifice; the Yaoundé Convention might, for that reason, appear to be an inferior agreement.[57]

Nigeria's proposed solution to this problem was to offer only nominal compliance with the principle of reciprocity. All customs duties were to be abolished *erga omnes* except for 26 commodities on which the Community would enjoy a 2 percent to 5 percent advantage. These were commodities for which Community members were already the major suppliers; the introduction of a preferential margin would consequently have had no significant impact on Nigeria's other trading partners. Since customs duties made a major contribution to government revenue and also served to protect domestic industry, fiscal entry charges would be imposed *erga omnes* on all imports, including those 26 items on which tariffs were retained.

Nigeria had been one of the most outspoken critics of the Yaoundé Convention, challenging its legality under GATT rules (much to the displeasure of the French).[58] Arguments against reciprocity were reinforced in 1964 by UNCTAD's declaration of hostility to such impositions and, perhaps more importantly, by the addition in 1965 of a new Part IV to the GATT Treaty, which stated explicitly that reciprocity should not be expected in trade negotiations with developing countries. France did not, however, subscribe to the principles that underlay the new Part IV of the Treaty, arguing instead that the interests of developing countries would be better served by managed markets. Accordingly, France demanded that Nigeria should give "real commercial advantages" to the Six—a sentiment that was echoed by the Yaoundé Associates.

For reasons concerned as much with squabbles within the Community as with the desire to protect the Associates, the French government stalled the negotiations; further delay occurred following the French boycott of Community institutions in July 1965. But Nigeria was in a relatively strong bargaining position, as well as represented by able negotiators. The Dutch and German governments were particularly anxious to reach an agreement since the Nigerian application represented a test case for the sincerity of the Declaration of Intentions. As the largest Anglophone African state, Nigeria's association with the Community would have had considerable symbolic importance besides potential economic significance.[59] The Convention, which was eventually signed by the Six and Nigeria on 16 July 1966, provided for duty-free access for Nigerian exports to the Community market, but four exports that competed with production from the Yaoundé Associates—cocoa, groundnut oil, palm oil, and plywood—were subject to quotas. In return, Nigeria granted the Community preferential access on the tariff headings that had been initially proposed. As a result of the Nigerian civil war the agreement was not ratified but was nevertheless of great importance in serving as a precedent, particularly for the Arusha Agreement with the East African states.

An exploratory memorandum had been submitted to the EEC by the member states of the East African Community before the opening of talks between the Six and Nigeria. Again the motivation was economic, and primarily defensive—in September 1962 Tanganyika had been in the vanguard of Commonwealth states in denouncing the political overtones of association status but under pressure from her regional partners agreed to a reconsideration following the failure of the British application. Of major concern was access to the European market for East African coffee. Considerable delay occurred in the negotiation of an agreement with the Six initially as a result of the East Africans' refusal to compromise on the issue of nonreciprocity and subsequently as a result of the German dispute with Tanzania over its proposed recognition of East Germany, the French boycott of Community institutions, the difficulties in coordinating a common position among the East African partners, and finally the Community's giving priority to the Nigerian Treaty.[60] Once the Nigerian Agreement had been signed, however, a framework existed that was easily adapted to the particularities of the East African case. Although an initial agreement signed in 1968 expired before it became operational, a similar agreement was signed at Arusha in September 1969, but delays in its ratification by European governments prevented its implementation until January 1971.

Both the Yaoundé Associates and France continued to insist on reciprocity. After considerable haggling it was agreed that the Community would receive preferences of from 2 percent to 9 percent on 59 items (the EEC had originally asked for 220, the East Africans initially offered 26), the total value of trade in which amounted to 8 million Kenyan pounds (15 percent of total East African imports from the Community).[61] As in the Lagos Agreement, East African exports would enjoy free access to the European market except for those products (unroasted coffee, cloves, and tinned pineapples) that threatened the production of the Yaoundé Associates where duty-free access was limited to specified quotas, at which point the Six had the option of reimposing duties.

## THE NEGOTIATION OF LOMÉ I

The likely success, following De Gaulle's departure, of Britain's third application for membership of the Community in 1970 once again reopened the question of the future relationship of its former colonies with the EEC. Over the previous decade, the environment in which the negotiations would take place had changed substantially. All of Britain's African colonies, with the exception of the illegal government in Rhodesia, had attained their independence: it would no longer be a question of Britain unilaterally determining the terms on which Commonwealth Africa might become associated with the EEC. Negotiation of the Lagos and Arusha Agreements attested to the declining suspicion held by Commonwealth Africa toward the Community and the increasing importance of the EEC market for these countries. One former British colony, Mauritius (which has a significant Francophone minority), actually applied for membership of the second Yaoundé Convention at the time of the opening of negotiations between Britain and the Community and was admitted in May 1973.

Divisions within the OAU were no longer as salient as in the early 1960s; with the demise of Nkrumah there were no significant advocates of a supranational African state, but attention had turned to the promotion of regional economic cooperation. Nigeria emerged from its painful civil war determined to build a framework for West African regional cooperation, which necessitated involving the Francophone states. Meanwhile, British attitudes during earlier negotiations with the Community had signaled clearly to the Commonwealth that their interests would be subordinated to British determination to achieve EEC membership: this was of particular concern to Caribbean and Pacific countries whose economies depended heavily on the Commonwealth Sugar Agreement. British patronage was no longer assured: if Britain entered the Community without making arrangements for Commonwealth countries, they would not only lose their preferences in the British market but would also be discriminated against in favor of the existing Associates. From the Commonwealth perspective, there were sound reasons for seeking the European Community as a collective patron.

A similar disillusionment with their traditional patron had affected the attitude of Francophone Associates. France had not succeeded in preserving their tariff advantages during the Yaoundé period; no satisfactory successor to the *surprix* system had been found. Recent signals from Paris had cast doubt on the willingness of France to continue to favor the Associates: government reports had argued that there was little economic benefit to be derived from close ties with African Associates and had recommended that French aid be redeployed in favor of developing countries whose economic prospects appeared brighter than those of the EAMA.[62] Introduction of the Community's Generalized System of Preferences (GSP) in July 1971 and the conclusion of preferential trade agreements with most countries bordering the Mediterranean provided evidence that the member states increasingly perceived the Associates as peripheral to their principal economic interests. Poor trade performance during the Yaoundé Conventions suggested to the Associates that their preferences over other African states might not be worth defending: if the Community would provide a sweetener as compensation, it might well be better to strengthen its bargaining hand by negotiating a new Convention in alliance with the Commonwealth associables.

From the Community perspective, the Yaoundé Conventions had proved somewhat of an embarrassment. Not only had they singularly failed in their objective of assisting the Associates to compete on equal terms on the open market, but, in the eyes of a number of member states, they had unnecessarily rendered the Community vulnerable to criticism. Member states had been accused of exercising a collective neocolonialism, of helping to perpetuate the balkanization of Africa, and, as a result of the insistence on reverse preferences, of undermining one of the fundamental principles of the postwar trade regime and, in the process, exploiting a group of the world's weakest states. Regardless of the veracity of such accusations, they were embarrassing for the member states. Germany and the Netherlands had long pressed for a Community development policy that went beyond the Yaoundé Associates. Even France, the long-standing defender of the Association arrangements, recognized that its economic interests were undermined by preserving the privileges of the Associates—even in Africa, where Nigeria was rapidly emerging as a major economic and political force. Successful negotiation of an agreement with the Commonwealth associables was certain to be perceived by the British government as a sign of the good faith of the original member states.

Meanwhile, the Commission of the European Communities perceived future British membership as an opportunity to considerably extend the scope of Community development policy. In a 1971 memorandum, it noted that for most LDCs "the Community only seemed to be a customs and agricultural organization liable to be an obstacle to the expansion of their trade and, in any event without the means of actively cooperating in the solution of their development problems." Since the Community pre-

sently had recourse to only one instrument in its development cooperation policy—the manipulation of tariffs and quotas—the possibilities for
Community action would be increasingly circumscribed.[63] More aid should
be channeled through the Community, support provided for international commodity agreements, and encouragement given to regional cooperation among developing countries.[64] A new Convention that included the Commonwealth associables would obviously provide a major
extension of the Development Directorate-General's bureaucratic task.

Despite the coincidence of interests between the parties, the negotiations had an unpromising start. Protocol 22 of the Treaty of Accession
of the four applicants to the Community offered the independent Commonwealth countries listed in Annex V three alternatives for ordering
their relations with the Community "in the spirit of the Declaration of
Intent" adopted by the Council at its April 1963 meeting. These African, Caribbean, and Pacific countries ("associables" in contrast to the
"untouchables"[65]—developing Asian countries whose superior manufacturing base rendered them, in the eyes of the Community, ineligible for
Association status) were given a choice of the following:

1. participation in the Convention of Association that would succeed the existing
   Yaoundé Convention with the EAMA;
2. conclusion of one or more special Conventions of Association on the basis of
   Article 238 of the Treaty of Rome comprising reciprocal rights and obligations, particularly in the field of trade; or
3. conclusion of trade agreements with a view to facilitating and developing trade
   between the Community and those countries.

None of the three options restated in the Protocol was regarded as particularly attractive by Commonwealth countries in 1972. The Arusha
Agreement concluded under Article 238 was perceived as an inadequate
model since it restricted exports that competed with those of the EAMA,
required reverse preferences to be offered to the Community, and made
no provision for the extension of financial and technical assistance by the
EEC. Nigerian Ambassador, E. Olu Sanu, who was to play a prominent
role in the negotiation of Lomé, stated that the Arusha Agreement "has,
to say the least, been regarded as a sad economic and political mistake."[66]

Given the three alternatives offered, most of the important Commonwealth countries were inclining in 1972 toward option three, a simple
trade agreement with the expanded Community. To adopt the first of

the options offered would result, many states feared, in a new Convention that would reproduce many of the flaws of the Yaoundé predecessors. From the Commonwealth perspective, any new comprehensive agreement would have to be based on new norms: nonreciprocity, equality, and security. The Yaoundé trade regime, with its insistence on reverse preferences, was anachronistic—particularly since the addition of Part IV of GATT in the mid-1960s. Yaoundé had also failed to provide security for the Associates: trade preferences had been eroded without the Associates' being consulted; no satisfactory guarantee of the security of their export earnings had been provided. Any future arrangement must have a contractual nature in order to guarantee the security of the arrangements. Finally, Yaoundé had manifestly been an unequal relationship with negotiations effectively taking place only within the Community, which subsequently handed down its decisions in imperial style to the Associates.

Although existing Associates in April 1972 had declared themselves willing to negotiate side by side with the Commonwealth, forging a united position proved difficult. Senegal and the Ivory Coast were reluctant to accept the position that an Agreement should not contain provision for reciprocity in any area on the part of the Africans (they acknowledged, however, that reverse trade preferences were unacceptable), and, secondly, they rejected the argument that there should be no link between the aid and trade provisions of a future convention. Here the EAMA apparently feared that in the event of failure to reach a solution satisfactory to all African states, the Commonwealth group would enter into a nonreciprocal trade agreement but would expect nevertheless to receive aid from the Community.

In the remainder of 1972 little progress was made. A Caribbean delegation had visited Lagos in September 1972, but proposed meetings between the Commonwealth Secretariat and the Brussels-based Association Secretariat failed to materialize owing to mutual suspicions. The Francophones, and apparently France itself, regarded the Commonwealth Secretariat as an American trojan horse. In February 1973, Nigeria took the initiative by calling a meeting of African Commonwealth states; it was decided that they would negotiate with the EEC as a single group with activities to be coordinated by the Brussels Secretariat of the East African Community. The Commonwealth group also decided that the topic of relations with the EEC would be removed from the official agenda of a meeting to be held later that month in Accra of the UN's Economic Commission for Africa (ECA), which had commissioned a report to examine "Intra-African Economic Cooperation and African Relations with the European Community." Ostensibly the Commonwealth group's decision to remove the question of negotiations with the EEC from the ECA agenda was taken in order to avoid "premature politicization" of the subject, which might have occurred if initial discussion had taken place at the ministerial level. Personal and bureaucratic rivalries also undoubtedly played a role, with the Nigerians anxious to reduce the influence of both the ECA and the Commonwealth Secretariat. In lieu of the ECA discussion, the Commonwealth African group proposed informal contacts with the EAMA Secretariat but apparently was still committed to nothing more than a trade agreement with the Community—at its February meeting the group in fact rejected the three options offered by Protocol 22.[67]

At this juncture, the European Commission made a decisive intervention with the publication of its memorandum on "Renewal and Enlargement of the Association with the AASM and Certain Commonwealth Developing Countries." Named after then Commissioner for Development, Deniau, this document in retrospect played a major role in ensuring the successful outcome of the negotiations. Prepared in the period since the Community's enlargement, the memorandum was well reasoned and politically astute, showing a keen awareness not only of the subtleties of Community policy making but also of the sensitivities of the proposed partners. By suggesting a major step forward in Community development policies (the publication of its proposals, which were in many instances a "creative" interpretation of the provisions of Protocol 22, made it very difficult for the member states to renege in any future negotiations on their main principles), the memorandum was successful in meeting the needs of both the Associates and the associables and in convincing them not only that their interests were compatible but also that they might be best pursued through joint negotiations with the Community. This innovative role was acknowledged by the Nigerian ambassador to Brussels, who commented that Nigeria had been attracted by the Deniau Memorandum "which represented a departure from Europe's usual conservative approach."[68]

Noting the decision of the Summit Conference of October 1972 (which included the heads of state of the new members) to implement a comprehensive policy of worldwide development cooperation, the Commission reminded the Associates and associables that the Community "did not wish to abandon the policy of association and replace it by a world-wide policy as yet to be formulated." Rather, the intention was to enlarge, enrich, and strengthen the Association in such a manner that relations with the EAMA would not be weakened. In a move that appeared to render obsolete the provisions of Protocol 22, the Commission declared that "there can be no question of limiting the scope of the negotiations by setting up any prior conditions." Membership in an enlarged Association was to be available not only to those countries listed in the Treaty of Accession but also to other African countries "with comparable products and structure."[69] This removed one of the objections of those who perceived Association as a neocolonialist arrangement available only to countries that were former colonies of Community member states.

On the controversial issue of reverse preferences the Memorandum also moved toward satisfying the objections of critics. Association would be based on the principle of a free trade area that would not oblige the associated states to grant preferences to the Community members. Associates could if they desired extend duty-free treatment to third countries; moreover, "wide-ranging derogations" of the kind provided for under Protocol 2 of the Yaoundé Conventions were envisaged.[70]

In reviewing the impact of Association under the Yaoundé Conventions the Commission noted that results in the trade sector had "failed to come up to initial expectations." One cause of this was "a fairly substantial" reduction of preferences for EAMA exports in the Community market. Consequently, the Memorandum reasoned, "the Community will have to take steps to revitalize and improve the commercial content of the Association, unless it wishes to see a large part of its commercial importance whittled away with the additional risk that within 15 years the Association will have ceased to be a framework for an effective policy of cooperation in the development field."[71] Since preferences in the trade sector offered little scope for further maneuver (although the Commission did envisage improved access for Associates' agricultural products and argued once again for the phasing out of consumption taxes), advantages for the Associates should be sought in other areas, including trade promotion and the stabilization of their export earnings. Provision in Protocol 22 that "the Community will have as its firm purpose the safeguarding of the interests of all the countries whose economies depend to a considerable extent on the export of primary products" was interpreted as a Community commitment to stabilizing the export earnings of these countries. This the Commission considered to be an area in which "it is quite clear that it has failed so far to provide a solution to the problems of the EAMA." It concluded that "This is all the more regrettable and disturbing as parallel developments on an international scale have been equally disappointing."[72] Accordingly, it proposed the creation of a compensatory financing scheme—which subsequently became known as STABEX (see chapter 3).

In the realm of financial and technical cooperation, the Memorandum made three principal proposals: (1) maintenance of the general priorities by sector "as confirmed by experience"; (2) "practical improvements to make cooperation more immediately effective"; and (3) more far-reaching and broader aid, which would include contributions to recurrent costs of projects, increased support for regional cooperation, and special priority to the least advanced associated states. Recognizing that Community aid had previously concentrated on the realization of medium- or large-scale operations, more aid was to be given to small firms within the associated countries and to microprojects for rural communities. The existing discretionary grant of a 15 percent preference to suppliers from an associated state was to be applied automatically. No specific recommendation was made on the future volume of Community aid except to propose that enlargement of Association must not interfere with the advantages gained by existing Associates (to be considered in real terms) while all countries in a future agreement should receive similar treatment for comparable situations. Finally, it was proposed to solve the problem of lack of continuity in aid commitments by including development assistance within the regular Community budget (which would have increased the Commission's autonomy from the member states).

In many ways the Deniau Memorandum answered the concerns of both the EAMA and the Commonwealth associables before these had been voiced in formal negotiations with the EEC. Associates were reassured that their existing benefits from European aid would be maintained and that the overall package would provide them with treatment that was no less favorable than that enjoyed under the Yaoundé Conventions. For the Commonwealth, the Memorandum promised a more flexible attitude on the issue of reverse preferences and, through the proposed STABEX scheme, offered the type of guarantee of security for their export earnings that they were seeking. By proposing that the new arrangements be available to countries that had not been colonies of European member states, the Commission also went some way toward assuaging criticisms of the divisive nature of its Third World policies.

Two problems were now faced by the Associates and the associables: first, to forge their own unity and, second, to ensure in the subsequent negotiations with the Community that the proposals made in the Memorandum be realized. The first formal contact between the EAMA and African associables came at a meeting of trade ministers sponsored by the OAU in Abidjan in May 1973. Also represented were the African states of "comparable structure": Ethiopia, Liberia, and the Sudan. Agreement was reached at this meeting on an eight-point platform that was to form the basis for negotiation with the Community. This was subsequently endorsed by the Addis Ababa meeting of the OAU Heads of State later the same month. But it was not until July, at a hastily called meeting under Nigerian auspices, that it was agreed that the African countries should go to Brussels with a single spokesman, secretariat, and common platform. Nigeria also took the initiative by inviting representatives from the Caribbean associables to the July preparatory meeting.

At the end of the month, negotiations with the Community formally opened in Brussels. Nigerian Trade Commissioner, Wenike Briggs, insisted that he was speaking in the name of all African countries in rejecting the three models of Association proposed by Protocol 22 and in reciting the eight-point program agreed by the OAU Heads of State.[73] In brief, this demanded:

1. nonreciprocity in trade and tariff concessions;
2. the extension on a nondiscriminatory basis toward third countries of the provisions on right of establishment;
3. revision of the rules of origin so as to facilitate the industrial development of African countries;
4. revision of the provisions on the movement of payments and capital to take account of the objective of monetary independence in African countries and their need for monetary cooperation;
5. dissociation of EEC financial and technical aid from any particular form of relationship with the EEC;
6. free and assured access to EEC markets for all African products, including processed and semiprocessed agricultural products whether or not they are subject to the common agricultural policy of the EEC;
7. the guaranteeing to African countries of stable, equitable, and remunerative

prices in EEC markets for their main products in order to allow them to increase their export earnings;
8. future arrangements that would have no adverse effect on intra-African cooperation.

A similar list of eight points was presented by the spokesman for the Caribbean countries while the statement by the Fiji Prime Minister on behalf of the three Pacific countries also rejected reverse preferences in arguing that "the reintroduction of reciprocal requirements would be a reversion to the trade patterns of the imperial and colonial era."[74]

In response, the European Community, much to the consternation of the Associates and associables, merely repeated the offer of the three options made available in Protocol 22. This was an early indication that the concessions proposed in the Deniau Memorandum would not be extracted easily from the member states. At the time of the initial negotiations the Nine appeared to be in disarray: although there were reports that an earlier Council meeting had agreed after considerable British pressure to drop the requirement for reverse preferences, the EEC spokesman conceded that the Community had not yet established its position on the future trade arrangements. The Council, in fact, had allowed the Commission to begin the negotiations without having reached agreement on the proposals in the Deniau Memorandum.

Coincidence of the interests of the three groups of developing countries participating in the negotiations was evident from their opening statements. An obvious next step in strengthening their bargaining hand was to reach agreement on a joint negotiating position. This was achieved before the negotiations resumed in October 1973: henceforth the ACP group, as it became known, was represented by a single spokesman. Of the points raised in the initial statements, only the question of access to the Community market for Commonwealth sugar did not figure in the Africans' eight points. Finding a satisfactory successor to the Commonwealth Sugar Agreement was a principal stumbling block in Britain's accession to the Community; for the developing countries most affected, the Caribbean and the Pacific, the forging of a united front with the African group (which was eventually to enable them to make a satisfactory settlement of the sugar issue a prerequisite for signature of a new Convention) was a particularly effective means of increasing bargaining leverage. ACP success in realizing and sustaining a common negotiating position was particularly impressive given the divisions between African countries that had existed only a few months before. It came as a surprise for Community negotiators and was by no means a welcome event to all of them. Even in the earliest stages of the negotiations: "the contrast of the coherence of the underdeveloped countries with the hesitancy of the European Community was striking."[75]

For the first six months little progress was made in the negotiations, even toward realizing the suggestions made by the Commission in the Deniau Memorandum. Trade issues proved to be particularly controversial. ACP negotiators complained that the EEC was using the Common Agricultural Policy as an excuse for wholesale denial of free access for their agricultural products and demanded that any *exceptions* to the principle of free access be justified on a case-by-case basis. On the subject of nontariff barriers to their exports, the ACP were critical of the Commission's claim that it had no mandate to negotiate in this area, which, it asserted, was within the competence of the member states. Little progress was made on the rules-of-origin issue: ACP negotiators proposed that a minimum of 25 percent of value added locally be recognized as sufficient to confer originating status. EEC spokesmen insisted, however, that adjustment to the present rules could be contemplated only on a case-by-case basis where damage to ACP interests caused by current rules could be documented.

Meanwhile, the ACP negotiating hand had been strengthened by developments in the international environment. Talks had begun in the month when OPEC imposed its oil embargo, an event that not only changed European perceptions regarding raw materials supplies but also hardened the negotiating position of the ACP. In April 1974 ACP representatives stated that the Deniau notion of a price stabilization scheme for export earnings was no longer attractive: "the parameters in the Commission's files have become false." Events had overtaken the idea of merely preventing fluctuations in export earnings, and the ACP were looking instead to Europe to pay remunerative prices related to their import costs of machinery and goods. "The ACP was learning from the energy crisis, and the trend now towards paying an economically just price for oil was an object lesson to the producers of raw materials." Guarantee of supply to Europe of raw materials as a condition for price stabilization was rejected.[76]

At the time, however, there was considerable doubt whether any of the innovative proposals of the Commission would be realized in any form.

Member states were deeply divided over what should be included in a new Convention: this was exacerbated by the election of a new government in Britain that proclaimed its intention to renegotiate Britain's terms of membership. Negotiations with the ACP became a pawn in this intra-Community game and at one stage were suspended for one month by demand of the Wilson government. Negotiations were complicated by a British demand that Community aid in the future be divided equally between Associates and nonassociates. Implementation of this proposal would either have reduced the amount being received by the Associates or have required a substantial increase in the Community aid budget. Both alternatives were clearly unacceptable to other member states. At this stage of the talks, it was the disputes between the Community member states, rather than between them and the ACP, that threatened the future of the negotiations. France continued to insist on the need for reciprocity in the future Convention, while on the eve of the ministerial meeting with the ACP, scheduled to take place in Kingston in July, Britain blocked agreement on a Community commitment in principle to a stabilization scheme for ACP export earnings in retaliation for French and Belgium refusal to agree to guaranteed annual access to the Community market for Commonwealth sugar.

Last-minute negotiations among the Nine produced the necessary compromise, for not only did the Kingston meeting go ahead but also agreement was reached in principle with the ACP on most of the important points outstanding. For the first time, the Nine conceded officially that a new Convention would not insist on reciprocity from the ACP and that there would be free access for ACP exports to Community markets with no corresponding commitments being required of the ACP. The Community also declared its willingness to undertake a further examination of the access of ACP agricultural products that competed with EEC production, a commitment formalized in Annex II to the Convention (before the Kingston meeting, the Nine had declared that they had made a final offer on this matter—one that failed to satisfy ACP states such as Botswana, which were heavily reliant on the UK market for the exports of their agricultural products). The Nine agreed in principle to the introduction of a scheme to stabilize the export earnings of the ACP (STABEX) although not on covering the real value of export earnings. In return for this commitment, the ACP conceded Community demands that reports should be made on how transfers received under the scheme were used. Agreement was reached on further examination of the rules-of-origin issue, and, finally, the Community accepted ACP demands that a new Convention should include a chapter providing for industrial cooperation between the two groups.

Two issues were left unresolved: the quantity of financial aid to be made available and the access of ACP sugar producers to the Community market. ACP negotiators had demanded a sum of 8,000 million units of account for the five-year period that the Convention was expected to cover: chairman of the European Council of Ministers, Jean Sauvagnargues had replied that the ACP could expect no more than 3,500 mua. As in the Yaoundé Conventions, this issue was determined primarily by debate among the Community member states. Aid for nonassociates complicated matters: France had conceded the principle of financial aid to nonassociates before the Kingston meeting, but the German government had stated categorically that it would not accept any blanket aid commitments. Bonn in fact effectively determined the final aid offer made to the ACP by informing its partners of the amount that it was willing to contribute and subsequently stating that the matter was nonnegotiable. The sum finally agreed (3,390 mua, including 390 mua in EIB ordinary loans) even fell short of the amount initially mentioned by the chairman of the EEC Council of Ministers.

Sugar represented a more complex problem. Of all the primary products in international trade, sugar is unique in that there are two competing varieties, one of which is suited to cultivation in temperate climates the other in tropical. Since only a small proportion of total sugar output is sold on the international market, the remainder being consumed domestically or traded subject to international agreements such as the U.S. Sugar Act, prices in the free market are extremely volatile.

Britain and the six original members of the Common Market had pursued antipodal policies in the sugar sector over several decades. Britain's sugar needs were supplied almost entirely from imports until the 1920s, primarily from cane sugar grown in Africa and the Caribbean islands but supplemented by imports of beet from Northern Europe. Government subsidies encouraged the establishment of domestic beet production in the 1930s and a subsequent growth of output. But domestic production was not at the expense of Commonwealth cane sugar exporters, who were given a guaranteed market for specific quantities following the outbreak of the Second World War. These guarantees were continued in the dollar shortage of the immediate postwar period and formalized in December 1951 with the signature of the Commonwealth Sugar Agreement (CSA). In the subsequent period the acreage under beet production in Britain was strictly controlled in order to maintain a market for cane producers, who satisfied approximately two-thirds of Britain's domestic consumption. Commonwealth suppliers benefited from a Negotiated Price Quota, revised every three years, under which a specified quantity of sugar was guaranteed a market at a price "reasonably remunerative to efficient producers." By the late 1960s the quotas provided for imports of more than 1.8 million tons, which were divided between the producing countries, Australia receiving the largest single quota of about 350,000 tons.[77]

In contrast, the Six had always been basically self-sufficient in sugar from domestic beet supplies, although Luxembourg did not grow sugar, and Germany and Italy sometimes supplemented domestic production with imports. Belgium, the Netherlands, and France were net exporters. As one of the most important agricultural commodities produced in Western Europe, sugar was an obvious candidate for inclusion in the Common Agricultural Policy. Construction of a Community sugar regime proved particularly difficult, however, as a result of the different pricing policies pursued by the five governments, reflecting the variations in the efficiency of the domestic producers (those in Germany and Italy being particularly high-cost). In order to enable German and Italian beet farmers to survive, the CAP price would have to be set at a high level, but this would certainly have encouraged overproduction in the other countries.

To counter this tendency, the sugar regime, unlike those for all other CAP products, provided for quotas for each country (that were supposed to be phased out by 1975) that did not restrict production per se but placed limits on the quantities for which markets and prices were guaranteed. Introduced in July 1968, the common policy provided for uniform prices throughout the Community and similar arrangements for specific quotas of cane production for the French overseas departments of Reunion, Guadeloupe, and Martinique. However, no concessions were made for producers among the Yaoundé Associates: France had previously guaranteed Congo and Madagascar a market for 93,000 tons at the prevailing French price, but this arrangement was terminated with the installation of the Community's common policy.

Agreement on the sugar regime in the Council of Ministers was reached only by setting both prices and production quotas at levels higher than those recommended by the Commission. In 1967/68 the Community's threshold price was 438 percent above its import (i.e., the world) price for sugar—the largest differential at the time for any of the important CAP products.[78] High price levels led to a substantial increase in production such that a considerable Community sugar surplus developed, reaching more than 1.7 million tons in 1971 (or approximately the volume of imports in Britain from the Commonwealth). This happy coincidence was certainly not lost on the Community producers, least of all the well-organized French beet farmers, who coveted the protected British market as a solution to their overproduction problems.[79]

Protection of the interests of Commonwealth producers had, however, been underlined by successive British governments during the accession talks. A successful outcome of the negotiations on sugar was essential if the government was to appear credible in its claims that the developing Commonwealth was not being deserted; in the renegotiation talks following the election of the Wilson government it represented an important element that might be used to "sell" Community membership to the British public. Sugar represented more than 90 percent of the export earnings of Mauritius, more than 70 percent of the exports of Fiji, and a similar proportion of those of some Caribbean islands. In addition to the concerns of the Commonwealth, there were substantial British domestic interests in the maintenance of cane sugar imports. Foremost among these was the sugar refining company Tate and Lyle, which had extensive interests in the production, shipping, and refining of cane sugar. Curtailment of cane sugar imports would also have had domestic political repercussions, since Tate and Lyle warned that this would inevitably lead to the dismissal of large numbers of workers from its port refineries dependent on cane sugar, two of which were located in economically depressed areas of Britain.

As Webb makes clear, however, neither private sector nor governmental interests were united in their support for Commonwealth producers. British beet growers used the opportunity to forge an alliance with their Community counterparts aimed at the exclusion of Commonwealth sugar from the enlarged Community market. Price differentials in recent years had moved in favor of the refining of beet rather than cane sugar to the extent that it had become necessary for the government to pay a subsidy to refiners of cane: those refiners who had the capability of processing both types (which included the British Sugar Corporation, in which the government held a substantial minority shareholding) consequently favored a shift in sources of supply to European beet. In the government itself there were marked differences in loyalties within the Foreign and Commonwealth Office and the Ministry of Agriculture.[80]

The configuration of governmental and business interests in the sugar sector at the time of the enlargement negotiations did not appear propitious for reaching a solution that would be satisfactory to all parties. Demand for sugar within the Commmunity was virtually stagnant and comparatively price inelastic; there was no prospect that the problem of too much sugar competing for a limited market would be solved through a growth in demand. The eventual outcome of the accession negotiations was a formula that essentially left the problem unresolved. After initially denouncing the offer as lacking the "bankable assurances" necessary for the Commonwealth, the British government accepted a commitment that "the enlarged Community will have as its firm purpose the safeguarding of the interests of all the countries referred to in this Protocol (No. 22) whose economies depend to a considerable extent on the export of primary products, and particularly of sugar."

Further discussion of the issue was postponed until the negotiations for a successor to the second Yaoundé Convention (the Commonwealth Sugar Agreement was due to expire in December 1974, one month before the Yaoundé Convention). This proved to be fortuitous timing, for in the interim period, an extraordinary transformation of the international sugar market occurred as a result of unprecedented simultaneous harvest failures in principal cane- and beet-producing countries, which eventually allowed a compromise that satisfied the interests of all parties.

In its initial proposals for a future Community sugar regime published in July 1973, the Commission had honored the commitment in Protocol 22 by proposing the import of 1.4 million tons of sugar from the associables and India, essentially at the expense of Community producers whose future production was to be curtailed in order to limit exports to the ISA quota of 800,000 tons. These recommendations brought forth a furious response from the Community beet lobby, strongly backed by the governments of France, Belgium, Germany, and Italy, and precipitated the worst crisis within the Community since the French nonparticipation of the mid-1960s. Jacques Chirac, then French Minister for Agriculture, publicly attacked the two French Commissioners for promoting a policy harmful to French interests. In their 1973 form the Commission proposals were clearly unacceptable, and in the ensuing months an acrimonious debate among the Nine failed to produce any agreement on future policy.

But in the fall of 1973 the price of sugar on the international market rose steeply so that in November 1973, for the first time since the Community's sugar regime was imposed, it exceeded the Community's internal price, necessitating a levy on the export of Community beet. A poor beet harvest in Europe and the United States in the winter of 1973–74 caused the price on the international market to escalate more rapidly: by March 1974 it had reached double the level of the previous November. Supply shortages were experienced in both Europe and the United States but particularly in Britain as some Commonwealth producers reneged on their commitments under the Commonwealth Sugar Agreement in order to sell their sugar at the higher prices prevailing on the international market. In these turbulent circumstances an unexpected reversal of alliances occurred: Community beet growers and Commonwealth cane exporters reached an informal agreement in May 1974 under which the European growers would not oppose the import of 1.4 million tons of Commonwealth sugar into the Community, in return for which the cane producers would refrain from opposition to the expansion of European beet exports. Meanwhile, the British government had lost enthusiasm for defending the interests of Commonwealth producers, whom it accused of holding consumers to ransom.

In these extraordinary circumstances the Community was able to issue—in the same month as the Kingston meeting with the ACP—revised proposals that satisfied all parties. These maintained the pledge to import 1.4 million tons of Commonwealth sugar but also provided for an increase in beet production within the Community, as opposed to the previously mooted decline. Long-term projections on the nature of the future Community sugar market were ignored as member governments rushed to fulfill their short-term objectives, foremost among which was security of supply.[81] At the Council meeting in November, by which time the world price for sugar had risen to 560 pounds per ton (in excess of four times the internal Community price), agreement was reached in principle on the importing of 1.4 million tons of Commonwealth sugar into the Community.

Having secured the principle of guaranteed access, the ACP producers then attempted to use their bargaining advantage to maximize the price they would receive not only for sugar supplied in the future to the Community market but also for supplies to the British market in 1975. On the first issue there was little bargaining to be done since the Community would not contemplate an arrangement whereby a third party, in this case the ACP cane growers, would receive prices in excess of those guaranteed to Community producers. Nevertheless, the ACP obtained an unprecedented agreement that not only breached the CAP principle of self-sufficiency but also linked the price they received for their exports to the Community to that paid to producers in the Nine. Agreement on the premium to be paid by Britain for supplies in 1975 was the last issue to be resolved in the negotiations, the Commonwealth Caribbean exercising claims on ACP unity in order to make signature of the entire Convention package subject to prior accord with Britain. Sugar prices on the international market, however, had already fallen substantially from their November peak, weakening the Caribbean bargaining hand. In the early hours of 1 February 1975, the day after the second Yaoundé Conventions expired, agreement was finally reached on the sugar issue—Commonwealth producers were to receive £260 per ton for sugar shipped to Britain in 1975, nearly double the Community internal price—and the new Convention was ready for signature in Lomé at the end of the month.[82]

## CONCLUSIONS

Even the more severe critics of Lomé could not deny that it represented a significant improvement over the Yaoundé arrangements.[83] Not only had the ACP Group been successful in removing the most objectionable aspects of the previous relationship, particularly the requirement for reverse preferences, but also Lomé represented a major expansion of the scope of cooperation to include the industrial field and the stabilization of export earnings from agricultural commodities. As important from the ACP perspective was that the Convention appeared to incorporate the principal norms they had sought: equality and security. These were of course interrelated—for aspirations for security referred not only to a guarantee of their subsistence through the STABEX scheme but also to the maintenance of the position of ACP exports in the European market. ACP states believed that the Community's acceptance of the principle of equality in a contractual relationship (which Community representatives have continually emphasized), together with the obligation imposed on the Community by Articles 5 and 6 of the Convention's trade chapter to consult with the ACP before effecting any change in its trade policies, would be sufficient to enable them to act effectively to protect their share of the European market.

A number of factors explain why the weak had been able to negotiate a markedly better deal from the strong. First, of course, was the dramatic change in the international environment that had occurred since the association of the colonies under Part IV of the Treaty of Rome. Representatives of the Community themselves often used the word *neocolonial* in describing these arrangements. In succeeding years, the relationship between France and its former colonies had been diluted; the paternalism acceptable in the early 1960s was no longer so in an era of growing Southern assertiveness. Lomé, in part, was a response to changing norms in the international community. The principle of nonreciprocity had been accepted by GATT in the mid-1960s and applied in the recently introduced GSP schemes. Reverse preferences in the Yaoundé and Arusha arrangements were an anachronism most Community member states found embarrassing.

Second, the probable success of Britain's application for Community membership necessitated a change in the Community's relationship with LDCs to accommodate the developing Commonwealth. From the Community perspective, successful negotiations with the Commonwealth associables not only offered the opportunity to show good faith to a skeptical British government and public but also a chance to considerably extend the scope of the Community's policies in the field of development cooperation. That the Community itself had considerable interests in ensuring a successful outcome to the talks obviously strengthened the negotiating hand of the ACP. And the Commission's interest in fostering a new development policy prompted it to issue the Deniau Memorandum, which played a significant role in bringing together the associables and the Associates and, by publicly proposing a number of improvements in the relationship, placed the member states in a position from which it was difficult to retreat.

Third, and not least, was the success of the ACP in forging a united negotiating front. Collective action paid dividends: not only did it place the Group as a whole in a much stronger bargaining position (collectively they were of greater interest to the Community than as regional groupings), but also a united stance enabled some countries to obtain concessions on items of particular interest that they might not have achieved on an individual basis. This was particularly the case for the Caribbean and Pacific sugar producers, which, calling on ACP solidarity, were able to make the satisfactory outcome of talks on prices in the British market a prerequisite for the signature of the Convention. Commonwealth countries, particularly Nigeria and Jamaica, had played a significant leadership role in forging and maintaining ACP solidarity. Meanwhile, changes in the international environment during the talks undoubtedly strengthened the ACP hand. OPEC's success provided a background of unprecedented concern over future security of supply of raw materials. Probably of greater importance was the upheaval in the international sugar market in 1973–74. Without this, it would have been unlikely that the original member states of the Community would have accepted a commitment to the import of Commonwealth sugar, as the reaction to the Commission's 1973 proposals had demonstrated. Prolonged negotiations on this matter after the other details of the Convention had been successfully negotiated would have sorely strained the unity of the ACP Group.

At a meeting in Lagos, one month after the conclusion of the negotiations, the ACP Group showed it was well aware of the limitations of the agreement. Little progress had been made on a guarantee of access for ACP agricultural products that competed with Community domestic production or on the rules-of-origin issue (although the Community agreed to periodic evaluations of their operation). Although STABEX was regarded as a major achievement, concern was expressed over its limited funds, limited product and market coverage, and failure to guarantee ACP import capacity. In the field of financial and technical cooperation, which, rather interestingly, was not perceived to be one of the most important aspects of the negotiations, the Group had accepted an arrangement that failed to maintain the real per capita value of the aid received by the Associates under Yaoundé and that excluded the Group from participation in the key financing decisions.

Overall, however, the Group had good reason to be satisfied with the achievements of its strategy of collective clientelism. Even if the Convention fell short of fully realizing their objectives, it was perceived as a significant foundation on which future improvements might be built. The ACP were confident that the Community would accept its generalized obligation to them under the spirit of Lomé and act to protect their interests. Almost immediately, however, as the following chapters show, it became apparent that the Community had a vastly different perception of its obligations under the Convention, which it tended to interpret in a narrow and legalistic manner.

# 3

# STABEX and SYSMIN

According to A. B. Beye, a former President of the ACP–EEC Council of Ministers, STABEX is "the main pillar" of the Lomé Convention.[1] Certainly, the compensatory financing scheme was the most innovative of the Convention's provisions. As the previous chapter noted, a principal weakness of the Yaoundé Conventions had been their failure to provide an adequate successor to the *surprix* scheme of the French colonial years. For the ACP, a guarantee of their subsistence through the stabilization of their export earnings was a core objective of their strategy of collective clientelism.

STABEX has often been misperceived as the EEC's response to growing fears regarding future security of supply of raw materials brought about in large part by OPEC's successful action in October 1973. In reality, as the European Commission points out, the STABEX proposal was put forward *in tempore non suspecto* as part of the Deniau Memorandum in April of that year. Although European thinking may well have been influenced by the commodities boom of 1971–73, the principal motivations underlying the STABEX proposal were to provide a major incentive to both Associates and associables to enter into an agreement with the enlarged Community while simultaneously resisting growing pressure from various actors in the Community for a return to managed markets.

STABEX represented a particularly innovative response by the European Commission to Part III of Protocol No. 22 of Britain's Act of Accession to the Community, which stated that "the Community will have as its firm purpose the safeguarding of the interests of all the coun-

The first part of this chapter draws on material first published in my article, "What is to be Done for Third World Commodity Producers: An Evaluation of the STABEX scheme" in *International Organization* (Summer 1984) 38 (3). Earlier versions of tables 3.1, 3.2, and 3.6. were reproduced with my permission by Joanna Moss in her book, *The Lomé Conventions and their Implications for the United States* (Boulder: Westview Press, 1982), tables 4-1, 4-2, 4-5, and 5-1. As a result of an editorial error, my manuscript was not cited as the source of these tables.

tries referred to in this Protocol [the Yaoundé Associates and Commonwealth "associables"] whose economies depend to a considerable extent on the export of primary products, and particularly of sugar." Although this clause was originally envisioned as a response to the concerns of Commonwealth sugar producers, the Commission "creatively" interpreted it to apply to all primary commodity exporters and thus as justification for the STABEX scheme. The publication of the Memorandum was also a shrewd tactical move on the Commission's part: although agreement on the details of STABEX was reached only after lengthy bureaucratic battles among the "Ten"—the Commission being the tenth partner—and between the Community and the ACP Group, the publication of the proposals placed the member states in a position from which it would have been extremely difficult to retreat. The principle of a Community contribution toward the stabilization of the export earnings of the ACP was thus established before the Lomé negotiations began in earnest.

STABEX was intended to be a form of development aid conceived in microeconomic and sectoral terms; i.e., the primary intention behind the scheme was that it would channel resources to commodity producers in countries whose earnings from the export of a particular commodity had declined (and thereby provide an incentive to continue production for export). A secondary objective was to aid governments whose revenues had suffered as a result of decline in export earnings (although STABEX transfers were not intended to be remedies for balance of payment problems). To ensure that these dual objectives were realized, detailed rules for use of transfers under the system would be stipulated in an agreement between the Commission and each beneficiary country. This agreement would establish:

the obligatory priority allocations, the conditions of utilization of the residual amounts and the development policy measures which each country intended to implement in order to make the best use of the guarantee accorded to it, for example to ensure stability of employment, the diversification of the economy, etc.[2]

One part of the transfer, the Commission envisioned, would permit the public authorities to guarantee commodity producers a minimum unit purchasing price; a second part would be earmarked for the public authorities "with the particular aim of improving the productivity and competitiveness of the product in question and diversifying the economy."

These functions might be performed by a government stabilization fund; any remaining credit could be used to finance projects of general interest that would otherwise suffer as a result of a fall in export receipts.

In its initial proposals the Commission envisaged that the scheme would work in the following manner. Reference prices (based on a moving average of world prices over the five years preceding the application) would be established for each commodity, together with reference quantities (each country's average exports to the Community in the five years before the entry into force of the agreement), which would be fixed for the duration of the Convention. Weightings would then be added to the reference price to reflect the situations of different recipient countries. A credit line would be opened *automatically* when actual earnings fell below the reference level; these transfers would be repayable, although derogations would be allowed for the poorest countries. The system would be given its own source of financing, *not subject to any ceiling*, and would be separate from other funds designated for development cooperation.

Commodities initially proposed for inclusion in the scheme were sugar, groundnuts, groundnut oil, cotton, cocoa, coffee, bananas, and copper. These were chosen as much for political as economic reasons—to satisfy various political constituencies in the Associates and Commonwealth associables. Sugar was put forward, not in the expectation that the member states would agree to its eventual inclusion, but in the hope that this proposal would force the Nine to provide the guaranteed access to the Community market for specified quantities of Commonwealth sugar that Britain and the Commonwealth producers were seeking. Copper was initially included to make the scheme attractive to Zaire; the Commission subsequently realized this was a tactical mistake since the proposals were published before a detailed analysis of the nature of the copper industry had been undertaken and before the consequences (including potential cost) of including a mineral in the system had been explored.[3]

During the negotiations, significant modifications to the scheme were made in order for it to meet the objectives of EEC member states and, to a lesser extent, those of the ACP. These had profound consequences for the manner in which the system operated, as will be detailed in the next section of the chapter. Four objectives were paramount from the perspective of the member states:

1. The scheme should not interfere with the workings of the market (a point already accommodated by the Commission in its initial design for the scheme).

2. ACP exports that competed with European production should not be encouraged by STABEX: in other words, the scheme should reinforce the existing division of labor between the two parties.
3. The scheme should be confined to trade relations between the EEC and ACP: STABEX would be part of the "privileged" relationship with the Community enjoyed by the ACP. The EEC's objective in constructing the exclusive relationship—to tie the ACP closer to the EEC—would be achieved by confining the scheme to coverage only of ACP earnings from exports to the Community. Consequently, it would be necessary to establish that any loss of earnings was not the result of trade diversion by an ACP state. Accordingly, rather than the beneficiaries automatically receiving a credit line when their earnings fell below the reference level, as proposed in the Deniau Memorandum, transfers were to be made at the discretion of the Commission.
4. The potential costs of the scheme should be limited. Member states unanimously rejected the idea of an open-ended commitment: instead of a separate budget STABEX would receive a predetermined amount from the overall commitment under the European Development Fund. On similar grounds of cost limitation, minerals would be excluded from the scheme. The dual reference quantity/reference price system was replaced by a single reference level—total export earnings for each commodity—a move that would make the system less expensive in circumstances where falls in exported quantities coincided with rising world market prices. Product thresholds were also introduced in order to limit the number of claims that might be made on the scheme.

Principal among the ACP objectives in the negotiations was the desire to maximize the benefits derived from the scheme while minimizing the constraints on the uses that might be made of such benefits. The Group was markedly more successful in the latter objective. Although they were able to persuade the Community to increase the number of products included in the scheme, they did not realize their demands that STABEX be made a full index-linked scheme for stabilizing real export earnings. However, in a political concession to ACP assertions of sovereignty, the ministers of the member states, in the face of Commission objections, agreed to the principle that the beneficiary of a STABEX transfer alone had the right to determine the purposes for which it might be used. This concession essentially robbed the scheme of its original *raison d'être*. Although the scheme would still be sectorally triggered, the link between a fall in the export earnings of a particular commodity and a transfer in favor of the producers of that commodity was broken. The consequences of this will be explored later.

## SHORTCOMINGS OF STABEX

STABEX is a concessional compensatory system that provides for transfers from the European Development Fund to ACP states if their earnings from exports to the EEC from a product included in the scheme fall below a reference level (calculated as the average from exports to the Community over the previous four years). To qualify for a transfer, the product in question must account for at least 6.5 percent of the country's earnings from exports to all destinations (2 percent for the least developed, landlocked and island countries [LLIC]), and the shortfall in a calendar year must be at least 6.5 percent of the reference level (2 percent for the LLIC).[4] The Commission must also be satisfied that the shortfall is not the result of trade diversion by the ACP state. During the operation of the system in Lomé I the Commission established the principle that no transfer would be made if total earnings from exports of a product to all destinations exceeded the average of its total export earnings in the preceding four years—this qualifying provision was written into the second convention. Transfers take the form of untied interest-free loans (grants for the least developed countries) made in an EEC currency of the choice of the ACP state in the amount of the shortfall in f.o.b. earnings from exports of the product to the Community.

In the period since STABEX was implemented a number of shortcomings have been evident. Rather than operating automatically with no interference with market mechanisms, STABEX has introduced a number of distortions into EEC–ACP trade. These have arisen in large part from the way in which the scheme was amended in order to accommodate the objectives of the participants as noted above. STABEX has fallen far short of its stated goal of providing comprehensive insurance to ACP primary producers. The problems with the scheme may conveniently be grouped as follows: (1) limited coverage of ACP export earnings; (2) discretionary administration of the system; (3) use of transfers; and (4) the limited impact of the system on ACP economies.

### 1. Limited Coverage of ACP Export Earnings

STABEX's utility as an insurance scheme to the ACP is determined by the proportion of their export earnings it covers. Four factors figure prominently here: the list of products included within the scheme, the thresholds that must be met in order to qualify for a transfer; the method

**TABLE 3.1.**

ACP Principal Exports and Share (%) of
Total ACP Export Earnings in 1975

(a) *Product Groups Included in*
*the STABEX Scheme (%)*

| | |
|---|---|
| 1. Groundnut | 3.1 |
| 2. Cocoa | 6.9 |
| 3. Coffee | 5.5 |
| 4. Cotton | 1.5 |
| 5. Coconut | 0.3 |
| 6. Palm | 1.6 |
| 7. Hides, skins, and leathers | 0.6 |
| 8. Wood | 4.6 |
| 9. Fresh bananas | 1.1 |
| 10. Tea | 0.8 |
| 11. Raw sisal | 0.6 |
| 12. Iron ore | 3.8 |
| Total STABEX | 30.4 |

(b) *Other Principal Exports Not Covered*
*by STABEX %*

| | |
|---|---|
| Petroleum | 34.5 |
| Copper | 9.5 |
| Sugar | 5.6 |
| Aluminum | 1.8 |
| Thorium and uranium ore | 0.6 |
| Calcium phosphates | 1.4 |
| Tobacco | 0.8 |
| Pineapple and products | 0.7 |
| Natural rubber | 0.5 |
| Meat | 0.4 |
| Clothes | 0.3 |
| Manganese ore | 0.5 |
| Tuna | 0.3 |
| Tin | 0.3 |
| Cotton fabrics | 0.2 |
| Crustaceans | 0.2 |
| Rum | 0.3 |
| Vegetables | 0.1 |
| Gum arabic | 0.2 |

Source: Derived from Eurostat, *Analysis of Trade Between the*
*European Community and the ACP States* (Luxembourg: Eurostat, 1979).
Note: Product shares of total exports fluctuate considerably
from year to year as a result both of changes in export volumes and in world market prices. Coffee's percentage contribution to ACP export earnings tripled in the next two
years, for example, but fell back to 7 percent by 1980.

of calculating reference periods and reference values, and the overall resources available to the system.

Since STABEX is triggered by fluctuations in the earnings from specific products, rather than overall export earnings, the utility of the scheme is determined in large part by the list of products it covers. During the negotiations for Lomé I, this list was changed significantly from that originally proposed in the Deniau Memorandum: sugar and copper were dropped from the scheme[5]; the ACP succeeded in persuading the EEC to add iron ore, coconut, palm and palm products, leathers, skins and hides, wood, and sisal.[6]

Table 3.1 shows the share of STABEX products in total ACP export earnings and the principal ACP export products not included in the scheme. During the first Convention, STABEX provided nominal coverage for products that together accounted for approximately 30 percent to 40 percent of total ACP earnings from exports to the European Community (the figure varies from year to year depending on the world market prices for STABEX commodities and other ACP exports). If petroleum is excluded from the calculations, STABEX nominally covered approximately 50 percent of other ACP exports. In reality, the system actually protected a smaller percentage of total ACP exports since eligibility for transfers is decided on an individual country basis, subject to that country's exports of a product's meeting the dependence and fluctuation thresholds. The European Commission estimates that the effect of these thresholds is to reduce the coverage of each product by approximately 15 percent to 20 percent.[7]

Three principal groups of products are excluded from STABEX: minerals, products included within the Community's Common Agricultural Policy (CAP), and processed and manufactured goods. Other sources of foreign exchange for ACP states, e.g., earnings from tourism and remittances from migrant workers, are also not covered. Minerals (with the incongruous exception of iron ore, added during the last stages of the negotiations to placate Mauritania, a principal ACP exporter, which held the chair of the STABEX negotiating committee at the time) were excluded on two grounds: the vertically integrated and oligopolistic nature of the industries, which, the Community feared, might enable transnational companies to manipulate the scheme to their benefit; and, second, the potential cost to the system of their inclusion—which the Community termed "prohibitive."[8] Besides the consideration of cost, the other principal Community objective that has had the effect of limiting product coverage is the desire to ensure that STABEX will not encourage ACP exports where these compete with European production.

Whereas for most agricultural products there is a certain coincidence of interests between the Community's desire to ensure supplies and the aspirations of the ACP to stabilize export earnings, in products covered by the CAP there is a direct conflict of interest between producers in the ACP and those in the Community. CAP products thus represent a test case for the Community's professed commitment to ACP development, a test on which the Community has performed poorly to date. In its negotiations with the ACP the Community has argued that it cannot extend STABEX coverage to CAP products, since this would offer ACP producers better terms than those provided to domestic agriculture (because STABEX would provide financial compensation in the event of loss of earnings from a fall in output). Whether Community producers would be bothered by a guarantee of export earnings to ACP states is open to question: they are much more concerned with the principle of whether there should be any access to the Community market for third-country exporters of products included in the CAP.

In this instance the Commission has used the equity issue as a means of sidestepping the more fundamental question of access for third-country producers. This is seen very clearly in the negotiations on tobacco's inclusion within STABEX; tobacco is the only major ACP agricultural export other than sugar that the system currently does not cover. At the time of the signature of Lomé II, the Commission announced:

The Community has undertaken to examine the possibility of including unmanufactured tobacco within the limits of a quantitative ceiling for exports to the Community, to be fixed at the current level, provided that this arrangement does not disturb the Community tobacco market.[9]

The key clause is obviously the last, which effectively signals that the Commission intends to restrict ACP countries to the role of residual suppliers for CAP products. In its initial position paper for the member states, the Commission asserted that a negative response should be given to the request for the extension of STABEX coverage to tobacco: the Commission had investigated the possibility that special provisions be made for ACP varieties of tobacco noncompetitive with those grown in the EEC but found that the major part of ACP exports were in fact directly competitive.[10] CAP products are excluded from STABEX simply because the

Community is concerned that any incentives toward their production will be perceived as guaranteeing a market share to ACP exporters and inevitably lead to increased competition for domestic producers.

A third major group of products excluded from STABEX are those that have undergone more than a very limited degree of processing. At present the only processed and manufactured products included in the scheme are certain oils (groundnut, palm, coconut, and niaouli and ylang-ylang); cocoa paste and butter; extracts, essences or concentrates of coffee; leathers; cotton linters; and sawn wood. Exclusion of other processed products (including current ACP exports such as plywood, cotton cloth, flour, and canned fish) deters investment in downstream activities—one of the most realistic means through which ACP states might increase the domestic value added to exports and thereby reduce their vulnerability to fluctuations in export earnings from primary products. Even where a processed product is included in STABEX, the system of product thresholds deters processing, since a move from exporting the raw material to the export of a processed product may mean that both products fail to meet the dependence threshold. Under the Convention, the Commission is obliged to reduce transfers where it can be demonstrated that a decline in export earnings resulted from a domestic policy measure on the part of the ACP state. Included in the list of such measures is domestic processing—in 1975 the value of a STABEX transfer to Niger was reduced by the Commission on these grounds.[11]

This is a further instance where the extent of product coverage in STABEX and thus its utility was determined primarily by domestic political considerations in the Community. This is seen clearly in the Community's response to ACP requests for the inclusion of sisal products in STABEX. In suggesting that the member states reject the ACP proposal the Commission stated (in an internal memorandum):

sisal products, notably twine, are sensitive for the Community and their inclusion is liable, at the present time, to present the sisal processing industry within the Community with grave problems.

Since the exclusion of processed products from STABEX acts indirectly to increase the level of effective protection enjoyed by European processing industries, the Commission and the member states have been subject to pressure from groups representing European industry that have declared themselves adamantly opposed to the extension of STABEX to include additional processed products.[12] In its proposals for a third Convention, the Commission asserted that the system should maintain its "agricultural bent"; there should be no extension of the list of products covered.

*Thresholds.* STABEX's dependence and fluctuation thresholds have been justified by the Community on the grounds that they ensure that the system concentrates its efforts on problems that are "important" (significant dependency on particular products) and "serious" (a substantial fall in the level of receipts). Thresholds prevent the Commission from being faced with a multitude of claims for transfers involving relatively small sums. Community spokesmen have argued that since the dependence threshold is recalculated each year, it provides an exact reflection of the evolution of ACP exports and establishes a narrow link between each product and the total of exports. But with a given threshold firmly enforced, the system inevitably acts in an arbitrary manner—a shortfall of 6.3 percent in an export whose share of the total earnings of an ACP state is 80 percent would not be compensated, for instance, whereas a shortfall of 6.5 percent in an export accounting for 6.5 percent of total earnings would be eligible for a transfer. Large percentage falls in earnings from a minor crop thus will be compensated although the absolute sums involved may be small, whereas a small percentage fall that produces a large absolute decline in earnings from a major export will not qualify a country for a transfer. Substantial volumes of export earnings may be lost in this manner without activating the system.

The present system of dependency thresholds can serve as a disincentive to diversification of exports. This could occur in circumstances where a country had several important exports whose contribution to total earnings was roughly equivalent and one dominant export. The introduction of a new export might reduce the percentage share of all exports except the dominant one beneath the dependence threshold. An example would be a country for which a mineral constitutes 80 percent of export earnings and that has three other exports that all fulfill the current dependency threshold. The introduction of a fourth minor export would, if all four now had equal shares in total exports, bring all four products beneath the 6.5 percent dependency threshold. In these circumstances none of the country's exports would be eligible for coverage by STABEX—not only do the four minor products not qualify but the mineral is excluded from the system. Although this type of situation might be rare, the problem of meeting the dependency thresholds for minor exports is a real one for mineral and petroleum exporters.

Furthermore, in a situation where the increasing dependence on one product pushes other exports below the dependency threshold, STABEX does nothing to discourage the trend of these countries toward becoming one-product economies; the rigidity of the threshold prevents the scheme from providing an incentive to governments to maintain their interest in small and relatively declining sectors. A case in point would be Nigeria, where cocoa's share of total exports fell from 15 percent in 1970 to 4 percent in 1976. Cocoa remains an important cash crop and significant source of employment in Nigeria, which as late as 1977 provided 30 percent of Britain's imports of the product. Although the value (but not the quantity) of cocoa exports rose during this period, its share in total earnings declined owing to the expansion of oil exports. This precluded assistance from STABEX to a sector where overall output was declining.

Nigeria is obviously an exceptional case by virtue of its petroleum earnings—which the EEC might well argue should be invested in part in agriculture. Nevertheless this illustration does demonstrate that the potential problem of the exclusion from STABEX of the products of the minor export sectors of mineral producers is not merely a hypothetical one. Belated recognition of this problem was given by the Commission in its proposal that the dependency threshold be waived "in exceptional circumstances" in Lomé III for countries heavily dependent on mineral exports but also significant agricultural producers. While increased flexibility would be desirable, this would increase the discretionary power of the Commission in the absence of clearly defined criteria for "exceptional cases."

A principal reason for the maintenance of thresholds is their effect of reducing the costs of the system. This effect is demonstrated clearly in a Commission study. The Commission found that if the dependence threshold was abolished (as demanded by the ACP during the negotiation of Lomé II) or substantially reduced, the coverage of ACP exports by the system would be greatly increased, but there would be a concomitant increase in the risks of export earnings fluctuations for which additional financial resources would have to be provided. Countries currently excluded from the system because of their heavy dependence on earnings from exports of a single mineral would become beneficiaries. Calculations by the Commission for two such countries—Nigeria and Zaire—

show that whereas neither benfited from a transfer in respect of the products covered by STABEX in the period 1974–78, given the failure of their nonmineral exports to meet the 6.5 percent threshold, if the dependency threshold had been abolished, then Nigeria would have received transfers amounting to 252 mua, and Zaire, 40 mua. Abolition of the dependency threshold would have brought similar gains to nonmineral exporters. For the Ivory Coast, which currently has three products covered by STABEX, the suppression of the dependency threshold would have extended the coverage to 18 products and represented an additional risk for the system of 152 mua for 1977 alone. Kenya and Tanzania would have enjoyed coverage for an additional 15 products; Kenya alone would have received transfers amounting to approximately 30 mua for the period 1975–77.[13]

Thresholds cause STABEX to function in an arbitrary and discriminatory manner, reducing its value to ACP countries and, indeed, limiting the system's ability to achieve its stated objectives. Together with the selective list of products covered, the thresholds combine to produce marked variations between ACP states in the percentage of exports to the Community that STABEX covers and, consequently, in the benefits they derive from the system (table 3.2). Calculations in a French government study show it is rare indeed for STABEX to approach total coverage of a country's exports; for the forty-three of the original forty-six signatories to the Convention for which data were available, STABEX covered more than 75 percent of total exports to the Community for four countries, between 50 percent and 75 percent for thirteen, between 25 percent and 50 percent for eleven, and less than 25 percent for seven countries. Eight countries had no products eligible for STABEX coverage.[14] Inevitably, a system that offers only partial coverage of exports can at best provide partial compensation for loss of earnings.

On various occasions the Community has responded to these criticisms by arguing that the thresholds were instruments that enabled the Community not only to concentrate its efforts on important problems but also to give a special advantage to the least developed countries among the ACP. Accordingly, the levels of thresholds had been established by country rather than by product (with the exception of sisal, the special threshold for which is redundant since Tanzania, the only ACP producer that meets the dependence threshold, is classified as a least developed country). But the validity of the argument that eligibility for ben-

**TABLE 3.2.**

ACP Country Product Coverage—Transfers Under Lomé I

| Country | Income Per Head $ | STABEX Products | | STABEX Transfers | | |
| --- | --- | --- | --- | --- | --- | --- |
| | | Number | % Total Exports | Number | Volume 000 UA | % Total |
| Gabon | 2,813 | 1 | 32 | 1 | 6,703 | 1.8 |
| Bahamas* | 2,184 | 0 | 0 | 0 | 0 | 0 |
| Trinidad and Tobago* | 2,113 | 0 | 0 | 0 | 0 | |
| Barbados* | 1,500 | 0 | 0 | 0 | 0 | 0 |
| Jamaica* | 1,328 | 1 | 4 | 0 | 0 | 0 |
| Surinam | 1,297 | 0 | 0 | 0 | 0 | 0 |
| Fiji* | 1,151 | 1 | 5 | 2 | 2,115 | 0.6 |
| Ivory Coast | 617 | 3 | 67 | 1 | 15,000 | 4.0 |
| Seychelles*†a | 572 | 1 | 21 | 0 | 0 | 0 |
| Mauritius* | 552 | 0 | 0 | 0 | 0 | 0 |
| Guyana | 512 | 0 | 0 | 0 | 0 | 0 |
| Congo | 509 | 1 | 42 | 1 | 7,362 | 2.0 |
| Swaziland*†a | 457 | 1 | 3 | 3 | 13,225 | 3.5 |
| Zambia* | 453 | 0 | 0 | 0 | 0 | 0 |
| Botswana*†u | 414 | 1 | 9 | 0 | 0 | 0 |
| Nigeria | 412 | 0 | 0 | 0 | 0 | 0 |
| Tonga*†a | 391 | 1 | 50 | 4 | 1,208 | 0.3 |
| Grenada*† | 379 | 2 | 41 | 0 | 0 | 0 |
| Ghana | 372 | 2 | 80 | 1 | 5,176 | 1.4 |
| Cameroon | 363 | 3 | 61 | 2 | 4,065 | 1.1 |
| Mauritania† | 350 | 1 | 73 | 2 | 37,000 | 9.9 |
| Senegal | 345 | 1 | 35 | 2 | 65,106 | 17.4 |
| Liberia | 343 | 1 | 71 | 1 | 7,587 | 2.0 |
| W. Samoa*†a,u | 300 | 2 | 73 | 5 | 2,837 | 0.8 |
| Sudan†u | 296 | 2 | 65 | 5 | 41,776 | 11.1 |
| Eq. Guinea | 294 | n.a. | n.a. | 0 | 0 | 0 |
| Uganda*†u | 294 | 3 | 86 | 8 | 20,595 | 5.5 |
| Kenya | 252 | 2 | 33 | 0 | 0 | 0 |
| Madagascar* | 217 | 2 | 33 | 3 | 5,748 | 1.5 |
| Zaire | 212 | 0 | 0 | 0 | 0 | 0 |
| Lesotho*†a,u | 203 | 1 | 26 | 0 | 0 | 0 |
| CAR*†u | 200 | 3 | 62 | 4 | 7,830 | 2.1 |
| Sierra Leone† | 199 | 2 | 15 | 1 | 3,977 | 1.1 |
| Togo† | 187 | 2 | 39 | 2 | 3,626 | 1.0 |
| Comoros*†a,u | 180 | 3 | 83 | 0 | 0 | 0 |
| Gambia†u | 178 | 1 | 94 | 3 | 7,512 | 2.0 |
| Tanzania†u | 176 | 3 | 41 | 4 | 20,702 | 5.5 |
| Benin†u | 170 | 1 | 34 | 12 | 20,367 | 5.4 |

**TABLE 3.2.** *(Continued)*

| Country | Income Per Head $ | STABEX Products | | STABEX Transfers | | |
|---|---|---|---|---|---|---|
| | | Number | % Total Exports | Number | Volume 000 UA | % Total |
| Guinea†ᵘ | 162 | 3 | 15 | 0 | 0 | 0 |
| Niger*†ᵘ | 146 | 2 | 24 | 6 | 22,654 | 6.0 |
| Rwanda*†ᵃ,ᵘ | 146 | 2 | 65 | 1 | 609 | 0.2 |
| Guinea Bissau†ᵃ,ᵘ | 140 | 1 | 43 | 5 | 11,288 | 3.0 |
| Malawi*†ᵘ | 134 | 2 | 25 | 0 | 0 | 0 |
| Chad†ᵘ | 120 | 1 | 69 | 2 | 7,336 | 2.0 |
| Upper Volta*†ᵘ | 117 | 2 | 30 | 5 | 7,262 | 1.9 |
| Somalia†ᵘ | 112 | 1 | 26 | 2 | 1,932 | 0.5 |
| Burundi*†ᵃ,ᵘ | 110 | 3 | 95 | 2 | 1,486 | 0.4 |
| Ethiopia†ᵃ,ᵘ | 97 | 2 | 51 | 2 | 14,420 | 0.9 |
| Mali*†ᵘ | 94 | 2 | 46 | 4 | 9,781 | 2.6 |

Source: GNP per capita from *ACP: Statistical Yearbook* (Luxembourg: Eurostat, 1980)
STABEX products as percent of exports calculated from data in *ibid.*
STABEX transfers from *Comprehensive Report on the Export Earnings and Stabilization System Established by the Lomé Convention for the Years 1975 to 1979*, (Sec [81] 1104).
   * Denotes landlocked or island ACP state.
   † Denotes country designated as "least developed" for the purposes of the Convention.
   ᵃ Denotes country whose exports to all destinations are covered by STABEX.
   ᵘ Denotes country designated as "least developed" by the United Nations.

efits is determined by need is undermined by the peculiar classification of countries adopted for the purposes of this chapter of the Convention. For STABEX purposes, Equatorial Guinea is classified as an island, while the Seychelles, one of the top ten ACP countries in terms of income per capita, benefits from the terms offered to the least developed. These groupings, which the Overseas Development Institute has termed "bizarre," were the outcome of sensitive political compromises made during the negotiation of the first Convention.[15] There is little logical justification for affording the same preferential treatment with respect to the dependency and fluctuation thresholds to a wealthy island state, such as Trinidad and Tobago, as to a least developed, landlocked country such as Upper Volta.[16] It is the selective product coverage rather than discrimination by level of development that excludes some of the countries with the highest per capita income from the system (their economies being dependent on exports of petroleum, minerals, and/or sugar), but this also prevents access to the system by low-income countries such as Zaire and Zambia.

A second argument made by the Community in defense of the thresholds is that the intention of STABEX is to support specific sectors rather than the overall balance of payments of a country. If the thresholds were removed and STABEX extended to all ACP exports, then, in the words of a Community spokesman, "one would arrive at the IMF system" (the Compensatory Financing Facility).[17] But, again, this argument is unconvincing and, indeed, is in conflict with statements that the Community has made elsewhere in support of the creation of a worldwide STABEX scheme, which, it argues, could easily be coordinated with the IMF facility "on which it would be an improvement."[18] Indeed, STABEX differs from the IMF Facility on several crucial dimensions, as will be detailed later in this chapter.

*Reference Periods.* Eligibility for a STABEX transfer is dependent on export earnings' falling below a threshold percentage of a reference value, which is the trend value calculated in nominal terms as the average of export earnings from that particular commodity in the previous four years. Two principal criticisms can be made of this method of calculation. First, it precludes transfers when a rising trend in export earnings (expressed in current values) is interrupted, a situation that might be as serious for a country as an actual fall in export receipts. Unlike the system employed by the IMF for its Compensatory Financing Facility, the calculation of the reference value for STABEX does not take into account projections of future earnings. By computing the reference values as an average of export earnings over the last four years, the expected trend value in STABEX in relation to any shortfall year refers in fact to earnings two and one-half years before the period in which the shortfall has occurred. Unless the situation is one in which the value of world trade is declining, the method of calculation is unfavorable to the ACP. An advantageous aspect of the present system, however, is the relative ease of calculation: any projection such as that used by the IMF is inevitably discretionary given the "inexact science" of forecasting trends in export earnings.[19]

A related criticism is the failure of the scheme to calculate changes in ACP export earnings in real rather than nominal terms. Indexation of the prices of raw materials to those of LDC imports of manufactured goods has figured prominently in the demands for a New International Economic Order, and the maximalist position of the ACP in the negotiations for both Lomé I and its successor was that STABEX should guarantee their export earnings in real terms. In an era of inflation the present

STABEX system inevitably covers a smaller portion of the risk experienced by the ACP states than an indexed system would. Each year the unit value of exports of the commodity in question will tend to rise, so that a smaller volume of exports will be sufficient to maintain export earnings at a level in excess of the average receipts during the reference period and thereby render the state ineligible for a transfer. This has in fact been the experience during the implementation of the system: the Court of Auditors of the European Community noted that "the unit value of the exports in the statistics applied was nearly always higher than the reference unit value."[20] This is consistent with the Commission's findings, discussed below, that most of the transfers made during Lomé I were the result of local production problems; that is, earnings shortfalls were caused primarily by declines in quantities exported rather than by falls in unit prices.

A method of calculating reference values in real terms obviously would significantly increase the volume of transfers and probably also raise the administrative costs of the scheme. Estimates of the actual sums involved are hazardous given the lack of complete data in the public realm. On the basis of partial data, the Commonwealth Secretariat calculated that for 1975 and 1976, transfers on the basis of real earnings would have been greater than those actually made on a nominal earnings basis by a factor of between 3.26 and 5.00. Stated in another way, STABEX transfers made during these years on a nominal earnings basis protected only 20 percent to 31 percent of real earnings exports. If coverage was extended to all ACP merchandise exports to all markets and transfers calculated on a real earnings basis, the cost of the system for the years 1975–76 would have been more than seventeen times that actually incurred. While these figures must be treated circumspectly owing to the incomplete data and the problems involved in calculating a suitable index for manufactured goods imports, they do provide an approximation of the magnitude of the costs involved in real earnings stabilization.[21]

*The System's Resources.* One of the major differences between the system introduced in the first Lomé Convention and that initially proposed by the Commission was the imposition of a ceiling on total resources available—380 mua in the first Convention (a figure raised to 550 mua in Lomé II). One consequence of this was a clause in the Convention that empowered the EEC Council of Ministers to reduce transfers in the event of the system's resources' being exhausted (Article 17, 4). This proved not to be necessary during the first Convention. However, enthusiasm for the system's performance led participants to ignore a number of danger signals: despite the reductions in transfers made by the Commission (see below) and the failure of two states to take full advantage of the transfers to which they were entitled, fully 99 percent of the system's resources were used. And this occurred in years when the prices of some STABEX commodities rose significantly on the world market. In aggregate, close to 70 percent of transfers made during the first Convention were occasioned by local circumstances, i.e., a decline in volumes exported, rather than by price falls. More than 80 percent of the transfers were made in respect of commodities that accounted for less than 40 percent of the "risk" insured; some of the major commodities in ACP-EEC trade, e.g., coffee, cocoa, and tea, made few demands on the system in this period. STABEX had not been tested by a situation where export earnings from a number of major commodities declined simultaneously or by one in which significant local disasters coincided with a decline in demand in the European market.

Developments in the international economy immediately following the signature of the second Convention demonstrated that the funds available were inadequate to cope with a combination of circumstances of this type. Largely as a result of declining international prices for coffee plus continuing local problems in groundnut production, requests for transfers in respect of the 1981 financial year amounted to 261 mua, whereas the resources available to the system totaled only 138 mua (including monies brought forward from the system in Lomé I, and a 20 percent advance on the following year's transfer). Requests for additional funding from the EEC member states met with an unenthusiastic response. Following consultations with the ACP Group (which itself was unable to agree on a formula for reducing transfers), the Commission decided that transfers would be reduced by 40.5 percent for the least developed ACP states and by 52.6 percent for others (transfers less than 1 mua were paid in full). In 1982 the problem was more severe: requests found to be justified amounted to 453 mua while funds available to the system were little more than 112 mua. An additional 70.7 mua was provided for the system from interest payments on EDF assets and from the proceeds of special loan repayments by ACP states. These funds, however, were made available on condition that they be used for projects approved by the EEC. Even with these additional funds, resources available amounted to less than 43 percent of justified requests. Again, it proved necessary to reduce transfers—this time by 53.5 percent for the least developed, and by 58.1 percent for other states (all transfer requests under 1 mua again being met in full).

Although the European Commission has claimed that the difficulties that the system has faced during Lomé II are in large part cyclical (the product of an unusual combination of price falls and local production difficulties), in reality the problems appear to be more structural: the outcome of the Community's decision to limit the resources available to the system. The experience of the operations in 1981 and 1982 points to the inability of the system at its present level of financing to cope with a significant fall in world market prices for one of its major products. Reduction in legitimate transfer requests has meant that the system has been unable to fulfill one of its principal stated objectives—to provide the security of a guarantee of earnings to the ACP.

## 2. Discretionary Administration

One of the principles established by the Community in the negotiations for Lomé I was that STABEX would apply only to ACP exports to the EEC. This provision was inserted not only because of cost but also because STABEX would provide an incentive to maintain existing patterns of ACP exports to the EEC. There were a few minor exceptions to this principle: under Article 17(4) of the first Convention, STABEX coverage was extended to the exports to all destinations of a number of countries that traditionally sent the bulk of their exports to non-EEC member states.[22] According to the European Commission, however, all-destinations coverage was a "flagrant derogation" from the principles that underlay the scheme. In response to ACP requests that this treatment should be extended to all members of the ACP Group, the Commission stated bluntly that "there is no reason why the Community should assume financial responsibility for mitigating the ill-effects of events taking place on markets other than its own."[23] The Community's attitude is quite understandable, but the problem here is that the rules of the system may serve as a disincentive to ACP economic diversification—in this instance, acting to discourage a search for new markets.

As important as the possible disincentive to ACP market diversification is the discretionary power the Commission gains from the failure of the system to cover all exports and all export markets. Although the

Convention provided that transfers would not be made where a fall in export earnings was the result of a deliberate trade policy on the part of an ACP state, it did not specify the criteria to be used to determine whether a discriminatory policy had been pursued. By default, this task fell to the European Commission. In the first year of the system's application the Commission established the principle that an ACP state would not be eligible for a transfer in respect of a reduction of earnings from exports to the EEC if its total earnings from exports of that product to all destinations for that year were greater than the average of its earnings from exports to all destinations for the previous four years. This decision was based on a narrow interpretation of Article 17(4). The Commission argued that the intention of this article was to give more favorable treatment to states enjoying all-destinations coverage of earnings; to provide transfers to other ACP countries in circumstances where there was no fall in their total export earnings would have the effect of placing these privileged states at a disadvantage.

This was a peculiar and very restrictive definition of trade divergence. Earnings from the Community relative to those from other markets might fall in a number of circumstances beyond the control of the ACP, e.g., a general downturn in EEC economic activity compared with that in other markets, strikes in European processing industries or at European ports, etc. Although nominal earnings from all destinations might not have fallen (which, as noted above, would be unlikely to occur in a period of world inflation), the loss in earnings to the EEC might be sufficient to cause the real purchasing power of the ACP state's exports of a particular product to decline. To deny a transfer in these circumstances, although technically justifiable, reduces the system's potential to stabilize ACP export earnings. The importance of this principle to the scheme's administration is seen in that 12 of the 138 transfer requests submitted by the ACP during Lomé I were rejected on the grounds that there was no fall in earnings from all destinations.

Article 19, 4(b) of the first Convention provides for consultations to be held between the Commission and the requesting State "should examination of the total exports of the requesting ACP State show a significant change." One obvious problem with this provision was that the Convention did not define what was understood by "significant change." This was left to the Commission to interpret. Its report on the implementation of the system in 1975 announced that this phrase was understood as divergence of earnings by 10 percent in relation to the situation that prevailed during the reference period.

Subsequently, no fewer than forty-two situations were identified that might lead to "significant changes" in total exports. Fourteen of these (e.g., civil war in an ACP state, imposition of a nontariff barrier by the EEC, reduction in Community demand) would not lead to a reduction in transfers, since the ACP state could not be held responsible for them. Six situations would automatically lead to a reduction: dumping of the product that reduced the unit value of exports, frontier movement of goods between ACP states, the impact of barter arrangements between an ACP state and a third party, a general export ban on a STABEX product, speculative stock building, and measures designed to delay the normal disposal of production. A ban on exports to the Community or a quota limitation on such exports would render the request inadmissible. Finally, there were twenty-one situations in which consultations would be necessary to determine whether a reduction in transfer was justified. These included such diverse factors as quality changes, exhaustion of production, nature protection measures, strikes in an ACP state, imposition of an export tax, an international boycott against an ACP state, increased domestic consumption, and increased domestic processing.[24]

The importance of these provisions was seen in the implementation of the system in the first Convention. Each year the Commission entered into consultations with ACP governments in approximately one-third of the cases in which transfer requests were made. Reductions were made in 27 of the 99 cases that the Commission decided had met the various requirements of the system.[25] These were justified for reason such as a considerable increase in domestic consumption (Benin, 1977), a devaluation of the local currency (Sudan, 1978), or, most frequently, a decline in exports below the share traditionally exported to the Community. In 1978 the Commission established another precedent by reducing the transfer made to Senegal on the grounds that a domestic purchase of the product had been financed by "exceptional aid" from the EEC provided under Article 59 of the Convention. In the case of iron ore, the Commission dictated a further ground for reduction: since mining normally entailed the expenditure of foreign exchange on imported items, transfers would be reduced in the event of a temporary or permanent halt to mining activities by the size of the estimated savings in current expenditure on foreign exchange.

Reports by the Commission on the system's operation suggest that the actual value of a transfer was more a result of bargaining between the Commission and the ACP state than the application of any rigorous procedure. For instance, in 1978, the Commission decided to reduce a transfer in respect of Tanzanian sisal exports on the grounds that a decline in the share of the total exports traditionally supplied to the Community had occurred; this reduction itself was then reduced when the Commission decided that a cause of the decline in the Community's share was a drop in Community demand for the product. Community discretion in the administration of the system is thus extensive: although consultations take place, the Commission alone has the ultimate authority to decide why a decline in exports to the Community occurred and subsequently to determine the volume of the transfer. ACP states have frequently expressed their displeasure that they have not understood the Community's reason for reducing particular transfers. Where a process of bargaining takes place, ACP states are of course at a disadvantage in that they cannot afford the luxury of lengthy negotiations over what are often desperately needed transfers. The only recourse available to an ACP state in a dispute is to politicize the matter by bringing it before a meeting of the ACP–EEC Council of Ministers.

On a number of other important administrative issues, the Commission has also exercised a considerable amount of discretion. One of the more fundamental administrative problems concerns the statistics used. Since the purpose of the system is to respond rapidly to shortfalls in export earnings, conventional sources of trade statistics (given the time lag before their publication) cannot be employed. Consequently, the Commission relies on a combination of data on imports furnished by the member states and export data received from various government departments of ACP countries. One problem in reconciling the two (or more) sources is that the import figures are expressed in c.i.f. values whereas those for exports are f.o.b. Since the Commission has decided to use f.o.b. values as the basis for the system, import data have to be subjected to a c.i.f./f.o.b. deflator. Some interesting observations on this were made by the Communities' Court of Auditors:

The c.i.f./f.o.b. factor . . . consists, in fact, of an "estimate" based on fictitious values in respect of the years 1971 to 1974 but projected to the years 1975 to 1977. This factor is determined in a happy-go-lucky manner, although it is of great significance for the operation of the system.

An examination intended to determine the c.i.f./f.o.b. factors used by the Commission . . . has revealed previously established anomalies, such as negative factors, i.e., lower than unity, which practically amounts to saying that goods delivered c.i.f. at Hamburg would be worth less than at f.o.b. shipment from the ACP State.[26]

The Court found that there were "considerable discrepancies" between the statistics furnished by different government departments in ACP countries and between these figures and those derived from import data from the member states even after the c.i.f./f.o.b. deflator had been applied. No consistent policy was adopted by the Commission with regard to which set of statistics to use:

In one case the ACP data was [*sic*] used to calculate the transferred sums; in another the EEC statistics were used and in a third case it was the mean average of these two statistical values.[27]

In reply, the Commission confirmed the considerable discretionary authority it exercises on this issue; resolution of problems appeared to be a matter of bargaining with the ACP state concerned:

Cross-checking . . . takes the form of negotiations where considerable discrepancies are found. A measure of flexibility is essential in order to secure an acceptable outcome from such negotiations. In such cases an optimum solution has to be found which, in the light of considerations of time-saving and financial resources, is satisfactory both for the Commission and for the ACP State.[28]

The Commission does not make the results of the cross-checking public, nor even the f.o.b. statistics employed as the basis for calculating transfers. This secrecy, not surprisingly, has aroused suspicions about the veracity of its calculations.[29]

One of the favorite claims of the Commission made in response to ACP demands for a greater role in the management of STABEX has been that the system operates in a largely automatic manner. The experience of the system's implementation in the first Convention, detailed above, belies this assertion. The discretionary latitude afforded the Commission by the Convention not surprisingly has given rise to allegations that the decision-making procedures have been manipulated for political purposes.[30] This cynicism was reinforced by the results of the implementation during the first Convention when expenditure corresponded very closely to the total funds available; positive responses to ACP requests led to transfers totaling 377.5 mua, equivalent to 99 percent of the resources available to the system. Reductions made after consultations amounted to 85 mua, equivalent to 22 percent of the system's resources. No request was turned down by reason of insufficiency of funds during Lomé I, but curiously, a number of countries did not request transfers when their circumstances would have entitled them to do so. Senegal agreed in 1979 to forego a transfer of 16.6 million units of account to which it was entitled. Similarly, in 1975, the Ivory Coast did not claim a large transfer in respect of a shortfall in earnings from exports of wood, which would have amounted to 20 percent of that year's total allocation of STABEX funds. If either of these claims had been submitted, then the system's resources would have been exhausted. There is no definitive evidence about whether the Commission exerted pressure on these or other states not to submit claims or whether manipulation occurred in calculating other transfers. But at present, the decision-making in the system obviously lacks transparency. The discretionary powers available to the Commission give rise to uncertainty and leave it vulnerable to claims that decisions are influenced by factors other than those of a strictly statistical nature, which are supposed to determine whether an ACP state meets the technical requirements for a transfer.[31]

## 3. Use of Transfers

According to Article 16 of the first Convention, the system has the aim of "remedying the harmful effects of the instability of export earnings and of thereby enabling the ACP States to achieve the stability, profitability, and sustained growth of their economies." By this definition alone it is not unreasonable to conclude, as the Community's Court of Auditors did, that "the aim of STABEX is ultimately the stabilization of the State's export revenue, and not of the producer's prices."[32] This interpretation of the purposes of the system has been repeatedly rejected by the Commission, which has instead emphasized the sectoral nature of the scheme. According to the Commission:

To some extent, STABEX's main objective is socio-economic; the transfer should be regarded as a contribution to maintain the flow of funds to the production sector of an ACP State hit by economic or natural difficulties. The financial resources transferred are intended to underpin the efforts of the State concerned to ease or eliminate the difficulties encountered by the sector hit. STABEX has to intervene as regards both employment and earnings. It is this focusing on specific sectors which is the original feature of the system and differentiates it from all other systems.[33]

A favorite analogy employed by the Commission is that STABEX performs the function of unemployment and sickness insurance for ACP primary producers—unemployment in the case of a decline in earnings resulting from the economic situation, sickness where local factors have caused a decrease in quantities exported. An example of a model operation of the system was outlined by the Commission as follows: a fall in export earnings would require an ACP state to reduce expenditure, tax other producers (which would result in a decline in domestic savings, print money (resulting in inflation), or enter into foreign debt. Some share of a transfer might legitimately be used, therefore, to offset the budgetary loss from a decline in state revenues and foreign exchange earnings, but the bulk should be employed to offset the drop in income in the private part of the production sector, perhaps through the transfer of funds to a stabilization office.[34]

If the intention to directly aid primary producers was to be attained, then some means needed to be provided to ensure that funds transferred would reach the affected sectors. Originally this was to be determined through the signature of an agreement when the transfer was made, which would specify its use. But this provision was bargained away during the negotiations for the first Convention, whose Article 20 provides only that: "The recipient ACP State shall decide how the resources will be used. It shall inform the Commission annually of the use to which it has put the resources transferred." Furthermore, as the Community's Court of Auditors has noted, "the reports are not necessarily binding on the beneficiary country."[35]

The Court also recorded the replies to Commission enquiries regarding the use of transfers "have been rather evasive." Sudan, for instance, replied that its transfers had been used to "help finance state expenditure"; the Comoros government reported that the records of its predecessor on the use of transfers had been destroyed after its overthrow. The proportion of transfers used to develop the production, marketing, and export of STABEX products and ancillary services was reported by the Commission to be 37 percent in 1975, 20 percent in 1976, and 51 percent in 1977. Members of the European Parliament protested when the government of Upper Volta announced it had used CFA francs 100 million of a 1975 STABEX transfer to purchase seventy vehicles for use by government departments, the national security force, and the police. Reports suggest that much less than half of the transfers made during the first three years of the system's operation were utilized in the sectors concerned. In the first year fully 20 percent of the transfers were used to boost the cash revenues of recipient governments. Transfers had also been used for infrastructural and other capital projects, for debt-servicing payments, and for subscriptions to international banks and other financial institutions.

This report, and others that have shown the use of STABEX transfers for purposes other than those for which the Community intended them, have displayed—depending on one's perspective—either a touching honesty on the part of ACP states or the lack of sophistication of their bureaucracies in failing to make the accounting adjustments necessary to switch money from one department to another. For STABEX transfers are sources of foreign exchange whose fungibility can be utilized to disguise the uses made of transfers. Ultimately this fungibility ensures that in the absence of a binding agreement on the use of the transfers (which would appear to necessitate EEC involvement in the local administration of the funds), the Community can never be certain they will find their way to producers in the affected sectors.

But if the Commission was successful in ensuring that transfers reached the affected sectors, it would then render the system vulnerable to the accusation that it is harmful to ACP states in that it encourages the preservation of outmoded production structures. Here one encounters a dilemma that Singer pointed out thirty years ago: high prices for the primary products of developing countries give them the means to import capital goods and to diversify their economies but reduce the incentive to do so; conversely, when revenues from primary product exports fall, the necessity of export diversification is most obvious but the means for attaining it are lacking.[36] Compensatory finance, like higher prices, would tend to preserve existing production structures if transfers were solely directed toward commodity producers in the sectors that have suffered export losses.

Charges that STABEX serves to freeze the international division of labor have caused the Commission to display a schizophrenic attitude toward the use of transfers for diversification of production structures. In its longest published "think-piece" on the system's purposes, the Commission asserted the primary aim was to contribute toward making the affected sectors "viable and economic." Since structural changes and the diversification of production were processes requiring considerable volumes of finance and long periods of time, they were tasks "which far exceed the relatively modest financial resources and periods of application of STABEX." Furthermore, the Commission added, it would be shortsighted to term a production sector outmoded when, given the rapid changes in raw material markets, it might become of primary economic importance in the near future. An ACP state also had to pay attention to social objectives; since many jobs and livelihoods might depend on labor-intensive production within a temporarily uneconomic sector, the country cannot afford to allow it to disappear. Consequently, the report avers, transfers should predominantly be directed toward the affected sector: "Only if a realistic assessment of the situation shows that this is not justifiable in the specific case may the funds be directed to other appropriate sectors for the purposes of diversification."[37]

In an earlier report, however, the Commission had written enthusiastically of the use of transfers in schemes aimed at maintaining agricultural production in sectors not covered by the system, or for purposes of industrialization. This report concludes:

This channelling of transfers towards diversification and industrialization is of particular interest and goes some way towards dispelling the idea that the effect of the system would be to freeze existing economic structures.[38]

Ultimately, an outmoded production structure cannot be preserved indefinitely by the system, since the moving average of the reference period on which transfers are based would tend inexorably toward zero. But considerable harm could be done to the economy of an ACP state before this final crisis arises. Western Samoa, for instance, used a STABEX transfer from the loss of earnings from banana exports to create a new banana plantation. But this was an economically nonviable export sector: the benefits of the transfer thus indirectly subsidized New Zealand consumers of the bananas.[39]

Since STABEX has not succeeded in channeling revenues directly toward producing sectors, the principal function of the system has been to serve as a supplementary source of finance on concessional terms to ACP states (which on occasion has amounted to more than the beneficiary's receipts from programmable Lomé funds). The European Commission has stated quite clearly that "STABEX is not a trade policy instrument but a development aid instrument."[40] This conception of STABEX as a form of aid was reinforced by the member states' refusal to create a separate fund for its financing. Rather, STABEX is funded from the resources of the EDF (accounting for approximately 12 percent of the total). Furthermore, the original hope that the scheme would, at least in part, be self-financing as ACP states repaid loans from the fund has disappeared with the greatly liberalized repayment criteria introduced in the second Convention. By the end of 1980 only six repayments had been made, amounting to less than 2 percent of total STABEX transfers.

In the contemporary situation of financial stringency, STABEX competes for funds with other EDF activities (which are normally allocated according to conventional aid criteria determined by the member states). The latter have been particularly concerned at the manner in which the system has operated to favor a limited number of ACP states. The present system with its incomplete product coverage and arbitrary thresholds excludes some of the poorest ACP states, e.g., Zaire, from the system completely, while providing only limited coverage to the exports of others. As table 3.2 shows, a total of twenty-nine countries received transfers during the first five years of the system's operation. As might be expected, given the unequal opportunity for access as a result of differential product coverage, and the role of *fortuna* in triggering the system, the country distribution of transfers was unrelated to level of development (measured in per capita GNP). Of the three principal beneficiaries—Senegal, Sudan, and Mauritania—which together accounted for 38 percent of total transfers, only Sudan is classified as a least developed state for the purposes of the system. In aggregate, however, those countries classified as least developed (61 percent of the ACP Group) received 67 percent of the payments during Lomé I.

Results of the implementation of the system during the first Convention also demonstrate the extent to which its operations can be determined by a limited number of products as a result of natural adversities. Fully 42 percent of all transfers during the first five-year period were accounted for by one group of products—groundnuts, groundnut oil, and groundnut oilcake—primarily as a result of drought in West Africa. Three other commodities—iron ore, cotton, and timber—accounted for a further 37 percent (table 3.3). Actual transfers under the scheme will always be determined by factors outside the control of participating states or of the Commission; there are limits to the extent to which the scheme can be manipulated to serve developmental purposes. Both because of this and because of the inability to determine the use to which transfers are

**TABLE 3.3.**

Aggregate Figures by ACP Products

| Product | Aggregate Amounts (in UA) from 1975 to 1979 | Percentage |
|---|---|---|
| 1. Groundnuts | 71,338,766 | 19.03 |
| 2. Groundnut oil | 68,021,513 | 18.15 |
| 3. Iron ore | 61,789,536 | 16.48 |
| 4. Cotton | 43,359,441 | 11.57 |
| 5. Wood in the rough | 38,191,812 | 10.19 |
| 6. Sisal | 20,577,410 | 5.49 |
| 7. Oil cakes | 16,568,442 | 4.42 |
| 8. Coffee | 14,494,289 | 3.87 |
| 9. Raw hides and skins | 8,401,983 | 2.24 |
| 10. Tea | 8,376,330 | 2.23 |
| 11. Palm-nut and kernel oil | 4,940,220 | 1.32 |
| 12. Bananas | 2,920,422 | 0.78 |
| 13. Vanilla | 2,903,720 | 0.77 |
| 14. Palm oil | 2,232,940 | 0.60 |
| 15. Copra | 2,163,264 | 0.58 |
| 16. Coconut oil | 2,114,974 | 0.56 |
| 17. Cloves | 1,139,516 | 0.30 |
| 18. Cocoa | 1,057,603 | 0.28 |
| 19. Groundnut oil cakes | 1,026,143 | 0.27 |
| 20. Gum arabic | 848,489 | 0.23 |
| 21. Sawn wood | 696,646 | 0.19 |
| 22. Palm nuts and kernels | 626,966 | 0.17 |
| 23. Pyrethrum | 608,802 | 0.16 |
| 24. Cocoa paste | 463,558 | 0.12 |

Source: Katharina Focke, *From Lomé 1 towards Lomé 2*, (Luxembourg: ACP–EEC Consultative Assembly, 1980), p. 24.

put, member states have lost enthusiasm for the scheme. This was demonstrated when the EEC refused to make up the shortfall in STABEX funds in 1981 and 1982 by using funds earmarked for other purposes in the EDF.

## 4. Impact on ACP Economies

The potential impact the system can have on ACP economies is inevitably constrained by the selective product and market coverage STABEX provides and has been further limited by the reductions in transfers necessitated by the shortfall in total funds available in 1981–82. Since

STABEX payments have generally been made on an *ex post facto* basis,[41] their effect has typically been to *destabilize* revenue receipts from the exports of the products concerned.[42] And it is not surprising, given that the design of the system reflects the original intention of aiding specific sectors, transfers have not stabilized the total earnings of ACP states from exports to the EEC. A cursory examination of the application of the scheme in its first three years shows that, for two of the three, STABEX transfers probably contributed toward a destabilization of total export revenue, since the majority of recipients in these years enjoyed an increase in their total earnings from exports to the Community.

STABEX transfers on occasion have been of considerable economic importance to individual recipient states. Transfers in various years have contributed as much as 89 percent of the total earnings from all exports to all destinations of Tuvalu, 44.4 percent for Mauritania, 37.1 percent for Guinea Bissau, 27.6 percent for Mali, and 24 percent for Benin. Transfers received during the first Convention accounted for 16 percent of all of Senegal's foreign aid receipts during the period and covered 10 percent of its foreign trade deficit. In terms of a percentage of export earnings for a particular product the figures are even more impressive: in 1978 transfers were 158.8 percent of earnings from groundnut exports for Mali; 154 percent of copra earnings for Tuvalu; 150 percent of banana receipts for Tonga; and 122 percent of revenue from the export of groundnut oil for Senegal.

While the significance of these figures for the states concerned should not be dismissed, these cases appear to be exceptional. STABEX transfers have generally had a minor economic impact on recipients, as both the Commission and the Court of Auditors have acknowledged. In perhaps its bluntest statement the Commission concluded:

> It is fitting to note that, in the majority of cases, the amounts paid over are not high enough to reach a critical mass which would make it possible to have permanently a significant influence on the economic policy of the recipient countries, especially as the transfers are normally used to benefit a number of sectors, thereby minimizing their sectoral impact.
>
> While transfers therefore certainly do have a favourable influence, notably on foreign trade, their influence cannot be quantified nor can it be described as spectacular.[43]

In assessing the economic impact of STABEX transfers it is interesting to compare ACP receipts from this scheme to their drawings on the IMF's Compensatory Financing Facility (CFF). The Facility was established by the IMF to provide additional assistance to member countries experiencing balance of payments problems arising from export shortfalls, provided that these were temporary and largely attributable to circumstances beyond the member's control. Accordingly, unlike STABEX, the CFF covers only net shortfalls on total export earnings (but includes manufactured exports and earnings from services). As previously noted, the IMF employs a reference value centered on the shortfall year that, even though calculated only in nominal terms, produces much larger shortfalls than the STABEX formula when applied to the same circumstances (and in 1981 the IMF set a precedent for import price indexation when it extended the CFF to include compensation for excesses in the cost of cereal imports). Under the IMF scheme, unlike STABEX, a country is eligible for compensation when a decline in the rate of growth of export earnings occurs; an absolute decline in earnings is not necessary to qualify for assistance. But under the IMF scheme, drawings are limited by the size of the member state's quota; potential beneficiaries must also demonstrate a balance of payments need and must pledge to cooperate with the IMF in seeking a solution to their balance of payments difficulties. All drawings are subject to interest and must be repaid within three to five years. Early repayment is required if export performance is better than expected, but no automatic extension is given in the event of earnings' failing to reach projected levels.

From the perspective of developing countries in general, and ACP states in particular, there are two principal disadvantages to the IMF's scheme. First, drawings are limited to 100 percent of country quotas (which for many ACP states are quite small) and, second, are subject to conditionality—a requirement to cooperate with an IMF-approved stabilization program. The test of cooperation is more severe when use of the Facility raises the member's outstanding borrowing from the fund to more than 50 percent of its quota: in these circumstances the Fund must be satisfied that past cooperation has been adequate. According to a Fund pamphlet on the Compensatory Financing Facility:

Although the extent of the cooperation required has not been codified, satisfactory performance in the context of a financial program supported by the Fund would be considered as evidence of past cooperation.[44]

Close to 70 percent of purchases by all countries from the CFF from 1976 to 1980 were designed so as not to raise the countries' total drawings above

50 percent of their quotas. As table 3.4. shows, this was also true for many members of the ACP Group. In recent years, however, at a time when the needs of developing countries for international liquidity have been greatest, CFF drawings have often been accompanied by standby credits: the whole package thereby becomes subject to conditions imposed by the IMF.

There are some interesting contrasts in the transfers to ACP states under the two schemes during the first Convention (table 3.4). In total, the IMF made available approximately twice the funds transferred under STABEX (811.8 million SDRs in comparison to 379.1 mua).[45] ACP states that benefited from both schemes drew 323.9 million SDRs from the IMF and 286 mua from STABEX. Most of the difference between the total resources made available by the two schemes is accounted for by nine countries, which borrowed 487.9 million SDRs from the IMF but were not recipients of STABEX transfers. These nine (Barbados, Guyana, Jamaica, Kenya,Malawi, Mauritius, Papua New Guinea, Zaire, and Zambia) include only one least developed ACP state; most of them are among the larger of the ACP economies and thus have IMF quotas above the ACP average. Not surprisingly, several are heavily dependent on earnings from minerals exports, which were not covered by STABEX.

By contrast, eleven countries received STABEX transfers but made no drawings from the CFF.[46] Seven of these are classified as least developed for the purposes of the STABEX system; most have relatively small and undiversified economies. The significance of the IMF quota size for limiting the contribution of its facility to smaller developing countries is seen in that Gambia, Guinea Bissau, Mauritania, Niger, Senegal, the Solomon Islands, Swaziland, and Western Samoa all received STABEX transfers of a value in excess of 100 percent of their IMF quotas (and these transfers, it should be recalled, in most cases represented only partial coverage of export earnings shortfalls). STABEX has obviously been of principal benefit to the smaller ACP economies.

## SYSMIN

By the time that negotiations for the first Convention were under way the Commission was regretting its initial proposal to include copper within a future export earnings stabilization system. Two principal reasons determined this change of attitude. The first was the estimated cost—pro-

**TABLE 3.4.**

Use of STABEX and the CFF by ACP States During Lomé I

| Country | CFF Drawings (SDR millions) | STABEX Transfers (mua) |
|---|---|---|
| Barbados | 3.5 (27%) | 0 |
| Barbados | 3.0 (23%) | |
| Benin | — | 20.4g |
| Burundi | 9.5 (41%)* | 1.5g |
| Cameroon | 17.5 (50%) | 4.1 |
| Cape Verde | — | 1.2g |
| Central African Republic | 5.1 (39%) | 7.8g |
| Chad | 6.5 (50%) | 7.3g |
| Congo | 6.5 (50%) | 7.4 |
| Ethiopia | 18.0 (50%) | 14.4g |
| Ethiopia | 18.0 (50%)* | |
| Fiji | 6.5 (50%) | 2.1 |
| Gabon | — | 6.7 |
| Gambia | 3.5 (50%) | 7.5g |
| Gambia | 4.5 (50%) | |
| Ghana | — | 5.2 |
| Guinea Bissau | 1.1 (28%) | 11.3g |
| Guyana | 10.0 (50%) | 0 |
| Guyana | 8.8 (35%) | |
| Guyana | 6.3 (25%) | |
| Ivory Coast | 26.0 (50%) | 15.0 |
| Jamaica | 13.3 (25%) | 0 |
| Jamaica | 13.3 (25%) | |
| Jamaica | 15.8 (21%) | |
| Jamaica | 31.8 (43%)* | |
| Kenya | 24.0 (50%) | 0 |
| Kenya | 69.0 (100%)* | |
| Liberia | — | 7.6 |
| Madagascar | — | 5.7 |
| Malawi | 9.5 (50%) | 0 |
| Malawi | 9.5 (50%)* | |
| Mali | 5.1 (19%)* | 9.8g |
| Mauritania | 6.5 (50%) | 37.0g |
| Mauritania | 10.5 (62%)* | |
| Mauritius | 11.0 (50%) | 0 |
| Niger | — | 22.7g |

| Country | CFF Drawings (SDR millions) | STABEX Transfers (mua) |
|---|---|---|
| Papua New Guinea | 10.0 (50%) | 0 |
| Senegal | 21.0 (50%) | 65.1 |
| Sierra Leone | 7.0 (28%) | 4.0g |
| Sierra Leone | 5.5 (22%) | |
| Solomon Islands | 1.0 (50%) | 2.2g |
| Somalia | — | 1.9g |
| Sudan | 18.0 (25%) | 41.8g |
| Sudan | 26.7 (37%) | |
| Sudan | 21.3 (24%) | |
| Sudan | 36.0 (41%)* | |
| Swaziland | — | 13.2g |
| Tanzania | 21.0 (50%) | 20.7g |
| Tanzania | 20.3 (37%) | |
| Togo | 7.5 (50%) | 3.6g |
| Tonga | — | 1.2g |
| Uganda | 20.0 (50%) | 20.6g |
| Uganda | 5.0 (10%)* | |
| Uganda | 25.0 (50%)* | |
| Upper Volta | — | 7.3g |
| Western Samoa | 0.5 (25%) | 2.8g |
| Western Samoa | 0.5 (25%) | |
| Western Samoa | 1.3 (42%) | |
| Zaire | 56.5 (50%) | 0 |
| Zaire | 28.3 (25%) | |
| Zambia | 19.0 (25%) | 0 |
| Zambia | 19.0 (25%) | |
| Zambia | 19.0 (25%) | |
| Zambia | 48.8 (35%) | |

Sources: Data on the CFF from Louis M. Goreux, *Compensatory Financing Facility* (Washington, D.C.: International Monetary Fund Pamphlet Series No. 34, 1980) Table 16; data on STABEX from Commission of the European Communities, "Comprehensive Report on the Export Earnings Stabilization System Established by the Lomé Convention for the Years 1975 to 1979" [SEC(81) 1104] Table I, 3.

In 1977 one European unit of account (ua) was worth 1.15 SDRs. This exchange rate can be employed as a means for approximate comparison of the two sets of figures.

*Purchases since liberalization of the scheme in 1979

g STABEX transfers in grant form

Figures in parentheses refer to the percentage of the country's total IMF quota.

jected at more than 300 mua, close to the total budget of the system that was eventually implemented. Second was the nature of the industry: dominated by vertically integrated TNCs that controlled most important decisions, including the levels of production. Inclusion of minerals within a STABEX-type scheme was problematic also in that mines are exploiting a nonrenewable resource: revenue would be expected to fall inevitably over time.

ACP copper producers put up remarkably little resistance to the Community decision not to include their product within STABEX. It was all the more surprising to the Commission, therefore, that the EEC Council of Ministers agreed to the inclusion of iron ore in the system during the final ministerial negotiating sessions. This, of course, breached the principle that STABEX was to be a system confined to agricultural products; consequently it was not unexpected that the ACP Group demanded that other minerals be added to the scheme at the first ACP-EEC Council of Ministers meeting in June 1975.

Although the Community continued to resist such an extension, concern for the situation of ACP mineral producers was growing on two counts. First was the fear of serious economic and possibly political instability in the two principal ACP copper producers, Zaire and Zambia, both located in strategically sensitive parts of Africa. Neither was eligible for assistance from the existing STABEX scheme; although Zaire's dependence on copper earnings was not as great as that of Zambia (55 percent as opposed to more than 90 percent of total export receipts), Zaire's other principal exports were also minerals and thus excluded from STABEX. In June 1978, West Germany's Chancellor Schmidt greatly aided the ACP cause when he declared, while on a state visit to Zambia, that copper should be included in STABEX. This pronouncement proved politically embarrassing for both the Community and the German government; the latter subsequently put forward a proposal for a hybrid STABEX-type scheme designed exclusively to benefit copper producers (discussed below).

Security of supply of raw materials was the second concern of the Community. The Commission had shown increasing alarm at the decline in European investment in minerals exploration and exploitation in general and that in Africa in particular. Spending on exploration by European mining companies had fallen from a peak of 57 percent of overall expenditure in 1961 to 13.5 percent for the period 1973–75.[47] European mining companies estimated that to maintain supplies of main nonferrous metals to Europe over the next decade, an annual investment of £2.4 billion was needed, whereas actual expenditure during the 1960s and 1970s averaged only £400 million p.a.[48] Developing countries' shares in the total exploration expenditure of European mining companies fell precipitously from about 40 percent in the late 1960s to an average of 13 percent between 1972 and 1977. Black Africa—the principal mineral-supplying region in the ACP—had fared even worse. With the exception of uranium, exploration expenditures had dropped to levels in the period 1974–77 that were less than one-twelfth of the average figure for the years 1966–73.[49] As table 3.5 shows, expenditure on exploration and on production in Africa remained relatively low in the period 1976–81 and certainly disproportionate to black Africa's 20 percent share in total Community mineral imports (by value) and its 13.5 percent share in total world mineral reserves.

Given the greater European dependence on imported raw materials than that of the United States (an average of 75 percent in contrast to 15 percent), the Commission had good reason to be concerned with the general downward trend in overseas investment by the mining companies, and, in particular, its diversion away from sub-Saharan Africa where European companies had long been dominant and the "special relationship" engendered in the Lomé Convention had been expected to reinforce Community advantages. Table 3.6 shows the share of ACP countries in EEC imports of minerals in 1980: for a number of minerals these countries held a substantial share of known world reserves; in that the mineral potential of many African countries in particular is relatively unexplored they had the potential to make an even more significant contribution to Community supplies in the future.

Community thinking on this subject is set out in a background memorandum for the Lomé III negotiations. This noted that the desire of European mining companies to obtain supplies as cheaply as possible, and to minimize risks, had led to investment being directed primarily at deposits in other industrialized countries where "Europe could hardly expect to be a priority customer" and with which the Community could not easily balance its mineral imports by industrial exports. Furthermore, the memorandum noted:

There is a clear tendency on the part of European companies to invest in, or conclude supply contracts with, countries not linked to the Community by a spe-

**TABLE 3.5.**

Geographical Distribution of Expenditure by EEC Mining Companies

(a) *Capital expenditure on all projects excluding uranium (in $US 000)*

| Countries | 1976 | 1977 | 1978 | 1979 | 1980 | 1981 |
|---|---|---|---|---|---|---|
| *Developed Countries* | | | | | | |
| Africa | 67,219 (10.5%) | 45,296 (6.2%) | 49,990 (7.0%) | 68,447 (14.5%) | 28,448 (4.3%) | 17,300 (1.9%) |
| Australia | 50,657 (7.9%) | 183,602 (25.1%) | 197,367 (27.7%) | 103,530 (22.0%) | 192,843 (29.4%) | 241,505 (27.2%) |
| Europe | 243,448 (38.1%) | 258,361 (35.3%) | 216,000 (30.3%) | 148,837 (31.6%) | 202,771 (30.9%) | 274,961 (31.0%) |
| North America | 146,801 (23.0%) | 134,847 (18.4%) | 153,188 (21.5%) | 99,819 (21.2%) | 111,543 (17.0%) | 102,692 (11.6%) |
| Others | — | 4,412 (0.6%) | — | — | — | — |
| *Less Developed Countries* | | | | | | |
| Africa | 31,772 (5.0%) | 2,628 (0.4%) | 3,443 (0.5%) | — | 14,887 (2.3%) | 23,192 (2.6%) |
| Asia | 3,528 (0.6%) | 13,437 (1.8%) | 45,958 (6.5%) | 7,201 (1.5%) | 481 (0.1%) | 751 (0.1%) |
| Latin America | 68,188 (10.7%) | 56,897 (7.8%) | 23,340 (3.3%) | 24,478 (5.2%) | 98,175 (14.9%) | 204,085 (23.0%) |
| Oceania | 27,648 (4.3%) | 31,303 (4.3%) | 22,544 (3.2%) | 18,826 (4.0%) | 7,531 (1.2%) | 21,900 (2.5%) |
| TOTAL | 639,261 | 730,783 | 711,830 | 471,138 | 656,719 | 886,368 |

(b) *Exploration expenditure on all projects excluding uranium (in $US 000)*

*Developed Countries*

| | | | | | | | | | | | |
|---|---|---|---|---|---|---|---|---|---|---|---|
| Africa | 11,701 | (4.9%) | 12,389 | (5.2%) | 9,129 | (4.2%) | 9,310 | (3.8%) | 15,133 | (4.5%) | 13,636 | (4.0%) |
| Australia | 45,322 | (18.9%) | 45,579 | (19.0%) | 49,846 | (23.0%) | 58,289 | (23.9%) | 100,899 | (29.7%) | 95,209 | (28.1%) |
| Europe | 83,620 | (34.9%) | 89,933 | (37.6%) | 73,949 | (34.1%) | 82,300 | (33.7%) | 100,826 | (29.7%) | 85,569 | (25.3%) |
| North America | 50,015 | (20.9%) | 44,412 | (18.5%) | 43,627 | (20.1%) | 43,627 | (17.9%) | 70,702 | (20.8%) | 83,843 | (24.7%) |
| Others | 21,861 | (9.1%) | 26,201 | (10.9%) | 5,510 | (2.5%) | 5,726 | (2.3%) | 436 | (0.1%) | 227 | (0.1%) |

*Less Developed Countries*

| | | | | | | | | | | | |
|---|---|---|---|---|---|---|---|---|---|---|---|
| Africa | 327 | (0.1%) | 754 | (0.3%) | 6,370 | (2.9%) | 8,140 | (3.3%) | 9,511 | (2.8%) | 6,778 | (2.0%) |
| Asia | 5,809 | (2.4%) | 8,651 | (3.6%) | 11,353 | (5.2%) | 15,702 | (6.4%) | 8,880 | (2.6%) | 7,797 | (2.3%) |
| Latin America | 10,176 | (4.2%) | 20,577 | (8.6%) | 17,038 | (7.9%) | 20,167 | (8.3%) | 32,464 | (9.6%) | 44,423 | (13.1%) |
| Oceania | 601 | (0.2%) | 2,000 | (0.8%) | 1,012 | (0.5%) | 623 | (0.3%) | 581 | (0.2%) | 1,255 | (0.4%) |
| Others | 10,053 | (4.2%) | 12,368 | (5.2%) | 3,144 | (1.5%) | — | | — | | — | |
| TOTAL | 239,485 | | 262,864 | | 216,670 | | 243,884 | | 339,432 | | 338,787 | |

Source: Calculated from data in Commission of the European Communities, *Relations between the European Community and the ACP States in the Mining Sector* [COM(83) 651 fin] (8 November 1983) Annexes 8 and 9.

**TABLE 3.6.**

ACP Share in EEC Imports of Selected Minerals

| Mineral | EEC Import Dependence (%) | ACP Share (%) in Total Value of EEC imports (1980) | ACP Share of World Reserves (%) |
|---|---|---|---|
| *(a) Minerals included within SYSMIN* | | | |
| Aluminum | 65.2 | 22.7 | 50.7 |
| Cobalt | 95.4 | 82.7 | 32.8 |
| Copper | 67.2 | 30.7 | 14.7 |
| Iron ore | 45.4 | 14.5 | 1.5 |
| Manganese | 98.0 | 14.5 | 5.5 |
| Phosphates | 71.8 | 14.5 | 1.0 |
| Tin | 77.8 | 7.9 | 2.3 |
| *(b) Other Minerals* | | | |
| Chromium | 92.6 | 2.1 | 28.4 |
| Fluorine | 28.9 | 8.5 | 4.8 |
| Lead | 45.0 | 1.8 | 2.6 |
| Nickel | 79.6 | 22.4 | 20.5 |
| Titanium | 99.3 | 0.2 | 2.7 |
| Tungsten | 72.9 | 3.8 | 0.4 |
| Zinc | 52.0 | 3.2 | 0.9 |

Source: Calculated from data in Commission of the European Communities, *Relations between the European Community and the ACP States in the Mining Sector* [COM(83) 651 final] (9 November 1983).

cial relationship of the sort that exists with the ACP States. This means that there is often no element of interdependence to offset the drawbacks of dependence. In this respect the Community is behaving differently from the other industrialized countries—the United States, with its enormously strong position throughout the whole American continent, the USSR and the Eastern bloc countries, which have so far been self-sufficient, and above all our main competitor on the world market, Japan . . . [which] has used long-term contracts and unwritten but irrevocable undertakings . . . to forge close ties of interdependence with Asian and Pacific countries, including Australia, giving it real security of supply.[50]

As the examples cited in this paragraph suggest, the Community's notion of interdependence is one that is more than a little unbalanced.

European mining companies gave their explanation for the declining trend in investment in a lengthy memorandum submitted to the Commission in May 1977. Their principal complaint was that their investments were being exposed to a:

fundamentally new order of political risk. What is new is the manner in which host governments can exploit a mining company's necessary vulnerability (in the early stages of a project when very large funds are immobilised in the mine) to impose major changes in the operating conditions with complete impunity and the general acquiescence of the international community.[51]

Two tendencies were perceived as combining to produce this effect. One was internal to the industry: falling mineral grades and substantially increased infrastructure costs caused a considerable increase in the scale and lead time of the typical mining project such that the (much larger) investment was at risk for longer and the economic profile of the typical mine in its host country was "much more obtrusive." Concurrently, extraindustry developments, most notably the ascendance of the Third World in the United Nations, "combined with the universal *[sic]* public sympathy with the economic claims of LDCs," facilitated the repudiation of agreements by these governments without undue cost in foreign aid (and, the memo continues, in investment deterred—which is a rather surprising conclusion since the purpose of this paragraph appears to be to explain precisely why investment by European companies had been deterred).[52]

Noting that raw materials questions were becoming of increasing importance to Western governments, the companies asserted that it was unlikely that the flow of investment and entrepreneurial interest necessary to meet Europe's future mineral needs would be forthcoming unless the investor could be given some security from these new dangers. The companies thought this might best be achieved through a politicization of any investment dispute: governments might become involved through guaranteeing the terms of mining agreements by entering into intergovernmental treaties with LDC host states and thereby ensure "equitable treatment for investors," by financial participation in mining ventures or by providing guarantees for private capital invested in these, and/or through an insurance system against any losses incurred by European investors as a result of political action taken by host governments.[53]

Government participation would be even more effective it if occurred on a European Community basis:

The greater diversity of economic relationships between the EC and any particular host countries will make not only for more powerful but also more subtle leverage. The European bloc can also bring into play its importance as a market for the materials in question—a natural development in the face of current attempts to unite commodity producers along the lines of OPEC. Its association with or sponsorship of particular overseas mining enterprises could give the relevant terms of exploitation a degree of international legitimacy which has not previously been possible.

The certainty that the government will use all the leverage available to it to secure the agreed rights of its overseas mining investors should be very helpful in stabilising the relationship with the host government through the vulnerable period when the host government has most to gain and the investor most to lose in the event of a breach of the agreement.[54]

Initial Community discussion of a minerals policy within the context of the Lomé relationship arose from the submission of a German government memorandum on copper following Schmidt's statement in Zambia. A special regime for this product was justified, it was suggested, for three reasons: the economic situation in the principal producing countries (Zaire and Zambia) was becoming more difficult, meanwhile, their dependence on copper was on the rise; there was little chance that a satisfactory international agreement on the product would be concluded in the near future; and finally, exclusion of copper from all stabilization measures risked the creation of discrimination between copper-producing countries and other ACP states. The scheme would have provided for compensation for a fall in export revenue where earnings from copper fell below a reference level and a simultaneous fall occurred in total primary product export earnings. The total transfer to be received would have been the smaller of the two shortfalls.[55]

Reaction of other member states and the Commission to the proposals was negative. Concern was expressed that there would be "slippage" in the system; i.e., having accepted the principle of special measures for copper producers, it would be very difficult to deny the claims of exporters of, for example, phosphates or bauxite. There was also the cost factor: the Belgian government estimated that the German proposals would cost 350 mua for copper alone; inclusion of other products would considerably increase the financial risks. These were particularly severe since there was a danger of price manipulation by the transnational companies that dominated the minerals industries.

By January 1979, by which time negotiations with the ACP had begun for a successor to the first Convention, the Community had decided that any future provisions for minerals should not be limited to copper alone and that the STABEX system, whose characteristics should remain unaltered, was unsuitable for the inclusion of mineral products. In justifying its position to the ACP, the Commission drew upon the experience gained from the inclusion of iron ore in STABEX in Lomé I. Particularly problematic was the Sierra Leone case, where a company terminated production of iron ore when the grade of mineral fell from 74 percent to 40 percent; continued production would have necessitated substantial additional equipment expenses. Costs of exploitation would have risen; the company's financial problems were exacerbated by higher taxes imposed by the Sierra Leone government. In a speech to the ACP–EEC Comité Paritaire in Bordeaux at the end of January 1979, Commissioner for Development Claude Cheysson stated:

If the STABEX-agriculture was applied to minerals, by a curious paradox Africa would be the first victim. And so that one cannot say that I invent: we have had the experience with the mineral, iron, which figures by error, in my opinion, among the products covered by STABEX. We have seen, and the President of the ACP Council knows this well, how an American company with iron mines on several continents has given priority to the closure of its mine in Sierra Leone, whereas there wasn't compensation in South America.

In other words, by offering to the multinational, which is going to be finally responsible for the price of the mineral, the strategic possibility of choosing the continent on which it can impose the burden of its errors of investment or of overproduction, it is assured that Africa will be the continent where the closures are made when they are necessary.[56]

When the Commission finally published its proposals relating to minerals in Lomé II, these were concerned, not with the stability of export earnings of ACP producers, but with the security of supply of Community imports. Terming current European investment in Third World minerals a "complete catastrophe,"[57] the Commission urged the Council to acknowledge the need for greater diversification of sources of supply. European investment lagged behind that of the United States and Japan, and although the latter was as dependent on imported supplies as the Community, it "has put into effect a supply policy that is perfectly coordinated with the private initiatives of its industry; this has not yet been done by the Community."[58]

Diagnosis of the problem by the Commission, and its proposed remedies were almost identical to those put forward by the European mining companies. Noting that investments in Third World minerals exploration had been paralyzed by the lack of effective protection against investment risks, the Commission made the following proposals:

1. community participation in the creation of national or regional mining exploration funds, which, the Commission argued, on the basis of World Bank ex-

perience in Bolivia, would reduce the risks involved in financing exploration expenditure;

2. direct Community participation through the investment of risk capital in exploration and prospecting (primarily through additional investment by the European Investment Bank from its own resources);
3. signature of agreements between the Community and host countries that would create standard rules of conduct for the hosts and investors;
4. a supplementary Community insurance scheme to cover noneconomic risks not included in national schemes (the model for the proposed scheme was to be the U.S. Overseas Private Investment Corporation as the mining companies had suggested in their memorandum);
5. provision of finance to enable ACP states to acquire shares in the capital of mining companies operating in their territories;
6. technical assistance to ACP governments to strengthen their geological and mining departments.[59]

This memorandum marked a significant shift in the Commission's emphasis regarding the policies that it suggested should be pursued toward ACP mineral producers, a testament to the extent to which the mining companies' memorandum had struck a responsive note.[60] An earlier Commission communication on the problems of raw materials supplies had mentioned the topic of political instability only peripherally.[61] The mining companies' memorandum, however, enabled the Commission to combine its long-standing interest in the provision of a Community-wide investment guarantee scheme (which would have extended its own jurisdiction) with the raw materials question.[62] Emphasis was now being placed entirely on security of supply for the European market; the immediate problems of ACP mineral producers who were suffering from the effects of export earnings instability were ignored. In fact, the only mention of export earnings in the new proposals was with regard to the expectation that a viable minerals industry resulting from additional European investment would increase the volume of ACP receipts in the future.

The Commission's proposals became entangled in a lengthy debate within the Council over investment guarantees in the new Convention (see chapter 7) before agreement was finally reached on proposals for an "insurance scheme" to safeguard mineral production. Community intentions were stated with unusual candor in its original proposals to the ACP:

The aim of the solution envisaged by the Community is to help the ACP countries . . . to cope with the harmful effects of certain circumstances beyond their control which seriously affect their capacity *to produce for the Community market or to export the products in question to that market.*[63]

Although the statement of the system's objectives that appeared in the new Treaty was more politic, a reference to "export earnings" being inserted at the insistence of the ACP,[64] the latter were extremely upset at what they regarded as the failure of the system to address the short-term needs of ACP mineral exporters, its uneven-handed emphasis on European interests, and the inadequate resources provided to the system for attaining even its limited objectives. Unlike STABEX, and unlike the German government's proposals, the new minerals system (SYSMIN) does not automatically safeguard ACP export earnings. In the negotiations that followed the submission of the Community's memorandum, the ACP Secretariat proposed that the system should have a "second window," whose resources would be employed to help stabilize the export earnings of mineral producers, but this was rejected. So angered by the outcome of the negotiations was the Premier of Papua New Guinea, a significant minerals exporter, that he dispatched a personal letter of complaint to the President of the Commission.[65]

SYSMIN is intended to allow Community intervention in the form of financial aid when the ACP mineral exporter faces production problems resulting, e.g., from damage to installations, and/or when internal or external political difficulties interrupt its ability to export to the European market, the problems being sufficiently grave that normal emergency aid provided by the Convention is considered inadequate. The system in Lomé II was supported by financing amounting to 280 mua, divided into a number of equal annual installments. Rather complicated conditions must be fulfilled before the Community will consider the provision of assistance: the mineral concerned must have accounted for at least 15 percent of the country's export earnings over the previous four years (10 percent for the least developed, landlocked, and island states),[66] and a 10 percent decline in production or export capacity must occur in an "otherwise viable and economic line of production." If these conditions are met, an ACP state may apply for assistance. Unlike the STABEX scheme, a transfer is not guaranteed if the preconditions are fulfilled (and the Commission is satisfied that trade diversion has not occurred) but is dependent on Community approval of the ACP state's proposals for the use of a transfer in projects and programs aimed at restoring production and/or exports. Finance takes the form of loans repayable over 40 years with a 10-year grace period and an interest rate of 1 percent (0.75 percent for the least developed countries). Under no circumstances will an individual

**TABLE 3.7.**

Products and Producers Covered by SYSMIN

|  | Producer Country | Dependence Threshold (Average % 1972–76) | EEC Share of Exports (Average % 1972–76) |
|---|---|---|---|
| Copper | Zambia | 91 | 60 |
|  | Zaire | 55 | 91 |
|  | Papua New Guinea | 51.7 | 40 |
| Phosphates | Togo | 59 | 92 |
|  | Senegal | 17.6 | 54 |
| Bauxite | Guinea | 90 | 34* |
| Alumina | Jamaica | 67 | 19* |
|  | Surinam | 70 | 29* |
|  | Guyana[a] | 40 | 9* |
| Manganese | Gabon | 15 | 32* |
| Iron ore | Liberia | 69 | 74 |
|  | Mauritania | 71 | 75 |
| Tin | Rwanda | 13 |  |

Source: Mimeo Community document.
  *Figure is for 1976 only
  [a] EEC share refers to 1976 bauxite exports

ACP country be permitted to receive more than 50 percent of the funds available from an annual installment.

Included within the scheme are the following products (see table 3.7): copper and cobalt (produced by Zambia, Zaire, and Papua New Guinea); phosphates (Togo and Senegal); bauxite and aluminum (Guinea, Jamaica, Surinam, and Guyana); manganese (Gabon); and tin (Rwanda). Any new mines producing iron ore will be included within SYSMIN; those in production at the time of the signature of the second Convention are included within STABEX for the first five years of the system's operation, at which time they will be transferred to SYSMIN. ACP demands for the system to cover uranium (which currently constitutes 60 percent of the export revenue of Niger and 13 percent of that of Gabon), diamonds (15 percent of the Central African Republic's export earnings), clinker, graphite, and chromium (the latter of obvious relevance with the accession of Zimbabwe to the Convention) were rejected.

Although it is premature to judge the implementation of SYSMIN, which Development Commissioner Cheysson has termed an "adventure" into "virgin" territory,[67] some preliminary evaluative comments can be made. Total financial resources available would appear to be inadequate even to attain the limited objectives of SYSMIN, given the immense sums involved in minerals production. But the system is more notable for what it does not attempt to achieve than for its own objectives.

By comparison with STABEX, the minerals system is directed predominantly toward satisfying European needs. Interdependence in the minerals sphere is given a narrow definition, applying only to the actual production and export of the minerals concerned and not to the revenue that is earned by the ACP state. The system caters to only one of the two problems that prompted European interest in ACP minerals: security of supply. Problems of political and economic instability resulting in part from fluctuations in export receipts are touched on only tangentially by the mechanisms of the system, which in itself appears peculiarly shortsighted given European interests in the stability of the strategically located copper producers in Africa.

In another respect SYSMIN represents a retreat from the "spirit of partnership" supposedly embodied in the creation of STABEX in Lomé I. In the new system the discretionary power available to the Commission is considerably augmented; not only is it responsible for determining levels of dependence and fluctuation of earnings, which, as has been noted in the context of the STABEX system, allows it considerable decision-making leeway, but also in SYSMIN the Commission considers the uses to which the transfers will be put as a criterion for determining whether a transfer should be given. The ACP Group took the unusual step of attaching a unilateral declaration on the system as an annex to the Convention, to express its discontent with the manner in which the system operates.[68]

By the end of 1982 only two SYSMIN operations were under way: for the copper sectors in Zambia and Zaire. In the Zambian case, the maximum amount permissible for a single loan from the scheme was authorized: 55 mua—a sum that falls far short of the country's recent export earnings losses from declining prices. For the Zaire case, the loan was set at 40 mua, the lower figure apparently being determined by the Commission's perceptions that Zaire's dependence on copper is less than that of Zambia and that the conditions of mining were easier than in Zambia, ores of a higher grade being obtained. The Zaire loan illustrated the discretionary power the system gives to the Commission: as preconditions for the loan, the Commission insisted that the Zaire government adopt a new fiscal regime for the copper sector and reorganize relations between itself and the mining company, Gecamines. As an UNCTAD study notes, SYSMIN began without clearly defined rules, which have subsequently been devised by the Commission on an *ad hoc* basis.[69]

A second chapter in the Lomé II Convention's Title on mineral products relates to the development of the mining and energy potential of ACP states. Proposals by the Commission for increased technical assistance for strengthening ACP technical and scientific capacity in geology and mining were accepted with little amendment by the Council. Similarly, the new Convention provides that Community funds may be used to cofinance the establishment of national or regional exploration funds in ACP states and provide risk capital for research and investment preparatory to the launching of mining and energy projects. A further innovation in the second Convention was provision for the European Investment Bank to "commit its own resources on a case-by-case basis beyond the amount fixed [in the Convention] in mining investment projects and energy investment projects recognized by the ACP state concerned and by the Community as being of mutual interest."

Provision for increased assistance in the minerals field was, in fact, the principal innovation of the second Convention. This was a reflection of Community concern at developments in this sphere—and of the manner in which the bargaining power in the relationship had changed once the ACP had formally become parties to it in 1975. In the first round of renegotiations the Community was able to pursue those areas of cooperation that held out most interest to it rather than having to attempt to attract ACP participation by offering incentives to satisfy the particular interests of the various subgroupings. It is a reflection of the relative bargaining power of the parties that the initiative for collaboration in the minerals field came from the Community—which was the party most satisfied with the provisions for cooperation in this field in the second Convention. Although ACP minerals exporters may make a significant contribution to the satisfaction of Community imports needs, no single ACP producer nor the Group as a whole was in a position to hold the Community to ransom: as tables 3.6 and 3.7 show, ACP producers rarely supply more than 20 percent of the value of total Community imports of a mineral while, in many cases, the ACP supplier is more dependent on the Community market than vice versa. And, in the period since the first

Convention was negotiated, the position of most ACP minerals exporters had been severely weakened as a result of declining world market prices.

According to the Community, "cooperation in the mining sector underwent a rapid and remarkable expansion" in the second Convention.[70] By May 1983 financial commitments to the mining sector (187.6 mua) were more than three times those for the five years of the Lomé I period. The principal sources for this increase were the SYSMIN operations in Zaire and Zambia, and unsubsidized loans from the EIB. In 1981 nearly half of the total funds committed by the EIB to ACP states went to the mining sector. Even allowing for the multiplier effects of these sums (since they were often used to cofinance projects with other agencies), the amounts involved were small in comparison to the financing needs of the sector. Africa, in particular, continued to be shunned by mining companies.

One reason for this was the fear of political risk involved in investing in the continent. The Commission had failed in the Lomé II negotiations to attract the support of the member states for its investment guarantee proposals. After months of debate within the Community the outcome was a rather meaningless provision that "pursuant to the general aims of the treatment of investments" the Community and the member states, on the one hand, and the ACP states, on the other, may "conclude agreements relating to individual projects where the Community and possibly European undertakings contribute towards their financing" (Annex VIII). This issue will certainly be raised again in the negotiations for the successor arrangement to Lomé II.

While there is no doubt that greater certainty of treatment of mining investments would benefit all of the parties concerned, the approach adopted by the Commission has lacked the necessary sensitivity and subtlety to play a constructive role in this area. Ostensibly, the Commission accepted the argument of the European mining companies that irresponsible behavior on the part of host governments was at the heart of investment disputes—the result of the latter's attempts to change the terms on which the mining companies operated.

While there is certainly evidence that some developing countries have behaved irresponsibly (and even from their own long-term perspective irrationally) in this regard, the mining companies' perspective is dangerously one-sided. For, as a number of studies have shown, the balance of bargaining power between investor and host country changes over the lifetime of the investment cycle.[71] During the period in which the host government is seeking finance for exploration and initial exploitation of a mineral deposit its bargaining position is very weak. This is particularly the case where the host government may have little knowledge of the extent of minerals deposits and lacks familiarity with the structure of the minerals industry concerned. These weaknesses are exacerbated by the increasing costs and longer lead times involved in minerals exploitation.

In this period a mining company may be able to obtain an agreement from the government that provides extremely favorable terms for its operations. Once the company has made a large investment in the host country, then the relative bargaining power of the two parties will obviously change. Not unsurprisingly, many host governments take the opportunity to renegotiate agreements so that they may capture some of the "rent" being enjoyed by the mining companies. This practice is by no means confined to LDCs, as British and Norwegian behavior with respect to the exploitation of their North Sea oil fields demonstrates.

An attempt by the European Community to enter a dispute between host government and investors at this stage of the investment cycle may be unwise unless the Community is willing to acknowledge that the host country may have a genuine grievance. There was no sign in the proposals it submitted to the Council that the Commission was willing to do this. While it is desirable for all parties that a more secure environment be created to encourage investment in the minerals and energy sectors of ACP states, the imposition of sanctions on the host government by the EEC in uncritical support of its mining companies is not the best method of attaining this objective and actually may be counterproductive to the long-term interests of both the companies and the EEC (as would appear to have been the US experience with the Hickenlooper and Gonzalez amendments).

ACP countries have been slow to capitalize on the obvious European interest in their mining sectors. In part this has been the product of the relative weakness of the economies of the mineral exporters since the early 1970s. A further explanation is the unwillingness of the ACP countries concerned to enter into long-term arrangements with the Community and to provide the type of security necessary to attract overseas mining companies. Again this results from a preoccupation with maintaining their sovereignty, and from their relatively ineffective negotiating capacity. While generally being unwilling to enter into agreements with the EEC, the ACP have shown once again their perception of the exclusive nature of the relationship established by Lomé by their behavior in the minerals field: ACP countries protested vigorously against EEC participation in the Carajas iron ore project in Brazil where, in return for a loan of $600 million from the European Coal and Steel Community, the Community will benefit from guaranteed long-term supply contracts of 13.7 million tonnes of iron ore a year. ACP countries have been slow to learn that whatever the mutual interests they may have with the Community in this sphere, they will continue to lose out to third parties unless they are able to offer the long-term guarantees that Community investors seek.

## CONCLUSIONS

ACP states perceive STABEX with mixed feelings. On the positive side, it remains the only system created by a group of industrialized countries to provide compensatory finance for the commodity exports of a group of developing country trading partners. STABEX has provided substantial transfers for some ACP states that, unlike virtually any other development assistance they receive, are unconditional foreign exchange made available on exceptionally soft terms and untied to any particular project. On the other hand, STABEX has failed to give the ACP the guarantee of their subsistence they sought through their strategy of collective clientelism. Not only is the product coverage limited with the consequence that the major mineral exporters are effectively excluded from the system, but also the amounts available to the system have proved inadequate in circumstances where declining world market prices coincided with local production difficulties. Consequently the scheme has not provided the security the ACP had hoped and the Europeans had claimed would result from this insurance policy. Although the system has generally disbursed funds with exceptional speed—the average time lag between application and receipt of transfer being a little more than four months—the administration of the system lacks transparency, the Community enjoying considerable discretion in interpretation of the rules.

Community member states have been less enthusiastic about the system, regretting in particular that they gave way on the conditionality issue at the Kingston conference in 1974. As a consequence, some states feel it is a less effective form of development assistance than conventional European project aid, and the limited product coverage results in disproportionate assistance going to a handful of relatively favored states. Lack of enthusiasm on the part of the Europeans for the scheme was evident in their refusal to provide additional funding in 1981–82. Similarly, the insistence on SYSMIN loans' being tied to the execution of Community-approved projects reflects the continuing concern about the uses of STABEX transfers. Since the majority of the transfers under STABEX were not used in the sectors in which they were generated, their principal purpose was to serve as general balance of payments support, a function most member states believe is best left to the IMF.

Community concern over this issue was reflected in its proposals that STABEX transfers in the period after Lomé II be subject to prior discussion between the Commission and the ACP state concerned on the causes of the transfer and on the uses to be made of the transfer. ACP countries will, however, resist this move, objecting that it is an attempt to increase conditionality in the relationship and to infringe "acquired rights" in the partnership—in this case the agreement in Kingston in 1974 that the ACP states alone would have responsibility for determining the use of STABEX transfers. At the time of writing, the outcome of negotiations in this sphere for the post-Lomé II period was uncertain. In the absence of agreement over the use of transfers, the future of the system may be in some doubt. Strict tying of the transfer to use within the affected sector would appear to be illogical in that, first, not all the products included within the system are the product of peasant farmers—transfers in respect of rubber and timber, for instance, would go predominantly to plantations that are often foreign-owned, and, second, there is a danger of discouraging diversification and preserving outmoded production structures.

Nevertheless, a strong case can be made that it is in the mutual interest of the ACP and EEC that more of the funds go back to the affected sectors. As noted above, the majority of the transfers during the first Convention were caused by local production difficulties. And, as both the World Bank and a Community study have shown, the share of Africa in world exports of tropical products has fallen substantially over the last decade: except in the case of tea, Africa fell behind in its share of world production of all other major commodities included within STABEX in the 1970s.[72] In part this has been due to inappropriate policies, especially as regards pricing, which STABEX transfers were originally designed to help correct. Although their use of transfers in other sectors can be explained by the extremely acute foreign exchange shortages experienced during the last ten years, a reflection of the inadequacy of low-condition liquidity available to the poorest countries, ACP states are in danger of damaging their own long-term interests by ignoring the sectors from which transfers have originated.

# 4

## Commercial Cooperation

In negotiating the Lomé trade regime, the ACP Group sought arrangements that would provide security of access for their exports to the European market in the expectation that this would facilitate a diversification of their economic structures. ACP countries had benefited only marginally from the new international division of labor that has enabled the newly industrializing countries to rapidly expand their exports of manufactured goods. In most ACP states, manufacturing sectors remain small and unsophisticated; typically at least three-quarters of the value added in domestic manufacturing is derived from import-substituting industries, particularly food processing, beverages, textiles, cement, and paper and printing. Even the relatively more developed Caribbean members of the ACP Group export few manufactures to the EEC, these being principally processed minerals such as chemicals and alumina.[1]

A continuing dependence on primary products for the majority of their export earnings would condemn ACP countries to a relatively slow rate of economic growth. As the World Bank has noted, whereas demand for imports of primary products in industrialized countries grows at approximately the same rate as incomes, that for imported manufactured goods grows approximately twice as fast. Developing countries have increased their share of world trade in manufactures whereas their share of trade in nonfuel primary commodities has fallen.[2] Lack of success in diversifying their economies had been a major factor underlying the limited growth of the exports of Associated states under the Yaoundé Conventions. A similar slow rate of growth in the traditional exports of the ACP might be anticipated under the Lomé relationship, given the protection afforded European agriculture by the Community's Common Agricultural Policy, the substantial share that ACP countries already enjoyed in EEC imports of tropical products, and the slow increase in demand in Europe for these items. Any increase in total exports of primary products would probably occur largely by displacing current nonACP suppliers, rather than as a result of significant increases in aggregate European demand. On the basis of rather heroic assumptions, McQueen estimated that the maximum short-term increase in the export earnings of ACP states from seven tropical products in which they enjoyed a tariff advantage would be 6 percent.[3]

In pursuing their strategy of collective clientelism, the ACP hoped to see three new norms incorporated in their trade relations with the EEC. The first was the principle of nonreciprocity, which would minimize the opportunity costs to the Group of entering into the relationship and pose no obstruction, for instance, to the protection of their infant industries or to entry into regional free trade areas with third parties. Second, they sought to establish the principle that their exports would enjoy preferential access to the European market over those of third countries. Finally, their expectation was that the contractual nature of the relationship would underwrite the norm of security of access for their exports despite the growth of the New Protectionism and the continuing extension of the Community's Common Agricultural Policy.

As chapter 2 noted, the ACP were successful in their pursuit of the first norm. In the Lomé negotiations the issue of reciprocity had great symbolic importance for the ACP; their task was facilitated in that the norms of the GATT had been changed with the addition of Part IV in 1964, which provided that developing countries were to be exempted from requirements for strict reciprocity. Under Lomé, ACP states are obliged only to refrain from discriminating among Community member states and to provide them with treatment no less favorable than that granted to the most-favored industrialized trading partner.[4] The other norms to which the ACP aspired in their strategy of collective clientelism proved much more controversial, however. Arguments over the extent to which the Community was committed to them by the terms of the Conventions caused much of the bitterness that has arisen during their implementation.

One of the most forthright statements of ACP aspirations to establish the norm of preferred access for their exports, and subsequent disillusionment with the manner in which the Community had interpreted its obligations on this matter, was provided by the Zambian President, Kenneth Kaunda:

In our view, we negotiated that Lomé Convention in the belief that it will confer on our exports terms and conditions more favourable than those granted to the products of other countries. After some two years of implementation of the Convention, we now have many reasons to doubt that this is the understanding and the policy of the Community.

The situation is not helped by the information which we receive from time to time of the Community signing some preferential agreements with third countries—without the ACP member states receiving the necessary prior information as required by the Convention for the safeguard of the interest of ACP member states. Neither are we comforted by the Community's haste in extending its Generalized System of Preferences without adequate safeguard for the ACP's trade benefits under the Lomé Convention, which face the threat of equally rapid erosion through such extension.[5]

In fact, by the time the Lomé Convention was signed, much of the preferential advantage afforded the original Associates under the Treaty of Rome had been eroded. There were four principal sources of this erosion: a general lowering of the Community's Common External Tariff (CET) resulting from successive rounds of multilateral trade negotiations conducted under GATT auspices; the implementation of the Community's Generalized System of Preferences, whose coverage had been significantly extended since its introduction in 1971; the extension of EEC preferential trading arrangements to other states, including members of EFTA and most Mediterranean countries; and *ad hoc* trade promotion agreements signed by the Community with a wide variety of other states. These last agreements were often the product of political initiatives by the Community: for instance, the establishment of diplomatic links with the Peoples' Republic of China was followed by the extension of a quota for textile products; preferences were given to jute producers in India and Bangla Desh following natural disasters there; and Rumania received preferences on fertilizer exports to the Community after the earthquake of 1977. While these political and humanitarian gestures have been a logical contribution to the Community's development policies, they presented additional competition for existing or potential ACP exports and a further erosion of their privileged position in the European market.

According to Wall, the reduction in most–favored–nation (MFN) rates and the introduction of GSP schemes "have reduced tariff barriers on imports into developed from developing countries to insignificant levels and coverage."[6] Even in the absence of the Lomé provisions, more than 75 percent of ACP exports would enjoy duty-free access to the Community market either by virtue of a zero tariff rating (mostly primary products) or through the Community's GSP. Only a small proportion of current ACP exports thus enjoy tariff advantages in the Community market over third country suppliers—and these occur only vis-à-vis LDCs that do not have preferential agreements with the Community (mainly the states of Southeast Asia and Latin America) only in respect of goods not included within the GSP scheme, and towards non-EFTA OECD countries.[7]

As a result of MFN reductions, the preferential margin enjoyed by ACP products is extremely small—for manufactured products the average incidence of the CET is from 8 percent to 9 percent. To place this in proper perspective, it might be compared, for example, with the administrative costs connected with the import of goods (documents, transits etc.). A Community study estimates that these alone can amount to 8 percent of the c.i.f. price of the import. Consequently, the document concludes, although exact calculations cannot be made, a margin of preference such as that enjoyed by the ACP is rarely decisive in an importer's decision. And even where a preferential margin is enjoyed, the ACP state itself may not benefit from the customs duty forgone by the EEC since this amount has to be shared with the importer:

The margin of preference of the ACP on the Community market is above all a consecration of a traditional commerce, and its benefit, in many cases, seems to go above all to the Community importers. In the ACP domain as in the others (GSP), it is in a large measure a gift by the European economy to itself, to the detriment of the resources of the Community budget (600 mua per year, approximately, for the total of preferential trade with LDCs).[8]

While tariffs on agricultural products are generally much higher and of a wider dispersion in their incidence, not all ACP agricultural exports qualify for duty-free and unrestricted access to the Community market.

Although the general level of the CET may be insufficient to provide a significant advantage to the ACP as a result of the Lomé Convention, the Group has argued there are specific items of interest to them in which their position is being adversely affected by further liberalization of the Community's tariff policies, particularly within the framework of the GSP. Since 1971, when the Community's GSP was introduced, the volume of its offer for duty-free imports in the industrial sector had been increased from 478 mua to reach 6,900 mua by 1980. Of greatest immediate concern to the ACP, however, was the expansion in the number of processed agricultural products covered by the scheme—from 147 in the period 1971–73 to a total of 310 in 1979. In its memorandum on the

Community's proposed GSP offer for 1978, the ACP Group included data on a sample of 28 ACP exports from chapters 1–24 of the Brussels Tariff Nomenclature (BTN) (agricultural and processed products), which had been the object of EEC offers under the GSP in previous years. In nineteen products it was found that GSP beneficiaries increased their exports at a rate equal to or above that defined as significant. Twelve of these increases coincided with decreases in ACP market shares both in the quantity and value of trade in that product at a rate equal to or above that defined as significant; three were accompanied by a small decline in ACP market shares, and the remaining four, by significant increases in the ACP market share.[9]

While these correlations do not provide definitive evidence of a causal relationship between the extension of the GSP and a decline in the ACP's market share (other factors, such as declining ACP output, diversion of production to domestic consumption or other markets may have played a role, as the EEC argued was the case with ACP exports of plywood), the predominance of negative correlations does suggest that the GSP may have adversely affected ACP interests. As ACP spokesmen have pointed out, beneficiaries from the GSP were often countries more competitive than the ACP and better able to market their products. It was precisely this need to defend their position in the European market against more efficient, higher income LDCs that had been a principal motivation underlying the strategy of collective clientelism.

In defending their privileged access to the European market the ACP have been vulnerable to criticism from other LDCs that their behavior threatens the much-vaunted unity of the Group of 77 and facilitates a European strategy of *divide et impera*. European negotiators have made much of this problem, constantly stressing that the Community has obligations to all developing countries besides those to its "privileged" partners in the Lomé relationship. In recent years, however, the Group of 77 has been more sympathetic than in the past to the needs of its poorest members: whereas the Yaoundé Conventions had been frequently condemned, criticism of Lomé has been much more muted. In its position statements the ACP Group was careful to assert that it supported the principle of improving the Community's GSP. Nevertheless, they argued, this should not come at the expense of the legitimate interests of the ACP, who were being made to pay the cost of the Community's indiscriminate extenion of its offer through an uncompensated loss of their market preferences. Their case was supported, the ACP spokesmen argued, by resolutions passed by the United Nations with the support of other developing countries. UN Resolution 96 (iv) adopted at the UNCTAD IV Conference in Nairobi in May 1976 stated that:

The generalized system of non-reciprocal, non-discriminatory preferences should be improved in favour of the developing countries, taking into account the relevant interests of those developing countries enjoying special advantages as well as the need to find ways and means of protecting their interests.[10]

According to the ACP Group, the spirit of the Convention (and certainly its intention as far as they were concerned) was to guarantee the group a preferential margin over all third parties. Their interpretation was based on Article 2, 2 (a), which states that "as a general rule" the Community will ensure that ACP exports that do not enjoy duty-free access to the EEC market will enjoy treatment more favorable than MFN rates. For the ACP, this implied that ACP exports enjoying duty-free access would be placed in an even more preferential position over exports from third countries than the treatment accorded to those ACP exports subject to duties. Accordingly, the ACP Secretariat concluded that:

the Community should cease to use its considerable political might to ride roughshod over the ACP's legitimate interest, should protect their position in the Community market and in the rare case that this may not be adequately protected by selective extension of the GSP, that appropriate compensation should be paid to the ACP. If the Community continues to ignore these requests, the ACP is in little doubt that its trade, which has already not been showing significant progress, would fare even worse.[11]

In a 1977 memorandum the ACP claimed that the EEC had in fact made a commitment to abide by the spirit of the Convention and to safeguard its interests when considering an extension of the GSP. The Group quoted a report of the Interim Committee, which had stated that "consideration be given to the possibility of withdrawing the (GSP) offer in whole or in part in order to remedy any unfavorable situation that might arise with ACP States as a result of applying the system." But this statement certainly was not representative of the predominant thrust of Community opinion and was not reflected in subsequent Community behavior.[12]

Part of the problem for the ACP was that they were victims of a bureaucratic battle within the Commission. Responsibility for administering the Community's Generalized System of Preferences lay with DG I, the External Affairs Directorate, whereas DG VIII, the Development Cooperation Directorate, was responsible for managing the Lomé relationship. Opinion within DG I was much more "globalist" in its orientation, predominant emphasis being placed on the Community's relations with the totality of developing countries, especially those newly industrializing countries that were emerging as important trading partners for the Nine. By contrast, DG VIII had traditionally been concerned only with relations with the Associated states and subsequently the ACP. With the extension of Community development assistance to non-associates in the mid-1970s, the interests and geographical scope of DG VIII had widened, but this in itself had served only to provoke resentment in DG I, which perceived this as an encroachment on its territory by DG VIII and its ambitious Commissioner, Claude Cheysson.

There was widespread sentiment in DG I that the Lomé relationship had been given undue emphasis in Community foreign economic policy and that the time had arrived to extend the benefits enjoyed by the ACP to other developing countries. In addition, some concern existed that elements of DG VIII were acting as a protectionist Trojan horse within the Commission by supporting the French concept of managed markets as a means of guaranteeing the ACP a market for their products at a stable price.

But even within DG VIII there was little sympathy for the ACP position that the Community was obliged, under either the letter or spirit of the Lomé Convention, to preserve the tariff advantages that the Group enjoyed. And as the ACP's argument became more insistent, the relationship grew more bitter and EC representatives became increasingly hostile. According to an internal memorandum, the primary responsibility for the erosion of their preferences lay with the ACP Group itself, which, it was argued, had been too backward in voicing their interests in the international arena. Initially they had participated in the LDC consensus, which demanded a lowering of EEC tariffs: in September 1973 the spokesmen of the African group at the United Nations had demanded that the EEC improve its GSP, notably in the domain of agricultural products (where the Associates enjoyed their greatest tariff advantages). This behavior, the memorandum suggested, could be explained by the ignorance and timidity (the "Yaoundé complex") of the one group and by the strategy of the Anglophone associables who, doubting for a long time that a Convention would be concluded with the EEC, prepared, like other nonassociated LDCs, an alternative regime. When the ACP finally attempted to defend their privileged position and succeeded in persuading the United Nations that their interests should be safeguarded in any further extension of the GSP, the resolutions that were passed arrived "too late in an evolution towards the contrary direction."

As a consequence:

The tendency to take account of the negative remarks of the ACP in consultations on measures of commercial policy has weakened (if ever it was strong). It is at the level of Commission propositions that accommodation occurs between the divergent interests of our different categories of commercial partners. Discussion between Member States only truly integrates elements arising from national interests; the tendencies to open the market of the United Kingdom and the Federal Republic of Germany to the products (notably tropical) non-associated LDCs are neutralized by the objections of France, Belgium and Italy, and the real discussion, product by product, is reduced to the level of protection of local European industries. The "consultation" consists of listening afterwards to the grievances of the ACP and selling to them in a more or less convincing fashion the limitations introduced to the benefit of the Dutch refiners of vegetable oils, or of French, Italian and Belgian etc. canning industries.[13]

Even in discussions taking place within the Commission on the formulation of the GSP offer, clearly there had been no strong advocate of ACP interests.

From the Community's perspective, the intention of the Lomé regime was to provide free access for ACP products: "to the extent that there exists customs duties or quantitative restrictions for third country products there exists a preferential situation for ACP States but this is the consequence and not the object (of the free access provisions)."[14] If preferences were indeed being eroded, as Commissioner Cheysson admitted,[15] the ACP should seek compensation in other areas of the "privileged" relationship the Group enjoyed with the EEC. According to the internal Community memorandum quoted at some length above, it is on a second dimension of the free access provisions of the Convention that the fundamental advantage of the ACP States resides—all their competitive products can find an outlet on the Community market.

This, the memorandum notes, is a commercial security that can favor their industrial development in all domains, and at this level no other LDC or group of LDCs benefits from this advantage, even if the associated countries of the southern Mediterranean approach it. Security for the ACP is provided by the absence of tariff quotas or ceilings that are integral to the GSP. By virtue of its complexity, and the insecurity it had created, the GSP had itself become a nontariff barrier to LDC exports. In contrast, the simplicity of the Lomé regime was enviable. Concessions made under the GSP scheme were unilateral and thus could be withdrawn at any time, whereas Lomé, at least nominally, was a negotiated contractual arrangement.[16]

On the question of preferential access for their exports—which the ACP regarded as the most promising way of securing their share of the Community market—the strategy of collective clientelism clearly failed. As an alternative, the EEC emphasized the other norm sought by the ACP: security of access. This, the Community asserted was guaranteed since the relationship was "based on a *de jure* system resulting from a contract freely negotiated between equal partners."[17] But, as will be documented below, this much-vaunted security has been lacking in substance when put to the test.

## SECURITY OF ACCESS

Nominally, the Convention's trade provisions appear to offer the free and assured access ACP countries sought through their strategy of collective clientelism. Products originating within the ACP are granted duty-free access to the EEC market not subject to "any quantitative restrictions or measures having equivalent effect other than those which the Member States apply among themselves" (Article 3 of the first Convention). But the liberalism and security of the trade regime is undermined by a number of important restrictions: (1) regulations regarding products included in the Community's Common Agricultural Policy; (2) rules of origin; (3) measures taken to limit the imports of products regarded as "sensitive"; and (4) the existence of safeguard mechanisms.

### 1. The ACP and the Common Agricultural Policy

Through its representatives and publications, the Community has given great weight to the claim that 99.5 percent of current ACP exports (by value) enter the Community market duty-free. The remainder are CAP products where ACP production competes directly with that of Community farmers; for these, the Convention commits the Community to provide treatment more favorable than MFN terms. The comparatively small volume of ACP trade denied duty-free access might appear to support the Community's contention that the barriers faced by ACP exporters of these products are "not a serious handicap."[18] But to dwell at length on these figures would be misleading. To do so ignores the deterrent effect that the CAP has on ACP producers desiring to increase their exports of these products to the Community—in other words, if the CAP was not in place, then exports of these products might be expected to contribute substantially more than 0.5 percent of ACP export earnings. As is not uncommon in its discussion of the trade relationship, the Commission has taken an overly static view. Aggregated figures of this type also obscure the importance that these restrictions may have for the export earnings of individual ACP states.

What is at issue here is the very nature of the trade relationship. In essence ACP states are being told they may freely export to the EEC only as long as no conflict of interest arises—a dangerous qualification that, as will be shown, has been applied to items other than those included within the CAP. In the negotiations for a new Convention, ACP spokesmen turned the Community's argument on its head and demanded to know why, if the amounts involved were so insignificant, the Community would not make a "political commitment" to the principle of total free access for all ACP exports.

In response, the ACP were subjected to a long and rather paternalistic statement by the Community's chief spokesman on commercial cooperation in which emphasis was placed on the existence of a genuine conflict of interest on this matter. He concluded: "you must not ask us to scorn our own interests, that is not possible."[19] This conception of the Lomé "partnership" as inoperative when a conflict of interest arises is peculiarly one-sided but often appears to underlie Community conceptions of the relationship.

As currently constituted, the CAP presents a significant barrier to an increase in agricultural exports from Third World countries. Birnberg estimated that a liberalization of its system of variable levies would add $385.4 million per year to the exports of LDCs.[20] To expect, however, to achieve a major reform of the CAP through the Lomé relationship is unrealistic. With limited success having been achieved in establishing Community-wide decision-making in other issue areas, the CAP has become a sacred cow: the Commission's negotiating mandate for the Toyko Round of Multilateral Trade Negotiations stated that "its [the CAP's] principles and mechanisms should not be called into question and therefore do not constitute a matter for negotiation."[21] In this context the ACP Group might be deemed to have been remarkably successful in breeching the fundamental principles of the CAP by negotiating the Sugar Protocol of the Convention.

For other products in which a conflict of interest occurs, the Community has been less generous toward its Lomé partners despite the fact that (with the exception of sugar) the ACP generally account for less than 10 percent of the total value of extra-EEC imports of agricultural products.[22] While the ACP understand they cannot expect to take advantage of the benefits provided by the Common Agricultural Policy without accepting some of the constraints to which European and other suppliers are subject, they hold the perception that the European Community has not acted in the "spirit" of Lomé in its less than generous attitude toward the small volume of agricultural imports ACP countries provide.

Bitterness between the two parties has arisen in particular over the regimes established for the import of ACP beef and for certain fruits and vegetables. In all cases a direct conflict of interest exists between the ACP and producers in member states or their associated territories.[23] Special provisions for the import of ACP beef were announced unilaterally by the EEC during 1975 that were designed to freeze ACP exports to the EEC at the existing level. Duty-free quotas and exemption from 90 percent of the EEC's variable import levy were granted to four African producers—Botswana, Madagascar, Swaziland, and Kenya—to enable them to continue to export to their traditional markets, primarily the United Kingdom (export to other member states has been limited since the four exporters failed to meet the animal health/food hygiene regulations that these states imposed, regulations the ACP allege have been employed as a nontariff barrier against their exports).[24]

Exports from the four ACP countries constituted only 6 to 7 percent of EEC imports of beef and but 0.4 percent of total Community beef and veal consumption—equivalent to roughly one day's supply of the Community market. These exports were nevertheless of importance to the ACP states concerned—particularly Botswana for which beef constituted 56 percent of total export earnings. In light of the small share of the ACP in extra-Community imports, the treatment accorded them under the Lomé I beef regime appeared particularly mean-spirited. First, no growth was built into the quota for exports benefiting from reduced levies—the ceiling remained low and static. Second, the regime provided no security for

ACP producers: the special provisions had to be renegotiated each year. In commenting on Community policy toward ACP beef exporters the Select Committee of the House of Commons on Overseas Development noted:

The way in which the negotiations are handled, with the deliberate maintenance of uncertainty for the maximum legal period, have [*sic*] done nothing to convince the ACP States affected of the EEC's good faith or generous intention. Your committee can see no justification for squandering political goodwill over issues that are so minor in the total economic context of the EEC.[25]

This advice was apparently heeded by the Community in the renegotiations, for, despite the reservations of the Irish and French representatives a new beef regime was established for Lomé II that guarantees the levy reduction for the five-year period of the Convention for a larger initial quota (30,000 tonnes), with allowance made for an annual growth of 7 percent. More flexibility was introduced in the arrangements by allowing the ACP exporters to reallocate shortfalls on the country quotas among themselves or to make up a shortfall that arises from *force majeure* in the following year. This outcome was apparently acceptable to the ACP states concerned.[26]

This new-found generosity of spirit did not carry over to other CAP products exported by the ACP. A list of more than sixty agricultural products on which new or additional concessions were sought was sent by the ACP to the Community during the renegotiations. In many of the items trade was of very small magnitude or nonexistent: what was of concern to the ACP was to attain some guarantee of access so that production might be encouraged in the future by the security provided. Again, however, the Community refused to treat its relations with the ACP outside the context of its total external relations in the agricultural sphere. For instance, in the case of tomatoes, where the ACP had supplied less than 1 percent of total extra-EEC imports during the first Convention, Senegal (currently the only significant producer among the ACP) was permitted a 60 percent reduction in customs duties (but no exemption from levies) in respect of a total of only 2,000 tonnes and limited to months outside the Community's own growing season. This reduction was similar to that extended by the Community to the Maghreb countries (Morocco, Algeria, and Tunisia), but these three benefited from much larger quotas for their products.

What is very evident in this matter is that there is no potential for a significant growth in ACP exports of CAP products in the future. Some concessions were made in the Lomé II Convention on certain vegetables and fruits, but in most cases a very low ceiling was set and beneficiaries' access to the Community market was subject to seasonal limitations. Anyone familiar with the haggling that went on in the meetings of the EEC Council of Ministers and COREPER during the renegotiations could not but be struck by the ungenerous Community attitude; lengthy debates occurred about whether exporting seasons for ACP producers should be extended by one or two days and whether tonnages benefiting from reduced duties might be increased by marginal amounts. Representatives of the Italian government, and to a lesser extent the French, were the most obdurate.

As is also the case with industrial products, ACP states suffer from being latecomers to the international market. Although some members of the ACP Group enjoy climates suitable for the cultivation of fruits and vegetables for the European market, potential for increasing their exports is blocked not only by the Community's own surpluses (which will almost certainly be exacerbated if the EEC is expanded to include Spain and Portugal, as well as Greece) but also by the presence of other exporters that enjoy privileged access to the Community market. After six years of frequently bitter negotiations, the ACP Group are aware that the special relationship they enjoy with the Community by virtue of the Lomé Convention is not going to guarantee their agricultural products more generous treatment than that given to other third-country suppliers; the CAP consequently represents a serious obstacle to an expansion of ACP exports and undermines the supposed security provided by the trade regime.

## 2. The Rules of Origin

A second major qualification to the principle of free access for ACP exports to the Community market arises from the restrictive definition of "originating products" applied in the Lomé regime—rules that constituted 43 of the 84 pages of printed text of the first Convention. Establishment of rules of origin in a preferential trade relationship is to the benefit of all parties since their intention is to ensure that benefits arising from the preferential provisions are shared only by the signatories. In any trading relationship the aim is to establish a balance between two objectives: rules that are sufficiently restrictive to prevent third countries from utilizing preferential beneficiaries as mere conduits for their products yet that are sufficiently flexible that they do not prevent the development of export industries within the beneficiary states. The ACP states contend that the Lomé rules of origin have been biased so heavily toward the first objective that they have frustrated attainment of the second.

In principle, originating status is conferred on products wholly produced within an ACP state or on those items whose tariff heading under the nomenclature of the Customs Cooperation Council (CCCN) (formerly the Brussels Tariff Nomenclature) has been changed by virtue of domestic processing. But, the Community argues, since the CCCN was originally devised to facilitate the implementation of MFN status and was not intended to apply to preferential trading regimes, additional restrictions are necessary before originating status can be conferred in the Community's preferential trading.

Two types of exception are made to the principle that a change in tariff heading will confer originating status. List A, appended to the Convention, notes a number of products during whose manufacture a change of tariff heading takes place but where the Community judges insufficient transformation of the product has occurred for originating status to be conferred. List B, on the other hand, notes a number of products where there has been no change of tariff heading but the Community considers a sufficient transformation has taken place for the product to be given originating status.

Two criteria are applied in each list in deciding whether originating status can be conferred. The percentage criterion stipulates the maximum percentage value of the finished product that can be constituted by imported inputs. A second criterion relates to processing and requires that certain operations must be carried out in the beneficiary country (and also refers to a number of processes deemed to produce an insufficient transformation to permit the confirmation of originating status).

In the Lomé regime, List A specifies close to 300 items for which the general rule that a change in tariff heading confers originating status does not apply—this eliminates approximately one-third of the tariff headings under the CCCN. In general, the percentage requirement stipulates imported inputs should not exceed 40 percent or, more often, 50 percent of the value of the final product. In some instances additional restrictions are imposed that specify maximum import levels of particular materials and parts from third countries, these percentages not being cumulative within the overall value-added requirement. Many of the processes required by List A (referring primarily to textile products) are multistage operations that do not confer originating status unless *all* stages of the operation are conducted within the exporting beneficiary country.

For many textile products, consequently, the domestic value added necessary for the confirmation of orginating status is very high. McQueen has calculated, for instance, that the percentage of value added required by the Lomé rules for cotton fabrics is not less than 320 percent. For finished garments, where yarn is the only permitted nonoriginating material, the origin rules require that an ACP state add more than 600 percent to the value of the raw material.[27] These processing requirements demand a much higher level of value added than the percentage criterion in List A.

ACP states have argued the rules of origin are so restrictive as to constitute a nontariff barrier to their exports. They appear to place Anglophone ACP states at a disadvantage in comparison to the access to the U.K. market they enjoyed under the Commonwealth Preferences System. This made no reference to multistage processing requirements, and its percentage criterion was, with a few exceptions, substantially lower than that required by the Lomé regime. In contrast to the EEC's use of the process criterion and frequently the percentage criterion as an additional requirement, Australia, New Zealand, Canada, and the United States employ only the percentage criterion for the purposes of their GSP schemes to determine whether products have been sufficiently transformed to enjoy originating status.[28]

Given their low levels of per capita income (32 ACP states had a per capita GNP of $350 or less in 1975), their small populations, and their inadequate infrastructure, the ACP Group has argued the high value-added requirements set by the Lomé rules of origin are completely unrealistic. McQueen cites figures from the *UN Yearbook of Industrial Statistics* showing that, taking the manufacturing sector as a whole, only three countries (Congo, Ghana, and Somalia) succeeded in adding domestically as much as 50 percent of the value of the finished products. All other countries in the ACP Group for which data were available recorded levels of between 20 percent and 46 percent. Disaggregating the figures by product group at the three-digit level of the International Standard Industrial Classification, of a total of eight hundred fourteen possibilities (thirty-seven product groups and twenty-two countries), only in sixty-three product groups (7.7 percent of the total) was value added of 50 percent to 59 percent, and forty-six product groups (5.7 percent of the total) recorded levels of 60 percent or more.[29] In considering this evidence, the House of Commons Select Committee commented:

It seems that the Rule requiring that 50–60 percent of value added originating in the ACP States is taken to be a serious infringement of both the spirit and letter of Article 1 of the Convention. It is clearly absurd to expect a country like Niger or Barbados to add 60 per cent to the value of manufactured products *in situ*.[30]

In response to ACP criticisms, spokemen for the EEC have argued, somewhat paternalistically, that the rules are necessary to protect the advantages enjoyed by the ACP, and rather than constitute an obstacle to industrialization in these countries, are of a nature that would stimulate a "true industrialization."[31] A relaxation of the value-added requirement would encourage "footloose" industries to locate in the ACP, industries that would be insufficiently integrated in the economies of the host countries to make a significant contribution to these countries' development.[32] In addition, it was pointed out, problems ACP states experienced in meeting the value-added requirements were addressed by the provisions in the Convention for a cumulation of value added and for derogations to the rules.

In the negotiations for the first Convention, the ACP states had succeeded in winning a concession from the Community that allowed for all ACP countries to be treated as a single territory for the purposes of calculating domestic value added; i.e., value added in the process of manufacturing a product in more than one ACP state could be cumulated toward meeting the percentage and processing criteria. This concession by the Community gave the ACP countries an advantage, at least in theory, over GSP beneficiaries for whom cumulation was not permitted and was intended to encourage regional industrial cooperation among groups of ACP countries.

Of greater practical significance was the provision that:

When products wholly obtained in the Community or in the countries and territories undergo working or processing in one or more ACP States, they shall be considered as having been wholly produced in that or those ACP States.[33]

This provision again gives the ACP countries an advantage over GSP beneficiaries for whom cumulation of donor country content has not been permitted. But the primary benefit from this regulation is derived by EEC companies placed on an advantageous footing in ACP states in comparison with the transnational corporations of third countries. This discrimination against third-country producers applies as much to other developing countries as to developed, thereby erecting a barrier to greater cooperation among LDCs. In addition, by enabling ACP countries to meet the requirements of the rules of origin by using imported components from the EEC, this provision reduces the incentive to the ACP to take advantage of the rule allowing for cumulation of value added across ACP countries.

Evidently, the Community's intention is to use the donor country cumulation provision as a lever to exert pressure on the ACP to utilize inputs from the Community. Nowhere is this more obvious than in the regulations pertaining to the definition of originating product for ACP fishing industries. Annex I to the first Convention provides that ACP fish products will enjoy originating status provided the vessels from which the fish are caught fulfill all of the following requirements: registration in a member state or ACP state; sail under the flag of a member state or ACP state; are owned to an extent of at least 50 percent by nationals of states party to the Convention or by a company with its head office in one of the countries, of which the majority of board members and the chairman and company manager are nationals of states party to the Convention, and at least half the capital of which belongs to states party to the Convention; and, finally, at least 50 percent of the crew, captain and officers included, are nationals of states party to the Convention.

These curious, lengthy conditions, the ACP Group has argued, are utterly unreasonable for countries at their levels of development, especially the provisions relating to ownership, since the most practicable method of exploiting marine resources for many ACP states is to lease fishing vessels from other countries. Where ACP states are located at considerable distance from the Community, they can expect little contribution from Community vessels in the development of their fishing resources.[34] In response, Community spokesmen have stated merely that:

To the extent that ACP States cannot yet ensure by their own means the fish catches necessary to supply their processing industries, the Convention foresees that they can develop a partnership with boats flying the flag of Member States of the Community, without losing the benefit of originating status for fish captured by these means.[35]

The principal purposes of the regulations would appear to be, first, to help maintain the dominant position of certain member states, most notably France, in the exploitation of the fishery resources of West African countries and, second, to prevent competitors of European fleets from gaining access to the domestic Community market.

An emphasis on securing inputs from European industries has also been evident in the Commission's administration of the derogation provisions of the chapter on originating status. These, the Community has argued, are a second means by which ACP states can circumvent difficulties that arise in meeting the value-added requirements of the rules of origin. Article 27 of Protocol No. 1 to the first Convention allows for the EEC's Council of Ministers to permit derogations from the rules of origin provisions if the Commission decides, in response to a request by an ACP state, that these are warranted for the establishment of new industries or the development of existing industries. But derogations are only temporary—with the clear implication that the intervening period should be used by ACP countries to search for Community sources for the inputs concerned.[36]

Rather than work primarily to the benefit of the ACP, the provisions in the Convention for cumulation of origin and for derogations appear to have been of greatest benefit to the industries of the member states of the European Community. Currently, intra-ACP trade is at an extremely low level, transport links between the countries being rudimentary. Even among ACP countries currently joined in customs cooperation agreements and whose transportation links are comparatively sophisticated, the quantity of inputs from other ACP countries within the region is very small. A study conducted by the CARICOM Secretariat found that materials derived from other states within the regional grouping represented only 0.3 percent of f.o.b. prices for 286 products where separate information was available for labor costs and overheads and profits, and 0.2 percent for a further 212 products where disaggregated information of this nature was unavailable.[37]

At present, therefore, the Community's concession on cumulation of value added among ACP states represents only a potential advantage that may be realized at some time in the future. But the allowance for donor country cumulation has immediately accorded real benefits to European industry that may stand in the way of the future realization of intra-ACP cooperation. Although the Lomé Convention dispensed with requirements for reverse preferences in the field of trade, the effect of the donor country cumulation procedure has been to reintroduce the principle of reverse preferences by the back door. In concluding its critical review of the Convention's rules of origin, and of the lack of flexibility displayed by the Community in their application, the Select Committee of the House of Commons on Overseas Development asserted the present system "seeks to bias choices of industrial development and technology transfer in favour of the EEC. If Your Committee are not enthusiastic about tied aid, they are even less disposed to its industrial equivalent."[38]

That there were only a small number of requests for derogations during the first Convention (five had been granted, and three were under consideration at the time of the renegotiations) was used by the Community to argue the rules of origin had not been a significant problem for ACP states. F. Durieux, chief Community spokesman on commercial cooperation, stated at the outset of the negotiations that "the Community's general position . . . is fairly simple, being based on the factual observation that the existing system has not given rise to major difficulties."[39] But this is yet another instance in which the Community adopted an overly formalistic and static perspective.

As the ACP countries have argued, the restrictive impact of the rules of origin occurs essentially on an *ex ante* basis. There should be no surprise at the small number of derogation requests since consideration of the rules occurs when potential investors are undertaking their feasibility studies; at this time there is the realization that the rules exclude the planned exports from trade preferences. Since the negative decision is likely to be taken at this stage, it (and comments on the deterrent effects of the rules) will probably never be communicated to the ACP country concerned. Accordingly, the Group aver, it is unreasonable of the community to demand the ACP Group produce evidence on an *ex post facto* basis of the deterrent effect of the rules.

Furthermore, the Community's response to the derogation requests made during the first Lomé Convention had done little to convince potential investors of the efficacy of the procedure. Applications for derogation proved to be time-consuming and their results unsatisfactory for the requesting states. Decisions had not been reached in some cases until nine months after the request had been submitted, and the eventual derogations covered on average only one-half the quantity and one-half of the time period requested. All derogations were temporary and had been granted for only one year.[40]

Derogations, the ACP Group argued, were no substitute for realistic rules of origin according with the spirit of Article 1 of the Convention, which stated that its object was "to promote trade between the Contracting Parties, *taking account of their respective levels of development*, and, in particular, of the need to secure additional benefits for the trade of ACP States" (emphasis added). In the present Convention the rules were so restrictive as to go far beyond what was necessary to ensure that third countries did not exploit the preferential access enjoyed by the ACP. Accordingly, the ACP Group asserted, greater flexibility should be introduced into the rules to take account of levels of economic development, in particular, those of the least developed, landlocked, and island countries.

Community spokesmen in the renegotiations consistently resisted attempts to adjust the rules to make allowance for level of development (a proposal that at one time apparently had the support of the British government). The Commission's position rested on two arguments: significant amendment to the Lomé rules of origin (which are very similar to those that the Community employs in its other preferential agreements, including the GSP), on the one hand, would be discriminatory, and, on the other, "would complicate in an unsupportable manner the administrative task of the customs authorities."[41] Neither argument is particularly convincing. The very essence of the Lomé relationship is discriminatory: no new principle would be involved in modifying the rules, and, in any case, certain adjustments had already been made between one preferential agreement and another. Although the argument that a greater flexibility in the rules would complicate the task of the customs authorities has some merit, the ACP asserted this was a fairly insignificant administrative problem (since the same general procedures would be employed) and should not be allowed to stand in the way of improving the rules. As was pointed out, the ACP countries themselves have to cope with different rules of origin under 16 different preferential schemes as beneficiaries of various GSP arrangements.

Commission intransigence carried the day. This position was not without its supporters among the member states—for instance, the Irish demanded consistency in the rules, in part because they feared any further relaxation might cause them to lose some of the foreign investment they had succeeded in attracting as one of the lower wage areas of the Community. Rather than agree to any significant changes in the rules themselves, the Community offered a more flexible procedure for derogations in the second Convention. Requests from ACP countries would be examined more expeditiously—a decision must be reached by the ACP–EEC Customs Cooperation Committee within three months of submission of the request—and would take into account, in particular, the level of development or the geographical situation of the ACP state concerned, the economic and social impact where the decision involved a least developed ACP state, and the possibility of conferring originating status on products that include components originating in neighboring developing countries with which one or more ACP states have special trade relationships. Derogations "generally" would be for two years and might provide for renewals for one year without a new decision of the Committee being necessary, provided the ACP state(s) concerned submitted evidence of inability to comply with the rules.

It is unlikely that these more flexible procedures will lead to a significant increase in the number of requests for derogation. The fundamental problem—the deterrent effect of the rules—remains, and improved provisions for derogations do little to provide the security investors seek before committing their money. As McQueen has argued, the rules are "manifestly unsuitable for trade with countries at the level of development of the ACP States."[42] In their present form the rules represent a nontariff barrier adding further protection to European industries. Their restrictiveness undermines the claim of the Community that the Convention provides secure access to the EEC market for ACP states and their domestic and foreign investors.

### 3. Lomé and ACP Exports of "Sensitive" Products

ACP countries, being among the least developed in the world, have few options for increasing their exports. This is especially true for those countries that lack significant mineral deposits. An ACP study prepared at the time of the renegotiations considered the various alternatives available to ACP states for future industrialization and concluded the most feasible options are the development of processed and/or labor-intensive products within the category of light industry.[43] Given the low per capita income of many ACP states and their small populations, the domestic market is insufficient to support viable industries of this type. An assured export market was therefore regarded as crucial for the industrial development of most ACP states.

Considerable potential appears to exist for further processing by ACP states of their raw material exports—an activity singled out for special

**TABLE 4.1.**

Relationship Between Exports of Unprocessed and Processed
Commodities in ACP Trade with the EEC

| *Unprocessed* | *Semiprocessed and Processed* |
| --- | --- |
| Cocoa beans (87%) | Cocoa powder, paste & butter (12.7%), chocolate & other preparations containing cocoa (0.03%) |
| Raw hides, & skins (72%) | Leather (26%); leather finished products, including footwear (2%) |
| Rubber (99.2%) | Rubber goods (0.8%) |
| Crude palm oil (91%) | Refined palm oil (9%) |
| Wood in rough (64.8%) | Simply worked (23%); planks, plywood, improved/reconstituted wood (11.6%); finished wood products (0.6%) |
| Raw cotton (69%) | Cotton yarn & thread (4%), cotton fabrics (12%), knitted cotton accessories (9.8%), cotton clothing (5.2%) |
| Fresh vegetables (94.7%) | Preserved vegetables (5.3%) |
| Fresh fruit (60%) | Preserved fruit (40%) |

Source: ACP memorandum.
Note: Percentage figures refer to the share of product subgroups in all exports from the ACP to the
EEC of the product group.

emphasis by Article 29 of the first Convention. Table 4.1 shows the small
share processed products have in the exports of ACP raw materials. Even
one of the more developed ACP states, the Ivory Coast, still exports 80
percent of its three principal products—coffee, cocoa, and timber—in
unprocessed form.[44] As a GATT Report noted: "the lower the degree of
processing, the better placed the ACP countries appear to be in the
Community market."[45] Increased domestic processing would enable the
ACP to increase the value added locally, to capture oligopsony rents, and
to reduce their vulnerability to fluctuations in the terms of trade.

As Wall has argued very persuasively, it is hazardous to generalize regarding the feasibility of increasing local processing, given the variability
of processing chains between different raw materials. Contrary to popular misconceptions, the effective protection afforded domestic production
in industrialized states does not always increase in successive stages of
the processing chains. In some chains effective protection actually declines.[46] Since most ACP exports are admitted to the European market
duty-free, they are not threatened by the problem of escalating effective
tariffs. However, a related but inverse argument can be made regarding

the tariff advantages enjoyed by the ACP over other developing country suppliers to the European market: whereas virtually all the exports of ACP countries enter the Community market duty-free, the GSP scheme that provides duty-free access for many manufactures from other LDCs does not cover all raw materials and agricultural products. Increased processing of some raw materials by ACP states may therefore reduce their "effective protection" against third-country suppliers in the European market. At the present time, however, agricultural products which have undergone only limited processing are often excluded from the EEC's GSP in order to protect European processing industries.

Other factors may also complicate a strategy of increased domestic processing. ACP states may not enjoy a comparative advantage in these activities if they require large capital investments, sophisticated technology, or large numbers of skilled personnel or if transport or communications costs favor location close to the product's final market. CAP countries have also argued that they are victims of a discriminatory pricing policy by international shipping cartels—freight rates for Africa being substantially above those for Latin America, for instance. Since ACP states appear to lag behind other LDCs in the processing of their raw materials exports, however, there would appear to be considerable scope for increasing domestic value added before these technical factors come into play. This is particularly true of the processing of agricultural products, including beverages. For a number of these, e.g., canned fruits and fruit juices, ACP states enjoy significant tariff advantages over beneficiaries of the GSP system. But in these instances ACP states frequently encounter other problems arising from the trade-distorting policies and restrictive practices pursued by European governments and their corporations.

Many processing industries in Europe are the beneficiaries of subsidies from national governments and/or the European Community. Among these are the processors of tomatoes, citrus fruit, and sugar. Ironically, one reason for these subsidies was to provide "compensation" for the tariff concessions given to Mediterranean countries and ACP states. A number of preserved or processed fruit and vegetable products are considered "sensitive" in the European market—these include peeled tomatoes, tomato juice, preserved peaches, preserved peas, preserved beans, and preserved pears.[47] Where European processing industries provide significant employment opportunities, and where European farmers are faced with saturated markets for "sensitive" products, any attempt by ACP states to establish their own processing industries will create a direct conflict of interest with the Community. To date, when such conflicts have occurred in other areas, the EEC has backed away from its commitment to its ACP partners; it is unlikely to view ACP efforts to establish competitive processing industries any more favorably.

ACP countries have also experienced problems in attempting to expand their exports in a second category of "sensitive" industry: that which involves labor-intensive manufacturing. One consequence of the restrictive rules of origin is to exclude products of simple labor-intensive operations in which some ACP states have a comparative advantage. In a memorandum to the House of Commons Select Committee on Overseas Development, McQueen cited figures from recent studies of labor-intensive industries in Britain and the United States showing that wages and salaries of production workers in a wide range of electrical goods industries in the United Kingdom account for between 8 percent and 18 percent of the value of gross output; in labor-intensive processes in the U.S. electronics industry, wages and salaries of production workers account for between 13 percent and 25 percent of the value of output.[48] Given that wages in ACP states are likely to be considerably lower than those in the United Kingdom or United States and consequently account for an even lower percentage of the value of output, the requirements of the Lomé rules of origin that local value add between 50 percent and 60 percent of the f.o.b. cost of the finished product clearly exclude this type of simple labor-intensive industry (unless European components are used).

As noted above, the Community has asserted these industries are not desirable for the ACP, since they are "footloose" and "insufficiently integrated" into the economies of the host countries. But, as McQueen argued, this perception of the contribution of offshore production to the development of LDCs is excessively static and short term in focus. Although footloose assembly industries may not bring substantial industrial benefits immediately, they do provide employment and training to what might otherwise be an idle work force and also bring foreign exchange benefits. Furthermore, over the long term, additional stages of production are often transferred to the developing country and backward linkages established with the local economy. Over a period of time a gradual shift occurs in bargaining power away from the transnational companies in favor of the host government, especially if the country is able to attract a number of competing transnationals.[49]

Community apprehension regarding the effects of footloose industries on ACP economies has not extended to EEC companies of this nature. As the House of Commons Select Committee noted:

The truth is that it (the cumulation provision) makes it more difficult for Japanese or American footloose industries to be established in the ACP States; it makes it easier for European footloose industries to be established there . . . furthermore, it is not the EEC's business to tilt the pattern of development of ACP States in one direction or another.[50]

By preventing ACP countries from attracting third-country multinationals on the same terms available to EEC industries, the Convention has weakened the bargaining position of ACP governments.

Donor cumulation under the Lomé rules of origin has the same effect as the offshore assembly arrangements offered by the United States whereby the tariff rate on imports of products assembled outside the United States is reduced if U.S. components are used in their manufacture.[51] The European Community has also taken initiatives on this matter, most notably with the outward processing of textiles. Although the Council of Ministers has yet to reach final agreement on the details of a Community-wide policy, its outline has become clear: beneficiary states are to receive quotas that will be in addition to country quotas already granted for the direct import of textile products from these countries. In contrast, the ACP countries in theory enjoy unrestricted access to the European market for products in which the cumulation of donor components has been utilized.

Again, however, this advantage has proved to be more apparent than real. During the first Convention, the EEC was explicit in its statements that as far as imports of "sensitive" products into the Community were concerned, it would not be able to afford the ACP treatment different from that given to other suppliers. Nowhere was this more evident than in textiles and clothing.

The rapid expansion of the export capacity of LDCs for textile products has caused severe adjustment problems for developed countries. LDCs are currently bearing the cost of the failure of certain national industries within the European Community—most notably those of Britain and France—to modernize in anticipation of changes in world market conditions and production structures. LDCs have also been adversely affected by the failure of the European Community to act decisively when the Multifiber Arrangement (MFA) was first negotiated.

In contrast to the United States, which immediately instituted global quotas for most textiles imports, the Community acted only to limit imports on selected "sensitive" products. The consequence was that LDC exporters diversified their production into those items whose access to the European market remained unrestricted and, in addition, switched exports from the American to the European market. Although LDCs may have experienced short-term benefits from this strategy, the undesirable consequence was that when the EEC eventually reformulated its policy at the Community level, the restrictions on LDC exports were probably more severe than they would have been if a more effective policy had been adopted at an earlier stage.[52]

ACP countries, latecomers to all fields of industrial activity, have only recently begun to export textiles. Few ACP states possessed textile manufacturing plants at independence; their subsequent establishment was due in part to the desire of European companies to breach the tariff walls erected after independence to promote import substitution and was often encouraged by generous investment codes and low tariffs for imported inputs offered by the host states. Subsequent manufacturing for export had its origins as much in European developments as in those in ACP states, namely, the rationalization and verticalization of production structures within European industries that caused them to engage in international sourcing. This development was precisely the type the Lomé rules were expected to encourage. Initially, French textile companies were predominant but were later followed by German and Dutch, often in partnership with host governments (and sometimes assisted by the European Investment Bank, the European Development Fund, and national aid agencies).[53]

ACP exports of textiles, because of the sensitivity of many of these products for the European market, provide an interesting test case of the security of access to the European market the Lomé Convention is claimed to guarantee. Formulating a policy toward ACP textiles that would be part of a coherent global framework has proved to be elusive for the European Community. The main outlines of its textiles policy were drawn up before the Lomé Convention—with its assurance of free access for the ACP to the European market—and before the emergence of some ACP states as (potentially) significant textiles exporters.

Although ACP exports of textile products and clothing increased substantially in the second half of the 1970s, they still constitute only a very small share of total EEC imports. Exports of cotton cloth from all ACP states increased in volume terms by more than 50 percent in the period 1975–79 (the increase in value was about 250 percent), but the ACP Group as a whole did not significantly increase its share of extra-EEC imports. By 1979, ACP states accounted for only 1.8 percent of all EEC imports of textiles.

Nevertheless, the Community found it necessary to warn the ACP states regarding the level of their exports. In November 1977 a Community spokeman informed the ACP that the EEC Council had "recognized that *all* imports from low-wage countries were contributing to the disruption of the market." Even for countries enjoying preferential access to the Community market, if they were deemed to be " 'significant suppliers' of sensitive products, which means in general that they supply at least 1 percent of the Community's total imports, the Community considered that they contributed to cumulative disruption of the market and should therefore be subject to restrictions similar to those imposed on third countries."[54]

At the time this ultimatum was issued, no ACP state fell into the category of "significant supplier"; consequently, the Community did not impose a limit on the exports of any particular ACP state. However, a thinly veiled warning was issued:

In a spirit of cooperation and frankness, it behoves the Community to inform the ACP States that there is an acute crisis in this production sector and to tell them which products would create serious market disruption if there were too sudden and too large an increase in imports.[55]

And, in December 1977, when the EEC Council established global internal ceilings for imports from suppliers covered by the MFA, an "ACP line," i.e., a set of indicative quotas for sensitive items from the ACP Group, was also established. No consultations had taken place with the ACP before the quotas were established, despite the pretense that the Lomé relationship represented a partnership among equals. The global quotas were not subdivided by individual ACP supplier and therefore were not intended to establish limits on the exports to the European market for any individual ACP exporter. Rather their function was primarily for internal Community purposes: to share the burdens of absorbing ACP exports between the member states, to assist these countries in monitoring their imports from the ACP, and to provide a vehicle for raising complaints with ACP states if exports grew at a rate more rapid than that provided for by the indicative quotas.

A memorandum sent from the Commission to the Chairman of the Committee of ACP Ambassadors in October 1978 stressed the importance of consultations on the matter of textile exports and informed the ACP that overall ceilings for their exports of sensitive products would be imposed. How a member state would react to the ACP Group's exceeding its quota would obviously be determined by the quantities involved and by the health of its domestic industries.

Mauritius was the first ACP state to encounter serious problems from its exports of clothing to the Community. French customs authorities in 1977 began to delay Mauritian clothing shipments, ostensibly to check for fraudulent certificates of origin. Under this less than subtle pressure, Mauritius agreed to voluntary export restraints on its shipments of pullovers, shirts, blouses, trousers, and gloves. It then switched a number of these exports to the UK market. In 1978 and 1979 Mauritius accounted for approximately 3 percent of all EEC imports of knitted goods. But whereas in 1978, the export of sweaters had been fairly evenly distributed between markets in France, Benelux, and the United Kingdom, in 1979 approximately 55 percent of the exports were sent to the United Kingdom. In that year, Mauritian exports were eight times the indicative quota assigned to Britain for T-shirts from *all* ACP countries and more than four times the quota for sweaters. For Ireland the disparity between its imports and the "ligne ACP" was even greater. Both countries, whose textile industries were among the weakest in the EEC, complained to the Commission about this additional threat.

Negotiations between Commission representatives and the Mauritian government failed to bring agreement; this provoked unilateral British action. On the day the second Lomé Convention was signed, the British government, with a remarkable lack of tact, threatened to impose the safeguard clause of the Convention to curtail Mauritian textile exports unless agreement was reached on "voluntary" export restraints. This move, undertaken at the cost of considerable political goodwill and at the expense of exposing the insecurity of the Lomé guarantees, had the desired effect of bringing the Mauritian government to the negotiating table. In January 1980 agreement was reached on limitations for two years on Mauritian exports to Britain and Ireland, which included a 20 percent reduction in the number of sweaters exported to the United Kingdom;

at this time the Mauritian authorities "expressed the regret that the question had not been dealt with until after the negotiations for the new Lomé Convention."[56]

These developments within the Community's policy toward ACP exporters of textiles have been discussed at some length because of their important implications for the Lomé relationship. On products the Community regards as sensitive, a clear signal has been communicated to the ACP that they will not be treated in a manner different from other suppliers. In the arguments that followed the announcement of the EEC position on textiles, the Community's chief spokesman on trade matters, F. Durieux, asserted that:

It is not possible for the Community to make exception for certain countries within the framework of this global policy even if the exports of these countries only constitute, at this stage, a small percentage in relation to the total imports of the EEC.[57]

Despite the fact that the ACP countries themselves were not to blame for the problems faced by the EEC's textile industries, despite the free access to the EEC market provided by the Lomé Convention, despite the "success" of ACP states in exporting textiles having occurred with the partnership of European finance (and predominantly European machinery)—the very type of development Lomé was intended to promote, and despite the EEC's enjoying a substantial trade surplus in textiles with the ACP (as the latter's spokesmen were quick to point out),[58] the Community undertook unilateral action against ACP exporters.

The implications of the EEC's actions on textiles extend beyond this sector. Given their low levels of development, there are severe constraints on the type of manufactured goods ACP states might feasibly export: the products of simple labor-intensive industries or of processing and assembly plants appear to be their best possibilities. But for many of these industries the European market is already saturated by exports from other developing countries (which are frequently more competitive suppliers than the ACP). The only significant advantage enjoyed by the ACP by virtue of the Lomé relationship appeared to lie in their security of access to the European market. But these illusions were shattered by the Community's behavior on the textiles issue.

Whereas the Community has repeatedly emphasized the need for ACP governments to create a secure environment for foreign investment, its own behavior in restricting access to the European market for ACP textiles has created considerable uncertainty among potential investors in ACP projects. Obviously, this is particularly true within the textiles sector itself—as a result of Community policy the second stage of the large UTEXI complex in the Ivory Coast was canceled, and a second producer, Gonfreville, was forced to reorient production to the domestic market—but the impact has been more generalized. A spokesman for the Centre for Industrial Development, interviewed in June 1980, asserted potential investors in ACP manufacturing projects in a number of sectors had been deterred by the lack of certainty their products would be allowed access to the Community market.[59]

Community refusal to make an exception to its global textiles policy in favor of ACP states has encouraged other developing country suppliers of other "sensitive" products to take a hard line vis-à-vis the ACP. In May 1980 Portugal, Brazil, and Mexico refused to negotiate voluntary export restraints on their exports of rope and string to the European market unless the principal ACP supplier, Tanzania, was also included in the talks with the European manfacturers' organization, Eurocord.[60]

An obvious unwillingness on the part of the Community to grant secure access to its market for ACP exports has cast serious doubt on the assertions made by some academic commentators that the Lomé Convention was designed "to encourage those structural changes most in keeping with the new international division of labor." Mytelka argues, for instance, that

By agreeing to treat the ACP countries as a single customs territory . . . the EEC demonstrates that it is interested in facilitating a rationalization of EEC MNC production across the ACP countries thus making it possible for a French, German or British multinational firm to pursue its least cost-profit maximization point by manufacturing components in different ACP countries, assembling them in still another ACP country, and then exporting the finished product back to the EEC duty-free.[61]

In reality, the provision for cumulation across ACP countries was a concession that ACP proponents of regionalism succeeded in extracting from a reluctant EEC after hard-fought negotiation. Given the present low level of trade between ACP states, and the rudimentary transportation links between them, it would have been a very far-sighted TNC and European Commission to have lobbied energetically in favor of this provision. Certainly, the EEC was concerned to preserve the advantages enjoyed by European companies in their operations in ACP countries—hence the provision for cumulation of value added to be applied to components of EEC origin. But the Commission and member states have never taken seriously the idea that ACP states would be significant exporters of manufactured goods. Free access to the Community market was made available because there was no perception the ACP would threaten Community interests. There was never an intention, however, of giving ACP states carte blanche with regard to their access to the EEC market. Indeed, the internal memorandum quoted earlier in this chapter argued the Community would probably wish to reconsider its commitments to the ACP states if any of them should acquire the potential to become significant exporters of manufactured goods. Lomé was more concerned with perpetuating the existing division of labor than fostering a new one. Access for ACP exports was secure only as long as they did not threaten EEC interests: when this occurred they were vulnerable to an imposition of the Convention's safeguarded clause.[62]

## 4. The Safeguard Clause

One of the statements the Community is fond of repeating is that the safeguard clause of the Convention has never been applied and therefore is of little significance. This argument conveniently ignores the consensus among most economists that the very existence of safeguard clauses, given the threat of their use, is sufficient to generate welfare losses for exporting countries as a result of the uncertainties created.[63] Although the safeguard clause may not have been implemented, its imposition has been threatened as a means of extracting voluntary export restraints from ACP governments. Citing the case of the textiles industry, an ACP spokesman at the renegotiation of the Convention asserted "the very existence of the safeguard clause inhibited the development of industries in the ACP States, even if the clause was not applied."[64]

ACP states initially proposed there should be no safeguard clause whatsoever in Lomé II, given the disparity in economic development between the EEC and its partners. This aim was quickly rebuffed by the Community, however, as was the fallback position of the ACP, which sought immunity from the safeguard for the least developed, landlocked, and island states. Neither were the ACP successful in linking the safeguard clause to a commitment from the EEC to hold regular consultations on structural adjustment within the Community. On this matter the Community spokesman at the Bahamas ministerial meeting "urged that ACP States try to avoid raising questions of principle on matters which had not only operative but also political elements."[65] Not surprisingly, the ACP were a little perplexed by this new distinction between the "operative" and the "political."

Some concessions were made toward the ACP position in the second Convention. Whereas the Community's initial proposal was that the ACP would merely be "informed" before a safeguard action was taken, they agreed to the ACP proposal that prior consultations would take place and that the clause would not be used "for protectionist purposes or to hamper structural development" (Article 12, 2). This agreement on prior consultation was undermined, however, by a later clause asserting the consultations "shall not prevent any immediate decisions which the Community or its Member States . . . might take where special factors have necessitated these decisions" (Article 13, 3). Attempts by the ACP to limit the application of the safeguard to cases where the Community could demonstrate that ACP exports were responsible for the disruption of the Community market also failed.

Nominally, the ACP's position was improved by virtue of the limitations on Community action imposed by the new Convention. On the question of consultations, the Commission's own legal department counseled: "The internal procedures applied must be drawn up in such a way that they do not prevent this international obligation from being fulfilled."[66] In reality, the second Convention did little to ease the insecurity of the ACP on this matter. Either the Commission or a member state could impose the safeguard without prior consultation if (undefined) "special factors" were deemed to warrant it. Given the institutional constraints on Commission action, the ACP are probably more vulnerable to unilateral action on the part of a member state—as was the case with Britain's threatened imposition of the safeguard against Mauritian textiles. And, certainly, the recent behavior of the member states toward each other, e.g., the lamb "war" between Britain and France, gave little reason to expect that the member states would honor the commitments in the Convention—international obligations or not—if they perceived a threat to their domestic interests.

## SOME IMPLICATIONS

Implementation of the trade chapter of the Convention belied the expectations of the ACP regarding the benefits that would be derived in the trade sector from a strategy of collective clientelism. During the Convention they saw the advantages they enjoyed over third countries eroded; far from enjoying a veto over European decisions that might adversely affect their interests, they found that the EEC was not even willing to respect the commitment it had made in the Convention to consult with the ACP on issues affecting their interests.

Rather than provide the security the ACP had hoped for, the important qualifications to the principle of free access written into the Convention enabled the Community to take arbitrary actions that unsettled not only the governments of ACP countries but also potential investors. And rather than provide an insurance against the New Protectionism, the ACP found collective clientelism had brought them no significant benefits over other exporters of products deemed as "sensitive" by the Community.[67]

Inevitably, given the fragility of the trade regime and the reduction in the ACP Groups's preferential margins, there was little reason to expect that the Lomé provisions would have a major impact on the course of commercial relations between the Community and the ACP. The evolution of the trade relationship during the first Convention is examined in the next chapter.

# 5

# Trade Between the EEC and ACP During the Lomé Period*

According to one of the Convention's most enthusiastic proponents: "the duty-free access enjoyed by the ACP states to EEC markets could be potentially decisive for their economic development."[1] On an a priori basis, however, there were a number of reasons why a less optimistic assessment might have been made. As we have seen, similar duty-free access to the EEC market for the Yaoundé Associates had not resulted in a dramatic improvement of their trading position in the European market in comparison to that of other LDCs. Second, by the time that the first Lomé Convention was negotiated, the value of the tariff preferences accorded by duty-free access to the Community market had been eroded by the general reduction in international tariffs as a result of successive rounds of GATT negotiations and of the implementation and extension of the Community's Generalized System of Preferences (GSP). In addition, as chapter 4 has documented, the apparent liberalism of the Lomé trade regime is circumscribed by a number of significant restrictions, most notably the levies and quotas on products falling under the Community's Common Agricultural Policy (CAP), the rules of origin, and the provisions for safeguard action against imports of products regarded as "sensitive" by the Community.

This chapter is a substantially revised and updated version of a study conducted jointly with Dr. Joanna Moss, whose results were published in "Trade Developments Under the Lomé Convention," *World Development* (Oct. 1982), 10.(10): 841–856 and in "Trade Between the ACP and EEC During Lomé I," in Christopher Stevens, ed., *EEC and The Third World: A Survey 3. The Atlantic Rift* (London: Hodder and Stoughton, 1983), pp. 133–51. The research assistance of Ravi Thomas is gratefully acknowledged. The complete results of the data analysis of the original study, which covered the period 1970–79, are printed in Joanna Moss, *The Lomé Conventions and their Implications for the United States* (Boulder, Colo.: Westview Press, 1982), appendix C. Dr. Moss has asked me to record that, as a result of an editorial error, acknowledgment of the joint authorship of this study was inadvertently omitted from the first printing of her book.

A final reason why one would not have expected the Lomé Conventions to have a marked effect on trade relations between the Community and the ACP is that for many members of the latter grouping, the majority of the trade provisions represented merely a continuation of existing arrangements. Eighteen countries had enjoyed duty-free access to the preenlargement EEC by virtue of the Yaoundé Conventions; for them, the Lomé arrangements created new preferences only with respect to the three new Community member states. Similarly, Commonwealth countries had enjoyed duty-free access to their principal market, the United Kingdom, via the Commonwealth Preferences Scheme. In their case, the Convention provided new preferences in the markets of the original six member states plus Denmark and Ireland. Three Commonwealth countries—Kenya, Tanzania, and Uganda—however, had previously attained duty-free access to the Community market for their principal exports, albeit subject to quantitative restrictions, through the Arusha Convention. Only in the case of ACP countries that had not been colonies of one of the member states of the enlarged Community were new preferences created in the markets of to all nine countries. Some ACP countries may actually have experienced a deterioration of the conditions for access for their products as a result of Lomé: this would appear to be the case, for instance, for certain Commonwealth producers of agricultural products whose access to the British market was now restricted by virtue of the product's being covered by the Community's Common Agricultural Policy.

This chapter presents a detailed examination of the trade relationship between the ACP countries and the EEC during the years 1975–81.[2] In the first part, data on Community shares in the imports and exports of ACP states in the period 1975–81 are compared with data for the five years preceding the signature of the Convention. The second part of the chapter examines changes in the commodity composition of trade in the years since the initial Convention was signed.

In order to determine statistically significant changes in trading patterns between the EEC and the ACP, export and import data (derived from IMF sources) are transformed into market shares for each year in the period 1970–81. For example, in 1979, ACP exports to the world totaled $47.0 billion, of which $18.7 billion went to the EEC; thus, the EEC share in ACP exports was 40 percent. Each year's share is then ranked on a scale from 1 to 12, the lowest share being ranked as 1. Rankings are then aggregated in two groupings: for the years 1970–74, and 1975–81. A nonparametric test, the Wilcoxon-Mann-Whitney (W) test is employed to detect whether a statistically significant change in the average of the market shares occurred in the two sample periods. A nonparametric test is employed largely because the sample size is small. Appendix B provides a more detailed rationale for the test and an explanation of the procedures used. Again a null hypothesis (that no statistically significant change in market shares occurred), two alternative hypotheses are tested: that market shares increased and that market shares declined. An alternative hypothesis is accepted where there is a 95 percent certainty that market shares either increased or decreased.

If the Lomé provisions were to exert a major influence on the trading patterns, then one would expect, other things being equal, that the share of ACP exports going to the Community would increase in that ACP countries enjoyed a tariff advantage in that market over other developing country exporters of similar products, an advantage not available to them in other markets. And while the Convention does not demand "reverse" preferences on the part of the ACP, the provision that EEC countries receive at least most favored industrialized country status might be expected other things being equal, to lead to an increase in the Community's share in ACP imports.

Of course, other things are not always equal. In the 1970s considerable change occurred in the trading patterns between industrialized and developing countries. The oil price explosion and high rates of inflation in industrialized countries greatly increased the value of world trade as measured in current prices and changed long-established trading patterns. World trade grew at an annual rate of 29 percent in the period 1970–73 and then at an annual rate of 31 percent in the remainder of the decade. Whereas in the period 1970–73 the share of oil-exporting countries in world exports was 9 percent, in the period 1974–79 it averaged 14 percent.

Any study of the trade patterns of ACP countries during the years 1970–81 will thus inevitably be biased by structural changes in the world economy. The methodology employed in this study has a number of advantages in removing these biases. Examining market shares rather than the volume of exports/imports or the rate of growth of export/imports is advantageous in that the results are not biased by large percentage figures that in reality reflect only a small absolute increase over an even smaller base. (The EEC, for instance, is fond of citing growth figures for certain categories of ACP manufactures, which look impressive if not placed in the context of the small absolute quantities involved). By examining data for ACP exports and imports, it is also possible to "control" for changes in local circumstances. Since the principal items in ACP exports are primary products, whose production is very vulnerable to local natural and man-made disasters, it is likely that local circumstances rather than changes in demand in the industrialized countries in many cases will be the predominant factor in determining export values. Certainly, this was found to be the case for products covered by the Convention's STABEX scheme (see chapter 3). Changes in local circumstances, for instance, would not be expected, *ceteris paribus*, to affect the direction of exports.

This methodology also permits a comparision of the ACP performance with that of relevant "control" groups. Since oil is the predominant factor in aggregate ACP exports to the Community and plays a major role in the imports of non-oil ACP countries, the performance for ACP countries as a whole is compared with that of "non-oil" ACP states. Two other groups are used for comparison: in the case of EEC share in exports, data are presented for non-oil developing countries; and in the examination of EEC shares in ACP imports, results are recorded for another major ACP trading partner, the United States.

## SOME PRELIMINARIES

In the period 1970–81, the value (in current prices) of ACP exports to the world[3] and imports from the world increased by a factor of five. Exports expanded at an average annual rate of 50 percent and imports at 46 percent. In these years ACP countries consumed between 2.4 percent and 3.1 percent of total world exports (table 5.1) ACP shares of world exports peaked at 4.0 percent in 1974, in large part the result of oil price increases. ACP states' share in total world trade dropped, however, from 3.5 percent to 2.8 percent in the period 1970—81. This decline was most marked for the non oil-exporting countries. By 1979 only 1.5 percent of world exports came from the "non-oil" ACP countries compared with a peak of 2.3 percent in 1970. In contrast, other non-oil developing countries retained their share of total world exports over the decade; consequently, the share of non-oil ACP in the total exports of non-oil LDCs fell from 22 percent to 10 percent over the period 1970–1981.[4]

**TABLE 5.1.**
*ACP Share of World Trade (%)*

| | Exports | | | | Imports | | | |
|---|---|---|---|---|---|---|---|---|
| | *1970* | *1974* | *1978* | *1981* | *1970* | *1974* | *1978* | *1981* |
| ACP share of world trade | 3.9 | 4.0 | 3.3 | 3.0 | 3.1 | 2.7 | 3.0 | 2.7 |
| ACP share of LDC trade with world | 18 | 12 | 12 | 9 | 16 | 11 | 11 | 9 |
| Share of Non-OPEC ACP states in non-OPEC LDCs' trade with world | 22 | 18 | 15 | 10 | 16 | 12 | 9 | 7 |

Source: Eurostat, *EC-ACP Trade: A Statistical Analysis 1970–1981* (Luxembourg: Eurostat, 1983) pp. 29–30.

Results of any aggregate analysis of trade between the ACP and the EEC must be interpreted with some caution since they are predominantly determined by only a handful of countries. Nigeria alone accounts for more than one-quarter of ACP exports to the Community, and more than one-third of ACP imports from the EEC. The eight most important ACP exporters (Nigeria, Ivory Coast, Zaire, Cameroon, Kenya, Ghana, Zambia, and Gabon) provide nearly 70 percent of the Group's exports to the Community; the eight leading importers (Nigeria, Ivory Coast, Liberia, Sudan, Gabon, Kenya, Zaire, and Cameroon—in descending order of importance) together account for a similar percentage of ACP imports from the EEC. Looked at from another angle, more than 30 ACP countries together account for less than 1 percent of ACP-EEC trade. The twenty-four most important bilateral flows between EEC member states and ACP countries contribute more than 60 percent of total trade.[5]

A similar concentration is found in terms of the composition of ACP exports. The ten principal products (whose composition has varied in the period under examination, as will be detailed later in the study) together have accounted on average for close to 80 percent of ACP exports to the Community during the decade.

Finally, a few words in this section should be devoted to the trade balance between the Community and the ACP states. For both sides to the Conventions, the balance has been viewed as a barometer of the effec-

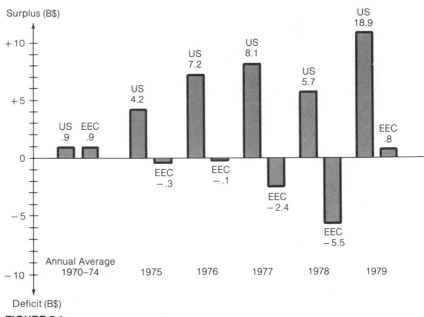

**FIGURE 5.1.**
ACP Trade Balance with the U.S. and the EEC ($ billions)

tiveness of the trade provisions. The Community has proudly proclaimed it has run a balance of trade deficit with the ACP for most of
the period of the first Convention. However, this is misleading in that
the Community naturally uses data that employ c.i.f. values for imports
from the ACP and f.o.b. values for Community exports. If we examine
the relationship from the ACP perspective, then we find (figure 5.1) that,
using c.i.f. values for ACP imports and f.o.b. values for ACP exports,
the ACP have run a deficit in their trade with the Community in all years
under the Convention except 1979. Transportation and insurance charges
are a sufficiently large component of import costs that both groupings
can be running a trade "deficit" at the same time. But even if the balance
of trade is not as favorable to the ACP as the Community has maintained, this is not necessarily to the former's disadvantage; e.g., the deficit may be covered by capital transfers from the EEC in the form of
foreign aid.

**TABLE 5.2.**

EEC Shares In ACP Exports

| | 1970–74 Average | 1975–81 Average | Statistically Significant |
|---|---|---|---|
| ACP | 45.6% | 39.8% | Decline |
| Non-oil ACP | 46.4 | 44.9 | No change |
| Yaoundé ACP | 62.8 | 52.5 | Decline |
| Non-oil Yaoundé ACP | 63.3 | 54.7 | Decline |
| Commonwealth ACP | 40.3 | 33.0 | Decline |
| Non-oil Commonwealth ACP | 37.9 | 37.6 | No change |
| PNA ACP* | 41.3 | 40.6 | No change |
| Developing countries (excluding oil exporters) | 25.4 | 21.9 | Decline |
| Major oil exporters (including Nigeria) | 43.9 | 31.2 | Decline |
| Latin America | 27.5 | 22.3 | Decline |

*ACP countries not previously enjoying preferential trading arrangements with one or more EEC member states.

## ACP EXPORTS TO THE EEC

Table 5.2 presents data on the EEC share in the exports of ACP countries and, for comparison, of subgroupings within the ACP and of other developing countries. This table shows that for most developing countries, the EEC was a less important market at the end of the decade than at the beginning. Despite the provisions of the Lomé Convention, the EEC share of all ACP exports also declined. A major reason was the expansion of ACP oil exports to other markets, especially the United States.[6] For non-oil ACP exporters, the Community maintained its market shares. In fact, the Community share of ACP nonpetroleum exports increased marginally over the decade, except for those countries previously associated with the preenlargement EEC. There was no significant change in the EEC share of exports of ACP countries that previously had no preferential access to any of the markets of the Nine; an increase might have been anticipated if the Lomé provisions had provided significant advantages to these countries *vis-à-vis* their position in third markets.

As previously noted, the apparent lack of impact of the Lomé provisions on aggregate ACP exports was expected, in that they did not represent a radical departure from existing trade relations for many of the

**TABLE 5.3.**
Share of the Original Six EEC States in ACP Exports

|  | 1970–74 Average | 1975–81 Average | Statistically Significant |
|---|---|---|---|
| ACP | 31.5% | 30.2% | No change |
| Non-oil ACP | 33.4 | 34.1 | No change |
| Commonwealth ACP | 21.2 | 23.6 | No change |
| Non-oil Commonwealth ACP | 17.1 | 19.2 | Increase |
| PNA ACP | 37.4 | 37.3 | No change |
| Yaoundé ACP | 58.2 | 48.4 | Decline |
| Non-oil Yaoundé ACP | 58.7 | 50.3 | Decline |
| Other non-oil LDCs | 18.0 | 16.7 | No change |

countries. To examine the effect of the *new* preferences created as a result of Lomé, it is necessary to move beyond a discussion of the share of the Nine taken as a group in the aggregate exports of the ACP.

In an attempt to isolate the effects on Commonwealth countries of the United Kingdom's entrance into the EEC, the trade relationship with the original six members of the Community was examined. Data on this are provided in table 5.3. For the Commonwealth as a whole, the share of the original six member states in their exports increased slightly but not sufficiently to be statistically significant. For non-oil Commonwealth countries, however, the share of the Six did increase significantly. It is impossible to say whether this occurred at the expense of previously associated African states, which lost their preferential margins over the newcomers, but it is of interest that the Six's share of the exports of both Yaoundé and non-oil Yaoundé groupings declined in a statistically significant manner.

Table 5.4 isolates the U.K. share in ACP exports in order to examine the trading relationship between ACP countries that had previously not enjoyed Commonwealth preferences and the United Kingdom. For the ACP as a whole, and for the non-oil ACP Group, Britain's share of their total exports declined in a statistically significant manner. The discrepancies between the market shares of the two groups can be explained largely by Britain's transition from being an oil importer to being self-sufficient. This has had a particularly marked effect on its share in Commonwealth exports (largely because of the decline in Nigerian oil exports to Britain). For the beneficiaries of new preferences in the British mar-

**TABLE 5.4.**

U.K. Share in ACP Exports

|  | 1970–74 Average | 1975–81 Average | Statistically Significant |
|---|---|---|---|
| ACP | 13.5% | 7.4% | Decline |
| Non-oil ACP | 12.6 | 10.3 | Decline |
| Commonwealth ACP | 18.3 | 8.9 | Decline |
| Non-oil Commonwealth ACP | 20.0 | 17.8 | Decline |
| PNA ACP | 3.7 | 2.8 | Decline |
| Yaoundé ACP | 4.4 | 3.8 | No change |
| Non-oil Yaoundé ACP | 4.4 | 3.9 | Decline |
| Other non-oil LDCs | 7.2 | 4.6 | Decline |

ket, the previously nonassociated states and the Yaoundé Group, the record was mixed. New preferences did not prevent a statistically significant decline in the share of Britain in the exports of the previously nonassociates, while Britain's share in the exports of the Yaoundé Group registered no statistically significant change. The continuing relative decline of the British economy was evident in the evolving pattern of relations. Whereas there was no statistically significant change in Britain's share of exports from the non-oil Commonwealth and non-oil Yaoundé Groups in the period 1975–79, a significant decline was recorded for both groups for the period 1975–81.

Denmark and Ireland were the only countries in the EEC, before the accession of Greece, that had no special trading relationships with any ACP state before the signature of the Lomé Convention. Because of this it is interesting to examine the changes that have occurred in their trade with the ACP since the implementation of the Convention, even though the volumes involved are small. New preferences in the Danish and Irish markets might have been expected to lead to an increase in their share of ACP exports. This proved to be the case for the non-oil ACP and for both the Yaoundé and non-oil Yaoundé Groups (table 5.5). In contrast to the other EEC countries, the Danish and Irish share declined for only one ACP Grouping.

Table 5.6 provides a summary of the changes in market shares for EEC member states and for the United States. Its most striking feature is the increasing importance of the United States as a market for the ACP in the years under consideration. Not all of this can be explained by ACP

**TABLE 5.5.**

Danish and Irish Shares in ACP Exports

|  | *1970–74 Average* | *1975–81 Average* | *Statistically Significant* |
|---|---|---|---|
| ACP | 0.6% | 0.5% | No change |
| Non-oil ACP | 0.4 | 0.6 | Increase |
| Commonwealth ACP | 0.8 | 0.6 | Decline |
| Non-oil Commonwealth ACP | 0.7 | 0.7 | No change |
| PNA ACP | 0.2 | 0.4 | Increase |
| Yaoundé ACP | 0.2 | 0.4 | Increase |
| Non-oil Yaoundé ACP | 0.2 | 0.5 | Increase |
| Other non-oil LDCs | 0.6 | 0.6 | No change |

oil exports, since the United States also consumed an increasing share of non-oil Commonwealth exports. In that the ACP as a group, or individually, do not receive preferences vis-à-vis other developing countries in the U.S. market (although most ACP states are beneficiaries of the U.S. GSP Scheme), while doing so with respect to the EEC market via the Lomé Convention, this result is contrary to expectations.

Within the EEC itself, it does appear that the Convention has had a positive impact on the trading relationships between countries that had previously not been linked in preferential agreements. In reading across table 5.6, one finds that the share of the Six in Commonwealth ACP exports registered no change, whereas for Britain there was a decline; and

**TABLE 5.6.**

Comparison of Changes in EEC Shares of ACP Exports

|  | *EEC9* | *EEC6* | *U.K.* | *DK & IR*** | *U.S.* |
|---|---|---|---|---|---|
| ACP | Decline | No chg. | Decline | No chg.* | Increase |
| Non-oil ACP | No chg. | No chg. | Decline | Increase* | No chg. |
| Commonwealth ACP | Decline | No chg.* | Decline | Decline* | Increase |
| Non-oil Commonwealth ACP | No chg. | Increase* | Decline | No chg.* | Increase |
| PNA ACP | No chg.* | No chg.* | Decline* | Increase* | No chg. |
| Yaoundé ACP | Decline | Decline | No chg.* | Increase* | Increase |
| Non-oil Yaoundé | Decline | Decline | Decline* | Increase* | No chg. |
| Other non-oil LDCs | Decline | No chg. | Decline | No chg. | No chg. |

*Denotes relationships where Lomé created new trade preferences for the entire subgrouping.
**DK: Denmark; IR: Ireland.

**TABLE 5.7.**
EEC Member States' Shares in ACP Exports to the
Community

|  | 1970 | 1975 | 1981 |
|---|---|---|---|
| Belgium/Luxembourg | 10.4% | 6.8% | 10.3% |
| Denmark | 0.7 | 1.4 | 1.4 |
| France | 19.6 | 24.4 | 24.9 |
| Germany | 13.3 | 14.7 | 20.7 |
| Ireland | 0.2 | 0.3 | 0.4 |
| Italy | 10.6 | 8.0 | 14.0 |
| Netherlands | 12.8 | 16.1 | 15.4 |
| U.K. | 32.4 | 28.3 | 12.8 |
| Hirschman index of concentration | 44.7 | 44.5 | 41.9 |

for the Yaoundé Group, there was an increase or no change in the shares
of the new member states in their exports, in comparison with the decline in that of the Six. Statistically significant increases in EEC shares
of ACP exports occurred only in those relationships where Lomé created
new preferences. This points to a diversification of ACP trading partners
within the Six, a development that certainly would be perceived by most
ACP states as a positive result of the Convention. Table 5.7 presents data
on the shares of individual EEC member states in ACP exports to the
EEC. The most prominent feature is the marked decline in the U.K. share:
from being the leading European importer of ACP products, the U.K.
fell to fifth position, behind France, Germany, the Netherlands, and even
Italy. Diversification within the EEC market is reflected in a decline in
the concentration of trading partners, measured by a Hirschman index.[7]

## EEC SHARES IN ACP IMPORTS

The terms of the trade chapter of the Lomé Convention itself provide no
grounds to lead one to predict that its implementation would result in an
increase in the share of the Community in ACP imports. ACP states are
not required to offer reciprocal trade preferences. Their only obligation
under the Convention is to provide the member states with treatment
equally favorable to that offered to the most favored industrialized trading partner. Since for many ACP states this was already an EEC mem-

**TABLE 5.8.**
EEC Shares in ACP Imports

|  | 1970–74 Average | 1975–81 Average | Statistically Significant |
|---|---|---|---|
| ACP | 41.9% | 41.5% | No change |
| Non-oil ACP | 42.4 | 40.3 | No change |
| Commonwealth ACP | 34.1 | 36.5 | No change |
| Non-oil Commonwealth ACP | 31.7 | 28.8 | Decline |
| PNA ACP | 37.8 | 40.3 | No change |
| Yaoundé ACP | 63.9 | 57.3 | Decline |
| Non-oil Yaoundé ACP | 62.6 | 55.5 | Decline |
| Developing countries (excluding major oil exporters) | 25.6 | 22.1 | Decline |
| Major oil exporters | 40.4 | 40.1 | No change |
| Latin America | 23.8 | 17.9 | Decline |

ber, the only significant change that might have been anticipated would have been a multilateralization of treatment among the member states; e.g., Commonwealth countries would be obliged to give as favorable treatment to imports from Denmark, Ireland, and the Six as they accorded to imports from the United Kingdom. In that oil-importing ACP states faced a dramatic increase in the costs of their energy imports in the period since 1973, it would be anticipated that the share of energy in their total imports would rise and that, consequently, the share of EEC member states would fall (except where ACP states imported refined pe-

**TABLE 5.9.**
Share of the Original Six EEC States in ACP Imports

|  | 1970–74 Average | 1975–81 Average | Statistically Significant |
|---|---|---|---|
| ACP | 27.3 | 28.8 | No change |
| Non-oil ACP | 29.5 | 30.1 | No change |
| Commonwealth ACP | 15.2 | 20.7 | Increase |
| Non-oil Commonwealth ACP | 13.7 | 14.0 | No change |
| PNA ACP | 25.3 | 27.9 | No change |
| Yaoundé ACP | 59.8 | 53.3 | Decline |
| Non-oil Yaoundé ACP | 58.4 | 52.2 | Decline |
| Other non-oil LDCs | 18.0 | 16.7 | Decline |

**TABLE 5.10.**

U.K. Share in ACP Exports

|  | *1970–74 Average* | *1975–81 Average* | *Statistically Significant* |
|---|---|---|---|
| ACP | 13.9% | 11.9% | No change |
| Non-oil ACP | 12.2 | 9.5 | Decline |
| Commonwealth ACP | 18.3 | 15.0 | No change |
| Non-oil Commonwealth ACP | 17.4 | 14.0 | Decline |
| PNA ACP | 11.7 | 11.0 | No change |
| Yaoundé ACP | 3.7 | 3.6 | No change |
| Non-oil Yaoundé ACP | 3.9 | 3.8 | No change |
| Other non-oil LDCs | 7.0 | 4.8 | Decline |

troleum from the EEC). If the Community maintained its share in the total imports of ACP member states, then this alone might be considered to be a favorable performance.

Tables 5.8 through 5.11 present data on the share of the Community as a whole and its member states in total ACP imports. Contrary to expectations, the share of the Community as a whole in the imports of all ACP states registered no change over the period. Until 1979, in fact, as the Moss and Ravenhill study shows, the Community maintained its market share in all ACP groupings. After 1979, however, as the effects of the second round of major increases in oil prices had a devastating effect on the economies of oil-importing developing countries, the share of the EEC in the markets of the non-oil Commonwealth and non-oil Yaoundé

**TABLE 5.11.**

Danish and Irish Shares in ACP Imports

|  | *1970–74 Average* | *1975–81 Average* | *Statistically Significant* |
|---|---|---|---|
| ACP | 0.6% | 0.8% | Increase |
| Non-oil ACP | 0.6 | 0.7 | No change |
| Commonwealth ACP | 0.7 | 0.8 | Increase |
| Non-oil Commonwealth ACP | 0.6 | 0.7 | No change |
| PNA ACP | 0.9 | 1.4 | No change |
| Yaoundé ACP | 0.4 | 0.4 | No change |
| Non-oil Yaoundé | 0.4 | 0.4 | No change |
| Other non-oil LDCs | 0.6 | 0.5 | Decline |

groupings, as well as that of the whole Yaoundé group (where only Gabon is a significant oil exporter), declined in a statistically significant manner. Similar declines were experienced in the EEC share of the markets of other oil-importing developing countries.

For the various subgroupings of EEC member states, there were only two statistically significant declines: in the share of the original Six in the imports of the two Yaoundé Groups and in the share of the United Kingdom in the imports of non-oil ACP states and of the non-oil Commonwealth. The data for the original Six member states appear to confirm the prediction that the Convention would lead to a diversification of sources within the Six as a result of the multilateralization of most favored nation treatment. The Six increased their share of the total imports of Commonwealth countries in a statistically significant amount, yet in those countries to which they had been linked via the Yaoundé Conventions, their share of total imports declined in a statistically significant manner (table 5.9). Denmark and Ireland, previously having received no preferential treatment from ACP states, registered either an increase or no change in their share of the total imports of the ACP as a whole and the subgroupings in contrast to their declining share of the markets of other non-oil LDCs (table 5.11).

Table 5.12 provides a summary of the changes. Statistically significant increases in EEC shares of ACP total imports occurred only in relationships where, prior to Lomé, there had been no special economic ties between the ACP subgrouping and the relevant EEC member states. But

**TABLE 5.12.**

Comparison of Changes in EEC Shares of ACP Imports

|  | EEC9 | EEC6 | U.K. | DK & IR** | U.S. |
|---|---|---|---|---|---|
| ACP | No chg. | No chg. | No chg. | Increase* | Decline |
| Non-oil ACP | No chg. | No chg. | Decline | No chg.* | No chg. |
| Commonwealth ACP | No chg. | Increase* | No chg. | Increase* | Decline |
| Non-oil Commonwealth ACP | Decline | No chg.* | Decline | No chg.* | No chg. |
| PNA ACP | No chg.* | No chg.* | No chg.* | No chg.* | No chg. |
| Yaoundé ACP | Decline | Decline | No chg.* | No chg.* | No chg. |
| Non-oil Yaoundé | Decline | Decline | No chg.* | No chg.* | No chg. |
| Other non-oil LDCs | Decline | Decline | Decline | Decline | Decline |

*Denotes relationships where Lomé created new trade preferences for the entire sub-grouping.
**DK: Denmark; IR: Ireland.

perhaps the most marked difference between this table and that which examined changes in the EEC share of ACP exports is the poor performance of the United States. For none of the ACP subgroupings did the United States register a statistically significant increase in its share of imports. In comparison to the U.S. performance, the results of trade during the first Convention would appear to be remarkably favorable to the EEC, especially in the context of ACP states' facing increasing costs for imported energy.

A number of factors can be cited that might account for this relatively favorable EEC performance. Among those not specifically related to the Convention are traditional trading links, including membership in currency areas (especially the franc zone), and the presence in ACP states of EEC commercial firms, shipping lines, etc.; language ties; geographical proximity; and the tying of bilateral European aid to purchases from the member states. In addition, there are factors specific to the Convention itself, such as the rules of origin, which encourage ACP countries to purchase inputs from Community suppliers; the most favored industrialized nation treatment, which ACP countries are obliged to extend to the Community; the tying of EDF aid; and the possibility that the Convention might have created a "climate" favorable to the expansion of EEC exports to the ACP.

Some diversification of sources of imports from the Community did occur during the period 1970–75 but very little during the implementation of the Lomé Conventions. In these years it was not so much a matter of a reduction of concentration in trading partners but of France replacing the U.K. as the dominant source of imports from the Community (table 5.13). France was remarkably successful over the decade in penetrating new markets in ACP countries; by 1980 Nigeria had overtaken the Ivory Coast as France's principal ACP customer, accounting for more than 20 percent of total French sales to the Group.[8]

A Hirschman index of partner concentration registers only a very small decline during the lifetime of the Convention. Trade with Community member states continues to be less diversified in imports than exports. The marked decline in the EEC share of total ACP exports is not reflected in its share of ACP imports. For ACP imports from all sources, the EEC share fell from 44.2 percent in 1970, to 39.1 percent in 1975 but rose to 40.2 percent by 1979. Over the decade the U.S. share fell from 15.8 percent to 9.4 percent; that of the rest of the world rose from 40.0 percent to 50.3 percent, which can be attributed to the growth in

**TABLE 5.13.**
EEC Member States' Shares in ACP Imports from the
Community

|                         | *1970* | *1975* | *1981* |
|-------------------------|--------|--------|--------|
| Belgium/Luxembourg      | 6.7%   | 5.8%   | 5.7%   |
| Denmark                 | 1.3    | 1.4    | 1.8    |
| France                  | 25.1   | 27.8   | 29.3   |
| Germany                 | 15.8   | 18.6   | 18.3   |
| Ireland                 | 0.3    | 0.3    | 0.7    |
| Italy                   | 8.5    | 9.1    | 9.1    |
| Netherlands             | 7.0    | 6.7    | 7.2    |
| U.K.                    | 35.5   | 30.3   | 27.9   |
| Hirshman index of concentration | 48.0 | 46.9 | 46.3 |

the value of oil imports. In the period 1970–1980, the EEC share in industrialized countries' exports to the ACP rose from 50 percent to 61
percent.[9] Despite the absence of requirements of reciprocity in the Convention, the Community has been far more successful in maintaining its
share of ACP markets than have the ACP in their exports to the Community.

**ACP SHARE OF THE EEC MARKET**

An alternative approach to evaluating the impact of the Convention on
ACP–EEC trade is to examine the ACP share of the European market.
Whereas the analysis in the first part of this chapter has the advantage of
"controlling" for changes in supply conditions, this second method "controls" for changes in market conditions that affect all potential suppliers.
While the decrease in the Community's share of their exports noted above
might have been perceived as desirable by the ACP Group in that it represented market diversification, this trend would be welcomed only if it
was accompanied by maintenance of their share in the European market.
Indeed, as chapter 1 noted, one of the fundamental objectives of the ACP
in their strategy of collective clientelism was to obtain a guarantee that
their primary products would at least maintain their share of European
imports.

In general, this has not been the case. Table 5.14 shows that the ACP

**TABLE 5.14.**

Developing Countries' Shares in EEC Imports 1970–1981 (%)

| Grouping | 1970 | 1971 | 1972 | 1973 | 1974 | 1975 | 1976 | 1977 | 1978 | 1979 | 1980 | 1981 |
|---|---|---|---|---|---|---|---|---|---|---|---|---|
| ACP | 7.8 | 7.2 | 7.3 | 7.2 | 8.0 | 7.2 | 6.7 | 7.3 | 6.8 | 7.0 | 7.1 | 5.6 |
| Non-oil-exporting ACP | 6.1 | 4.9 | 4.9 | 5.0 | 4.5 | 4.4 | 4.2 | 4.9 | 4.5 | 4.1 | 3.7 | 3.2 |
| LDCs | 36.0 | 36.9 | 36.7 | 37.5 | 47.1 | 44.6 | 44.5 | 44.1 | 40.6 | 41.4 | 42.9 | 42.9 |
| Non-OPEC LDCs | 20.9 | 19.2 | 18.9 | 19.5 | 17.4 | 17.7 | 18.0 | 19.5 | 19.1 | 19.0 | 18.2 | 18.2 |
| Non-ACP Non-OPEC LDCs | 14.4 | 14.0 | 13.6 | 14.0 | 12.3 | 12.9 | 13.3 | 14.2 | 14.2 | 14.5 | 13.9 | 14.5 |
| ACP Share of EEC Imports from LDCs | 21.8 | 19.5 | 19.9 | 19.2 | 17.1 | 16.1 | 15.1 | 16.6 | 16.8 | 16.8 | 16.6 | 13.0 |
| Non-oil-exporting ACP share of EEC Imports from non-OPEC LDCs | 29.1 | 25.3 | 25.9 | 25.7 | 25.7 | 24.8 | 23.6 | 25.2 | 23.7 | 21.3 | 20.3 | 17.3 |

Source: Calculated from data in Eurostat, *EC-ACP Trade: A Statistical Analysis* (Luxembourg: Eurostat, 1983) p. 127.

share of total EEC imports fell dramatically during the 1970s despite the preferential access provided by Lomé. This aggregate figure might be misleading, however, owing to the increases in the price of EEC imports of oil and manufactured goods during this period. More relevant is a comparison of the performance of ACP countries with that of other developing countries, particularly non-oil exporters. Even on this comparison, the ACP fared badly. Their share of Community imports from LDCs dropped precipitously. An even sharper decline occurred in the share of non-oil ACP in EEC imports from all nonmajor oil-exporting LDCs. The decline in the ACP share of the European market clearly cannot be simply attributed to the rise in petroleum imports from extra-ACP sources. Non-oil ACP countries have not kept pace with the exports from other non-oil developing countries. As table 5.15 shows, the ACP performance in EEC markets over the period 1970–81 was markedly inferior to that of other developing countries: the ACP countries alone suffered a statistically significant decline in their share of the European market.

In aggregate, the ACP fared better in the U.S. market than in that of the EEC, more than doubling their share from 3.2 percent in 1970 to 7.1 percent in 1979. In Japan, however, their market share dropped from 3.4 percent to 1.8 percent in the same period; in other industrialized countries a similar fall in market share was recorded (from 1.6 percent to 1.0 percent).[10] These figures attest to the need for extreme caution in interpreting aggregate data: the increase in the ACP share of the U.S. market

TABLE 5.15.
Changes in Developing Countries' Shares of EEC Imports

|  | *1970–1974 Average (%)* | *1975–1981 Average (%)* | *Stat. Sign. Change* |
|---|---|---|---|
| Developing countries | 40.3 | 42.8 | Increase |
| Non-OPEC LDCs* | 18.8 | 18.5 | No change |
| Non-ACP Non-OPEC LDCs | 13.4 | 14.0 | No change |
| ACP | 7.6 | 6.8 | Decline |
| Non-oil-exporting ACP | 4.9 | 4.0 | Decline |
| ACP share of EEC Imports from LDCs | 18.8 | 15.8 | Decline |
| Non-oil-exporting ACP share in EEC Imports from non-OPEC LDCs | 26.2 | 21.7 | Decline |

was solely the result of increased petroleum exports. The single most important reason why the EEC share in total ACP exports fell over the decade is simply that the EEC imported a smaller share of ACP petroleum exports than of their other principal exports.

Since trade flows can be distorted by changes in a single important commodity, aggregate data can be misleading. More definitive conclusions regarding the effects of Lomé can be drawn if aggregate analysis is supplemented by a review of changes in ACP exports to the Community of those commodities in which the ACP have a particular interest. Table 5.16 presents data for the period 1973–1982 on the ACP share in EEC imports of the 25 most significant (mean 1977–1980) ACP commodities exported to the Community. A striking feature of this table is the last column, which shows the Common External Tariff rates for these commodities as of 1/1/80. Only 7 of the 25 most important ACP exports enjoyed any tariff advantage whatsoever over imports from third countries, and for four of these, the advantage was reduced since the product was included in the Community's GSP. Consequently, one would not expect the tariff preferences accorded by the Convention to have a great effect on ACP exports of these commodities (although other provisions of the Convention favorable to the ACP, such as the STABEX scheme, might influence them).

These commodities may conveniently be divided into three categories: those in which the ACP states experienced a sustained increase in their market shares after the implementation of the Lomé arrangements; those where the ACP share registered a sustained loss; and those where the ACP share fluctuated around the mean with no obvious movement in one direction or another. In only five commodities—bananas, tea, aluminum ore, sugar, and tobacco—were ACP exporters successful in sustaining an increased share of the European market. For three of these products— bananas, sugar, and tobacco—ACP exporters enjoyed tariff advantages over third parties. Sugar and tobacco are both subject to variable levies under the Common Agricultural Policy. The increasing ACP share in European tobacco imports can be attributed in large part to the accession of Zimbabwe to the Convention. Probably more important than tariff advantages for the success of ACP exports of bananas and sugar were the special regimes for their import established by the Convention. These regimes are the subject of the following chapter.

In seven other commodities—refined copper, blister copper, iron ore,

**TABLE 5.16.**
ACP Percentage Share in Total EEC Imports of the 25 Most Valuable ACP Exports 1973–1982

| | 1973 | 1974 | 1975 | 1976 | 1977 | 1978 | 1979 | 1980 | 1981 | 1982 | Product Share* | CET 1/1/80 |
|---|---|---|---|---|---|---|---|---|---|---|---|---|
| Crude petroleum | 7.0 | 10.4 | 8.8 | 7.4 | 7.6 | 8.1 | 10.7 | 12.1 | 7.9 | 9.6 | 33.8 | 0 |
| Coffee | 31.7 | 37.8 | 36.2 | 42.0 | 44.7 | 39.6 | 38.6 | 38.4 | 33.9 | 35.4 | 10.4 | 5 A |
| Cocoa beans | 92.0 | 85.8 | 87.5 | 91.1 | 85.5 | 90.7 | 88.3 | 87.0 | 89.7 | 90.9 | 9.1 | 3 |
| Refined copper | 42.0 | 44.4 | 40.9 | 38.3 | 39.8 | 31.5 | 32.7 | 32.4 | 30.5 | 32.3 | 4.5 | 0 |
| Non-coniferous wood | 75.7 | 74.3 | 75.4 | 70.0 | 70.9 | 72.2 | 72.9 | 73.9 | 73.8 | 73.3 | 4.5 | 0 |
| Petroleum derivatives | N.A. | N.A. | 3.5 | 6.0 | 7.6 | 9.3 | 8.4 | 8.5 | 4.7 | 4.1 | 3.9 | 0 |
| Sugar | N.A. | 36.0 | 49.3 | 59.3 | 67.1 | 72.5 | 71.2 | 75.0 | 83.4 | 89.5 | 2.8 | L |
| Iron ore | 21.5 | 21.1 | 19.4 | 17.8 | 19.7 | 18.0 | 16.9 | 17.2 | 18.1 | 17.5 | 2.4 | 0 |
| Cotton | 19.2 | 18.4 | 18.2 | 17.6 | 22.9 | 18.5 | 22.4 | 18.8 | 22.3 | 17.2 | 1.2 | 0 |
| Blister copper | 43.0 | 45.0 | 37.1 | 40.0 | 42.2 | 40.3 | 43.4 | 32.5 | 38.9 | 35.0 | 1.2 | 0 |
| Tea | N.A. | 24.7 | 25.9 | 27.0 | 33.8 | 41.6 | 39.1 | 33.9 | 36.4 | 35.6 | 1.1 | 0 B |
| Aluminum oxide | N.A. | 70.0 | 70.6 | 55.2 | 53.1 | 65.2 | 79.3 | 70.1 | 69.3 | 67.9 | 1.0 | 5.5 D |
| Aluminum ore | 33.6 | 39.0 | 46.1 | 58.8 | 59.1 | 61.6 | 54.5 | 50.8 | 57.9 | 48.9 | 0.84 | 0 |
| Groundnut oil | 60.2 | 61.9 | 83.7 | 80.0 | 79.9 | 53.4 | 53.0 | 36.2 | 25.3 | 59.3 | 0.82 | 10 C |
| Fresh bananas | 18.7 | 18.5 | 19.7 | 19.0 | 19.4 | 19.0 | 20.0 | 21.5 | 20.8 | 21.4 | 0.82 | 20 E |
| Wood simply worked | N.A. | 2.7 | 3.7 | 3.4 | 3.0 | 3.3 | 2.9 | 3.0 | 2.9 | 2.8 | 0.80 | 0 |

| | | | | | | | | | | | 23 LF |
| --- | --- | --- | --- | --- | --- | --- | --- | --- | --- | --- | --- |
| | | | | | | | | | | | 0 G |
| Raw tobacco | 6.9 | 7.6 | 8.6 | 8.9 | 8.4 | 11.2 | 8.7 | 12.6 | 18.4 | 17.5 | 0.74 |
| Thorium and uranium ores | 96.9 | 95.6 | 97.7 | 98.7 | 96.2 | 82.5 | 95.7 | 1.1 | 0.5 | 2.1 | 0.71 |
| Diamonds | N.A. | 15.8 | 12.9 | 4.4 | 4.8 | 7.1 | 3.1 | 2.8 | 5.8 | 9.4 | 0.65 |
| Copper ore | 46.3 | 31.4 | 58.7 | 51.1 | 46.6 | 46.3 | 45.0 | 45.5 | 50.7 | 53.8 | 0.63 |
| Calcium phosphate | 21.7 | 24.9 | 19.8 | 18.0 | 19.1 | 19.4 | 19.9 | 16.4 | 14.5 | 15.6 | 0.61 |
| Raw skins | N.A. | 14.6 | 13.0 | 11.0 | 10.5 | 11.4 | 11.4 | 13.7 | 13.1 | 13.0 | 0.49 |
| Natural rubber | 12.3 | 12.1 | 12.6 | 11.6 | 10.9 | 11.4 | 11.3 | 9.8 | 11.4 | 12.8 | 0.48 |
| Groundnut cake | N.A. | 58.4 | 67.3 | 48.5 | 43.9 | 42.4 | 34.7 | 37.1 | 35.4 | 63.1 | 0.40 |
| Groundnuts | N.A. | 46.2 | 50.9 | 56.9 | 41.6 | 27.1 | 9.5 | 9.2 | 11.3 | 16.6 | 0.36 |

Sources: Data on ACP shares in EEC imports of products from Commission des Communautés Européenes, *Evolution des échanges commerciaux entre le Communauté et les états A.C.P.* [VIII/378/78-F] (3 Avril 1978); and *Importations CEE des principaux produits en provenance des états ACP* [VIII/842/83] (Août 1983). CET rates from "Preferential Tariff Treatment Applied by the Community (Position as on 1 January 1980)," *Official Journal of the European Communities* (10 April 1980) 23:C88. GSP rates from Commission of the European Communities, *The European Communities Generalized Tariff Preferences Scheme for 1980* [COM(79) 348 final] (12 July 1979).

*Product share in total EEC imports from ACP; average 1977–1980.

A: GSP rate for coffee is 0 for designated "least developed" beneficiaries.

B: If packaged in containers of more than 3 kilograms. Tea packaged in containers of less than 3 kilograms is subject to a CET rate of 5 percent; the GSP rate is 0.

C: GSP rate for palm oil (a competitive substitute) is 7 percent.

D: GSP rate for aluminum oxide is 0.

E: An annual quota of bananas enjoying exemption from the CET is negotiated each year for Germany.

F: GSP rate for tobacco is 6 percent plus reduced levy.

G: The apparently dramatic drop in the ACP share of EEC imports of thorium and uranium ores in 1980 was the result of a reclassification of Gabon's and Niger's exports as "uranium and its compounds."

L: Product subject to CAP variable levies.

N.A.: Not available

diamonds, calcium phosphate, groundnuts, and groundnut cake—ACP exporters experienced a deterioration in their share of extra-EEC imports. None of these products enjoyed a tariff preference. The experience with the groundnut products illustrates the caution with which all these figures must be interpreted, given the predominance of primary products in ACP exports. A succession of poor harvests in West Africa caused a marked decline in total ACP groundnut exports—the index of quantity (1975 = 100) had fallen to 16.9 by 1979.

Table 5.16 reinforces the findings of the aggregate study that the results of the Convention in the trade sphere have been extremely disappointing for the ACP Group. One of their principal objectives in embarking on the strategy of collective clientelism was to at least maintain, or preferably increase, their share of the European market for their principal commodity exports. Declining shares of the EEC market of course might have been caused by factors entirely extraneous to the Convention—as was the case with groundnuts. Nevertheless, what is important here were the perceptions of the ACP Group—and there is no doubt that the trade results convinced them that the Community was making insufficient effort to live up to its obligations as patron in the Lomé relationship.

Table 5.17 presents data on changes in the commodity composition of ACP exports for 1975 and 1982. Petroleum is, of course, the single most important ACP export, its share of total ACP exports since the signature of the Convention never falling below 25 percent. The share of oil derivatives in total ACP exports tripled in the period, a result of increases in both the quantity exported and the unit value (in 1979, quantity = 257.3, unit value = 206.3, base 100 in 1975). Exports of aluminum oxide rose by 81.5 percent in quantity and 20.7 percent in unit value over the period. One new ACP export merits particular attention—natural uranium and its composites. It was not until 1977 that the EEC recorded any imports of this commodity from the ACP, but since then the quantity involved more than quadrupled; by 1980 it had become one of the ten most valuable ACP exports and contributed 1.5 percent of total ACP export earnings.

Data in table 5.17 suggest that the Lomé arrangements have also not enabled the ACP to realize another of their objectives in pursuing a strategy of collective clientelism: a diversification in the composition of their exports. A Hirschman index was constructed in order to measure the

**TABLE 5.17.**

Shares of the 25 Most Important Commodities in ACP Exports to the EEC 1975 and 1982 (Values in Thousand UA)

| 1975 | Value 000 EUA | Share % | 1982 | Value 000 EUA | Share* % |
|---|---|---|---|---|---|
| 1. Petroleum | 2,890,012 | 33.17 | 1. Petroleum | 7,369,943 | 37.31 |
| 2. Cocoa | 599,888 | 6.88 | 2. Coffee | 1,394,046 | 8.14 |
| 3. Refined copper | 582,468 | 6.68 | 3. Cocoa | 1,164,489 | 7.76 |
| 4. Sugar | 488,303 | 5.60 | 4. Oil derivatives | 723,955 | 4.15 |
| 5. Coffee | 479,941 | 5.50 | 5. Refined copper | 680,364 | 4.04 |
| 6. Iron ore | 327,251 | 3.75 | 6. Sugar | 554,066 | 2.89 |
| 7. Wood | 300,914 | 3.45 | 7. Wood | 502,045 | 3.26 |
| 8. Blister copper | 148,104 | 1.70 | 8. Iron ore | 461,338 | 2.44 |
| 9. Calcium phosphates | 122,496 | 1.40 | 9. Uranium and compounds | 305,758 | 1.46 |
| 10. Groundnut oil | 121,800 | 1.39 | 10. Diamonds | 256,905 | 0.95 |
| 11. Oil derivatives | 118,390 | 1.35 | 11. Tobacco | 246,307 | 1.04 |
| 12. Cotton | 116,981 | 1.34 | 12. Blister copper | 212,504 | 1.21 |
| 13. Groundnuts | 103,065 | 1.18 | 13. Cotton | 181,228 | 1.10 |
| 14. Bananas | 95,461 | 1.10 | 14. Bananas | 178,746 | 0.89 |
| 15. Copper ore | 94,710 | 1.08 | 15. Tea | 171,489 | 0.96 |
| 16. Palm oil | 86,984 | 0.99 | 16. Aluminum oxide | 168,027 | 1.04 |
| 17. Tobacco | 74,547 | 0.85 | 17. Copper ore | 152,670 | 0.72 |
| 18. Tea | 73,560 | 0.84 | 18. Aluminum ore | 144,373 | 0.86 |
| 19. Sawn wood | 68,261 | 0.78 | 19. Sawn wood | 114,466 | 0.74 |
| 20. Aluminum ore | 64,138 | 0.73 | 20. Canned tuna | 109,432 | 0.50 |
| 21. Aluminum oxide | 62,260 | 0.71 | 21. Calcium phosphates | 108,503 | 0.59 |
| 22. Raw skins | 56,333 | 0.64 | 22. Aluminum | 107,888 | 0.49 |
| 23. Thorium, uranium ores | 52,831 | 0.60 | 23. Groundnut oil | 97,531 | 0.56 |
| 24. Groundnut cake | 49,125 | 0.56 | 24. Clothing | 89,412 | 0.46 |
| 25. Manganese ore | 43,663 | 0.50 | 25. Palm oil | 85,717 | 0.39 |
| Cumulative Percentage | | 82.77% | Cumulative Percentage | | 83.95% |

*mean for the years 1978–1982
Sources: Same as for table 5.16.

commodity concentration of ACP exports to the EEC in the period 1975–
82. Rather than a diminution in the reliance on a few commodities occurring, as ACP states would have desired, the index in fact showed a
greater concentration for the years 1978–82 than for 1975 (mean 39.87
for the years 1978–82 compared with 36.05 in 1975). Again this is primarily a reflection of the rise in the share of petroleum in ACP exports
over this period. (The index reached a peak of 45.25 in 1980 after the oil
price rise of the preceding year.)

Given the magnitude of petroleum in total ACP exports, changes at
the margin may bᴜ obscured. Table 5.17 shows, for instance, that clothing and canned tuna by 1982 had become among the 25 most important
ACP exports. Further disaggregation of the data is necessary in order to
assess the importance of changes at the margin. Table 5.18 presents data
on all manufactured products that constituted at least 0.05 percent of total ACP exports to the EEC during the first Convention. Since the ACP
Group has been particularly concerned with its performance relative to
that of other exporters, the table also includes data on the share of the
ACP in European imports of these products. Increasing the share of
manufactures in their exports is regarded by the ACP as the best hope
for achieving greater stabilization and an eventual increase in their export
earnings. There is little encouragement from the aggregate performance
during the early Lomé period. Although ACP exports of "manufactures"
increased by 106 percent in value over the five years of the Convention,
more than 55 percent of this figure was accounted for by natural uranium and its composites, which the EEC classifies as a "manufactured"
product. A further 21 percent of the increase was derived from aluminum oxide. Besides these two products, only in the case of ropes and
cords was a substantial increase in market share experienced during the
first Convention but this fell back dramatically in 1981 and 1982. Although the value of ACP exports of clothing and leather rose rapidly, the
exports of other countries kept pace—with the result that there was no
significant change in the ACP share of the European market. In veneers,
plywood, vegetable alkaloids, and "other chemicals", the ACP suffered a
substantial loss of their market share.

Even when broken down by individual products, aggregation of data
may obscure changes at the national level, e.g., the emergence of new
producers, diversification of a country's exports, etc. Only by examining
the experience of individual ACP countries can such changes be identi-

**TABLE 5.18.**

ACP Exports of Manufactured Goods to the EEC 1973–1982 (Values in Thousand UA)

| | 1973 | 1974 | 1975 | 1976 | 1977 | 1978 | 1979 | 1980 | 1981 | 1982 |
|---|---|---|---|---|---|---|---|---|---|---|
| Aluminum oxide | 64,012 | 77,474 | 89,126 | 80,883 | 102,551 | 143,056 | 136,448 | 189,972 | 201,412 | 168,207 |
| | | (70.0) | (70.6) | (55.2) | (53.1) | (65.2) | (79.3) | (70.1) | (69.3) | (67.9) |
| Uranium | (—) | (—) | (—) | 2,897 | 25,252 | 35,756 | 148,150 | 395,770 | 290,715 | 305,758 |
| | | | | (—) | (3.1) | (3.1) | (9.5) | (26.4) | (18.2) | (20.0) |
| Clothing | 2,582 | 8,338 | 19,769 | 31,396 | 45,911 | 49,107 | 55,330 | 65,779 | 97,955 | 89,412 |
| | (—) | (—) | (0.6) | (0.7) | (1.0) | (1.1) | (1.0) | (1.0) | (1.2) | (1.0) |
| Leather | — | 16,185 | 18,002 | 38,577 | 30,414 | 34,900 | 64,298 | 46,768 | 38,391 | 49,600 |
| | (—) | (5.4) | (6.0) | (7.6) | (5.5) | (6.3) | (7.0) | (6.9) | (6.6) | (6.2) |
| Cotton fabrics | — | — | 13,901 | 25,344 | 31,167 | 27,285 | 32,790 | 28,422 | 31,535 | 40,723 |
| | (—) | (—) | (2.3) | (2.7) | (3.4) | (2.9) | (2.6) | (2.4) | (3.0) | (3.3) |
| Veneers & plywood | 26,009 | 24,792 | 15,576 | 21,132 | 15,113 | 18,478 | 24,292 | 21,073 | 23,459 | 24,041 |
| | (6.3) | (7.1) | (3.3) | (4.3) | (3.1) | (3.3) | (3.4) | (3.2) | (3.3) | (3.3) |
| Veg. alkaloids | — | — | — | 14,461 | 14,668 | 12,001 | 7,018 | 3,558 | n.a. | n.a. |
| | (—) | (—) | (—) | (9.4) | (9.2) | (6.7) | (4.9) | (n.a.) | | |
| Other chemicals | — | — | — | 15,521 | 12,958 | 6,817 | 5,180 | 9,568 | 10,998 | 8,312 |
| | (—) | (—) | (—) | (5.7) | (5.8) | (2.8) | (1.7) | (2.6) | (2.4) | (1.6) |
| Essential oils | 7,128 | 9,253 | 4,351 | 9,302 | 8,393 | 8,960 | 9,635 | 8,613 | 8,777 | 8,705 |
| | (—) | (—) | (5.2) | (7.0) | (6.1) | (6.7) | (6.9) | (6.0) | (5.5) | (5.1) |
| Natural hormones | — | — | — | 8,666 | 7,193 | 10,481 | 9,554 | n.a. | n.a. | n.a. |
| | (—) | (—) | (—) | (11.4) | (9.9) | (13.9) | (13.5) | | | |
| Ropes and cords | — | — | — | 1,343 | 7,636 | 8,793 | 15,281 | 14,983 | 6,869 | 7,310 |
| | (—) | (—) | (—) | (5.4) | (17.9) | (18.9) | (25.6) | (22.8) | (11.7) | (10.4) |

Sources: Calculated from data in: Commission des Communautés Européennes, *Évolution des échanges commerciaux entre la Communauté et les États ACP* [VIII/373/78-F] (3 Avril 1978); and *Importation CEE des principaux produits en provenance des états ACP* (VIII/842/83) (Août 1983).

Note: Units in thousands of UA; figures in parentheses indicate the percentage share of the ACP in total EEC imports of that good.

fied. Stevens and Weston have made an initial survey of ACP countries that sold nontraditional exports to the European market during the first Lomé Convention.[11] At this level of disaggregation, the performance of the ACP is somewhat more promising: between 1975 and 1980 the value of exports of twenty-two product groups of manufactured, processed agricultural, and temperate agricultural goods increased in real terms. There were eight products (totaling 14 mua) where no exports had been recorded in 1975, and twenty products where an increase in the number of exporting countries had occurred.

In terms of total ACP exports or the total imports of the EEC of these products from developing countries, however, the quantities involved were minute. And, as the analysis in the last section demonstrated, the growth in ACP exports of most of these products did not keep pace with exports from other developing countries, most notably the group of newly industrializing countries. These figures do demonstrate, however, that ACP countries are not incapable of taking advantage of their access to the European market in order to diversify their exports. On the other hand, these new exports tended to be products regarded as "sensitive" in the European market: textiles, clothing, processed leather goods, and off-season temperate agricultural products. Despite the small quantities involved, ACP states have already faced protectionist opposition within the Community to these new exports. As was noted in the case of Mauritian textiles, Lomé has not ensured exemption for the ACP from the imposition of voluntary export restraints. It is also noteworthy that a number of the new exports are manufactured in export-processing zones, toward which the European Commission has expressed opposition in the past. If ACP countries should continue to enjoy success in promoting nontraditional exports, a direct clash with European interests is likely to emerge that will provide a more decisive test of the security of the trade provisions of the Convention.

## CONCLUSION

From the perspective of the expectations of the ACP in pursuing their strategy of collective clientelism, trade with the Community during the first Convention was a severe disappointment. None of the principal ACP objectives was attained: their share of total EEC imports and of EEC imports from non-oil-exporting developing countries fell precipitously; for a number of their most important traditional exports, their share of the European market also declined; and little progress was made in aggregate terms in upgrading and diversifying the composition of their exports. Even allowing for the manner in which aggregate results are distorted by the dramatic increase in the share of petroleum in ACP exports, my most optimistic assessment of the trade provisions of the Convention would be that they were a "qualified failure."

As noted at the beginning of this chapter, this result was not unexpected: the experience of trade between the Community and the Yaoundé Associates under terms similar to those of the Lomé Convention was very similar; few of the principal ACP exports continue to enjoy a tariff advantage; access for new exports proved to be less certain than the Community appeared to have guaranteed in 1975; and, in any event, no dramatic transformation could have been expected, given the short period of time in which the Convention's provisions had been in operation. In the absence of the Convention, the performance of the ACP of course may well have been even worse. But this perception was outweighed by the feeling that the Convention had failed to live up to the expectations that the ACP held for it.

From the ACP Group's perspective, these disappointing results had two implications for the realization of the objectives of their strategy of collective clientelism. First, provisions for access to the European market should be further liberalized and guaranteed in order to provide security for products that threatened to compete with domestic Community production. Second, if it was the case (as the Community argued), that the reasons for the declining share of the ACP in the European market for some of their traditional exports lay predominantly in supply problems (in terms both of declining quantities produced and noncompetitive costs and qualities), then the ACP share of the Community market could be ensured only by some form of managed markets. Here, the sugar protocol provided an example: a guaranteed market for a specified quantity of ACP production at prices linked to those paid to domestic Community producers.

Demands along these lines were made by the ACP Group when the Convention was renegotiated in 1979–1980 and again in 1983–84. As chapter 9 argues, an extension of the relationship in this manner was completely unacceptable to the Community, given the constraints that this would have imposed on its choice of domestic and foreign economic policies. From the Community perspective, the trade provisions of the first Convention had gone as far as was practicable and/or politically feasible. Accordingly, the Community began to place a much greater emphasis on the aid provisions of the Convention—which imposed far fewer constraints on the Community's freedom of action.

# Appendix A To Chapter 5

## ACP COUNTRIES

Bahamas, Barbados, Benin, Botswana, Burundi, Cameroon, Cape Verde, Central African Republic, Chad, Comoros, Congo, Djibouti, Dominica, Equatorial Guinea, Ethiopia, Fiji, Gabon, Gambia, Ghana, Grenada, Guinea, Guinea Bissau, Guyana, Ivory Coast, Jamaica, Kenya, Kiribati, Lesotho, Liberia, Madagascar, Malawi, Mali, Mauritania, Mauritius, Niger, Nigeria, Papua New Guinea, Rwanda, St. Lucia, St. Vincent and Grenadines, Sao Tome and Principe, Senegal, Seychelles, Sierra Leone, Solomon Islands, Somalia, Sudan, Surinam, Swaziland, Tanzania, Togo, Tonga, Trinidad and Tobago, Tuvalu, Uganda, Upper Volta, Western Samoa, Zaire, Zambia.

## ACP SUBGROUPINGS

### 1. Yaoundé ACP

Benin, Burundi, Cameroon, Central African Republic, Chad, Congo, Gabon, Ivory Coast, Madagascar, Mali, Mauritania, Niger, Rwanda, Senegal, Somalia, Togo, Upper Volta, Zaire.

### 2. Commonwealth ACP

Bahamas, Barbados, Botswana, Dominica, Fiji, Gambia, Ghana, Grenada, Guyana, Jamaica, Kenya, Kiribati, Lesotho, Malawi, Mauritius, Nigeria, Papua New Guinea, St. Lucia, St. Vincent and the Grenadines, Seychelles, Sierra Leone, Solomon Islands, Swaziland, Tanzania, Tonga, Trinidad and Tobago, Tuvalu, Uganda, Western Samoa, Zambia.

### 3. Previously Non-Associated ACP

Cape Verde, Ethiopia, Equatorial Guinea, Guinea, Guinea Bissau, Liberia, Sudan.

### 4. Non-Oil ACP

ACP Group excluding Nigeria, Trinidad and Tobago, Gabon, the Bahamas, and Congo.

### 5. Non-Oil Commonwealth ACP

Commonwealth ACP Group excluding Nigeria, Trinidad and Tobago, and the Bahamas.

### 6. Non-Oil Yaoundé ACP

Yaoundé ACP Group excluding Gabon and the Congo.

## MAJOR OIL EXPORTING DEVELOPING COUNTRIES

Iraq, Iran, Libya, Nigeria, Saudia Arabia, Kuwait

## OTHER DEVELOPING COUNTRIES

World excluding industrialized countries, South Africa, European developing countries, major oil-exporting developing countries, and the ACP.

# Appendix B to Chapter 5

To examine the effect of the Lomé Conventions on trade between the ACP and the EEC an attempt is made to determine whether the levels of exports and imports for the period 1975–81 are different from those for the five-year period (1970–74) preceding the signature of the first Convention. Because of the worldwide inflationary trend during the seventies, both exports and imports display an upward trend throughout the years under review, when expressed in monetary units. In order to neutralize this effect, the exports or imports to or from an ACP grouping for any given year are divided by the exports or imports of that grouping to or from the entire world. These ratios are referred to as export and import "shares." All data, unless otherwise noted, are derived from the IMF *Direction of Trade Yearbook* (1976 and 1983 editions).

Any test of the null hypothesis (HO) (that there was no statistically significant change in ACP shares) is vulnerable to two types of error: Type I error when the null hypothesis is rejected when in reality it is true, and Type II error when HO is accepted when in fact it is false. Choice of a test for HO should be made with the objective to keep both types of errors as small as possible. In reality, it is impossible to minimize Type I and Type II errors simultaneously. The modest sample size does not warrant the use of a parametric test. Accordingly, a more robust non-parametric test particularly suited for this type of problem, the Wilcoxon-Mann-Whitney (W) test, which minimizes errors of Type II, is used.

## COMPARISON OF W TESTS WITH Z TESTS

The W and Z tests make one common assumption: that the two underlying populations from which the sample is drawn are identical except for possible differences in their means. The Z test makes an additional assumption: normality of the underlying population.

The Z test is the "best" test when the underlying populations are indeed normal. By "best" is meant that it is the test with the lowest Type II error when Type I error is fixed. The W test, however, compares well with the Z test in relative efficiency, that is, in the ratio of sample sizes required to give equal probabilities of Type I and Type II errors. In fact, when the underlying population is not normal, the W test actually surpasses the Z test in efficiency. An additional advantage offered by the W test is that it does not give undue emphasis to "outliers" resulting from imperfect data collection. This property is relevant to this particular study, as indicated by the frequent corrections that the IMF makes to its data on trade flows. For the above reasons, the W test was used in this study.

## EXAMPLE OF THE W TEST

Tables 5.14 and 5.15 can be used to illustrate the W test. ACP shares of EEC imports from LDCs reported in table 5.14 are ranked, with the lowest equal to 1, and highest equal to 12. This provides the following sequence: 12, 10, 11, 9, 8 for the years 1970–74; and 3, 2, 4.5, 6.5, 6.5, 4.5, 1 for the years 1975–81 (where tied ranks occur, the mean of the ranks concerned is employed). Where two groups of unequal size are used, as in this study, the aggregate of the ranks of the smaller of the two groups is employed to test for statistically significant change. In this example the decline in export shares is particularly pronounced over the 12-year period: it provides the maximum possible divergence of ranks. The Wilcoxon-Mann-Whitney tables show that by rejecting the null hypothesis—that ACP shares in EEC imports from LDCs have remained unchanged—a Type I error is risked with less than 0.005 probability. In general this study follows customary statistical procedures in requiring only that the risk of Type I error's being made should be less than 0.05. Accordingly table 5.15 records that ACP shares in EEC imports from LDCs have declined in a statistically significant manner.

This study does not attempt to test the trade-creating or trade-diverting effects of the Convention. There are grounds for questioning whether this would be a worthwhile exercise, especially given the low levels of tariff preferences enjoyed by the ACP. As important is the lack of availability of the type of data necessary for such a study, especially that relating to the elasticity of ACP export supply. Any study of this type would inevitably be heavily dependent on "informed guesswork." One work that attempted to measure the trade-creating and trade-diverting effects of the Yaoundé Convention—Delsi M. Gandia, *The EEC's Generalised Scheme of Preferences and the Yaoundé and Other Agreements* (Montclair, N.J.: Allanheld, Osmun, 1981)—served only to illustrate the futility of the task given the lack of necessary data.

# 6

# Three Problematic Protocols: the Political Economy of Sugar, Rum, and Bananas

European expansionism in the sixteenth through nineteenth centuries incorporated the Caribbean and Pacific islands into the world economy; sugar and rum were the basis of one leg of the three-cornered slave trade that provided the initial links between Europe, Africa, and the Caribbean. But the international division of labor was not entirely a matter of colonial convenience—the tragedy for many of the island producers of sugar and bananas is that their geographical characteristics render them unsuitable for the cultivation of many alternatives. Dependence on these products and on the European market remains high.

Sugar, rum, and bananas are all considered to be agricultural products by the European Community and consequently, under the terms of the Treaty of Rome, should be subject to a common organization of the market. Although this has been implemented only in the case of sugar, special regimes were introduced for all three products by Protocols attached to the Lomé Convention, whose result have been to compartmentalize the Community market in one way or another. Given the importance of these commodities for some ACP states and the fact that ACP interests conflict in all three with domestic interests in the member states—either with those of producers of competitive substitutes or with importers using other sources of supply—these three Protocols represent a critical test of the efficacy of a strategy of collective clientelism.

## SUGAR

Britain's commitment to safeguard the interests of developing country members of the Commonwealth Sugar Agreement proved to be the most difficult issue to resolve in the negotiations for the first Convention (see chapter 2). The consequences of the eventual solution adopted to this

**TABLE 6.1.**
Dependence of ACP Countries
on Sugar Exports: Earnings from
Sugar as % of Total Export
Earnings (mean 1974–76)

| | |
|---|---|
| Barbados | 33.7 |
| Fiji | 61.3 |
| Guyana | 43.3 |
| Mauritius | 83.0 |
| Jamaica | 13.7 |
| Kenya | * |
| Madagascar | * |
| Malawi | 11.3 |
| Uganda | * |
| Congo | * |
| Swaziland | 41.3 |
| Tanzania | * |
| Trinidad and Tobago | * |
| Surinam | * |

Source: Calculated from data in Eurostat, *Analysis of Trade Between the European Community and the ACP States.*
   *Less than 5 percent.

problem have haunted the ACP in the period since the Convention's implementation.

Sugar is the dominant export crop for five ACP states (see table 6.1) and, by virtue of its labor-intensive nature, is also a significant source of employment in several others. In Trinidad, for example, although sugar is relatively unimportant in the island's exports in comparison to petroleum, it remains the country's largest source of employment, providing work for about 40,000 people.[1]

LDC sugar exporters are faced by one of the world's most volatile commodity markets. On average only 20 percent to 25 percent of world sugar output enters international trade and of this as much as one-half is exported under special preferential regimes. Ninety percent of the sugar traded is cane, the volume being subject to the usual vicissitudes of natural and man-made disasters. Since 1900, the world sugar market has been oversupplied in eight of every ten years. As a result world market prices are frequently below the average costs of production of most producers.

In part this is caused by dumping by countries whose domestic price support systems have caused overproduction; it is also a function of the time lag between price changes and a supply response. Only beet growers can increase production rapidly when prices rise, since their product is an annual; cane is not ready for harvesting until up to two years after planting. But once cane has been planted, additional output can be supplied for several years before that cane is exhausted, during which time world prices will probably have fallen. This is the explanation of the predominantly cyclical pattern in world sugar markets in which brief periods of shortages and of high prices are followed by longer periods of marked oversupply.[2]

An important benefit of the Commonwealth Sugar Agreement (CSA) was to largely insulate suppliers in the colonies and dominions from these fluctuations. The agreement evolved out of wartime bulk-purchasing arrangements designed to conserve dollars and ensure sugar supplies to the British market.[3] At first these were on a year-to-year basis but from 1944 onward were renewed for periods of several years. In late 1949 the British Government announced its intention to negotiate a new long-term agreement with Commonwealth suppliers. Since sugar was to be purchased on an "average-cost-plus" price basis, it was necessary to impose quotas on exporting countries (the production potential of the Commonwealth being virtually infinite if costs could be ignored). Following protracted negotiations, price quotas were agreed in December 1951 and backdated to 1950. Initially the CSA was an eight-year rolling agreement renewed annually, but its last version was of infinite duration, subject to the escape clause that it could be denounced by Britain if its application for membership in the EEC was successful.[4]

Quotas for the colonies were 60 percent above those established by the 1937 International Sugar Agreement; for the Dominions the increase was 30 percent.[5] In the 1950s and 1960s quotas were expanded and additional suppliers admitted to the agreement. To some extent this occurred at the expense of British beet producers, whose acreage was strictly controlled by the Ministry of Agriculture (although in the 1950s and early 1960s British beet in fact was uncompetitive with CSA cane-sugar, whose costs of production were considerably lower). Commonwealth suppliers benefited from stable prices that were set at levels intended to be "reasonably remunerative for efficient producers" and were sometimes double those prevailing on the world market (developing country members of the CSA received an additional special payment that varied inversely with the world market price).[6] Of the twenty-four years in which the Agreement was in force, there were only eight in which the negotiated price was below the world market price. CSA costs were recouped from the proceeds of a levy on all sugar sold in the United Kingdom; since all costs were passed on to the consumer the CSA did not become a drain on public finance. British consumers and the country's large confectionery industry benefited on the other hand from stable supplies and from the fact that they did not pay for the protection of a domestic beet industry; retail sugar prices in Britain were half those prevailing on the European continent.

By the middle of the 1960s a dramatic change had occurred in the relative costs of production between developing country CSA suppliers and British beet growers. Although the acreage devoted to beet production in Britain increased by only 6.5 percent in the twenty years following the end of the war, yields rose by 38 percent.[7] By contrast, yields in the Caribbean fell steadily—which Smith attributes to a combination of factors: declining standards of cultivation and transportation, inadequate research into cane breeding, labor shortage and lack of mechanization, and technically obsolescent and suboptimum factories.[8] Consequently, whereas British beet producers received a higher price than CSA exporters in the 1950s and early 1960s (in order to compensate them for higher costs of production), by 1968 they were receiving the same price, while by 1973 the CSA price for developing countries had risen by necessity above that received by British producers. Naturally, this reinforced the demands of the British beet lobby that they be allowed a larger share of the domestic market, demands that coincided with the establishment of the EEC's sugar regime.

Negotiations to establish a sugar regime under the CAP were successfully concluded in July 1966. These had proved to be particularly difficult owing to the substantial differences in production costs between the member states and to the desire of each national government to preserve its domestic sugar industry. Costs of production in Italy were more than 50 percent above those in France; consequently if the Italian industry was to continue in production, EEC intervention prices had to be set at a high level. But a uniform high price throughout the Community would have encouraged massive overproduction by the more efficient French industry. The solution adopted was the installation of national production quotas. As Jones notes, this system marked a retreat from the pseudo-liberal conception that the CAP should create "an organic equilibrium between production and a market for products."[9] In essence, the CAP's sugar regime negates the concept of a common market.

Like other CAP regimes, that for sugar rests on a system of target and intervention prices and of variable levies on imports from third countries designed to exclude imports below the target price. A basic production quota for the Community as a whole is established that is divided first between the member states and then subdivided between individual factories responsible for offering contracts to growers. A market for all sugar produced within this basic quota (Quota A) is guaranteed at the intervention price. A second quota (Quota B) provides for an assured market for certain quantities beyond the basic quota (originally 35 percent of Quota A) but is subject to a production levy of up to 30 percent of the intervention price. Expenses of disposing of surpluses not covered by the production levy are met from the Agricultural Guarantee and Guidance Fund (FEOGA). Any sugar produced beyond a factory's B Quota is not allowed to be sold for human consumption within the Community and producers receive no assistance in disposing of it.

A key difference between the EEC sugar regime and the CSA is that the former has always aimed at slightly more than 100 percent self-sufficiency. The basic quota established for 1968–69 was 3 percent higher than estimated consumption requirements (which some contemporary commentators thought were also almost certainly too high).[10] Initial intervention prices were more than 25 percent above the prices received by CSA members. From its inception, the excessive acreages combined with high prices have consistently produced surpluses beyond EEC domestic consumption. By 1968–69, production was already 115 percent of self-sufficiency. The fortuitous exception to the pattern of surpluses was 1974— the year in which the principal provisions of the Lomé protocol were negotiated.

Negotiations for the first Lomé Convention, given the Community's commitment in the British Treaty of Accession "to have as its firm purpose *(aura a coeur)* the safeguarding of the interests of all the countries referred to in this Protocol whose economies depend to a considerable extent on the export of primary products, and particularly of sugar," offered the Commission an opportunity to propose reform of the Community's sugar regime to reduce its costs to the EEC budget. Initial intentions were to reduce production quotas to the levels that available market outlets could absorb, taking into account the 1.4m. tonnes of cane sugar that the United Kingdom had traditionally imported from developing countries under the CSA. This gave a basic quota of 8.4m. tonnes, Furthermore, the Commission proposed that the B Quota be reduced to 18 percent of the basic quota to enable the EEC to join the International Sugar Agreement.[11] These proposals met bitter resistance from Community beet growers, who objected not only to the quota reductions but to the principle of guaranteeing a market for ACP sugar, a move they regarded as contravening the very foundations of the CAP.

As chapter 2 noted, a fortuitous combination of circumstances enabled a (temporary) reconciliation of the interests of ACP exporters and European beet producers. Redirection of Caribbean sugar to the world market to exploit the higher world prices caused several countries to default on their commitments under the CSA and resulted in severe shortages in Britain. The position was exacerbated by panic buying in both Britain and Italy—the two principal deficit countries in the Community—leading to a significant increase in total EEC consumption in the period 1975–76. In the context of fears over the future security of supply of raw materials following the initial OPEC success, the EEC Council of Ministers opted to encourage domestic production.

Using the increased consumption in 1975 as the basis for their projections, the Council agreed to increase the A Quota by 16.8 percent to 9.136m. tonnes. Quota B was also raised—to 45 percent of the basic quota—giving a maximum quota of 13.25m. tonnes (an overall increase of 23 percent). In order to promote a rapid increase in production, the intervention price was raised by 15 percent (compared with an average for the CAP in that year of 10 percent), and the production levy on Quota B was suspended for two years.

This victory for the beet lobby occurred at the expense of European consumers and LDC suppliers (including, ultimately, the ACP). Apparently the Council of Ministers accepted the reasoning reflected in the following quotation from a contemporary article:

For sugar, as for other foodstuffs, the period of plenty appears to be over, and several of the orthodox notions about the world sugar economy have had to be questioned. One such was the belief that, except for brief periods of relative shortage, supply chronically outstripped demand.[12]

Unfortunately from the perspective of the ACP, the validity of the prevailing orthodoxy was upheld in the subsequent period.

## THE LOMÉ SUGAR PROTOCOL

At the conclusion of the negotiations for Lomé I, ACP spokesmen had reason to be satisfied with the provisions for sugar in the new Convention, for they had apparently succeeded in breaching a fundamental principle of the CAP—that no access should be allowed for imports from third countries if Community suppliers could reasonably meet domestic demands. Sugar producers in ACP countries were offered access to the Community market for up to approximately 1.3m. tonnes of sugar. Since this was almost identical to the quantities exported to Britain under the CSA, (see table 6.2), it appeared that the Community had accepted that the ACP countries should be allowed to maintain their traditional share of the British market.

A number of changes occurred in the country distribution of quotas in the transition from the CSA to the Lomé Protocol. In particular, the total allocated to the West Indies was reduced by 40 percent. In part this was the result of the difficulties that some countries had experienced in normal years in fulfilling their quotas under the CSA; it was also a conscious (but terribly shortsighted) decision by some Caribbean governments to attempt to capitalize on the prevailing high prices on the free market, rather than undertake a commitment that would oblige them to maintain supplies to the European market. Table 6.3 illustrates the nature of the dependence of ACP sugar producers on overseas sales in general and on the EEC market in particular. For most of them, the EEC is their single most important market: the unweighted mean share of the EEC in their total exports in 1977 was close to 70 percent.

Under the terms of the Protocol, ACP producers are guaranteed a market within the EEC for their sugar in the amount of their quotas at a price within the range prevailing in the Community (Article 5, 4). To the extent that the CAP price for sugar keeps pace with rates of inflation within the Community, ACP exporters enjoy a price closely indexed to the cost of their imports. The guaranteed price functions in the same manner as CAP intervention prices: ACP sugar is marketed at prices freely negotiated between buyers and sellers, but if no purchaser can be found at the guaranteed price, the Community steps in. Community buyers can pay more than the guaranteed price if they wish to ensure ACP sugar for themselves (as Britain did in 1975). ACP countries can also export in excess of their quotas, but the EEC has no obligation toward these supplementary quantities as regards purchase or prices.

**TABLE 6.2**
CSA and Lomé Convention Sugar Quotas
(metric tonnes white equivalent)

| *ACP* | *CSA* | | *Lomé* | |
|---|---|---|---|---|
| Mauritius | 374,438 | | 487,200 | |
| Swaziland | 83,980 | | 116,400 | |
| Fiji | 138,036 | | 163,600 | |
| West Indies & | 682,958 | | 409,100 | |
| Guyana, of which: | | | | |
| Jamaica | | 212,666 | | 118,300 |
| Trinidad & Tobago | | 123,630 | | 69,000 |
| Barbados | | 133,513 | | 49,300 |
| Guyana | | 180,254 | | 157,700 |
| St. Kitts–Nevis–Anguilla | | 32,895 | | 14,800 |
| Kenya | | | 5,000 | |
| Uganda | 7,000 | | 5,000 | |
| Tanzania | | | 10,000 | |
| Total Commwealth ACP states | 1,286,412 | | 1,196,300 | |
| Belize | 19,842 | | 39,400 | |
| Malawi | | | 20,000 | |
| Congo | Not | | 10,000 | |
| (Brazzaville) | members | | | |
| Madagascar | | | 10,000 | |
| Surinam | | | 4,000 | |
| Total ACP/OCT | 1,306,254 | | 1,279,700 | |
| India | 24,680 | | 25,000 | |
| Australia | 330,165 | | Not a member | |
| Total CSA | 1,661,099 | Total Lomé | 1,304,700 | |

Source: Calculated from data in Simon Harris and G. B. Hagelberg, "Effects of the Lomé Convention on the World's Cane-Sugar Producers,"
  *O.D.I. Review* (1975), 43

Although the Sugar Protocol is annexed to the first Convention (which covered a five-year period), its provisions are of indefinite duration. The Protocol explicitly allows for the arrangement to continue separately if the Convention itself is not renewed. Some controversy has arisen, however, over the meaning of the word "indefinite" since this can be interpreted as either "perpetual" or "not specified." Article 10 stipulates that the Protocol may be denounced by the Contracting Parties after five years,

**TABLE 6.3.**

Relation Between ACP Sugar Production and Lomé Quotas 1977

| ACP State | (1) 1977–78 Quota | (2) 1977 Production | (3) Exports to EEC 1977 | (4) Total Exports | (1) ÷ (4) % | (3) ÷ (2) % | (3) ÷ (4) % |
|---|---|---|---|---|---|---|---|
| Barbados | 49,300 | 119,836 | 62,500 | 106,247 | 46.4 | 52.5 | 58.9 |
| Fiji | 163,600 | 368,985 | 182,109 | 317,996 | 51.4 | 49.4 | 57.3 |
| Guyana | 157,700 | 253,127 | 177,955 | 217,609 | 72.5 | 70.3 | 81.8 |
| Mauritius | 487,200 | 704,762 | 567,736 | 673,981 | 72.3 | 80.6 | 84.2 |
| Jamaica | 118,300 | 297,714 | 135,525 | 205,455 | 57.6 | 45.5 | 66.0 |
| Kenya | 5,000 | 185,000 | — | — | — | — | — |
| Madagascar | 10,000 | 110,000 | 15,402 | 25,902 | 38.6 | 14.0 | 59.5 |
| Malawi | 20,000 | 95,273 | 18,629 | 63,006 | 31.7 | 19.6 | 29.6 |
| Uganda | 5,000 | 20,000 | 3,299 | 3,299 | 151.6 | 16.5 | 100.0 |
| Congo | 10,000 | 15,711 | 10,000 | 15,649 | 63.9 | 63.7 | 63.9 |
| Swaziland | 116,400 | 238,497 | 116,347 | 213,600 | 54.5 | 48.8 | 54.5 |
| Tanzania | 10,000 | 107,521 | 10,990 | 10,990 | 91.0 | 10.2 | 100.0 |
| Trinidad and Tobago | 69,000 | 178,004 | 91,642 | 140,239 | 49.2 | 51.5 | 65.3 |
| Surinam | 3,199 | 10,000 | 1,807 | 3,500 | 91.4 | 18.1 | 51.6 |

Source: Calculated from data in Commission of the European Communities "Sugar, The European Community and the Lomé Convention," *Europe Information* (1979) 19/79, p. 7

subject to two years' notice. But to confuse matters, an Annex to the Protocol states that this article is a formal legal provision for the purpose of juridical security and does not represent any qualification by the Community in its guarantees of access, duration, and price for preferential cane sugar.

There are two principal differences between the Lomé Protocol and the CSA, both of which have given rise to some dissatisfaction on the part of the ACP. Whereas the CSA price was f.o.b., that guaranteed by Lomé is c.i.f.: therefore the receipts for ACP states are reduced by the amount of freight and insurance costs. Consequently, and this has been a matter of considerable controversy, ACP producers tend to receive a lower price for their sugar than Community beet producers (owing to higher transport and storage costs). Under the CSA the British Government's Sugar Board had arranged a shipping program that took control once sugar had been loaded in an exporter's port.

Second, there are significant differences in the two agreements' provisions for dealing with shortfalls. Under the CSA considerable flexibility existed as a result of the "Chairman's Agreement." This was a "gentleman's agreement" entered into by the Chairman of the CSA exporters, which guaranteed that the total tonnage specified would be shipped regardless of the shortfall of any individual supplier. This was possible because of the presence in the CSA group of Australia—the largest producer in the Commonwealth, a reliable supplier able to make up the shortfalls arising when other countries experienced supply problems.

Lomé's provisions regarding failure to fulfill quotas are much more stringent. The principal reason for this was Community concern over security of supplies and is something for which some Commonwealth countries have only themselves to blame. Refusal by a number of the Caribbean exporters (most notably Jamaica and Guyana) to fulfill their CSA quotas in 1974–75 in order to exploit the higher prevailing world market price (in 1974 shortfalls in the CSA amounted to 325,336 tonnes), and the attempt to force the CSA price higher by withholding shipments, prompted the Community to insist that quotas be fulfilled unless a situation of *force majeure* prevails. If a shortfall occurs other than for this reason, the Convention provides that the future quota of an ACP country "shall be reduced . . . by the undelivered quantity" (Article 7, 3). On the other hand, there is no commitment in the Protocol to an automatic reallocation of quotas between ACP countries to maintain total tonnage in the event of one or more failing to fulfill its national quota. Rather, the Protocol states that "It may be decided by the Commission that . . . the undelivered quantity shall be reallocated between the other States" (Article 7, 4).

## THE SUGAR PROTOCOL IN OPERATION

In an era of low prices on the world sugar market (with the exception of 1980) the ACP have generally been appreciative of the security of income that the Sugar Protocol provides. Considerable controversy has arisen, however, over two aspects of its implementation: Community interpretations of the *force majeure* clause, and the annual negotiations to establish the guaranteed price. ACP states have also expressed their discontent that the Community has been unwilling to extend the terms of the protocol to new ACP suppliers.

In the case of *force majeure*, the terminology of the Convention is so vague that the Commission (which is responsible for judging whether circumstances of *force majeure* are applicable) exercises considerable discretionary power. So imprecise was the wording of the Convention that it was felt necessary to issue a clarification both of the conditions in which *force majeure* might apply and of the circumstances under which consultations should be held. In a 1977 letter, the EEC cochairman of the ACP-EEC joint subcommittee on sugar informed his ACP counterpart that the Community considered the criteria for *force majeure* to be the following: it must be impossible for an exporting country to fulfill its obligations without imposing "unreasonable" sacrifices; second, the circumstances must have been unavoidable, owing to unforeseeable causes beyond the control of the exporting country, and not the result of its own actions.[13] By way of illustration the following circumstances were listed as meeting the definition: natural disasters such as earthquakes, floods, droughts, or cyclones; wars or riots; shipwrecks; strikes leading to a reduction in production or delays in transportation; failure of the sugar cane harvest caused by plant diseases or insect pests; or fires.

The importance of the new definition was that it extended the obligations of the ACP. According to the Commission's specialist on ACP sugar the situation resulting in nondelivery had to be unforeseeable and unavoidable:

In other words, it is no longer a question of just a voluntary sale on the world market. Internal situations in the ACP countries, which their leaders should have coped with if they wanted to meet their delivery commitments, also come into it.[14]

Obviously this provides considerable discretion to the Commission in deciding whether an ACP government had taken all necessary precautions against possible supply interruptions.

Clarification of the definition of *force majeure* had proved necessary because the ACP Group had challenged the decision of the Commission in 1976 to reduce the quotas of four ACP states—Congo, Surinam, Uganda, and Kenya—as a result of their failure to meet their supply commitments under the Protocol for the 1975–76 period. After the ACP Group essentially "politicized" the dispute by taking it to the ACP-EEC Council of Ministers, the Community agreed at a ministerial meeting in Fiji in April 1977 to restore the quotas of the four states. At that time, the EEC spokesman stated that it was making this concession as a "unilateral political gesture without retroactive effect and that it could not call into question the validity of the Commission's decisions." This "particularly major concession" could not be invoked as a precedent, the Council warned, since the Community felt that it was taking into account the difficulties encountered by the ACP states in applying the provisions of the Protocol during its first year of application.

When the four states again failed to fulfill their quotas in the 1977–78 period, the Commission reduced them by the amount of the shortfall. Since these amounts were not reallocated to other ACP states, the action represented a saving to the Community budget of the costs of purchasing 15,874 tonnes of sugar.[15] The Commission's judgment that the shortfalls were the result of deliberate government policies, and its consequent quota reductions were protested by the ACP Group; two years after the issue was first raised at the ACP-EEC Council of Ministers no resolution had been reached, and the Convention's "good offices" procedure—providing for conciliation—was invoked by the ACP-EEC Council of Ministers. In 1981, however, the Community rejected the recommendations made by the two conciliators. In the meantime, Kenya and the Congo had applied for a "reallocation" under Article 7(4) of the Protocol: by the middle of 1982 the matter had still not been resolved.[16]

These disputes illustrate again the asymmetry in the distribution of decision-making power in the management of the Lomé partnership. As the letter from the EEC cochairman of the sugar subcommittee under-lined, it is the Commission alone that is responsible for applying the cri-teria to determine whether a situation of *force majeure* applies. Although the Commission consults with the ACP state before it reaches its deci-sion, and the criteria guiding its judgment were themselves jointly deter-mined by the ACP-EEC Council of Ministers, the ultimate decision is the Commission's alone. Again, this is an instance where the ACP *as a Group* are given no role in the decision-making process. The Sugar Pro-tocol is far from being a jointly managed operation.

The issue of management responsibility has also led to friction over the manner in which the guaranteed price to be received by ACP ex-porters is determined. According to Article 5,4 of the Protocol, this price is guaranteed within the price range prevailing in the Community. In a Declaration in the Procès-Verbal, the Community "undertakes that the Commission . . . will consult the sugar-exporting ACP States each year before making its proposals to the Council of the European Communities for the determination of sugar prices within the following campaign." ACP states have argued that contrary to the Protocol, the annual price has not been the subject of genuine negotiations; rather they had merely been informed of the Community's decision after the matter had been deter-mined by the Council in the CAP negotiations. Accordingly, the price proposed had been based primarily on data regarding costs of production within the Community and had failed to take into account the particular problems faced by the ACP, most notably, increases in production and transportation costs.[17]

In that the prices guaranteed to ACP producers under the Protocol generally have been considerably above those prevailing on the world market (the exceptions were 1975–76 and 1980–81—see table 6.4), the Community might justifiably feel aggrieved that ACP states have not shown sufficient appreciation of the benefits they have derived from the arrangement. As Community negotiators have pointed out, it is politi-cally impossible for the Community to envisage a price for the ACP higher than the net income guaranteed to Community producers. Nevertheless, the ACP states do have some grounds for complaint. Since prices under the Protocol are determined on a c.i.f. basis, the exporting states have had to bear the costs of transporting sugar to its European destination, costs that have increased considerably during the Convention's imple-mentation as a result of oil price rises. Consequently, ACP exporters do

**TABLE 6.4.**

A Comparison of World Market and
Lomé Protocol Prices
(in UA per 100 kilogram raw sugar)

|  | I.S.A. Daily Price | Lomé |
|---|---|---|
| 1975–76 | 27.39 | 25.53 |
| 1976–77 | 16.90 | 26.70 |
| 1977–78 | 13.06 | 27.25 |
| 1978–79 | 12.21 | 33.62 |
| 1979–80 | 15.62 | 34.13 |
| 1980–81 | 46.00 | 35.01 |
| 1981–82 | 33.55 | 38.94 |
| 1982–83 | 18.78 | 42.63 |
| 1983–84 | 20.95 | 44.34 |

Source: "Sugar, the European Community and the Lomé
Convention," p. 8; and data supplied by the Commission of the European Communities.

not receive an income equivalent to that guaranteed to Community producers.

On other pricing matters, the Community has also been accused by
the ACP of acting in a mean-spirited manner. One issue arises from the
different crop years for beet and cane sugar. Community prices are determined on the basis of the beet crop year—which runs from July to
June—whereas the CSA prices were fixed for the period January to December, the Caribbean growing season. ACP producers have demanded
that the guaranteed price under the Sugar Protocol be applied retroac-
tively to their production starting in the previous January (which, they
argued, would partially compensate for lower prices on the world market). This position was rejected by the Community. A second source of
irritation was the Community's introduction in July 1977 of a special self-
balancing storage levy system applicable to imported preferential sugar.
And, in 1980, the Community attempted to impose a lower price increase for imported ACP cane sugar than that granted to domestically
produced beet by proposing differential rates of increase for raw and white
sugar.

As an ACP spokesman noted:

The ACP cannot accept that the Protocol empowers the Community to unilaterally change the structure of the price range, redefines (sic) its intervention price,

deduct whatever changes [*sic*] it deems fit and then place the resulting figure before the ACP as its firm and final guaranteed price offer to the ACP. This is not by any interpretation honoring the letter of the protocol that there should be annual negotiations to determine the ACP guaranteeed price.[18]

More problematic in the long run for the ACP have been developments in the Community sugar market since the negotiation of the Protocol that threaten the future position of ACP sugar in the Community and that also have weakened their position on the free world market.

Community response to the sugar shortages of 1974–75 was to encourage an expansion of domestic production on the assumption that consumption would stabilize at the (historically unprecedented) level of 10.4m. tonnes. Taking into account the commitment to import 1.3m. tonnes from the ACP, the Council of Ministers raised the A Quota to 9.136m. tonnes. With the increase in the B Quota, the maximum output that enjoyed Community price supports was raised to 13.25m. tonnes— 30 percent in excess of the highest ever volume of domestic consumption. Response to the improved price incentives by European beet producers was immediate: the acreage planted rose by more than 19 percent in the succeeding two years. The consequence has been that European production in every year since the Sugar Protocol entered into force has been more than sufficient to meet domestic consumption (which has stabilized around the traditional level of 9.5m. tonnes).

At first, the full effect of the quota and price incentive increases was masked by adverse climatic conditions. In 1977–78, the first "normal" harvest, European production reached 11.53m. tonnes, 35 percent above the figure at the time the Sugar Protocol was negotiated and 22 percent in excess of consumption for that year. By 1979–1980, production had risen by a further 6.5 percent and was now close to 30 percent above European consumption (see table 6.5). Since ACP states continued to ship quantities close to their quota limits, the total supply to the European market was more than 40 percent above consumption requirements. Most of this total benefited from Community guarantees regarding prices and markets; consequently, the Community bore most of the costs of disposing of the surpluses. These were not inconsiderable: over the period 1977–79 they averaged over $750 million per year, representing close to 10 percent of the total expenditure of the agricultural support program and more than 4.5 percent of the total EEC budget.[19]

Not surprisingly, these costly surpluses brought demands for reform from consumer groups, some member states, and the Commission. Fol-

**TABLE 6.5.**

EEC Sugar Balance Sheet 1974–75 to 1979–1980
(000 tonnes white sugar equivalent)

| | Domestic Production of Which | | | Imports of which | | | |
|---|---|---|---|---|---|---|---|
| | Total | C | Within Max. Quota | Total | Preferential | Exports | Domestic Consumption |
| 1974–75 | 8,563 | 93 | 8,470 | 1,718 | CSA 568 ACP 590 | 171 | 9,561 |
| 1975–76 | 9,703 | 111 | 9,592 | 1,428 | 1,337 | 1,445 | 9,535 |
| 1976–77 | 10,003 | 183 | 9,820 | 1,444 | 1,417 | 1,696 | 9,036 |
| 1977–78 | 11,527 | 808 | 10,719 | 1,354 | 1,327 | 3,508 | 9,442 |
| 1978–79 | 11,714 | 804 | 10,970 | 1,221 | 1,189 | 3,214 | 9,507 |
| 1979–1980* | 12,274 | 1,432 | 10,842 | 1,430 | 1,358 | 4,123 | 9,548 |

Source: EEC Commission.
*Provisional.

lowing the old dictum that the best form of defense is to attack, EEC beet growers attempted to shift the blame for the surpluses onto the Community's commitment to import sugar from the ACP. By far the most aggressive and effective lobby was that of the French beet producers. A full-page advertisement in the *Financial Times* published by the *Comité Interprofessionel des Productions Sacchariferes* noted that "after ten years of perseverance" France had become the world's fifth largest sugar producer and second most important exporter and asked rhetorically: "Should France pay, through underemployment, for the degradation of the basic principles of the Common Agricultural Policy?"

Britain was accused of attempting to undermine the CAP:

One cannot join the Common Market and at the same time put "Commonwealth preference" before Community preference. . . . Nostalgia for low pre-war prices is maintained with internal electoral aims vis-a-vis the British housewife.[20]

If, as the "White Paper" proposed, the expense of "re-exporting" ACP sugar was to be considered outside the agricultural budget, then the actual costs of disposing of domestically produced surpluses would not appear to be unreasonable, the growers argued, given the benefits of security of supply.

European beet growers were thus pressing the case that ACP sugar had no place in the European market. And, much to the consternation of the ACP Group, the European Commission appeared to accept this argument. In May 1979 the Commission proposed to debit the development budget with the cost of exporting 1.3m. tonnes of sugar (equivalent to the amount imported from ACP countries) and to remove from the 1980 FEOGA budget estimate the cost of exporting the amount of sugar displaced by ACP imports.

In response, the ACP Group objected to the proposal's implications that the Sugar Protocol represented an aid rather than a trade arrangement and that part of the quantity of domestically produced sugar that is exported from the EEC should be regarded as attributable to imports of ACP sugar. A memorandum sent by the Chairman of the ACP Sugar Sub-Committee to the Commission noted a statement made by the Community's Agricultural Commissioner, Finn Gundlelach, in which he had stated explicitly that "The Protocol is, like the CSA was, an instrument of trade not of aid." At the time of the first enlargement, the memorandum noted, the United Kingdom brought into the Community a market for sugar more than sufficient to cover its traditional imports from developing countries; the Community itself had accepted the commitment to ACP sugar producers in Protocol No. 22 to the Treaty of Accession, while the U.K. government had confirmed that there would be "a firm and continuing market in the enlarged Community" for the sugar from developing countries. Paragraph 2 of Article 27 of the principal EEC sugar regulation introduced on 31 December 1974 had clearly stated that sugar imported on preferential terms from the ACP should be regarded as meeting part of the human consumption of sugar within the Community.[21]

ACP quotas were fixed and had not been increased since the signature of the Sugar Protocol; therefore the Group could not in any way be held responsible for the dramatic rise in EEC sugar exports caused solely by the increase in domestic beet production. ACP sugar in fact was not itself exported but rather consumed in the EEC (mainly in the United Kingdom).

Although the proposals were withdrawn by the Commission, considerable doubt remains regarding its long-term commitment to maintaining a place for ACP sugar in the European market. Recommendations for reform of domestic sugar policy continue to make reference to the costs of reexporting ACP sugar. And in an official pamphlet on the Sugar Protocol, the Commission noted:

The fact is that, despite the United Kingdom's sugar deficit, the EEC is itself essentially self-sufficient in this sector and even produces a surplus. The introduction of this preferential system therefore meant that the Community had to try to export quantities of sugar equivalent to its imports from the ACP States, an operation which has now become extremely expensive owing to low world prices.[22]

In its initial proposals for reforming the Community's sugar regime, the Commission argued that production quotas should be set at a level corresponding to Community consumption of 9.5m. tonnes p.a. plus "traditional" exports of 0.8m. tonne. Under this initiative, the total domestic demand for sugar could be met from internal sources. But even this proposal proved unacceptably restrictive to some member states (in particular the United Kingdom, whose beet growers sought an increased share of the Community market). As a result of these protests the Commission was obliged to propose a larger maximum quota. As Smith notes, the cuts in overall quotas from the 1975 regime put forward in the amended proposals would probably have little effect on actual production since most Quota B reductions would fall on member states which traditionally have not produced Quota B sugar. The Commission's plans also fail to deal effectively with the production of sugar beyond the maximum quota (category C sugar).[23]

Not only did the Commission fail to take into consideration the commitment to ACP exporters in calculating the level of domestic production necessary to meet consumption needs, but also the method of calculating the levy on Quota B sugar was changed in a manner suggesting that the Commission is determined to ignore the traditional share of the enlarged European market held by the ACP. Under the 1975 regime, for determining the volume of surplus production to be used in calculating the levy on Quota B sugar, imports of ACP sugar under the Protocol had to be deducted from total Community consumption figures. But in the new regime, no deduction of imports from the ACP is required—reference is made only to total domestic consumption. As a result, a quantity of domestically produced sugar equivalent to the level of imports from the ACP will no longer be subject to the production levy.

Long-term prospects for ACP sugar in the Community market have been made even more precarious by developments in the U.K. market.

Sugar supplies there are derived from three sources: domestic beet, which provides about 1.0m. tonne (and whose share of the market increased from 27 percent in 1975–76 to 49 percent in 1980–81, largely at the expense of other European beet growers); cane sugar (about 1.225m. tonnes, or virtually the entire ACP quota); and about 0.2 tonne of beet sugar imported from other member states. Consumption declined from 2.64m. tonnes in 1972 to 2.4m. tonnes in 1979.[24] Britain's cane refiners have faced an increasingly difficult situation as a result of their operating costs' being in excess of those of beet refiners. Since the refining margin fixed by the EEC is calculated on the basis of the beet process, beet refiners enjoy margins about five times as wide as those for cane. Consequently, the survival of cane refineries has been dependent on sugar on the British market being sold at a premium above the intervention price. This has been possible in the past only because the U.K. government has limited beet production and thereby ensured a noncompetitive domestic sugar market. But recently beet production has been expanded, following pressure from British beet producers, toward a target 25 percent above the 1979 production figure.

Given the decline in British sugar consumption and the reduction in cane imports following the termination of imports from Australia, the cane-refining industry has come under increasing competitive pressure, resulting in the closure of a refinery by Tate and Lyle, the principal cane sugar refiner. With this closure, the company can process a maximum of 1.04m. tonnes each year, 60,000 tonnes beneath the total of ACP sugar traditionally refined in Britain. As *The Economist* noted, the "ACP are right to see the refinery closure as the thin edge of a pretty thick wedge."[25] For if the additional ACP sugar is to be refined in Europe, it will now be dependent on processing in a beet refinery in the off-season (and thus essentially will be at the mercy of its rivals).

More likely is the prospect that the Community will make use of a declaration in the Procès-Verbal that "in exceptional circumstances and with the agreement of the exporting ACP States concerned, the Community may deliver sugar originating in the ACP States to a third country without preceding importation." This would result in ACP sugar being dumped on the world market, where it would compete directly with other ACP sugar exports. A precedent for this procedure already exists. When Zimbabwe (a beneficiary of the CSA whose quota was suspended during the Unilateral Declaration of Independence—U.D.I.—period) was admitted to the Convention in November 1980 it was agreed that the Community would commit itself to purchase 25,000 tonnes of sugar (the CSA quota) from Zimbabwe each year under the terms of the Sugar Protocol. But the total ACP quota in the Protocol will not in any way be increased. Zimbabwe's quota is to be met by transferring those quantities of sugar that have not been delivered by other ACP countries, but if these do not amount to the 25,000 tonnes' objective, the Community will purchase the difference from Zimbabwe and give it as food aid to the developing countries.

ACP countries fear that the Community will eventually renege on its commitment to the Sugar Protocol as a trade instrument by encouraging the exclusion of ACP sugar from the European market (or, at least, by doing nothing to counteract present market forces in this direction). If the Commission is successful in ending the present quota system in 1985 and replacing the management of the market by a system of guaranteed prices alone, it is likely that it will drive Tate and Lyle's cane refineries out of business. An insight into Commission thinking is provided by the rhetorical question posed by its expert on the Sugar Protocol:

The basic problem is to decide whether, six years after the start of the sugar protocol, the Community and the ACP countries are being pushed into taking a political decision. Faced with the impossibility of maintaining a commercial pact, which is struggling because of the divergence of interests of the different partners (14 ACP countries on one side and Tate and Lyle on the other), will they have to resort to transforming what is a commercial pact between equal partners into an aid convention in which, by definition, the forces are unequal?[26]

ACP interests have been adversely affected by European overproduction not only in the Community market but also from the resultant dumping of European surpluses on the world market. Given the small size of the world sugar market in relation to total production, changes in supply that are small relative to overall world production can give rise to substantial variations in price. As Smith notes:

The free world market is of little use to exporters interested in stable and remunerative prices or importers interested in security of supply, although it may be of considerable interest to the speculative operator.[27]

Over the years 1970–80 Community sugar production increased by 50 percent—acreage under cultivation increased by 25 percent while yields rose on average by more than 6 percent. In the meantime, however,

**TABLE 6.6**

EEC Share of the World Sugar Market
(000 tonnes raw value)

|  | Net World Exports | Net EEC Exports | Net EEC Exports as Percentage Net World Exports |
|---|---|---|---|
| 1973 | 16.5 | 0.8 | 4.7 |
| 1974 | 16.1 | 0.1 | 0.9 |
| 1975 | 13.2 | −0.2 | — |
| 1976 | 15.5 | 1.2 | 7.7 |
| 1977 | 20.7 | 2.3 | 11.1 |
| 1978 | 17.3 | 3.3 | 19.1 |
| 1979 | 18.0 | 3.6 | 20.0 |

Source: International Sugar Organization.

Community consumption rose by only 5.3 percent. As the surplus of domestically produced beet in the EEC climbed steadily beyond Community consumption needs, the EEC, already the world's number one sugar producer, became a significant exporter (see table 6.6). By 1981 the Community had become the world's second largest exporter and largest supplier of the free market, alone accounting for a staggering 27 percent of free market sugar.

EEC dumping on the world market has undermined the efforts of the International Sugar Agreement (ISA) to stabilize prices. When this agreement was concluded in Geneva in October 1977, the Community refused to accede to it—in part because other countries refused to accept that imports from the ACP under the Sugar Protocol should be taken into consideration in determining the size of the Community's export quota. While signatories to the ISA subsequently accepted a 15 percent cut in their quotas in an effort to raise prices, the Community continued to increase its exports and more than made up for the quantities withheld from the market by ISA members. By 1978 the Community accounted for more than 75 percent of sugar exports from non-ISA members. Continuous growth in EEC domestic production has prevented it from keeping its commitment to impose "parallel" restrictions on its exports in accord with the actions of ISA members.

The Community's own view is that:

As Community exports are large, the policy has certainly been instrumental in damping down the erratic movements in world sugar prices and has been beneficial to both importing and exporting developing countries.[28]

This perspective has not been shared by other sugar traders. EEC policies of using export subsidies in dumping sugar on the world market at below cost price caused Australia and Brazil to lodge a formal complaint with the GATT alleging that this practice had enabled the Community to gain an unfair share of the world market. The GATT Panel of Inquiry found that the EEC's policies had depressed world prices and concluded that they "constituted a permanent source of uncertainty in world sugar markets and thereby constituted a threat of serious prejudice in terms of Article XVI:1."[29] Furthermore, EEC exports of white sugar had narrowed the differential between white and raw sugar prices to such an extent that it no longer constituted a reasonable margin for costs of refining, packaging, etc. Massive dumping of Community exports on the world market has reduced the revenue for ACP sugar growers for that part of their production marketed outside of the Sugar Protocol.

Ironically, at the same time that the Community was increasing its exports to the world market, it was warning ACP states against expanding their own production. In a memorandum to the Council titled "Inconsistencies in the Policies Pursued by the Community and Member States: The Example of Sugar," the Commission noted that a number of ACP states were proposing "to step up their production considerably . . . in many cases with financial support and technical assistance from European firms, the financial support sometimes being provided by one or more of the Member states."[30] Of 66 known projects in the sugar sector in ACP states, 44 were backed by European firms. Noting that "it cannot contemplate any increase whatsoever in the (ACP) quota laid down in the Protocol," and that Zambia's request for a sugar quota had already been rejected, the Commission questioned whether it was sound development policy to promote investments in sugar production in ACP states, given the condition of the world market:

Finally, the Commission asks itself the following question: Can we go on accepting, by pretending the problem does not exist, the inconsistency between blanket export aid policies—which are in themselves perfectly understandable—and the responsibility which the Member States and the Community should exercise *vis-a-vis* their Third World partners, particularly as regards the selection of sectors of development.[31]

Although there is some validity in the Commission's argument, at least as regards the consistency of Community policies, its concern for the development needs of the ACP would be less disingenuous if it would first put its own house in order in the sugar sector. European failure to curtail domestic output essentially has exported the problems of adjustment to the ACP—and the Commission was now demanding that this be recognized by deterring ACP countries from expanding their sugar output. The Community's new regime (adopted in April 1981 after years of haggling) is nothing short of socially irresponsible. Production quotas remain essentially unchanged except for marginal adjustments in the B Quotas—those of France and Germany are actually raised. Quotas benefiting from Community guarantees were above the 1975 levels despite their having exceeded Community consumption by more than 20 percent. Similarly, the "co-responsibility" levy to cover the cost of exports was set at a lower level than the Commission had proposed.[32]

## RUM

Protocol No. 7 of the first Lomé Convention provided that "until the entry into force of a common organization of the market in spirits . . . (rum) originating in the ACP States shall be imported duty free into the Community under conditions such as to permit the development of traditional trade flows between the ACP States and the Community and between the Member States." Contrary to ACP demands, the Community treats rum as an agricultural product and consequently denies duty-free entry to unlimited quantities of the product. Each year the Community determines the size of the quota of ACP rum to be accorded duty-free access. This is calculated on the basis of the largest annual quantities imported in the last three years for which statistics are available, subject to an annual growth rate of 40 percent for the United Kingdom and 13 percent for the other national markets.

These quotas were necessary, the Community argued, since there was no common organization of the market for alcohol, the Community market was not expanding at the same rate in the various member states, and it was necessary to preserve the position of Community producers of competitive substitues, most notably the French Overseas Territories (which are treated as part of France). It was this last reason, in fact, that was dominant in the internal Community negotiations on the rum regime, the outcome of which represented a sensitive compromise between

French and British interests and their support for their respective traditional suppliers. In order to preserve the position of the French Overseas Territories, the market was compartmentalized by prohibiting the reexport of rum from Britain to other member states (Regulation No. 1464/76 of 21 June 1976). ACP states have maintained, to no avail, that this regulation is illegal under the Treaty of Rome since it reintroduces artificial barriers to exchange.

ACP states have complained, since the initial implementation of the Protocol, that Community procedures have not been in accord with the Protocol's "spirit." Initial consultations on the size of the quota and its distribution between the member states immediately produced friction:

The ACP States were of the view that the consultations were of limited value since they took place when the Community had completed its elaboration of the Regulation which the Community put into effect despite the outcome of the consultations.[33]

Spokesmen for the ACP Group questioned the accuracy of Community import statistics (determined on the basis of ex-bond reporting) and noted that significant discrepancies existed between them and export statistics of the ACP states concerned. These figures are of particular importance since they are the basis on which the size of future quotas are determined. Annual recalculation of quotas, the ACP have argued, introduces considerable uncertainty for exporters while, in several cases, the national quotas were so small that an export drive to penetrate the new market would not have been worthwhile.

ACP states have also complained that various procedural and other nontariff barriers have prevented them from fully using national quotas in some member states. This was particularly true of Germany, where importers had reported that they were having difficulty obtaining licenses to import rum of ACP origin (the ACP have alleged that the German government has been favoring the import of rum from Brazil, one of its principal Third World trading partners). Because they have been unable for one reason or another to fully take up all of the national quotas, the total quota for the final year of the first Convention's implementation was only 5 percent above that of the initial year—hardly a satisfactory growth rate for the ACP exporters. Overall take-up of the total quota did increase considerably, however, in the first four years of the Convention's implementation (see table 6.7) and should lead to increased quotas in the future.

**TABLE 6.7.**
Actual Take-up of the Tariff Quotas Opened for Rum

| Member State | 1975–76 Volume of Quota (bl) | 1975–76 Actual Take-up (bl) | (%) | 1976–77 Volume of Quota (bl) | 1976–77 Actual Take-up (bl) | (%) | 1977–78 Volume of Quota (bl) | 1977–78 Actual Take-up (bl) | (%) | 1978–79 Volume of Quota (bl) | 1978–79 Actual Take-up (bl) | (%) | 1979–1980 Volume of Quota (bl) |
|---|---|---|---|---|---|---|---|---|---|---|---|---|---|
| Benelux | 3,500 | 3,500 | 100 | 4,827 | 4,827 | 100 | 5,926 | 5,143 | 87 | 6,000 | 5,816 | 97 | 6,912 |
| Denmark | 2,900 | 1,943 | 67 | 2,700 | 2,115 | 78 | 4,000 | 1,577 | 39 | 3,698 | 1,448 | 39 | 3,722 |
| Germany | 26,000 | 21,076 | 81 | 24,643 | 23,188 | 94 | 24,000 | 20,956 | 87 | 24,706 | 24,706 | 100 | 33,979 |
| France | 6,000 | 6,000 | 100 | 12,051 | 4,881 | 41 | 11,395 | 5,509 | 48 | 9,022 | 3,551 | 39 | 6,449 |
| Ireland | 1,000 | 839 | 84 | 1,000 | 891 | 89 | 1,000 | 682 | 68 | 1,000 | 492 | 49 | 2,704 |
| Italy | 600 | 207 | 35 | 550 | 216 | 39 | 658 | 295 | 45 | 424 | 424 | 100 | 426 |
| United Kingdom | 128,000 | 62,676 | 49 | 125,395 | 79,617 | 63 | 126,030 | 83,337 | 66 | 116,957 | 103,872 | 89 | 122,645 |
| EEC | 168,000 | 96,241 | 57 | 171,166 | 115,735 | 68 | 173,009 | 117,489 | 68 | 161,807 | 140,309 | 87 | 176,837 |

Source: *Report of the ACP-EEC Council of Ministers (1 April 1976–29 Feb. 1980)*, p. 56.

A fundamental problem with the Protocol from the perspective of the ACP exporters is that it allows for the greatest growth in quotas to the market they have traditionally supplied (and whose growth potential therefore would be expected to be limited). As the House of Commons Select Committee on Overseas Development noted:

There is thus the absurd position of an unnecessarily large quota for the UK which domestic demand cannot possibly fill and an unnecessarily restrictive one for the rest of the EEC which, *ceteris paribus*, domestic demand could be expected far to outstrip. Your Committee would hope that this unfortunate oversight . . . may now be recognised openly and speedily corrected.

The fact that no such correction has been offered has inevitably confirmed ACP suspicions that rum producers are being deliberately excluded from the large and potentially profitable German market. Whatever the rights and wrongs of the process of the issue of licenses to import rum into Germany—and Your Committee heard much *circumstantial* but was able to examine no *concrete* evidence on this issue—the fact remains that a huge market has effectively remained closed to a high value export from a small group of ACP States, all of which face serious balance of payments problems. Your Committee finds this situation a revealing vignette of the reality behind much of the fine rhetoric that some EEC leaders have showered on the Lomé relationship.[34]

In its proposals for the renegotiation of the Convention, the Commission suggested that the compartmentalization of the market should be ended so that the rum regime might be more in conformity with the Treaty of Rome and that an annual ceiling for rum to be accorded duty-free access be drawn up that was "more adapted" to the existing exports of ACP states. This ceiling would be determined on the basis of exports for 1978, to be increased each year by a fixed quantity (which in the first year would amount to approximately 5 percent of the quota but as a predetermined quantity would obviously lead to lower rates of growth in succeeding years).

These proposals succeeded in alienating both the British and French delegations. For the British they marked a "considerable step backward" because the proposed growth rates were below those of the existing regime. For the French, they:

put into doubt the economic and political balance and can only, in fact, aim at the conquest of the French market by non-traditional ACP suppliers, to the detriment of the rum production of the overseas territories.[35]

Given this hostility of the two member states most concerned with the regime, the outcome was predictable: the Rum Protocol was renewed in essentially the same form with the modification that ACP quotas to their nontraditional markets would now enjoy a growth rate of 18 percent per year. The market remains compartmentalized.

A more serious threat to the ACP in the long term may be posed by Community attempts to establish a common organization of the market in ethyl alcohol of agricultural origin. ACP states are concerned that their rum will be excluded under the proposed definitions since these are based on a level of distillation met only by the products of the French Overseas Territories. Much will depend on the continued willingness of the U.K. government to reject a common regime unless this provides for a continued role for rum of ACP origin.[36]

## BANANAS

The inability of the countries having preferential trading arrangements with the EEC to increase their shares of the Community banana market has long been a cause of dissatisfaction. Part of the problem lies in the failure of the Community to establish a common organization of the market for bananas despite its obligations to do so under Article 40 of the Treaty of Rome, and the Charmasson Judgement. A completely free market, however, would almost certainly put all ACP banana suppliers out of business. At present the only common element in banana policy is the duty-free access guaranteed to ACP bananas in all EEC markets and the imposition of a 20 percent duty on third-country imports. But Germany is granted exemption from the duty under the Treaty of Rome for a quota whose size is determined annually by estimating total domestic consumption needs (which traditionally have been supplied by "dollar" fruit). In the French, Italian, and British markets, licensing arrangements originally established in the colonial period have been maintained to ensure that the market is reserved for traditional suppliers. Only in the Benelux countries, Denmark, and Ireland is the CET applied, and no other preferences are given to ACP producers.

Protocol Number Six of the first Convention stipulates that:

1. As regards its exports of bananas to the EEC, no ACP State will be placed, as regards access to the markets and market advantages, in a less favourable position than in the past or at present;
2. A joint endeavour will be undertaken by the ACP States and the Community to devise and implement appropriate measures particularly with respect to in-

vestment encompassing all stages of production to consumption in order to enable the ACP States, particularly Somalia, to increase their banana exports to their traditional Community markets;

3. Comparable endeavours will be undertaken to enable the ACP States to gain a foothold in new Community markets and to extend their banana exports to those markets.

As the Report of the ACP–EEC Council of Ministers on the implementation of the first Convention noted:

There was a fundamental difference of interpretation between the ACP States and the Community, mainly on the nature and scope of the obligations contracted by the Community.[37]

Divergent interpretations of the imprecisely worded Protocol in fact have been one of the principal causes of bitterness in relations between the Community and the ACP in the period since the implementation of the Convention. Ill feeling has been exacerbated by the inability of the ACP to penetrate the Community market in countries other than those in which they have traditionally been given preference. In 1976, ACP exporters sold a total of only 11 tonnes of bananas to the Benelux countries, Denmark, and Germany combined. In their traditional markets their shares in imports have been maintained (except for Somalia's share of the Italian market, which has increasingly been taken over by "dollar" bananas supplied by transnational corporations), and thus their share of the overall Community market has increased only marginally (see table 6.8). Quantities exported to the EEC have failed to regain their pre-Lomé peak.

According to the ACP, whose interpretation of the intentions of the Protocol can only be described as "creative," the first article implied the Community would create a regime for bananas similar to that for ACP sugar. They "could not understand what comprised the notion of a guarantee on their traditional markets if it did not provide certain undertakings regarding absolute quantities, the share of their exports in these markets, and the prices which they were accorded on these markets." They argued the Protocol obliged the Community to organize its banana market to guarantee that ACP exporters would benefit in their traditional markets from access facilities and preference over all other imported bananas, to reserve a minimum part of new markets in the Community for ACP states on profitable terms for their exporters, and to provide investment aid in addition to that offered in other chapters of the Convention. Noting that the ACP supplied only 25 percent of the bananas con-

**TABLE 6.8.**

EEC Imports of Fresh Bananas from the ACP

| | 1973 | 1974 | 1975 | 1976 | 1977 | 1978 | 1979 | 1980 | 1981 | 1982 |
|---|---|---|---|---|---|---|---|---|---|---|
| Value (000 ua) | 62,409 | 74,545 | 95,461 | 95,049 | 110,070 | 110,194 | 117,145 | 138,864 | 159,363 | 178,746 |
| Quantity (tonnes) | 378,584 | 345,530 | 342,960 | 321,566 | 345,570 | 329,745 | 337,817 | 334,308 | 324,795 | 339,236 |
| Unit Value | 0.165 | 0.216 | 0.278 | 0.296 | 0.318 | 0.334 | 0.346 | 0.415 | 0.491 | 0.527 |
| Value Index 1975 = 100 | 65.4 | 78.1 | 100 | 99.6 | 115.3 | 115.4 | 122.7 | 145.5 | 166.9 | 187.2 |
| Quantity Index 1975 = 100 | 110.4 | 110.7 | 100 | 93.8 | 100.8 | 96.1 | 98.5 | 97.5 | 94.7 | 98.9 |
| Unit Value Index 1975 = 100 | 59.3 | 77.6 | 100 | 106.5 | 114.3 | 120.1 | 124.5 | 149.3 | 176.6 | 189.6 |
| ACP Share in extra-EEC Imports | 18.7 | 18.5 | 19.7 | 19.0 | 19.4 | 19.0 | 20.0 | 21.5 | 20.8 | 21.4 |

Source: *Importations CEE des principaux produits en provenance des états ACP* (various years).

sumed in the Community, the Group asserted the measures taken by the Nine to implement the Protocol were "unsatisfactory, negative, and absolutely insufficient."[38]

From the Community's standpoint, the Protocol merely represented an understanding that "each Member State would continue to define its own market policy under the same conditions as those which existed when the Lomé Convention was signed." A common organization of the market as advocated by the ACP would not necessarily resolve their difficulties since at best this would assure ACP exporters of the application of the provisions for agricultural products subject to market organizations.[39] These were laid down in Article 2 of the Convention and provided merely that the Community would ensure "as a general rule" that ACP exports would receive more favorable treatment than that accorded MFN suppliers.

This reply sidesteps the main thrust of the ACP memorandum, which essentially is a demand for a market organization that would guarantee them a specific share of each national market. Interventionary measures of this type have been rejected by the German government as "totally unacceptable."[40] Community spokesmen have argued the problems of the ACP arise from their lack of competitiveness, particularly as regards prices and consistency of quality of their fruit. Community figures on prices prevailing in its market for bananas from various origins appear to validate this argument: in 1977 ACP bananas on average sold for 319 ua per tonne, whereas those from the rest of the world cost on average 263 ua per tonne. Within the different categories there were significant variations: ACP bananas fetched from 287 to 354 ua, whereas those from the rest of the world ranged from 207 to 294 ua per tonne. Even the most competitive of ACP bananas were at the top of the price range for imports from the rest of the world.

ACP exporters have argued, however, that their problems stem from the operations of transnational banana-trading companies that not only use their monopoly power to purchase bananas at low cost in Central and Latin America but also are able to exclude ACP bananas from their nontraditional markets in the EEC by virtue of their control over distribution and retailing networks. ACP exporters have also complained they are victims of discriminatory shipping rates. Some support for the ACP case was derived from the decision of the European Court of Justice in February 1978 upholding the greater part of the Decision of the European Commission against United Brands Company. The Court found that United Brands was guilty of abuses of its dominant position in respect of Chiquita bananas in Belgium, Denmark, Germany, Luxembourg, and the Netherlands. These abuses were as follows: (1) prohibiting the sale by distributors/ripeners of green bananas (in effect a prohibition against trade between member states since it is only in their green state that bananas may be shipped any distance without damage); (2) charging discriminatory prices in respect of equivalent transactions depending on the country of destination of the bananas; (3) refusing to supply a distributor in Denmark (on the grounds that he was participating in an advertising campaign for one of its competitors). A fourth accusation—of charging unfair prices—was dismissed, essentially because the Commission had failed to provide the necessary information regarding costs of production.

There is some truth to the arguments of both the Community and the ACP. German importers have noted their market is an open one; the failure of the ACP to penetrate it (despite trial purchases of ACP bananas in the past) has been caused by the lack of homogeneity of their bananas. This prevents importers from employing their customary methods for ripening.[41] If the ACP are to be competitive exporters, then more attention must be paid to quality control and to effective marketing of their products. ACP countries have lagged behind other producers (even the French Overseas Territories) in their investment in port facilities for refrigerated container vessels, which have cut the costs of transporting bananas from the Caribbean by as much as 50 percent. On the other hand, the Community might show more support for the ACP by more diligently enforcing its antitrust provisions to ensure that the ACP have an equitable chance of competing in those markets that have not traditionally provided preferences to their exports. If, as the Community suggests, ACP bananas cannot compete effectively with "dollar" fruit as regards price, then there is little justification for continuing to allow the Federal Republic to exempt its imports of "dollar" bananas from the full rate of duty under the Common External Tariff.

Discussions between the Community and the ACP on the Protocol have remained deadlocked. In its reply to the ACP memorandum, the Community noted:

What is not conceivable is to attain a Community-wide organization of the market of the type that ACP States desire, that is to say, one which would provide

guarantees of sales and of price. Neither is the Community in a position to envisage financial aids additional to those foreseen by the Lomé Convention.[42]

This stalemate resulted in the Protocol's being renewed in essentially the
same form in the Second Convention. Subsequently these arrangements
have been threatened by action in the courts of member states. In 1980
a small London-based fruit-importing company sued Britain's Ministry
of Agriculture, claiming its managed market for bananas contravened
Article 30 of the Treaty of Rome. Earlier, the Ministry of Agriculture
had refused the company, whose case was believed to be backed by the
American Del Monte Corporation, an import license for "dollar" bananas. If the case should prove successful—and a 1974 precedent exists
when the European Court found that the French system of managed
markets for bananas was illegal (a ruling France subsequently ignored)—
then the legitimacy of the Lomé arrangements will be struck down and
the position of ACP bananas in their traditional European markets
threatened.

## CONCLUSION

Only in the case of rum can the three Protocols be said to have operated
against ACP interests. Here they are in the position of being competitive
suppliers denied access to segments of the Community market in order
to protect either producers in the French overseas territories or other third-
party suppliers. In this case, liberalization of the market would probably
work to their advantage.

For the other two Protocols, the compartmentalization of the Community market has worked to safeguard ACP interests. For bananas, this
has been the result, not of the Protocol's adding anything to protection
received in traditional markets, but merely of the fact that it continues
to permit the traditional licensing that has protected Commonwealth
Caribbean producers in the British market and Francophone Africa and
the French overseas territories in the French market. Collective clientelism in this instance has brought no additional rewards to those gained
from historical ties with traditional patrons except that bananas are one
of the crops included within the STABEX scheme. ACP states have not
been successful in their demands that a managed market with guaranteed
ACP shares be introduced on a Community-wide basis. On the other hand,

they have not been exposed to free market competiton that, almost certainly, would have put them out of business.

Collective clientelism did bring payoffs in the negotiation of the Lomé Sugar Protocol, which represented a significant breach of the fundamental principles of the CAP. Subsequently ACP countries have benefited from the fact that prices on the Community market in all except one year have been substantially above those prevailing on the world market. On the other hand, high Community prices and the effects of the compromise negotiated 1974–75—increased levels of the Community quotas for domestic production—have rebounded to the disadvantage of the ACP. Not only have they found their markets in third countries—and prices— are being undermined by the dumping of Community surplus production, but also their position in the European market itself has increasingly been placed in jeopardy. Where there has been a direct conflict of interest between the ACP and a significant European domestic interest, collective clientelism and the Community's professed commitment to its Lomé partners have provided little protection of the ACP's interests. Despite the legal form of its commitment to purchase a specific quantity of ACP exports, the Community has at best grudgingly acknowledged its obligations and has frequently acted in less than good faith—not only in its attempts to blame the ACP for the difficulties caused by the CAP sugar policies but also in its discriminatory pricing treatment of ACP sugar. The mean-spirited way in which both the Sugar and Rum Protocols were interpreted by the EEC did much to sour the atmosphere in which the Lomé relationship was conducted.

# 7

# Industrial Cooperation

Next to STABEX, the most innovative chapter of the 1975 agreement was that pertaining to industrial cooperation. According to an ACP spokesman, "for some of their number this was the prime aspect of the Lomé Convention."[1] Like the issue of commodities' earnings stabilization, that of promoting industrial development in the Third World, in particular by permitting a transfer of those industries in which the South has a comparative advantage, has figured prominently in the demands for a New International Economic Order (especially the 1975 UNIDO Lima Declaration). ACP countries hoped their strategy of collective clientelism would enable them to exploit their close relations with the EEC in order to diversify their economies and thereby reduce their dependence on the export of raw materials and unprocessed agricultural commodities.

Within the Group of 77, ACP states are among those with the lowest levels of industrial capacity—even in those ACP countries classified as "middle-income" the share of manufacturing in GNP is extremely low (see table 7.1). Implementation of the Yaoundé Conventions had shown trade preferences were of little value unless the beneficiaries could export those goods that enjoyed the greatest tariff advantages (and these, with few exceptions, were processed and manufactured goods). And yet, as chapter 2 noted, industrial promotion had been one of the least successful aspects of the previous Association arrangements—in part because of Community aversion to becoming involved in a realm it believed to be primarily the responsibility of the private sector.

In their initial memorandum on the subject during the negotiations for Lomé I, the African Group had posed four principal questions:

1. Would our European partners be prepared to allow us free and unimpeded access to their wealth of knowledge and experience in the sphere of industrial development?
2. Would they be prepared to mobilise their scientific and technological infrastructure to meet the specific needs and requirements of ACP countries?

**TABLE 7.1.**

Share of Manufacturing in the GNP of ACP States (%)

| | | | |
|---|---|---|---|
| Barbados | 10.6 | Malawi | 12.5 |
| Benin | 8.6 | Mali | 11.1 |
| Botswana | 7.2 | Mauritania | 10.2 |
| Burundi | 9.8 | Mauritius | 18.3 |
| Cameroon | 12.7 | Niger | 16.4 |
| Cape Verde | 3.4* | Nigeria | 7.4 |
| Central African | | Papua New Guinea | 8.2 |
| Republic | 8.7 | Rwanda | 3.6 |
| Chad | 9.1 | St. Vincent | 8.8 |
| Comoros | 7.6* | Sao Tome and | 9.2* |
| Congo | 9.5 | Principe | |
| Djibouti | 10.1* | Senegal | 12.3 |
| Dominica | 4.0 | Seychelles | 3.9* |
| Equatorial | 5.3* | Sierra Leone | 5.8 |
| Guinea | | Solomon Islands | 1.4ᵃ |
| Ethiopia | 11.2 | Somalia | 9.6 |
| Fiji | 10.5 | Sudan | 9.7 |
| Gabon | 9.4* | Surinam | 7.1 |
| Gambia | 1.6 | Swaziland | 23.5* |
| Ghana | 9.2* | Tanzania | 10.4 |
| Grenada | 2.8* | Togo | 10.1 |
| Guinea | 9.4* | Tonga | 3.2ᵇ |
| Guinea-Bissau | 1.3* | Trinidad and | 14.1 |
| Guyana | 12.0 | Tobago | |
| Ivory Coast | 11.8 | Uganda | 6.9 |
| Jamaica | 16.8 | Upper Volta | 13.8 |
| Kenya | 12.4 | Western Samoa | 3.4ᵃ |
| Lesotho | 4.1 | Zaire | 9.9 |
| Liberia | 5.4 | Zambia | 17.1 |
| Madagascar | 13.7 | | |

Source: *ACP: Statistical Yearbook 1972–78* (Luxembourg: Eurostat, 1980).
Note: data are for 1975 except a for 1972, b for 1974.
*GDP

3. Would they be prepared to make the adjustments in their production patterns that would enable a new and more rational division of labour to be established between us?
4. And would they join us in establishing arrangements that would reconcile the interests of private industry and private investors in Europe with the declared policy of many of our countries to exercise increasing control over their industrial sectors?[2]

These questions were sufficiently broad that the Community could respond sympathetically without having to make any definite commitments. Community negotiators were, however, taken by surprise when the ACP Group returned to this subject at the Kingston negotiating meeting in July 1974 with a memorandum proposing the establishment of specific institutions to promote industrial cooperation in the new Convention.

Noting that, although industrialization was "a major component of the development stragegy of ACP countries and all of them without exception have given great priority to the industrial sector in their development plans during the past two decades," the memorandum asserted achievements during the past 15 years had been "very modest and great effort would have to be made if the targets for industrial development established for the second United Nations Development Decade are to be reached in many countries."[3] The limited industrial growth that had taken place was concentrated in a few isolated areas and had made only a modest contribution to economic development and the balance of payments, owing in part to the weak linkages between it and other sectors of the economy and owing also to its being based on imported foreign technology, the licenses for which had been made available only at very high cost. Attempts to manufacture finished consumer goods for export had been frustrated by tariff and nontariff barriers, marketing difficulties, and restrictive practices imposed by multinational corporations.[4]

Nine areas were identified in which specific measures might be taken:

1. expansion of the infrastructure necessary for industrial development, particularly in the least developed, landlocked, and island countries;
2. measures to enable ACP countries to gain preferential access to European technology;
3. adaptation of technology by European institutions for the special needs and problems of ACP states;
4. expansion of training and research facilities in ACP countries;
5. establishment of new industrial and commercial links between industries in Europe and those in the ACP "with the aim of bringing about a new international division of labour between the two sides" (included here would be measures to encourage the reduction of those domestic activities in the European industrial sector for which ACP countries were better endowed, and special provisions to deal with the problems that might result from this process of adjustment);
6. establishment of specific targets for the promotion of particular industries in areas such as the processing of raw materials for export, import substitution,

and heavy manufacturing requiring multinational arrangements on both sides;
7. special measures for small and medium-sized industries such as the establishment of industrial estates, provision of ancillary services, etc.;
8. special financing arrangements that would involve the participation of the EDF and EIB, as well as financial institutions in member countries;
9. training on a large scale of ACP personnel at shopfloor, supervisory, and managerial levels in European industries.

Since the subject of industrial cooperation was of such importance, the memorandum continued, a special chapter should be devoted to it in the new Convention that should provide for the establishment of a Committee on Industrial Cooperation and a Clearing House or Information Centre on Industrial Development.[5]

Eventual inclusion of a chapter on industrial development in the Convention represented a significant victory for ACP negotiators, especially since this was the only chapter that was the product of their own initiative—for the others it was principally a matter of Community proposals to which the ACP responded. Title III was in many respects very similar to the recommendations that the ACP had put forward in their July memorandum. Article 26 lists the following objectives for industrial cooperation between the Community and the ACP:

1. to promote the development and diversification of industry in the ACP States and to help bring about a better distribution of industry both within those States and between them;
2. to promote new relations in the industrial field between the Community, its Member States and the ACP States, in particular the establishment of new industrial and trade links between the industries of the Member States and those of the ACP States;
3. to increase the links between industry and the other sectors of the economy, in particular agriculture;
4. to facilitate the transfer of technology to the ACP States and to promote the adaptation of such technology to their specific conditions and needs, for example by expanding the capacity of the ACP States for research, for adaptation of technology and for training in industrial skills at all levels in these States;
5. to promote the marketing of industrial products of the ACP States in foreign markets in order to increase their share of international trade in those products;
6. to encourage the participation of nationals of ACP States, in particular that of small and medium-sized industrial firms, in the industrial development of those States;
7. to encourage Community firms to participate in the industrial development of the ACP States, where those States so desire and in accordance with their economic and social objectives.

In other articles in the Chapter, the Community pledged to assist the ACP in the provision of industrial infrastructure, the establishment of raw materials processing industries, the organization and financing of training, the making of contact with firms and institutions in possession of the appropriate technological "know-how," the selection and adaptation of available technology, and in the establishment and development of small and medium-sized industrial firms. A Committee on Industrial Cooperation and a Centre for Industrial Development were established.

Despite the similarities between the ACP memorandum and Title III of the Convention, a number of significant modifications had occurred at the behest of the Community. No reference was made in the Convention's text to specific targets for industrial development in ACP states, nor was any mention made of the need for adjustment on the part of Community industries and the provision of special aid in support of this. Similarly, although the Community promised to keep the ACP states "better informed" on technological matters and to assist them in the selection of technology best adapted to their needs, no commitment was made to enable the ACP to gain access to this technology on "favorable" terms as the ACP had requested.

While Title III echoes many of the aspirations expressed by the ACP in their memorandum and, as the Commission is fond of claiming, probably defines in greater detail than any other international agreement the ways in which developed and developing countries can cooperate in the field of industry, it is almost devoid of specific pledges and mechanisms through which these aspirations might be realized. Owing to the late stage in the negotiations at which the matter of industrial cooperation was introduced, many of the essential details regarding the institutions to be established (such as composition, size, and financing) were deliberately not specified in the Convention and later were to become the subject of (extensive) haggling. As Warnecke points out, the necessary instruments for implementing Title III were scattered throughout the Convention: in many of its provisions the Title was in fact redundant, merely making explicit that the means of financial and technical cooperation specified elsewhere in the Convention would be used to promote the objectives of the ACP in the industrial sector.[6] No separate financial allocation was provided for industrial cooperation; funds for this purpose were to be derived from the general allocation for the European Development Fund.

This lack of specificity in the Convention's provisions was the principal cause of the long delays that occurred before the Centre for Industrial Development became operational. Disputes involving the ACP states, the Nine, representatives of the European private sector, the Commission, and the European Investment Bank occurred over the financing, responsibilities, and staffing of the Centre. Eventually established on 1 January 1977, the third year in which the provisions of the Convention were operative, the responsibilities of the Centre according to Article 36 of the Convention were: to gather and disseminate relevant information on industrial opportunities; to arrange for studies to be carried out on the possibilities and potential for industrial development of ACP states, paying particular attention to the necessity of adaptation of technology; to identify opportunities for industrial training and applied research in the Community and the ACP; and "to organize and facilitate contacts and meetings of all kinds between Community and ACP states' industrial policy-makers, promoters, and firms and financial institutions."

A twelve-member Advisory Committee composed of individuals with industrial expertise drawn from states party to the Convention was created to assist the Centre's full-time staff. Guidelines for the Centre's operating procedures established by the Committee on Industrial Cooperation specified that in its selection of projects the first consideration should be viability, followed by social advantages, and finally the potential market outlets. Priority was to be given to the promotion of small and medium-sized businesses, the transfer and adaptation and development of appropriate technology, the selection of projects with a regional bias, the training of businessmen in ACP countries, and the articulation of industrial promotion programs for the least developed states.

Owing to the fact that the Centre had been in existence for only 18 months at the time when the renegotiation of the Convention began, it was difficult to accurately assess its performance. For, as the Centre itself noted, on average more than one year elapses between the identification of a project and signature of an investment agreement, and a further two to three years elapse before construction begins. Additional problems in evaluating its contribution are caused by the Centre's not being involved in all stages of a project—its provision of information over the phone, for instance, may lead to a scheme's successfully getting off the ground (e.g., by locating a source of finance), but this important act of assistance would not appear in the Centre's list of successful projects.

According to the Centre, during the first Convention a total of 125 project studies and expert appraisals were cofinanced and another 175 projects were assisted in one form or another. Seventy percent of the projects were related to agroindustries and food processing, building materials, timber utilization, tanning, the development of alternative energy sources (biomass, natural asphalt, solar heating, small hydroelectric power stations), and the recycling of used engine oil. In addition, the Centre published an inventory of adapted technologies that had been successfully used by developing countries, and profiles of a variety of industrial projects that ACP countries might feasibly undertake. Sixty-five technicians, managers, and members of production staffs were assisted through in-plant training (an activity limited by the Centre's inability to provide funding support beyond round-trip air fares).[7]

As officials of the Centre themselves admitted, however, there was a distressing failure of many of the projects identified as technically and financially feasible actually to be implemented. At the signing of the second Convention none had reached the operational stage; by mid-1980 the Centre could point to six that were functioning, and a further five began production during 1981.[8] Certainly, the claim made in a report by the European Parliament that the Centre had been responsible for the creation of 3,000 new jobs in ACP countries and a further 1,500 within the EEC appeared overly optimistic and could not be substantiated.[9] But the Centre itself by no means bears the entire blame for its relatively slow start. In many instances the failure to implement projects identified as potential commercial successes lay with the ACP states concerned and was often the result of the exercise of political pressures. One illustration may be cited: the Centre had positively evaluated a project for salt extraction from the sea using solar energy and had found a European partner for the two ACP states concerned. When the project failed to materialize, local investigation by the CID found that the project had been blocked because relatives of the Prime Minister of one of the states concerned were involved in the import trade for salt. Similarly, attempts at promoting regional projects had been stalled by the national jealousies between the prospective partners.

Generally, the ACP appeared to be more pleased with the Centre's operations than the Community was. In its memorandum on the role of the CID in Lomé II, the ACP Group commented:

the record of the CID can be considered globally and relatively positive . . . at the end of 1978, the CID had actively promoted a significant number of projects which are spread throughout all ACP regions.[10]

The Commission, on the other hand, showed considerable suspicion of the Centre from its initiation. The Centre was unique (until the creation of the Technical Centre for Agricultural and Rural Cooperation in Lomé II) in its position as a jointly managed institution in the Lomé framework. Since it enjoyed autonomy from the European Commission, the Centre's staff did not refrain from promoting projects in ACP states when these posed a potential threat to Community interests. This became evident in two sectors—the Centre's support of textile projects and of ACP countries' efforts to create export-processing zones (which the Community had attempted to discourage). Community dissatisfaction led to the dismissal of the Centre's first director in 1980. After a considerable period of bitter negotiations, a Dane was appointed as successor over the ACP candidate, a Nigerian who had served as deputy director since the Centre's establishment. ACP states failed to win Community acceptance of the principle of rotation of the directorship between nationals of the Community and of the ACP states. Staff at the Centre noted a new policy was imposed whereby the CID cannot act without prior coordination with the Commission and will refrain from promoting projects in the textiles sector.[11]

Evidence suggests the Community was less than fully cooperative with the Centre during Lomé I. Detailed instructions were sent by the Commission to its delegates in ACP states emphasizing the CID was not a *Community* institution and specifying the limits within which assistance should be rendered to the Centre. This lack of cooperation at the local level in ACP states was a significant problem for the Centre since, lacking its own local agents, one of its two project officers had to travel to attempt to resolve local difficulties. Staff of the Centre complained also that the Community had caused unnecessary difficulties in gaining the agreed immunities and diplomatic privileges the Centre's employees were to enjoy. A widespread sentiment existed among Centre staff and representatives of ACP states that some members of the Community were content to allow the Centre to flounder with inadequate support for the activities it had been assigned; the Community was perceived as not serious in its commitment to industrial cooperation and the Centre would serve as a convenient scapegoat for failures in this domain.

Beyond the political difficulties the Centre has experienced, its principal problem has been its inadequate financial resources. As the Centre itself noted in its evaluation of its activities during Lomé I, "due to its limited means, (it) was only able to make a modest scratch of the surface revealed by the enormous industrial development needs of the ACP States."[12] Its total budget for the first Convention amounted to 6.2 mua, which represented less than 1 percent of the total sectoral allocation to industrial cooperation under Lomé I. Overheads accounted for approximately 56 percent of its budget, which left less than 3 mua for program expenditures (an unusually high current/capital expenditure ratio). This funding supported a full-time staff of only nine professionals.

Both the ACP Group and the CID's staff have argued the Centre's effectiveness has been severely limited by its inability to offer financial support to interested parties. They note a lacuna exists within the array of European financial institutions in that none supported small-scale projects (the exception was the French *Caisse Central*, which has a special branch devoted to small and medium-sized enterprises but which can invest only in Francophone Africa). The European Investment Bank would not consider participation in projects where the capital was less than $2 million. The first annual report of the CID noted:

This lack of financing for the smaller enterprise is a serious weakness of Lomé if one considers (a) the role that can be played in ACP States by firms which are less important but which possess a relatively simple and easily adaptable "know-how," and (b) the high number of small EEC enterprises and their non-exploited potential which could be realized to the profit of ACP States.[13]

Under its present statutes, the Centre essentially has nothing to offer potential investors other than assistance in the identification of projects. It was particularly difficult to get small and medium-sized firms interested in the ACP states—the Centre argued it was necessary to provide them with incentives or else they would be inclined to choose to locate in one of the more advanced of the developing countries. This was particularly a problem now that potential investors realized that access to the Community market for ACP countries was not unlimited and that any new investments should first be cleared with the Community. The very fact that the Conventions themselves were of a five-year duration, with no guarantee their provisions would be renewed in the same form, similarly caused companies to doubt the security of the trade provisions. Given the less than enviable record of many ACP states as regards political stability and expropriation of foreign assets, a need was perceived for investment risk insurance for smaller firms (especially from the smaller EEC member states), which, lacking the resources and channels available to multinationals, were the most vulnerable. For these reasons, only larger European firms to date had been willing to participate in CID-sponsored projects, and the CID had not been successful in attracting companies to ACP states that had not previously had investments in one or more of these countries (although it had fostered new links, e.g., investment by French firms in projects in Anglophone countries). Staff members reported they enjoyed greatest success when they approached European firms privately before potential projects were advertised in the Centre's newsletter—a procedure that inevitably reinforced the failure to attract a more diverse group of European partners.

To remedy the problem of inadequate financial resources, the ACP Group proposed in a memorandum during the negotiations for Lomé II that a Fund for Industrial Development be created. Two rationales were put forward:

1. the need to reduce the financial resource gap for industrial development of the ACP States which has been widening considerably as a result of the decline in real terms of the private and official capital flows to the ACP, including those from the EEC;
2. the need to provide additional investment assistance and incentives for investors in the ACP States in recognition of the relatively difficult general investment conditions such as infrastructure, manpower, services, transportation etc., prevailing in those States.[14]

This demand was supported by the conclusions of the European Parliament's report on the renegotiation of the Convention, which noted "it is clear that the finances made available for industrial cooperation do not meet the needs of the ACP countries nor the goals set by the Convention."[15] Neither of the existing European agencies could perform the necessary financing according to the ACP. The EDF's experience had been only within the public sector, while the EIB was unacceptable since it was not accountable to the ACP under the Convention and therefore would not finance projects if these appeared to conflict with European interests.

The proposed Fund was to have two "windows": the first would be used for mobilizing private and other commercial capital resources for onlending on commercial terms; the second would provide resources for training, financial and technical incentives, and quasi-commercial resources, especially to small and medium-sized industries. Insurance cover for European investments would also be provided. Contributions from the Community and the ACP Group would be mandatory while voluntary contributions from the Nine member states and other governmental/intergovernmental institutions would also be sought. Finally the Fund would raise loan capital from the international capital market and national and international public and private institutions.[16]

Response from the Community to these proposals was predictably negative. An internal Community memorandum notes two grounds on which the proposals were unacceptable: the obligatory financial contribution to be made by the Community and the joint responsibility for management (which the ACP had proposed should fall to the Committee on Industrial Cooperation). The memorandum continued:

With respect to the CID, we must certainly declare our willingness to increase its budgetary resources to permit it to finance advice and expert evaluations, but we cannot accept that it will become responsible for direct industrial investment.[17]

This response is of great interest because of the light it throws on the reality of the "equal partnership." The Community has consistently resisted ACP attempts to attain an equal role in the management of the relationship (see also the chapters on STABEX and on Financial and Technical Cooperation). As far as the Community is concerned, since it alone provides the resources, then ultimately it must have the last say in the management of the relationship. The only area in which this principle had been breached was industrial cooperation with the establishment of the jointly managed CID. Its experience testified to the extent of Community resistance to creating institutions that would not be completely subordinate to the Community viewpoint. To provide this institution with financial resources (other than those derived from the EDF over which the Community had complete control) was totally unacceptable.[18]

This dispute also revealed the fundamentally different conceptions of the content of industrial cooperation held by the ACP and the Community. For the latter, industrial cooperation was never intended to go beyond the facilitation of links with the European private sector and the dissemination of relevant information to the ACP states. According to a Commission report, the Centre's "main role is to encourage European firms to participate in the execution of specific industrial projects."[19] For the ACP, the function of the Centre as a *bureau de mariages* should have been but one component of its role as the focal point of industrial cooperation within the Lomé framework. At the first meeting of the negotiating group on industrial cooperation in October 1979, an ACP spokesman noted that three of the objectives of industrial cooperation had been forgotten: the link with other sectors, notably agriculture; the transfer and adaptation of technology; and the promotion and marketing of new products. The role of the EIB in industrial projects in the ACP states had been very limited—amounting to 1.38 ua per head of ACP population. Meanwhile the Community, through subsidies, had artificially maintained outdated industrial structures which were no longer viable.[20]

In an attempt to remedy the lack of progress in industrial cooperation, which the chief ACP spokesman on the subject described as "peanuts if not non-existent," the ACP attempted once again to insert references in the second Convention to a specific target for growth of their industries and to the necessity for structural adjustment in the Community. A clause was proposed that would list as one of the objectives of industrial cooperation:

to encourage through the process of active and permanent redeployment within the Community, the restructuring of industries in the ACP and the Community Member States with a view to facilitating the production and export of manufactured and semi-manufactured goods.[21]

Even this very mild statement of the necessity of structural change within the EEC was rejected by the Community, largely because a link was made between such adjustment and ACP exports. A Community spokesman noted, in a statement as revealing as regards Community attitudes toward the wider North–South negotiations as toward the Lomé relationship: "the significance of general principles is different in global fora from ACP–EEC relations (which create concrete obligations)."[22] But if general principles were unacceptable, so were specific commitments—the Community rejected an article that would have inserted a firm political commitment by the Community to double (in relation to the existing situation) the percentage of processing of raw materials carried out within ACP states.

Community rejection of specific targets for industrial cooperation was inevitable given that control of the necessary instruments for effecting such a transfer of industry is not in their hands. Nevertheless, as the Community itself noted in a memorandum on industrial cooperation prepared for the Paris Conference on International Economic Cooperation:

Public power cannot substitute for direct economic operators; it is evident however that it controls a variety of means, often indirect, capable of orientating, accelerating or retarding the evolutions taking place.[23]

From the perspective of the ACP, it appeared the Community had used the means at its disposal solely to retard changes in the international division of labor.

A great imbalance exists between the Community's positive and negative powers in industrial cooperation. While the Commission has the power to cut off imports (since it is responsible for implementing the Community's external commercial policies), it has very little positive power in the sense of an ability to promote adjustment within the Community to allow for an increase in and diversification of ACP exports. Largely for this reason the ACP were very suspicious of Community proposals during the Lomé II negotiations that conflict of interest in the industrial field would be ameliorated if regular consultations were to be held. These were proposed not only at the intergovernmental level but also between representatives of economic and social groups of all parties to the Convention. Intergovernmental consultations in the industrial field, the ACP believed, given the imbalance in Community powers, would result merely in Community attempts to prevent them from expanding their activities where a potential conflict existed with EEC interests—especially since the Nine had displayed no willingness to promote internal adjustment in favor of ACP exports. The second Community proposal—for increased involvement of economic and social sectors to foster better understanding of common problems—was also greeted with considerable scepticism by the ACP. A Report to the Joint Committee of the ACP–EEC Consultative Assembly noted such involvement could be "counter-productive" to the ACP position, given the divergence of interests between the social and economic sectors of the Community and those of the ACP over such matters as transfer of technology.[24]

At present no Community-wide adjustment policy exists. Only the Netherlands among the member states has implemented a policy of assisting projects that abandon or modify domestic production structures in favor of building up industrial capacity in developing countries. Germany has achieved considerable success, however, by promoting adjustment through fiscal incentives. But other member states have used the various industrial and social policies at their disposal largely for preserving outmoded production structures.[25]

As the House of Commons Select Committee on Overseas Development asserted:

If there is a real desire to continue the idea that Lomé represents a model for North/South relations there must be evidence in the new Convention that the Community both accepts the inevitability of, and is prepared positively to encourage, an international redeployment of industry.[26]

No evidence of this emerged in the new Convention or in the internal negotiations within the Community that led to it. Industrial adjustment policy remains the prerogative of the member states and is jealously guarded. Germany, in particular, is hostile to the idea of creating Community-wide *dirigisme* in the industrial sector. But an adjustment policy in favor of developing countries need not take a *dirigiste* form; rather it could be fashioned after the German model of offering fiscal incentives. *Dirigisme* is more likely to appear in Community efforts to resist structural adjustment, e.g., the Community-sponsored cartel of steel producers. At present various Community and national subsidies are given to producers in the member states to sustain industries that might feasibly be developed by ACP states, e.g., various types of processing of raw materials, particlarly of agricultural products. Until the Community demonstrates a willingness to not only permit structural adjustment in favor of ACP states but also to actively promote it, the industrial cooperation provisions of the Convention will have little effect beyond the import substitution sector of ACP states.

If the ACP states are to succeed in attracting private investment in support of their aspirations in the industrial sphere, then they too must change their policies to provide a more secure investment climate. Given the recent independence of most ACP states, the question of investment guarantees is a particularly sensitive one in that it is perceived by many to threaten their sovereignty. Nevertheless, as flows of private capital declined precipitously following the often capricious expropriations of the 1960s and early 1970s, even the more radical states have come to appreciate the necessity of creating rules for the equitable treatment of foreign investment. Need for the provision of insurance coverage for European private investors was recognized both by the CID and by the ACP (and, as noted above, was incorporated as part of the Group's proposals for a Fund for Industrial Cooperation). That the outcome of the renegotiation of the Convention was less than fully satisfactory on this matter is due in large part to the clumsy handling of the issue by the Community.

As chapter 4 noted, the Commission as early as 1972 had proposed the creation of a Community-wide scheme for investment guarantees. Declining European investment in raw materials exploration and exploitation in developing countries had given the matter increased urgency. As the Commission noted in a January 1978 communication to the Council, "We are witnessing real blockage in this field."[27] Three member states had no investment guarantee schemes at all while other national schemes were necessarily incomplete, and coordination between them in the event of joint projects would be almost impossible (table 7.2 lists the investment promotion and protection agreements entered into on a bilateral basis between member states and ACP countries). Failure of the World Bank's

**TABLE 7.2.**

List of Agreements on the Protection and Promotion of Investments Signed Between EEC Member States and ACP Countries

| Member State | ACP State | Date of Signature | Date of Entry into Force R = Still under Ratification Procedure |
|---|---|---|---|
| Belgium | Zaire | 3/28/1976 | 1/1/1977 |
| Denmark | Malawi | 3/2/1971 | 3/2/1971 |
| Germany | Benin | 6/29/1978 | R |
| | Cameroon | 6/29/1962 | 11/21/1963 |
| | Central African Rep. | 8/13/1965 | 10/21/1968 |
| | Chad | 4/11/1967 | 11/23/1968 |
| | Congo | 9/13/1965 | 10/14/1967 |
| | Gabon | 5/16/1969 | 3/29/1971 |
| | Guinea | 4/19/1962 | 3/13/1965 |
| | Liberia | 12/12/1961 | 10/22/1967 |
| | Ivory Coast | 10/27/1966 | 6/10/1968 |
| | Madagascar | 9/21/1962 | 3/21/1966 |
| | Mali | 7/28/1977 | R |
| | Mauritius | 5/25/1971 | 8/27/1973 |
| | Niger | 10/29/1964 | 1/10/1966 |
| | Rwanda | 5/18/1967 | 2/28/1969 |
| | Senegal | 1/24/1964 | 1/16/1966 |
| | Sierra Leone | 4/8/1965 | 12/10/1966 |
| | Sudan | 2/7/1963 | 11/24/1967 |

**TABLE 7.2. (Continued)**

| Member State | ACP State | Date of Signature | Date of Entry into Force R = Still under Ratification Procedure |
|---|---|---|---|
| | Tanzania | 1/30/1965 | 7/12/1968 |
| | Uganda | 11/29/1966 | 8/19/1968 |
| | Togo | 5/16/1961 | 12/21/1964 |
| | Zaire | 3/18/1969 | 7/12/1971 |
| | Zambia | 12/10/1966 | 8/25/1972 |
| France | Liberia | 1/26/1979 | R |
| | Mauritius | 3/22/1973 | 3/1/1974 |
| | Sudan | 7/31/1978 | R |
| | Zaire | 10/5/1972 | 3/1/1975 |
| Italy | Ivory Coast | 7/23/1969 | R |
| | Guinea | 4/20/1964 | In force since signature, not yet ratified |
| | Chad | 7/11/1969 | R |
| Netherlands | Cameroon | 7/6/1965 | 5/7/1966 |
| | Ivory Coast | 4/25/1965 | 9/8/1966 |
| | Kenya | 9/11/1970 | R |
| | Uganda | 4/24/1970 | R |
| | Senegal | 6/12/1965 | 5/23/1967 |
| | Sudan | 8/22/1970 | 3/27/1972 |
| | Tanzania | 4/14/1970 | 7/28/1972 |
| United Kingdom | None | | |

Source: Fralon, *The New EEC/ACP Convention*, p. 205.

1972 proposal for the creation of an "International Investment Insurance Agency" and the ineffectiveness of the International Centre for the Settlement of Investment Disputes suggested no satisfactory solution would be found in global fora.

Two principal measures were proposed to remedy this problem. One would have provided for negotiation of agreements among the Community, the member states, and developing countries on the basic rules for the treatment of foreign investment. A second envisaged a number of specific protection agreements on a project-by-project basis where investments conformed to the priorities established by the Community (mining was mentioned as an illustration), were undertaken by companies from at least two member states, and involved large amounts of capital ($50 million or more). The more ambitious plan in its 1972 memorandum for a Community investment guarantee agency was dropped.[28]

When this proposal was submitted, the Commission successfully sought a mandate from the Council to enable it to propose the inclusion in the new Convention of a clause in which the contracting parties would affirm the necessity of promoting and protecting the investments of the other party and the importance of concluding reciprocal accords on this matter.[29] This was one of the few initiatives the Commission pursued in the Lomé II negotiations. It also proved the most controversial, as much because of the friction it engendered between the Community member states as because of friction between the Commission and the ACP Group.

Initially the Commission proposed a permissive clause that would allow for the conclusion of accords on investment protection between the contracting parties. Problems immediately arose over the wording of the clause. Backed by Denmark, Belgium, Italy, and Luxembourg, the Commission wanted a specific reference to the need for Community-level agreements. These four states also wanted the language of the clause strengthened to go beyond the permissive to specify that the contracting parties "must try to conclude" such agreements. Essentially the dispute boiled down to a question of national versus Community competence in investment guarantees—the rock on which the Commission's earlier proposals had foundered. Supporting a greater Community role were four smaller states that themselves had few bilateral agreements with ACP states and that had either no national investment insurance schemes or very limited ones. (Ireland, which had no significant overseas investments, stayed out of the debate since it had no interest in making ACP states a more attractive location for Community investments and thus more effective competitors). Two of the smaller member states had recently seen particularly unfortunate incidents between their companies and ACP states—Denmark with Ghana's expropriation of the Briscoe trading company and Belgium with Zaire's on-and-off nationalization of the copper mines.

Resistance to Community encroachment on an area of national competence was mounted by the Community's Big Three—France, Germany and the United Kingdom. Germany, with the largest number of bilateral accords with ACP governments, had no desire to share these advantages with other member states. France and Britain were most concerned with the question of national competence and also feared the consequences for their bilateral relations with ACP states if a "communitarisation" of investment disputes occurred. For a while the proposals were stalled as legal opinion was sought regarding the compatibility of Community and bilateral accords and regarding which would legally take precedence over the other. France threatened to take the whole question to the European Court of Justice; the smaller states, in retaliation, threatened to block the proposed minerals scheme (SYSMIN); meanwhile development Commissioner Cheysson complained of the "conspiracy of silence" of the member states on the question of investment protection.

What emerged from this disarray was a watered-down Community proposal to the ACP that would have provided that:

1. Contracting Parties affirm the necessity of promoting and protecting the investments of the other party in their respective territories, and affirm in this regard the importance of concluding, in the mutual interest, reciprocal accords on the promotion and protection of investments;
2. ACP States commit themselves to accord to the investments of each Member State of the Community or those subject to joint financing a treatment no less favorable than that which they granted, in the framework of accords relating to the promotion and protection of investments, to the most favored State.[30]

The second proposal was intended as a sop for the smaller states, which continued to be upset by the lack of specificity in the first clause.

As a result of the lengthy maneuvering within the Community, the proposals were sent to the ACP only a couple of weeks before what was scheduled to be the final ministerial negotiating session. ACP states had closely followed the debate over investment protection between the member states and realized now that the principal intention of the Commission's proposals was not so much the promotion of investments in ACP states as a multilateralization of the investment conditions granted to the most preferred member state—a move that would obviously give Community investors advantages over those of third parties. ACP suspicions were compounded when the Community sought to have this treatment applied to certain investments made *before* the Lomé II Convention came into force and to have these benefits conferred automatically through an exchange of letters between a member state and an ACP state rather than as a result of the negotiation of a bilateral agreement.

The manner in which the Community raised the issue of investment protection with the ACP made a negative response almost inevitable. ACP spokesmen rejected the idea of special investment protection measures for its EEC partners, arguing this would send an erroneous signal to all potential investors that there was such significant danger to investment in these countries that even their closest partners—the EEC—needed special protection. Retroactivity of the provisions was also rejected:

Their most serious concern arises from the Community's determination to seek to obtain the above rights (and be committed to the obligations) without having to enter into an *intergovernmental agreement* with the ACP States on this question. Thus in that way any Community Member State will have recourse to these rights by a simple process of declaration.

The ACP States, and indeed no sovereign state, can conceivably be expected to seriously contemplate such a procedure. The ACP States have made it clear from the beginning that they have no intention of so doing. They are equally certain that the Community Member States in a similar situation would not countenance such an obvious erosion of their sovereign status.[31]

Given the importance of these provisions to the smaller member states (Denmark threatened to refuse to sign a new Convention unless references to investment guarantees were incorporated), the Commission continued to press for ACP concessions. Bitter negotiations continued until two hours after the scheduled signature of the new Convention in Lomé on 31 October 1979 (indeed, a senior ACP negotiator stated that the ACP would have refused to sign the Convention if it had not been for the pleading of the President of Togo, who feared that a failure of the Convention to materialize after the lavish preparations would have caused a coup d'état to secure his ouster).[32]

As finally agreed, a joint declaration on investments was annexed to the Convention. This provides:

1. Where an ACP State has entered, or enters, into an inter-governmental agreement relating to the treatment of investments with any Member States, the ACP State concerned recognizes that the right of non-discriminatory treatment of investments coming from Member States of the Community in ACP States takes effect from the entry into force of the Convention.
2. (a) The application of this right shall be based on bilateral inter-governmental agreements which shall serve as reference agreements. (b) As regards such bi-

lateral inter-governmental investment agreements concluded before the entry into force of this Convention, the application of non-discriminatory treatment shall take into account any provisions in the reference agreement. The ACP State shall have the right to modify or adapt this treatment when international obligations and/or changed *de facto* circumstances so necessitate.

3. For the purpose of applying non-discriminatory treatment on the basis of paragraph 2(a), the Contracting States shall proceed to bilateral inter-governmental exchanges of letters or other appropriate form required by law of a Contracting State.

4. Any Contracting State has the right to ask for such an agreement. The agreement when concluded shall come into effect without delay in accordance with the law of the ACP State concerned.

5. Such agreements shall cover disputes relating to investments arising only after the entry into force of the new Convention.

6. The treatment of investments made before the entry into force of this Convention shall be examined by the two parties in the light of the provisions of the agreement of reference.

This declaration, itself hardly a model of lucidity, was made all the more confusing by an exchange of letters between the co-Presidents of the ACP–EEC Council of Ministers. Here it was acknowledged that the "right of non-discriminatory treatment" could not take automatic effect but can become operational only through bilateral intergovernmental agreements, that the application of such rights cannot infringe on the sovereignty of any state party to the Convention, and that retroactivity is not implied. The ACP insisted this exchange of letters be included in the minutes of the signing of the Convention.[33]

Although the smaller states of the Community could derive some satisfaction from the outcome of the negotiations, this provided little extra security for European investors and could hardly be regarded as a significant step toward attracting private capital to the ACP states. None of the parties to the Convention at the time of its signature had a clear idea of what the effects of the new provisions on investment would be in practice. While the ACP apparently had conceded that any EEC member state would be accorded most favored nation treatment as regards their investments if a bilateral intergovernmental agreement was concluded, an ACP state was under no obligation to maintain the terms extended in previous agreements. Rather than provide additional security for European capital, the result might be the opposite: if a member state that previously had no treaty with the ACP state requested to negotiate one, the effect would be to open the way for renegotiation of all existing treaties.

No reference is made in the Annex to the duration of any such treaties, again undermining their effectiveness as a means of providing security.

## SOME IMPLICATIONS

Cooperation in the industrial field was one of the aspects of their strategy of collective clientelism that most interested the ACP Group. Perhaps inevitably, given the aspirations and inflated expectations of the ACP Group, the results have been disappointing. As important as the modest nature of achievements in this sector is the manner in which the implementation of this Title has exposed the fallacy of notions of "equal partnership" on which the relationship is supposedly based.

As Commissioner for Development Cheysson himself acknowledged, the Title "lacks operational content."[34] ACP states were so delighted at their success in inserting a chapter on industrial cooperation that they neglected to insist at the time on the specification of the means by which its lengthy list of aspirations might be realized. Although the centerpiece of the framework for cooperation, the CID, has played a useful role, it has been handicapped by both a limited budget and a restricted mandate. In the second Convention the funding of the Centre was quadrupled to 25 mua (which continues to be derived from the EDF's allocation for regional cooperation projects), which its staff believed would be adequate for it to perform the limited role that the Community desires, that is, to provide liaison between European industries and ACP partners and to disseminate information.[35] But its autonomy has apparently been curtailed—in practice it will now be subordinate to the Commission, which rather makes a mockery of its status as a jointly managed institution.

As serious is the inability of the Centre to offer financial assistance to European firms in order to make the ACP states a more attractive investment proposition. There is a demonstrated need for a fund that could assist small and medium-sized firms in attaining development finance; such a fund could also play a useful role in providing investment risk insurance. ACP states have attempted to take a unilateral initiative by establishing an ACP Development Bank, without demanding obligatory Community contributions, but this proposal has yet to get off the ground.[36]

Ultimately, industrial cooperation depends on the private sector. But this does not imply the parties to the Convention have no means at their disposal through which they can influence the decisions of private investors. The types of industrial enterprise that ACP states might feasibly pursue are those that will threaten existing labor-intensive industries within the Community. An active policy of anticipatory adjustment assistance to encourage European industries to move out of those lines in which the ACP states have a comparative advantage would probably be the most useful contribution that the Community could make to ACP industrialization. Ultimately, it would be in the best interests of the Community also: a number of studies have shown that a failure to promote industrial adjustment has cost more jobs through obsolescence (as industries increasingly lag behind technological breakthroughs) than competition from developing countries has.[37] But existing policies at the Community level have been directed toward the polar opposite: the support of outmoded and inefficient production structures.

Industrial cooperation cannot, of course, be considered in isolation from other provisions of the Convention. The uncertainty of future security of access for ACP manufactures under the trade regime has discouraged foreign investment; similarly, the failure of STABEX to cover processed products has deterred a diversification into downstream activities. But the Convention itself is by no means the only reason for limited success in industrial cooperation. If ACP states are to exploit the advantages they enjoy by virtue of the Lomé Convention and, indeed, if they are to achieve their ambitious goals in the industrial sphere, then they must do much more to make themselves attractive locations for foreign private investment. Title Three would be more of a model for future North-South relations if the ACP states would commit themselves to seek independent third-party arbitration in the event of investment disputes. ACP countries in return would expect assurances regarding the conduct of foreign investors. To date, in accord with its narrow interpretation of the industrial cooperation chapter and its fear of setting a precedent for the global North-South dialogue, the Community has resisted the insertion of any reference to the conduct of European firms. ACP countries would almost certainly be more open to negotiations on the security of foreign investments if obligations were imposed on the investing parties to refrain from restrictive practices (e.g., by making reference to the OECD's Code of Conduct for transnational corporations). This is an area where the potential for cooperation for mutual benefit has not been realized, in part because of the Community's clumsy handling of the issue and in part because of the ACP Group's preoccupation with preserving its sovereignty.

# 8

# Financial and Technical Cooperation

In embarking on their strategy of collective clientelism the ACP Group had four principal objectives in relation to the arrangements for financial and technical cooperation. First, they hoped at least to maintain the value of per capita receipts of aid from the EDF in real terms; this would realize the commitment made to the Associates in the Deniau memorandum that any extension of the EDF to new parties would not place them in a position where their existing benefits would be jeopardized. The associables, of course, anticipated that they would gain as much from the new EDF on a per capita basis as the Associates.[1] Second, aid from the EDF should be additional to that currently received from EEC member states—a principle that went back to the Fund's establishment under the Treaty of Rome. Third, the Group sought improvements in the procedures of the Fund, especially in those areas (see chapter 2) identified as problematic during the Yaoundé Conventions—delays in disbursements, the small share of contracts awarded to companies in the recipient countries, and the lack of representation of the beneficiaries in the decision-making process. Fourth, many ACP states wished to see the Fund promoting more projects in sectors to which they gave priority, most notably industry, rather than the maintenance of its traditional emphasis on prestige projects and large-scale public works. And finally, the Group hoped to change the traditional preference of the Fund for countries with higher per capita incomes.

## ACP SHARES IN EEC AID

Any attempt to evaluate whether the ACP were successful in their objective of maintaining the real value of per capita aid receipts encounters the problem of which criteria should be used. For instance, should one employ the rate of inflation in the Community or that in ACP countries; what account should be taken of the rate of population growth in ACP countries and additions to their aggregated population as other countries accede to the Convention; and what allowance should be made for provisions for new areas of activity, e.g., the STABEX scheme, which some perceive as coming at the expense of traditional project aid?

In the negotiations for Lomé I, the ACP asked for a total of 8,000 mua for the fourth EDF, an eightfold increase over the previous Fund's value of 905 mua, which was clearly considerably in excess of anything that they might have realistically hoped to achieve. Initially the Commission had proposed a figure half that demanded by the ACP, a total calculated on the basis of inflation rates in the Community and the ACP since the Yaoundé Conventions were signed and adjusted for the increase in the recipient population as a result of the participation of Commonwealth states. But this figure was reduced by one-quarter by the Council, producing a revised sum of 3000 mua, which, according to Wall, represented a 25 percent fall on a per capita basis from the value of the third EDF.[2]

This hardly represented a favorable first test for the strategy of collective clientelism. Wall was not alone among critical commentators in suggesting it was unlikely that the EDF would prove to be additional aid for the ACP but rather would be subtracted from the bilateral aid programs of Community member states. Unfortunately the counterfactual proposition cannot be tested, since there is no knowing what would have happened to ACP aid receipts in the absence of Lomé. This question can be examined indirectly, however, by observing changes in the shares of ACP states in the bilateral programs of the member states during the first Convention.

Table 8.1a presents data on the ACP share in the total net bilateral overseas development assistance of EEC member states in the period 1971–1981. Rather than be "penalized" as recipients of European multilateral aid, the share of the ACP Group rose over the decade by a quarter and remained stable during this whole period of the Convention. If contributions to the EDF did indeed cause reductions in the bilateral programs of the member states, then this did not occur primarily at the expense of the ACP. Table 8.1b presents similar calculations for the share of Commonwealth ACP states in the British bilateral program. Although these results are more mixed, the share of the ACP in receipts actually rose during the lifetime of the Convention after having suffered a decline in the years immediately preceding its negotiation. For the former French

**TABLE 8.1.**

ACP Shares in EEC and British Bilateral Aid 1971–1981

(a) EEC Bilateral Net Overseas Development Assistance ($ m)

|  | 1971 | 1972 | 1973 | 1974 | 1975 | 1976 | 1977 | 1978 | 1979 | 1980 | 1981 |
|---|---|---|---|---|---|---|---|---|---|---|---|
| ACP | 578.6 | 683.1 | 808.9 | 1043.2 | 1306.9 | 1280.9 | 1378.9 | 1744.2 | 2424.5 | 2806.1 | 2675.5 |
| EEC total | 2400.2 | 2631.4 | 3099.2 | 3517.4 | 4302.7 | 4391.2 | 4584.5 | 6104.5 | 8054.3 | 9142.6 | 9005.3 |
| ACP share | 24.1% | 26.0% | 26.1% | 29.7% | 30.4% | 29.2% | 30.0% | 28.6% | 30.1% | 30.7% | 29.7% |

(b) British Bilateral Net Overseas Development Assistance ($ m)

|  | 1971 | 1972 | 1973 | 1974 | 1975 | 1976 | 1977 | 1978 | 1979 | 1980 | 1981 |
|---|---|---|---|---|---|---|---|---|---|---|---|
| Commonwealth ACP | 133.2 | 122.9 | 107.1 | 112.6 | 119.8 | 124.1 | 128.6 | 232.5 | 306.7 | 353.7 | 310.9 |
| Br. total | 487.8 | 480.9 | 442.1 | 509.2 | 566.5 | 580.8 | 555.4 | 854.0 | 1214.8 | 1326.2 | 1329.0 |
| Commonwealth ACP share | 27.3% | 25.6% | 24.2% | 22.1% | 21.2% | 21.4% | 23.2% | 27.2% | 25.2% | 26.7% | 23.4% |

(c) French Bilateral Net Overseas Development Assistance ($ m)

|  | 1971 | 1972 | 1973 | 1974 | 1975 | 1976 | 1977 | 1978 | 1979 | 1980 | 1981 |
|---|---|---|---|---|---|---|---|---|---|---|---|
| Ex-French colonies | 163.0 | 231.1 | 245.2 | 322.1 | 407.2 | 409.4 | 388.0 | 475.8 | 569.4 | 751.0 | 709.2 |
| French total | 1075.3 | 1320.3 | 1488.4 | 1615.6 | 2093.2 | 2145.5 | 2266.8 | 2705.3 | 3449.0 | 4161.7 | 4177.0 |
| Ex colonies' share | 15.2% | 17.5% | 16.5% | 20.0% | 19.5% | 19.1% | 17.1% | 17.6% | 16.5% | 18.0% | 17.0% |

Sources: OECD, *Geographical Distribution of Financial Flows to LDCs* (Paris: OECD, 1978, 1980, 1983); OECD, *Development Assistance* (annual).
Note: EEC data are for Belgium, Denmark, France, Germany, Italy, Netherlands, and the United Kingdom (Ireland and Luxembourg are not members of the DAC).

colonies, there is again no evidence of a decline in their share of French bilateral aid during this period (table 8.1c).

In that there is often little coordination between the EDF and the aid bureaucracies of the member states (with the exception of France), and given that the national aid agencies have particular interests in their traditional clients, these findings are perhaps not particularly surprising. Nevertheless, they do suggest that one objective of collective clientelism was realized: the Convention did not have an adverse effect on the ACP share in EEC bilateral aid.

It is also interesting to examine the share of the EEC in total aid given to the ACP—whether Lomé has, for instance, caused other donors to ignore the ACP, perceiving them as Europe's "Chosen Few." Tables 8.2a and b present data for the former Yaoundé Group and for twenty Commonwealth countries, respectively.[3] A striking feature of the data on the Yaoundé Group is the decline in the Community share of total aid receipts. This is primarily the result of the failure of EDF receipts to keep pace with other multilateral aid, since the Community share in total bilateral aid has remained relatively constant. As a result an increasing bilateralization of the aid relationship with the EEC has occurred over the decade. Yet while bilateral receipts from the EEC have become relatively more important in the EEC total, a considerable diversification of sources of this type of aid has taken place within the Community; the share of the former metropole (France, except in the cases of Rwanda, Burundi, and Zaire [Belgium], and Somalia [Italy]) has dropped consistently over the decade. Germany, in particular, has taken an increasing interest in the ACP countries; its concern with security of supplies of raw materials appears to have been reflected in its allocation of an increasing share of its bilateral aid to African states.

For the Commonwealth countries, the years since the signature of the Convention have seen the decline in the Community share of total aid receipts reversed and a similar trend in the EEC share of bilateral aid. As a result of the Convention, receipts from the EDF have led to a considerable increase in the share of Community aid in all multilateral receipts, a major factor in the rise in the EEC share of total receipts since 1975. For the Commonwealth countries the decline in the share of the former metropole in bilateral receipts has been dramatic (although, since it has already been shown that the share of the ACP in British bilateral aid has not declined, this is a reflection of the reductions in the total re-

**TABLE 8.2.**

EEC Share (%) in ACP Total Receipts of Overseas Development Assistance

(a) Former Yaoundé Associates

|  | 1971 | 1972 | 1973 | 1974 | 1975 | 1976 | 1977 | 1978 | 1979 |
|---|---|---|---|---|---|---|---|---|---|
| EEC share of total receipts | 72.4 | 73.4 | 72.8 | 66.2 | 63.9 | 63.8 | 58.6 | 57.8 | 61.3 |
| EEC share of bilateral aid | 79.6 | 82.0 | 84.2 | 81.0 | 80.3 | 79.0 | 77.5 | 79.5 | 76.9 |
| EEC share of multilat. aid | 60.3 | 57.4 | 59.3 | 57.0 | 52.9 | 45.3 | 37.2 | 36.7 | 44.8 |
| Former metropole share of bilateral aid | 62.7 | 70.4 | 64.4 | 60.8 | 60.4 | 57.8 | 54.4 | 51.2 | 49.0 |
| EEC bilateral aid as a % of EEC total aid | 67.0 | 72.1 | 68.9 | 65.8 | 65.7 | 72.7 | 77.2 | 74.7 | 72.2 |
| EEC multilat. aid as a % of total EEC aid | 33.0 | 27.9 | 31.1 | 33.2 | 34.3 | 27.3 | 22.8 | 25.3 | 27.8 |

Source: Calculated from data in OECD, *Geographical Distribution of Financial Flows to Developing Countries* (Paris: OECD, 1978, 1980, 1983).
Note: figures are *unweighted* means for the 18 Yaoundé countries.

(b) Commonwealth Countries

|  | 1971 | 1972 | 1973 | 1974 | 1975 | 1976 | 1977 | 1978 | 1979 |
|---|---|---|---|---|---|---|---|---|---|
| EEC share of total receipts | 48.7 | 48.3 | 39.9 | 38.1 | 34.9 | 33.4 | 38.4 | 40.5 | 45.9 |
| EEC share of bilateral aid | 62.7 | 60.1 | 49.8 | 51.7 | 55.3 | 50.4 | 51.1 | 52.9 | 63.5 |
| EEC share of multilat. aid | 6.3 | 11.7 | 3.1 | 11.6 | 11.4 | 14.2 | 19.8 | 25.2 | 28.4 |
| Former metropole share of bilateral aid | 52.7 | 46.5 | 37.8 | 38.0 | 36.0 | 30.2 | 26.7 | 33.0 | 27.5 |
| EEC bilateral aid as a % of EEC total aid | 101.3 | 98.2 | 99.7 | 98.1 | 97.4 | 93.7 | 82.8 | 75.1 | 79.3 |
| EEC multilat. aid as a % of total EEC aid | −1.3 | 1.8 | 0.3 | 1.9 | 2.6 | 6.3 | 17.2 | 24.9 | 20.7 |

Source: Calculated from data in OECD, *Geographical Distribution of Financial Flows to Developing Countries* (Paris: OECD, 1978, 1980, 1983).
Note: figures are *unweighted* means for the 19 Commonwealth countries.

sources devoted by Britain to aid programs in recent years rather than a diversion of British aid away from the ACP). Since the EEC share in total bilateral aid has increased since the signature of the Convention, it appears that Commonwealth countries have benefited from other EEC countries taking over the role previously played by Britain. The move to a collective patron through the signature of Lomé again appears to have had beneficial payoffs. As a group, however, Commonwealth countries are still less favored recipients of EEC bilateral aid than the Yaoundé countries. In part this might be a matter of geographical proximity, the Caribbean and Pacific countries being, of course, much further removed from the Community than the Yaoundé Group. But it is probably also a matter of historical ties and the relative lack of exposure of the Six to a number of these countries. Since over the period 1975–79 the Yaoundé countries on average received 20 ua per capita of European bilateral aid more than the Commonwealth Group, the latter might hope to improve their position in the future as a result of closer ties facilitated by the Convention.

These results show that although the real value of per capita EDF receipts may have fallen for the ACP, they have generally either maintained or increased their shares in total EEC bilateral aid. Collective clientelism thus might have paid dividends in a rather unexpected manner. It is not possible, of course, to attribute any causal effects to the Convention. Since the ACP include a large number of the world's least developed countries, which have been the major beneficiaries of the reorientation of aid agencies toward basic needs, the ACP might well have benefited from increased attention in European bilateral programs even in the absence of Lomé. But it is comforting for the ACP that some of the more dire predictions of critics of the Convention do not appear to have materialized. EDF aid as an addition to the contributions from the bilateral programs of member states has helped ensure that the ACP Group as a whole are relatively privileged beneficiaries of aid, receiving on average considerably more per capita than other countries at their levels of development.

## EDF PROCEDURES

In response to initiatives from both the ACP Group and the European Commission, the Lomé I Convention introduced a number of innovations into European Community aid. Principal among these were the reservation of 10 percent of the total programmable aid for regional projects, the financing of trade promotion, special measures for the least developed states, an allocation of 20 mua for supporting microprojects in local communities, a quadrupling of the ceiling on the value of contracts for which the accelerated tendering procedure applied, a 10 percent preference to ACP enterprises on works contracts of less than 2 mua, and a 15 percent preference to ACP firms on all supply contracts. These innovations notwithstanding, the principal criticisms of the Fund were depressingly familiar: the complexity of its administrative procedures and the time lag between signature of the Convention and the disbursement of aid.

In evaluating EDF procedures, choice of a relevant reference group is particularly important. If one chooses to compare the Fund to the procedures adopted by bilateral agencies, then it would be unsurprising if the comparison turned out to be negative. This, indeed, was the case when Hills compared the EDF to the Swedish International Development Agency and the British Ministry of Overseas Development.[4] Whether it is realistic to make such a comparison, given the apparently unavoidable additional procedural complexities where the donor is a multilateral organization is very doubtful. A study commissioned by the ACP as a background paper for the renegotiation of the Convention (and thus presumably unlikely to be unnecessarily charitable toward the EEC) was far more positive in its appraisal:

On paper at least the Commission's procedures constitute a massive advance compared with the majority of other agencies, in relation to a number of all-too-familiar procedural problems . . . in a number of areas, in which the practices habitually adopted by aid agencies as suiting their own convenience are demonstrably inimical to recipients' interests, the Commission appears to do better than most.[5]

In particular, the study noted, the procedures adopted by the Commission in aid programming, especially the significant role given to the recipients in their choice of programs and the subsequent administration of those projects selected for funding, if properly implemented, would reduce such common aid-induced distortions and biases as the propensity toward capital-intensive and import-intensive project designs, the requesting of projects that the potential recipient believes the donor favors but that do not enjoy the former's full support, and the propensity to favor large showcase projects in situations where multiple small projects might be more appropriate.[6] Whether these potential advantages were in fact realized is considered later in this chapter.

Community procedures were considered to be superior to those of many other agencies on a number of other dimensions. One of the most significant was the delegation of considerable responsibility to local representatives, thereby giving ACP states better access to the programming process and providing a local interpreter for the maze of procedural rules that have to be followed before a project is funded. The EDF's indicative programming and multiyear commitments, unlike the procedures of the U.S. AID, provide assurance as regards funding for long-term projects.[7] By comparison with many bilateral donors, the grant element in EDF aid remains very high (averaging 96 percent in 1976), and although aid is tied to purchases from the Community or ACP states, the ability to choose a supplier within any of the Nine member states enabled recipients to take advantage of competitive bidding and to diversify their sources. A willingness to subdivide contracts, coupled with the preferences given to local suppliers in small contracts, opens the way for local contractors to participate in EDF work. In fact, of the total contracts awarded for projects funded by the Fourth EDF by the end of 1982, ACP contractors had won in excess of 30 percent; for works contracts they had been awarded as much as 44 percent.[8] Although some of the beneficiaries were undoubtedly subsidiaries of European companies established in ACP states, this rather impressive performance goes some way toward answering criticisms that the EDF was in fact a *European* Development Fund.

One of the most advantageous features of the Community's aid program has been its willingness to engage in cofinancing of projects. More than 20 percent of the project appropriations under the Fourth EDF were used for this purpose. At the end of 1980, these totaled 598 mua, enabling work on 50 projects that had a total value of more than 3,600 mua. Similarly, the EIB provided more than 300 mua for 31 projects, which had a total value to ACP states of more than 2,600 mua. As a result of cofinancing (primarily with member states, the World Bank, and Arab funds), the Community's aid has had a significant multiplier effect, although ACP states have complained that the Community's preference for parallel rather than joint financing caused delays as a result of the need for extra negotiations and imposed an additional burden on ACP bureaucracies.

The multinational nature of the EDF itself has been the source of a number of problems. Awarding of contracts to EEC companies continues to be a highly political matter because of the desire of member countries to share in the spoils. This was acknowledged in an internal evaluation of the performance of the EDF:

There has to be a certain balance in the aid spin-off to the Member States, while for their part the recipient States insist the projects should as far as possible be implemented by their own authorities and national enterprises. These two considerations mean that the choice sometimes falls on a contractor with too little experience or insufficient resources, but of the "right" nationality. This has led to design faults in some schemes, and technical errors or delays in execution.[9]

According to the ACP, a search for technical assistance personnel of the "right" nationality not only caused delays but also led to the hiring of professionally incompetent personnel who did not know the language of a country and/or its particular circumstances.[10]

Yet despite the Commission's efforts to achieve an equitable distribution of contracts between the member states, the considerable imbalance characteristic of the Yaoundé Conventions continued. France continued to be the principal beneficiary (see table 8.3), although Italy also gained

**TABLE 8.3.**

Distribution of EDF IV Contracts among Member States at End of 1982

| Country | Share of Total Contracts (%) | Contribution to EDF IV (%) |
|---|---|---|
| Belgium | 8.7 | 6.25 |
| Denmark | 1.0 | 2.40 |
| France | 34.0 | 25.95 |
| Germany | 18.3 | 25.95 |
| Ireland | 0.5 | 0.60 |
| Italy | 17.2 | 12.00 |
| Luxembourg | 0.4 | 0.20 |
| Netherlands | 6.1 | 7.95 |
| United Kingdom | 13.9 | 18.70 |

Source: "Commission Report to the ACP-EEC Council of Ministers on the Administration of Financial and Technical Cooperation in 1982 Under the Lomé Convention," [COM (83) 486 fin] (July 1983) table XIa.

Note: ACP states and third countries accounted for 32 percent of total contracts awarded at end 1982. This amount is excluded from the calculation of country shares in total contracts.

a share of EDF contracts disproportionate to its contribution to the Fund. In part this might be attributed to the contract procedures of the EDF, which followed French national practice—a cause of considerable annoyance to the Commonwealth ACP countries and to British contractors. Continuing imbalances in the sharing of contracts among Community member states has done little to warm the more globalist members toward the special relationship with the ACP.

Delays in disbursement continued to be an unfortunate characteristic of the Fund. By the time that the first Convention expired, only 2,275 mua of the total of 3,400 mua of programmable aid had been committed and 984 mua disbursed (29 percent of the total aid available and forty-three percent of commitments).[11] Since the average rate of inflation in the Community was 10 percent annually, and that in the ACP countries 15 percent, at least 50 percent of the real value of the aid committed at the time of the signature of the Convention was eroded by inflation before the ACP received it.

There are few criteria by which this performance (however regrettable from an ideal viewpoint) might be judged from a comparative perspective (especially since the Community does not publish details of the indicative programs of the individual ACP states). No evidence suggests, for example, that the pipeline for EDF aid is significantly longer than that of other multilateral agencies. And by no means was the Community alone to blame for the tardiness of disbursement—ACP states themselves caused delays by submitting inadequately prepared project proposals and by failing to respond to Community requests for further information. Countries previously associated with the Community under the Yaoundé Conventions did significantly better in terms of early disbursements (table 8.4),

TABLE 8.4.

Commitments & Disbursements (EDF IV) at 31 August 1979 (in mua)

|  | (1) Commitments | (2) Disbursements | (2) as % (1) |
|---|---|---|---|
| Former Yaoundé Associates | 657 | 198 | 30.1% |
| New EDF Beneficiaries | 761 | 128 | 16.8% |
|  | 1418 | 326 | 23.0% |

Source: ACP-EEC Consultative Assembly, *From Lomé 1 towards Lomé 2* (November 1980) p. 58.

suggesting that lack of familiarity with each other on the part of the Community and the new beneficiaries contributed to the delays. As the Community itself noted, the change in emphasis on the part of donor agencies toward meeting basic needs, involving a concentration of efforts on rural areas, caused additional delays as projects became increasingly complex to design and administer. And where projects are of a long-term nature, as is the case, for instance, with many of the EDF's agricultural programs, it is unsurprising that aid is disbursed over a period of years.

On the question of procedures, therefore, the verdict on the EDF is a mixed one. While it falls far short of ideal standards, especially from the perspective of the recipient states, the EDF does not appear to be significantly worse than other multilateral agencies, and, on a number of dimensions, displays greater flexibility than many other donors.

## SECTORAL ALLOCATIONS

Among the principal complaints leveled at the first three European Development Funds was the allegation that too large a proportion of total resources was devoted to infrastructural projects and much too little to the development of directly productive schemes, especially manufacturing. EDF aid had traditionally favored prestige projects, and this sometimes resulted, in the words of the new Commissioner for Development Edgard Pisani, in the construction of "cathedrals in the sand."[12]

From the preliminary figures presented in table 8.5 (commitments made by the end of 1980), the conclusion can be drawn that there has not been a great change in the pattern of EDF allocations. These figures must be interpreted with some caution as a result of the rather idiosyncratic manner in which the Community breaks down its aid commitments, which tends to understate the share of infrastructural projects in total aid. First, the EDF includes energy projects under industrialization, whereas most other agencies classify these under economic infrastructure (and since close to 30 percent of "industrial" projects fell under this category, the result is a considerable overstatement of the contribution to this sector). Second, as White points out, the Community fails to distinguish between financial cooperation and technical cooperation; since the technical assistance component of economic infrastructure projects is relatively small compared to that of social projects, the aggregation of these figures again tends to understate the share of aid devoted to infrastructure.[13]

**TABLE 8.5.**
Sectoral Breakdown of EDF IV Commitments at 30
December 1980

| Sector | 000 ua | % |
| --- | --- | --- |
| 1. Industrialization | 392.3 | 19.2 |
| of which: | | |
| extractive industries | (9.5) | (0.5) |
| manufacturing | (85.9) | (4.2) |
| energy | (140.0) | (6.9) |
| 2. Tourism | 2.4 | 0.1 |
| 3. Rural production | 506.7 | 24.8 |
| of which: | | |
| plantations | (100.2) | (4.9) |
| 4. Transport and communications | 584.3 | 24.8 |
| of which: | | |
| roads and bridges | (457.8) | (22.4) |
| 5. Education and training | 227.8 | 11.1 |
| 6. Health | 47.4 | 2.3 |
| 7. Water/housing | 105.6 | 5.2 |
| 8. Trade promotion | 32.6 | 1.6 |
| 9. Other | 146.1 | 7.1 |
| of which: | | |
| Community delegations | (87.5) | (4.3) |

Source: Calculated from *Commission Report to the ACP-EEC Council of Ministers on the Administration of Financial and Technical Cooperation in 1980, Under the Lomé Convention* [X/46/1982-EN], table 12.
Note: Data include grants and special loans from the EDF but exclude funding from the EIB, exceptional aid, and STABEX transfers.

If energy projects are recategorized under the infrastructure heading, then the latter becomes by far the largest single sectoral grouping. Roads and bridges were the single most important consumer of EDF resources, alone accounting for close to one-fifth of the total commitments of programmable aid. White suggests that the EDF's concentration on infrastructural projects is possibly greater than that of any other agency, while at the same time, the Community's aid to the development of production is relatively small.[14] This is recognized by the Community itself: an internal assessment of EDF aid acknowledges a demonstrated reluctance to finance the industrial processing of raw materials "with the exception of large-scale agribusiness operations run by firms which are themselves integrated" where "most of the production involved was intended for markets outside Africa."[15] And where aid has been given toward industrialization it has come primarily from the resources of the EIB.

Since the EIB will not invest its own resources unless it is certain of attaining a commercial return (a minimum of 10 percent p.a.), many of the least developed ACP countries found that the Community was not willing to fund projects in the industrial sector. Only 25 percent of the loans from the EIB's own resources were made to least developed ACP states, and only 31 percent of total funds from the Bank (see table 8.6). Carlsen noted Tanzania had to reduce the share of industry in its indic-

**TABLE 8.6.**
Financing Granted by the EIB Under Lomé I—Breakdown by Country on the Basis of the Classification in Article 48

| | Loans from EIB Resources | | Risk Capital Operations | | | Incl. Credits from Global | Overall | |
|---|---|---|---|---|---|---|---|---|
| | MUA | % | MUA | % | Number | Loans | MUA | % |
| LEAST-DEVELOPED ACP STATES (ARTICLE 48) | 97.7 | 25.0 | 57.49 | 59.2 | 64 | 18 | 155.19 | 31.3 |
| Botswana | 6.5 | 1.7 | 1.75 | 1.8 | 4 | | 8.25 | 1.7 |
| Burundi | | | 0.50 | 0.5 | 2 | 1 | 0.50 | 0.1 |
| Cape Verde | | | 3.58 | 3.7 | 2 | | 3.58 | 0.7 |
| Comoros | | | 0.01 | | 1 | | 0.01 | |
| Djibouti | | | 1.00 | 1.0 | 1 | | 1.00 | 0.2 |
| Gambia | | | 2.39 | 2.5 | 2 | | 2.39 | 0.5 |
| Guinea | 4.4 | 1.1 | 0.15 | 0.2 | 2 | | 4.55 | 0.9 |
| Upper Volta | 8.0 | 2.0 | 7.93 | 8.1 | 4 | | 15.93 | 3.3 |
| Malawi | 14.5 | 3.7 | 1.15 | 1.2 | 12 | 7 | 15.65 | 3.2 |
| Mali | | | 6.15 | 6.3 | 2 | | 6.15 | 1.3 |
| Mauritania | 25.0 | 6.4 | | | | 1 | 25.00 | 5.1 |
| Niger | 6.0 | 1.5 | 0.90 | 0.9 | 3 | | 6.90 | 1.4 |
| Rwanda | | | 3.00 | 3.1 | 1 | | 3.00 | 0.6 |
| Seychelles | | | 0.58 | 0.6 | 1 | | 0.58 | 0.2 |
| Somalia | | | 0.25 | 0.3 | 1 | | 0.25 | 0.1 |
| Sudan | | | 6.50 | 6.7 | 1 | | 6.50 | 1.3 |
| Swaziland | 12.0 | 3.1 | 1.15 | 1.2 | 4 | | 13.15 | 2.7 |
| Tanzania | 5.0 | 1.3 | 7.75 | 8.0 | 14 | 10 | 12.75 | 2.6 |
| Chad | | | 7.50 | 7.7 | 1 | | 7.50 | 1.5 |
| Togo | 16.3 | 4.2 | 5.25 | 5.4 | 5 | | 21.55 | 4.4 |

**TABLE 8.6.** *(Continued)*

| | Loans from EIB Resources | | Risk Capital Operations | | | Incl. Credits from Global Loans | Overall | |
|---|---|---|---|---|---|---|---|---|
| | MUA | % | MUA | % | Number | Loans | MUA | % |
| OTHER ACP STATES | 292.3 | 75.0 | 39.79 | 40.8 | 155 | 78 | 322.09 | 68.2 |
| Cameroon | 32.7 | 8.4 | 4.60 | 4.7 | 8 | | 37.30 | 7.6 |
| Congo | | | 3.15 | 3.2 | 1 | | 3.15 | 0.7 |
| Ivory Coast | 47.3 | 12.1 | 2.92 | 3.0 | 14 | | 50.22 | 10.3 |
| Ghana | 16.0 | 4.1 | 2.25 | 2.3 | 4 | | 18.25 | 3.8 |
| Kenya | 52.4 | 13.4 | 1.17 | 1.2 | 26 | 16 | 53.57 | 11.0 |
| Liberia | 7.4 | 1.9 | 0.29 | 0.3 | 9 | 6 | 7.69 | 1.6 |
| Madagascar | | | 2.30 | 2.4 | 2 | | 2.30 | 0.5 |
| Mauritius | 12.5 | 3.2 | 0.04 | | 18 | 14 | 12.54 | 2.6 |
| Nigeria | 50.0 | 12.8 | | | 11 | 9 | 50.00 | 10.3 |
| Senegal | 12.0 | 3.1 | 8.07 | 8.3 | 6 | | 20.07 | 4.1 |
| Zaire | | | 5.26 | 5.4 | 5 | | 5.26 | 1.1 |
| Zambia | 10.5 | 2.7 | 3.43 | 3.5 | 13 | 8 | 13.93 | 2.9 |
| West Africa (regional) | | | 0.14 | 0.1 | 1 | | 0.14 | |
| Barbados | 7.5 | 1.9 | | | 8 | 6 | 7.50 | 1.5 |
| Guyana | | | 3.20 | 3.3 | 2 | 1 | 3.20 | 0.7 |
| Jamaica | | | 0.07 | 0.1 | 1 | | 0.07 | |
| Trinidad and Tobago | 10.0 | 2.6 | | | 18 | 16 | 10.00 | 2.0 |
| Caribbean (regional) | 3.0 | 0.8 | 1.0 | 1.0 | 4 | 2 | 4.00 | 0.8 |
| Fiji | 24.0 | 6.2 | | | 2 | | 24.00 | 4.9 |
| Papua New Guinea | 7.0 | 1.8 | 1.90 | 2.0 | 2 | | 8.90 | 1.9 |
| TOTAL ACP STATES | 390.0 | 100.0 | 97.28 | 100.0 | 219 | 96 | 487.28 | 100.0 |

Source: *Commission Report to the ACP-EEC Council of Ministers on the Administration of Financial and Technical Cooperation in 1980 Under the Lomé Convention* [X/461/1982-EN]

ative program from 55.1 percent to 40.7 percent since the EIB considered the country to be a bad investment risk and was unwilling to fund the proposed projects.[16]

By the end of 1980 only 22 ACP states had benefited from loans from the EIB's own resources—and, predictably, the principal beneficiaries were Kenya, the Ivory Coast, and Nigeria. More states received aid from the EIB in the form of participation in risk capital; some observers, however, have questioned the effectiveness of this support. Carlsen found the EIB had utilized funds in Kenya to finance projects by partly privately owned subsidiaries of transnational corporations. In this instance, European aid funds were used to subsidize the profits of TNCs and had no developmental effect since the companies were profitable and would have undertaken the investment without EIB support.[17] As was the case with EDF aid, the majority of finance for industrialization went to the energy sector, followed by agribusiness. Only 12 percent of the total resources from the EIB supported manufacturing industry in the ACP (table 8.7).

Neither has the EDF in its actual allocation of money placed a great deal of emphasis on meeting basic needs. Housing and urban infrastructure, health, and education together have received much less than the total allocated to infrastructure. Projects placed under rural production are often for the benefit of agribusiness rather than food production; Sharp calculated 40 percent of the money targeted for rural production was allocated to 47 large agri-industrial projects concentrated heavily on plantation crops for export—particularly cotton, palm oil, coffee, and tea—whose employment and general welfare effects on rural populations are not likely to be significant.[18]

Agri-industrial projects sponsored by the EDF have attracted particular criticism from the Community's Court of Auditors. The Court found that these projects often failed to achieve their purpose because they were on too large a scale, not properly integrated into the "primitive" rural economy, or failed to take account of human reactions to the disruption of the existing way of life or production methods. Projects which were intended to be export-oriented had become permanent consumers of scarce foreign exchange. Several were able to continue only because of continued EDF aid or government subsidies. Many were the victims of poor planning—palm oil projects in Togo and Benin were financed in areas with rainfall "seriously below" the requirements for the plant. Many projects also suffered from poor synchronization with the necessary industrial plant coming into service years after the plantation was in production. Finally, the Court noted, insufficient attention had been paid to food production in projects for commercial, especially perennial, crops. It concluded:

For all these reasons many agricultural projects make no great impact on national and regional development. Internally, their results are insecurity of employment, low incomes, farmers reduced to wage-earners, indifferent community facilities.

**TABLE 8.7.**
Subsidized Loans and Risk Capital (million UA) Committed by the EIB Under Lomé I (at end 1980). Breakdown by Sector

| Sector | Ordinary Loans from Own Resources | | | Risk Capital from EDF Resources | | | Total | | |
|---|---|---|---|---|---|---|---|---|---|
| | Number | Amount | % | Number | Amount | % | Number | Amount | % |
| General (including lines of credit) | 17 | 82.5 | 21.1 | 15 | 9.7 | 9.8 | 32 | 92.2 | 18.9 |
| Mines and extractive industries | 2 | 33.0 | 8.5 | 3 | 4.7 | 4.7 | 5 | 37.7 | 7.7 |
| Metal-working industries | 3 | 17.7 | 4.5 | 3 | 6.5 | 6.6 | 6 | 24.2 | 5.0 |
| Chemical industries | 3 | 17.4 | 4.5 | 4 | 9.2 | 9.3 | 7 | 26.6 | 5.4 |
| Manufacturing industries | 7 | 34.8 | 8.9 | 14 | 26.8 | 27.1 | 21 | 61.6 | 12.6 |
| Agri-industrial complexes | 11 | 64.9 | 16.6 | 15 | 30.9 | 31.2 | 26 | 95.8 | 19.6 |
| Projects with energy bias | 14 | 130.9 | 33.6 | 5 | 2.8 | 2.8 | 19 | 133.7 | 27.3 |
| *Total industrialization* | 57 | 381.2 | 97.7 | 59 | 90.6 | 91.5 | 116 | 471.8 | 96.5 |
| Tourism | 3 | 8.8 | 2.3 | 4 | 5.8 | 5.9 | 7 | 14.6 | 3.0 |
| *Total* | 60 | 390.0 | 100% | 63 | 96.4 | 97.4 | 123 | 486.4 | 99.5 |
| Blocked appropriations | — | — | — | /// | 4.3 | 4.3 | /// | 4.3 | 0.9 |
| Cancellations | — | — | — | /// | −1.7 | −1.7 | /// | −1.7 | −0.4 |
| Grand total | 60 | 390.0 | 100% | /// | 99.0 | 100.0 | /// | 489.0 | 100.0 |

Source: Same as table 8.6.

Externally, they have limited, or even unfavourable, effects on the balance of payments.[19]

Of course, it can be argued these projects were the choice of the ACP states themselves since in theory they alone are responsible for selecting which projects they wish to submit to the Community for consideration for financing. An examination of the formal procedures of the aid programming alone would lead to erroneous conclusions being drawn. For as the Community itself acknowledges, although it does not dictate projects, it is able to turn down particular requests. And, since the ACP know the type of projects the Community is likely to finance, it is probable that they tailor their programs accordingly to avoid delay and additional bureaucratic burdens. ACP countries have complained of the political pressures exerted by the programming missions noting that:

1. Some of the missions had not complied strictly with Article 51 of the Convention and had imposed their points of view on the ACP states, whose task was to define freely their objectives and priorities in the context of their national development plans.
2. Some ACP states had met with difficulty in persuading the Commission subsequently to accept additional information concerning individual projects or details relevant to project dossiers.
3. The Commission had on many occasions rejected vital technical amendments to projects already submitted to the EEC.[20]

Carlsen found in Kenya that the Community was reluctant to contribute to the financing of projects already in progress, preferring instead to undertake new schemes that could be identified as "European" projects.[21]

In general the previously noted biases in the sectoral distribution of EDF aid were maintained during the first Lomé Convention. As White comments, this pattern often does not meet the most pressing needs of the ACP:

The sectors in which EEC aid has been concentrated have been those which traditionally have been the easiest to finance. By the same token, from the developing countries' point of view, they have been the easiest for which to *mobilise* finance, so that a continuing concentration of EEC aid in these sectors would seem not to meet the most obvious needs or to give the Commission's aid programme any comparative advantage.[22]

## COUNTRY ALLOCATIONS

A prominent anomaly of the country allocations under the first three development funds was the high positive correlation between gross national product per capita of recipient states and aid per capita received from the EDF. Favoring the countries regarded as having better development prospects during the Yaoundé Conventions had continued a traditional bias in French colonial aid. Whereas the Yaoundé Conventions had not established criteria according to which country aid allocations might be determined, Lomé was explicit in placing emphasis on the least developed countries. Article 48 of the first Convention stated:

In the implementation of financial and technical cooperation, special attention shall be paid to the needs of the least developed ACP States so as to reduce the specific obstacles which impede their development and prevent them from taking full advantage of the opportunities offered by financial and technical cooperation.

This article represented a response not only to the aspirations of the ACP but also to the changing international climate regarding aid administration.

In aggregate terms, the distribution of commitments made by the end of the first Convention appeared to reflect the new emphasis. Least developed countries, as defined under Article 48,2, gained a share of programmable aid (except special loans and EIB loans from its own resources) disproportionate to their share in the total population of ACP states (64.1 percent of aid in contrast to 42.5 percent of total population). Yet the correlation between low per capita income and aid receipts was less perfect than these data might suggest, in large part because of the rather arbitrary designation of countries as "least developed." To examine the relationship more closely a detailed country-by-country breakdown is necessary. This is provided in table 8.8.

Data in this table are derived from total commitments of aid from the fourth EDF at the end of 1980 and from OECD data on the bilateral aid programs of Community members for the period 1975–79. Results are reported not only for total receipts of aid but also for programmable EDF aid. The latter is of greater interest in examining the Community's implementation of its commitment to the least developed, since total receipts include two categories—emergency aid and STABEX—not programmed in advance (and, thus, in one sense, outside Community control), plus the costs of maintaining EEC delegations in ACP states, which are

**TABLE 8.8.**

Country Receipts of European Aid 1975–79

| | Pop. (m) | GNP ($p.c.) | EDF (ua p.c.) | Pro (ua p.c.) | STABEX (ua p.c.) | Bilateral (ua p.c.) |
|---|---|---|---|---|---|---|
| Bahamas | 0.20 | 2184 | 9.21 | 9.0 | 0 | 2.5 |
| Barbados | 0.24 | 1500 | 19.41 | 16.1 | 0 | n.a. |
| Benin* | 3.11 | 170 | 17.06 | 9.9 | 6.5 | 28.7 |
| Botswana* | 0.69 | 414 | 36.06 | 30.9 | 0 | 124.6 |
| Burundi* | 3.93 | 110 | 13.87 | 12.5 | 0.4 | 31.5 |
| Cameroon | 7.53 | 363 | 7.76 | 6.4 | 0.5 | 48.0 |
| Cape Verde* | 0.30 | 138 | 32.25 | 23.6 | 4.0 | n.a. |
| Central Afr. Republic | 1.79 | 200 | 26.44 | 20.1 | 4.4 | 75.7 |
| Chad* | 4.03 | 120 | 14.51 | 12.0 | 1.8 | 36.9 |
| Comoros* | 0.30 | 180 | 31.51 | 20.9 | 0 | n.a. |
| Congo | 1.35 | 509 | 27.92 | 20.7 | 5.5 | 117.4 |
| Djibouti* | 0.11 | 2040 | 39.04 | 27.0 | 0 | n.a. |
| Dominica* | 0.08 | 343 | 53.42 | 46.8 | 0 | n.a. |
| Equatorial Guinea | 0.32 | 294 | 22.26 | 21.3 | 0 | n.a. |
| Ethiopia* | 27.47 | 97 | 3.87 | 3.1 | 0.5 | 4.0 |
| Fiji | 0.57 | 1151 | 34.50 | 30.0 | 3.7 | 63.6 |
| Gabon | 0.52 | 2813 | 32.13 | 16.1 | 12.9 | 220.7 |
| Gambia* | 0.52 | 178 | 43.65 | 26.3 | 14.5 | 64.0 |
| Ghana | 9.87 | 372 | 5.80 | 4.8 | 0.5 | 14.2 |
| Grenada | 0.10 | 379 | 25.16 | 19.9 | 0 | n.a. |
| Guinea* | 4.42 | 162 | 14.64 | 13.6 | 0 | 0.2 |
| Guinea-Bissau* | 0.53 | 140 | 59.32 | 34.9 | 21.3 | n.a. |
| Guyana | 0.78 | 512 | 21.13 | 21.1 | 0 | 15.2 |
| Ivory Coast | 6.71 | 617 | 9.25 | 6.5 | 2.2 | 48.1 |
| Jamaica | 2.04 | 1328 | 10.09 | 8.7 | 0 | 49.8 |
| Kenya | 13.40 | 252 | 6.39 | 6.1 | 0 | 28.9 |
| Lesotho* | 1.19 | 203 | 16.65 | 14.7 | 0 | 45.0 |
| Liberia | 1.57 | 343 | 21.53 | 15.9 | 4.8 | 22.3 |
| Madagascar | 7.68 | 217 | 10.41 | 9.0 | 0.7 | 13.8 |
| Malawi* | 5.04 | 134 | 14.02 | 12.9 | 0 | 32.3 |
| Mali* | 5.81 | 94 | 14.82 | 12.5 | 1.7 | 37.5 |
| Mauritania* | 1.42 | 247 | 51.27 | 22.3 | 26.1 | 54.0 |
| Mauritius | 0.86 | 552 | 22.35 | 15.3 | 0 | n.a. |
| Niger* | 4.60 | 146 | 22.10 | 14.4 | 4.9 | 49.9 |
| Papua New Guinea | 2.76 | 452 | 2.63 | 2.4 | 0 | 2.0 |

**TABLE 8.8.** *(Continued)*

|  | Pop. (m) | GNP ($p.c.) | EDF (ua p.c.) | Pro a p.c.) | STABEX (ua p.c.) | Bilateral (ua p.c.) |
|---|---|---|---|---|---|---|
| Rwanda* | 4.20 | 146 | 16.80 | 14.7 | 0.2 | 51.5 |
| St. Lucia | 0.11 | 508 | 16.91 | 7.8 | 0 | n.a. |
| Senegal | 4.98 | 345 | 27.61 | 12.6 | 13.1 | 66.2 |
| Seychelles* | 0.06 | 572 | 45.60 | 45.5 | 0 | n.a. |
| Sierra Leone | 3.05 | 199 | 10.37 | 8.7 | 1.3 | 12.9 |
| Solomon Isl.* | 0.19 | 302 | 34.97 | 34.9 | 0 | n.a. |
| Somalia* | 3.17 | 112 | 18.59 | 13.0 | 0.6 | 24.5 |
| Sudan* | 15.73 | 296 | 9.29 | 6.1 | 2.7 | 15.6 |
| Surinam | 0.36 | 1297 | 26.25 | 23.0 | 0 | n.a. |
| Swaziland* | 0.49 | 457 | 58.60 | 30.4 | 27.0 | 136.6 |
| Tanzania* | 15.31 | 176 | 7.63 | 6.1 | 1.4 | 36.8 |
| Togo* | 2.23 | 187 | 19.89 | 17.3 | 1.6 | 69.4 |
| Tonga* | 0.10 | 391 | 43.56 | 27.6 | 12.1 | n.a. |
| Trinidad and Tobago | 1.08 | 2113 | 8.57 | 7.4 | 0 | 2.7 |
| Uganda* | 11.55 | 294 | 4.83 | 2.6 | 1.8 | 2.3 |
| Upper Volta* | 6.07 | 117 | 12.51 | 10.9 | 1.2 | 41.0 |
| Western Samoa* | 0.15 | 300 | 50.75 | 31.8 | 18.9 | n.a. |
| Zaire | 24.90 | 212 | 4.87 | 4.0 | 0 | 26.1 |
| Zambia | 4.98 | 453 | 13.62 | 9.8 | 0 | 38.9 |

Source: Population and GNP p.c. from *ACP: Statistical Yearbook 1972–78* (Luxembourg: Eurostat, 1980).
EDF, Pro., STABEX calculated from data in Commission, *Fonds Européen De Développement: Situation Des Projets Du 4 ème FED à la Date Du 31.12.1980.* [VIII-E-2/109(79)-F Rev. 10].
Bilateral calculated from data in OECD, *Geographical Distribution of Financial Flows to Developing Countries* (Paris: OECD, 1978 and 1980).
Note: Data for bilateral aid were expressed in U.S.$ in the source document. To convert this to ua, the average value of the $ in ua was utilized for the years concerned. Since these figures refer to receipts rather than commitments, they are not strictly comparable to those for EDF aid. Nevertheless, the relative magnitude of the figures is of interest, as is the comparison between bilateral receipts of the various ACP countries.
Legend:
  Pop.: Population in millions.
  GNP: Gross National Product in $ per capita.
  EDF: Total commitments of EDF aid in au per capita.
  Pro.: Total commitments of programmable EDF aid in ua per capita.
  STABEX: Commitments of EDF aid under the STABEX scheme in ua per capita.
  Bilateral Combined net receipts of bilateral overseas development assistance from Belgium, Denmark, France, Germany, Italy, Netherlands, and the United Kingdom in ua per capita.
  *Country designated as least developed for the purposes of the Convention.
  n.a. Not available.

part of the administrative overheads of the EDF and therefore not considered by the OECD's Development Assistance Committee as overseas development assistance. Nigeria is not included in this table or in the subsequent calculations since its disproportionately low per capita receipts would distort the findings: when the Convention was negotiated it was agreed that Nigeria would not be a significant beneficiary of the EDF. By the end of 1980 its commitments from the Fourth Fund totaled only 18.244 mua, allocated primarily to technical assistance projects, scholarships for Nigerian students, interest rate subsidies, and for maintaining the local Commission delegation.

Correlation coefficients for the variables in this table are reported in table 8.9. Virtually no relationship exists between total receipts per capita or programmable aid per capita and GNP per capita; certainly the significant negative correlation one would expect if the commitment to the least developed had been effectively implemented is not present. However, the EDF performs better in this regard than the bilateral programs of the member states, where the relationship is more strongly positive (although not statistically significant). Gabon, which, as noted in chapter 2, had earlier been a favored recipient of EDF aid, remained disproportionately favored in the bilateral aid programs despite having the highest per capita income among Black African states.

What is most evident in this table is that in terms of per capita aid

**TABLE 8.9.**

Correlation Matrix of Aid Variables

|  | *GNPPC* | *POP* | *AIDPC* | *PRPC* | *STPC* | *BIPC* |
|---|---|---|---|---|---|---|
| GNPPC | — | 55 | 55 | 55 | 55 | 39 |
| POP | −.28 | — | 55 | 55 | 55 | 39 |
| AIDPC | .29 | −.56** | — | 55 | 55 | 39 |
| PRPC | .03 | −.57** | .81** | — | 55 | 39 |
| STPC | −.04 | −.20 | .68** | .42** | — | 39 |
| BIPC | .35 | −.35 | .67** | .62** | .53** | — |

Source: Derived from data in Table 7

** Denotes statistical significance at the 0.001 level.

GNPPC: Gross National Product per capita

POP: Population

AIDPC: EDF commitments per capita

PRPC: Programmable EDF commitments per capita

STPC: STABEX receipts per capita

BIPC: Receipts from bilateral EEC aid per capita

receipts it pays to be small. A strongly (statistically significant) negative relationship exists between population size and per capita receipts, both of total EDF money and of programmable aid. This bias toward small states is not unusual in aid agencies; in this instance it appears that the Commission placed as great an emphasis on country shares of the aid as on targeting the least developed populations. Two illustrations can be given of countries with similar per capita GNPs but whose populations and per capita aid receipts were notably divergent: Ghana, with GNP per capita of $372, population of 9.87 million, received per capita receipts of 5.8 ua which compared unfavorably with Grenada, whose figures were, respectively, $379, 0.1m, and 25.16 ua. Similarly Tanzania, with per capita income slightly below that of Togo, received commitments amounting to not much more than a third of the latter's on a per capita basis.

In terms of country allocations of aid, the record of the fourth EDF again is a mixed one. By comparison to its predecessors, much greater success was achieved in targeting the least developed countries. But the commitment to give special attention to their needs was far from fully implemented, at least in terms of the per capita allocations of aid between countries. A claim could be made by the Community that per capita GNP is not the only criterion on which to judge the level of a country's development and that it has better indicators for deciding relative needs. If this is so, then it would be useful for the Community to publish these. At present, the method of selecting which countries should be designated as least developed appears to be extremely arbitrary and, of course, subject to political influence. There appears to be little inherent logic in classifying Djibouti, whose citizens enjoy an average per capita income of $2,040 per annum as least developed while excluding, for instance, Equatorial Guinea, where the per capita income is $294.

## RENEGOTIATION OF THE AID PROVISIONS FOR LOMÉ II

ACP complaints regarding the implementation of financial and technical cooperation during Lomé I focused on two aspects: management procedures and the real value of aid received. On the management question two principal groups of complaints were raised: the first concerned ACP perceptions that the centralization of decision-making in the EDF led to delays and administrative clumsiness; to remedy this they proposed that the decision-making powers of the local EEC delegate in ACP states be reinforced. Second, they complained about their lack of influence over the question of which projects would be financed; their demand here was that they at least be allowed to be present when financing decisions were made so that they might be able to provide any additional information necessary for evaluating a project.

Renegotiation of the aid chapter proved to be one of the most bitter aspects of the negotiation for Lomé II. In part this was because the ACP started off by insisting that aspects of NIEO rhetoric be introduced into the Convention: a reference to their sovereignty (they rejected as unwarranted interference with their domestic policies a Community suggestion that the "most disadvantaged" of their populations be singled out for special attention in the new Convention) and a reference to the "international obligations" of the Community. A number of other demands were clearly unattainable: provision for a periodic adjustment of the aid total in order to preserve its real value during a Convention, the complete untying of aid, and the automatic award to ACP contractors of contracts of less than 5 mua. But the bitterness was also caused by the Community's unwillingness to discuss the possibility of a role for the ACP in the management of aid procedures at the most critical juncture: the actual financing decision.

The Commission produced an elaborate chart (Table 8.10) in an attempt to convince the ACP that they played a significant role in the administration of the EDF. And the new Convention stated explicitly "operations financed by the Community shall be implemented by the ACP states and the Community in close cooperation, the concept of equality between the partners being recognized" (Article 108,1). ACP states were given explicit responsibility in the new Convention for defining the objectives and priorities on which their indicative programs would be based, the choice of projects and programs, the preparation and presentation of dossiers, the negotiation and conclusion of contracts, the implementation of projects and programs, and the management and maintenance of operations. But the reality of the "equal partnership" was reflected succinctly in the fifth paragraph of the same article, which stated simply: "The Community shall be responsible for preparing and taking financing decisions on projects and programmes."

A certain amount of decision-making power on the approval of contracts was given to the representative of the ACP government, but this was made subject to review for 30 days by the local EEC delegate (whereas

**TABLE 8.10.**

European Development Fund Procedures—Lomé I

| | EEC | ACP | Explanatory Notes |
|---|---|---|---|
| 1. Programming | x | x | Community aid, programmed at the beginning of the period covered by the Convention, is incorporated in the economic and social development plans and programs of each ACP state. |
| Fixing of objectives and priorities | | x | Programs are drawn up on the basis of proposals from each ACP state in which the country concerned has established its own targets and priorities. |
| 2. Financing applications | | | |
| Preparation of applications | | x | Within the framework of the aid programs, ACP states are entirely responsible for their financing applications. They submit these on the basis of a project dossier drawn up by themselves. |
| Project dossiers | | x | The Community may, at the request of these states, provide technical assistance with preparation of the dossier. |
| 3. Appraisal | x | x | Upon receipt of the financing application the Commission proceeds to an appraisal of projects in close collaboration with the beneficiary ACP state and on the basis of criteria jointly defined in the Convention. |
| 4. Preparation of the Decision | | | |
| Financing proposals | x | x | For each project, the conclusions of the evaluation are summarized in a financing proposal drawn up in close collaboration between the Community and the ACP state. |
| Committee opinions | x | | Each financing proposal is submitted, depending on the nature of the financing, either to the EDF Committee or to the Article 22 Committee (EIB), both of which include representatives of member state governments (but not the ACP). |

| | Description | | |
|---|---|---|---|
| Appeal procedure | If the Committee turns down an application, the Community consults the ACP state on the desirability of resubmitting the dossier, possibly in a modified form. The ACP state may ask to be able to put its justification of the project to the Committee. (No ACP state has yet availed itself of the appeal procedure.) | | x |
| 5. Financing decision | The financing proposals and the opinion of the relevant committee are submitted to the Commission for decision in the case of subsidies and special loans and to the Board of the EIB in the case of reduced interest loans and risk capital. | x | |
| 6. Convention | All projects that are the object of a financing decision give rise to the preparation by the relevant department of the Community of a financing convention that is submitted to the ACP state concerned for signature. | | x |
| 7. Execution Responsibility Follow-up | ACP states are responsible for executing projects.<br>The Commission ensures that the projects are carried out in conformity with EDF rules and in the best economic and technical conditions. | x | |
| A. Preparation of supply and works contracts<br>A.1 Tenders<br> –Tender file | The file is prepared by the ACP state; it is reviewed and approved by the delegate and the Commission (normal procedure) or by the national delegate (accelerated procedure). | | x |
| –Invitations to tender | Timetable drawn up by mutual consent. | x | |
| –Opening of bids | The bids are opened at a meeting of the selection committee of the ACP state at which the delegate is present as an observer. | x | |
| –Selection | Approval of the ACP's choice by the delegate or the Commission as appropriate.* | | x |

**TABLE 8.10. (Continued)**

| | EEC | ACP | Explanatory Notes |
|---|---|---|---|
| –Preparation and conclusion of the contract | | x | The contract is negotiated and concluded by the ACP state and notified to the Commission through the delegate, who approves it. |
| A.2 Direct agreement | | x | The ACP state is free to undertake the discussions it feels are necessary and to award the contract to the company of its choice. The Commission is notified of the contract through the delegate, who approves it. |
| A.3 Execution by a national department | | x | The ACP state draws up an estimate that is notified to the Commission through the delegate, who approves it. |
| B. Preparation of technical cooperation contracts | | | |
| B.1 Selection of consulting firm or expert | x | x | The selection is made after individual negotiation or after an invitation to tender on the basis of a short list drawn up by the Commission (direct agreement) or by mutual consent between the Commission and the ACP state (tenders). |
| B.2 Negotiations and conclusion of contracts | | x | The contracts are drawn up, negotiated, and concluded with the ACP state in agreement with and with the participation of the delegate. |
| C. Execution of contracts and estimates | | | |
| C.1 From a technical standpoint | | | |
| –Adjustments and changes of detail | | x | |
| –Changes in the locations of multiunit projects | | x | |
| –Application or waiver of penalties for delays | | x | In the past these were all areas for which ultimate responsibility lay with the Commission or the delegate. They have now been transferred to the local authorities, although the delegate must be informed a posteriori. |

| Item | | | Notes |
|---|---|---|---|
| – Act discharging guarantors | | x | |
| – Purchases on the local market without origin conditions | | x | |
| – Use of machinery and equipment not originating in member states | | x | |
| – Subcontracting | | x | |
| – Provision and final acceptance | | x | |
| **C.2 From a financial standpoint** | | | |
| – Clearance and authorization of expenditure | | x | Generally speaking, the national authorizing officer handles clearance and authorization of expenditure. |
| – Financial control of expenditure authorization | | x | Approval of the delegate. |
| – Payment of expenditure | | | |
| · In national currency | | x | Executed by the central banks of the beneficiary states (paying agents). |
| · Other currencies | x | | Effected by The Commission after clearance and authorization by the national authorities. |
| **8. Evaluation** | x | x | Effects and results of completed projects are assessed regularly and jointly by the Community and the ACP state concerned. An assessment may also cover projects in process of execution. |
| **9. General orientation of financial and technical cooperation** | | | |
| – Reports and observations on implementation | | x | The ACP have never submitted any such comments. The Community's report is drawn up by the Commission. |
| – Review of the rundown of activity | | x | The responsibility of the EEC/ACP Council of Ministers annually. |
| – Resolution on the cooperation policy and guidelines | | x | The responsibility of the EEC/ACP Council of Ministers. |

Source: Community negotiating memorandum reproduced in Jose Alain Fralon et al., *The New EEC-ACP Convention: From Lomé I to Lomé II* (Bruxelles: Agence Européenne d'Informations, 1979), pp. 63–64.

*Companies in ACP states enjoy a price preference for works and supply contracts.

the ACP had wanted the decision to be made immediately). Ultimately Brussels was to remain in control of all financing and contractual procedures. An effort was made to accommodate ACP complaints regarding delays in project reviews and decisions by establishing a timetable for each project; whether this will have any effect on the problem of delays is dubious—officials of the Commission responsible for project reviews whom I interviewed were skeptical whether the new formality would bring any significant change. In its report, "Administration of Financial and Technical Cooperation," in 1982, the Commission admitted that commitments had failed to keep pace with the targets set for the new Convention.[23]

By far the most contentious (and, for both parties, probably the most significant) issue in the talks was the volume of the fifth EDF. In previous negotiations this had always been the last issue to be settled; it had never been a matter of real negotiation between the Community and the Associates but had been determined primarily by discussions among the EEC member states. Once a hard-fought compromise had been reached within the Community, it was very difficult for the Associates to extract any additional commitments: essentially the Commission was given no latitude to negotiate on this matter.

In the new negotiations the ACP attempted to force the Community's hand by demanding that talks on the volume of the EDF be initiated at an early stage and objective criteria be established for calculating the new amount. At the Freeport ministerial meeting in March 1979 the ACP proposed the following criteria: correction for erosion of the real value of aid in the period 1975–1985; preservation of the level of financial and technical resources transferred to the former Associates; growth in the number of ACP states and in their populations; the privileged and exemplary character of the ACP–EEC relationship; the erosion of their commercial preferences; the needs of the least developed, landlocked, and island countries; necessary funding for extension of STABEX; funding for new aspects of cooperation (including agricultural cooperation, a new approach to industrial cooperation, fishing, and energy); and the evolution of the Community's Gross National Product. On the basis of these criteria the ACP suggested, with more than a little optimism, that the volume of the new fund should be set at 12,000 mua (10.8 billion to update existing activities plus funding for SYSMIN and other new activities).

In response, the Community merely noted that the question of fixing the size of the aid fund was a "global problem of a political nature" that consequently would be taken up only in the last stage of the negotiations. As had been the case in previous negotiations, disputes among the member states delayed determination of the aid offer. Each negotiation of the EDF has been marked by resistance of one member state or another to paying its share of the Fund—on this occasion the British delegation was reluctant, given the financial problems of the country, to see any significant increase in its contribution. The actual aid offer was finally made at what was scheduled as the last ministerial talks, in Brussels, in May 1979: a total package of 5,107 mua, calculated on the basis of inflation within the Community in the previous five years.

It was not so much the size of the package—disappointing, as most ACP states had expected—but the take-it-or-leave-it manner in which it was presented that alienated the ACP and caused them to walk out of the negotiations. But within a month they had returned to the negotiation table and accepted a package whose total size had been raised to 5,607 mua. Only 5,226 mua of this was within the Convention; the remainder consisted of nonsubsidized loans from the EIB's own resources, plus a commitment to pay the expenses of the Commission's delegates in ACP states from the Community budget. Altogether, the walkout brought an increase of 6 percent in the Community's offer (possible only because a new "key" to member states' contributions was negotiated that reduced the British share). But none of the extra 300 mua was in the form of regular EDF programmable aid: more than one-half was the result of the removal of the cost of the Commission's delegations, which, as noted above, was not strictly aid in the first place; the extra funding resulting from this was insufficient to meet the cost of the new SYSMIN scheme. Most of the remaining additional funds were in the form of subsidized loans from the EIB.

The new package represented an increase in total resources of 51 percent over the first Convention. But in real terms this increase amounted to only 8 percent for the total package and 5 percent for aid administered by the EDF. And when the increase in the number of ACP countries and their populations is taken into consideration, the ACP found that they had negotiated a 7 percent decline in the per capita aid (see table 8.11).

**TABLE 8.11.**

Comparisons of the Real Value of Aid Under Lomé I and II

| | Lomé I | | Lomé II | |
| --- | --- | --- | --- | --- |
| | Total Resources | EDF Only | Total Resources | EDF Only |
| At current prices | 3,466 | 3,076 | 5,227 | 4,542 |
| % change | | | +51% | +48% |
| At 1975 constant prices | 3,466 | 3,076 | 3,734 | 3,244 |
| % change | | | +8% | +5% |
| On real per capita basis (eua) | 12.8 | 11.4 | 12.2 | 10.6 |
| % change | | | −5% | −7% |

Source: Calculated from data in Overseas Development Institute, "Lomé II", *Briefing Paper* no. 1 (February 1980).

## CONCLUSION

As a strategy of preserving the real value of the receipts of multilateral Community aid, collective clientelism must be judged a failure. From the perspective of the institutionalization of the Lomé relationship this is an important dimension, especially since the question of the sums to be available under the EDF have been central to the negotiations, and the Community's failure to preserve the real value of the aid not only broke the commitments it made to both the Commonwealth and the Yaoundé states before the signature of Lomé but also produced considerable bitterness and disillusionment.

This was reflected in a unilateral declaration by the ACP states attached as Annex XLIII to the new Convention:

While the ACP States have, in a spirit of cooperation accepted, for the purposes of this Convention, the total amount of assistance of 5,607 mua, the ACP States wish to record that in their opinion this amount is neither adequate nor fully reflects the understanding reached on the volume of financial assistance between the Co-Presidents of the Council of Ministers in the course of the negotiations in June 1979.

The extent of ACP bitterness is reflected in the tone of this statement, obviously more than just a bargaining ploy. This was hardly a propitious foundation on which to build ACP–EEC cooperation for the following five years.

Yet at the same time that the real value of EDF aid and its share in total ACP receipts was declining, the Group was improving its relative position in regard to bilateral aid from EEC member states. Exactly what might be made of this by an ACP decision-maker is far from clear. But insofar as EDF aid accounts for only 10 percent of total aid given by the Nine, and this percentage has been falling in recent years, these trends in the programming of bilateral EEC aid certainly could not be ignored. Was this increase in the ACP share an unexpected by-product of collective clientelism, or would it have occurred in any case, largely as a result of the increasing focus of aid agencies on least developed countries? For the Commonwealth states, at least, the increase in bilateral aid from Community sources other than the former metropole certainly appeared to suggest the Convention had brought additional payoffs beyond access to the multilateral funds of the EDF: other member states appeared to have accepted some responsibility for them as collective patrons. Collective clientelism had not led to a fall in their share in member states' bilateral aid programs. Similarly, for the Yaoundé states, the Community share of bilateral aid remained at approximately the same level over the decade, while the former metropole's share declined sharply. Again this appears to show other member states had accepted some responsibility for the former Associates in their bilateral aid programs. On the other hand, the share of Community multilateral aid, both as a percentage of total multilateral aid received and in all receipts from the EEC, fell over the decade, a reflection of the fall in the real value of per capita aid receipts from the EDF.

The results of financial and technical cooperation during the first Convention appear to raise as many questions as they answer. And this is before any evaluation is made of the actual welfare effects of Community aid programs on the populations of the recipient states. This was attempted by an unpublished Community document. In considering the conclusions this remarkably frank report reaches, consideration should be given to the probability that many of the weaknesses listed also apply to other aid agencies—the assessment of Community procedures undertaken above suggested they were certainly not significantly worse than those of other aid agencies and on a number of dimensions were probably somewhat better.

The Community report summarized here was the product of a comparative evaluation of the effectiveness of Community aid projects in four

West African countries—all previously associated under the Treaty of Rome and the Yaoundé Conventions.[24] In general the report found Community aid had made an effective contribution toward implementation of the main government policies for which aid had been requested. In particular it had exercised a beneficial effect on the growth and diversification of production, especially in agriculture; on integration of the different regions of countries; and on their balance of payments. With the exception of food aid and aid to producers under the second EDF, the funds had been employed with satisfactory efficiency.

Yet, a number of rather problematic tendencies were observed. Increases in national revenues resulting directly or indirectly from Community aid projects appeared to have done much less than was expected to improve the welfare of the local inhabitants, particularly in rural areas, but had boosted salaries in foreign companies or public national agencies more than was desired:

This results from—among other factors—the large share of heavy investments in the projects financed by the Community. As for operations aiming at agricultural development, it appears that an important part of the value added by peasant productions is drained off the rural population.

Long-term declines in the prices of produce, and a failure of peasant productivity to rise as much as had been anticipated, meant that the actual income accruing to producers had been less than expected. The principal beneficiaries tended to be rural landowners; women and the young gained little in the way of improved welfare. In food aid there were indications that the products supplied failed to meet real needs and that too high a proportion went to people other than those in the greatest need.

No effort had apparently been made to maximize local employment effects, which were often minimal because of the use of capital-intensive technology. A failure to involve local communities and, to a lesser extent, local administrative agencies, in the design and execution of projects led to many being viewed with suspicion by the local population as "foreign" impositions. Little effort had been made to use local resources. When aid was finally withdrawn from schemes, it left behind Western-type organizations and equipment that involved high maintenance costs (to which the Community has been reluctant to contribute). One consequence has been that the recipient governments have found themselves temporarily unable to operate certain facilities (e.g., hospitals), or they have written off capital projects, e.g., roads, when these needed funding for maintenance.[25] In too many cases, the report notes, technical assistance personnel tended to "do things for them" rather than to "assist them to help themselves"—another factor contributing to perceptions of projects as "alien" impositions.

While Community aid had made a contribution to the diversification of recipient economies, it had also had a number of undesirable effects. One of these was the demonstration effect on national salaries: the favorable conditions received by technical assistance personnel became the norm for national officials so that countries were spending an ever-increasing proportion of their administrative budget on paying, housing, and transporting their officials. Second, and perhaps most seriously, aid had actually made these states *more dependent* on external assistance as a result of the overwhelming amount of time and effort devoted to seeking it, rather than to mobilizing indigenous resources. The report's conclusion that "internal efficiency is reduced by this dependence on external reactions and decisions" warrants serious consideration by all LDCs.

# 9
# Conclusions

By the time negotiations began for the renewal of the Lomé Convention in 1978, ACP states were considerably disillusioned with the fruits of their special relationship with the EEC. Their strategy of collective clientelism had fallen short of their expectations on a number of critical dimensions. As the preceding chapters have shown, collective clientelism:

1. had failed to preserve the tariff advantages that ACP states enjoyed over third parties in the EEC
2. had failed to guarantee the ACP share of the European market
3. had not provided comprehensive "social insurance" to the ACP (Even before the inadequate level of funding of STABEX was exposed in the early years of the Second Convention, it was obvious that the scheme at best would have only a marginal impact on ACP economies.)
4. had not provided protection against the patron engaging in behavior detrimental to the clients' interests—particularly evident in the Community's response to ACP exports of textiles and in the Community's encouragement of domestic sugar production under the CAP
5. contrary to the pledges made to the Associated states before the Lomé I negotiations, had not maintained the real value of per capita aid to the clients
6. had not established a contractual relationship in which the clients' rights were unequivocally identified
7. had not initiated an equal partnership in which the relationship was jointly managed

Even if the hyperbole that accompanied signature of the initial Convention is put to one side, the ACP Group undoubtedly believed the agreement they had reached represented a significant advance over the Yaoundé Conventions. In particular, the Community had responded sympathetically to their preoccupation with issues of sovereignty by its acknowledgment of their equal standing in the relationship. The preamble to the Convention noted it had been concluded "on the basis of complete equality between partners"; henceforth there would be no "associates"—the Community's partners would be known simply as the ACP Group, and they would share in the management of the Convention. Success of the strategy of collective clientelism appeared to be ensured by the contractual nature of the Convention, which the Community itself was fond of emphasizing. And where the interests of the ACP were not protected by the contractual stipulations, the Group anticipated that the Community would live up to its generalized responsibilities as patron in the "spirit" of the Agreement. It soon became clear, however, that the parties had very different ideas of what constraints were placed on Community behavior by the partnership.

In reality, the ACP found that nothing in the relationship was guaranteed. The Convention was riddled with diverse escape clauses that permitted the Community to abrogate the agreement for reasons ranging from "the protection of health and life of humans, animals, and plants," to an insufficiency of funds (STABEX scheme). And there was nothing to prevent the Community from unilaterally redefining the "special relationship" by extending its benefits to third parties (as indeed happened with the GSP). Although the Community was obliged under the terms of the Convention to inform the ACP and consult with them "where Contracting Parties envisage taking any trade measures affecting the interest of one or more Contracting Parties" (Article 11, 1 of the first Convention), its compliance with this obligation seldom extended beyond a token gesture.[1]

Trade issues were particularly divisive. Divergent interpretations of the obligations the Community had assumed under the Convention were the major source of bitterness. For the ACP, free access for all their products (including agricultural exports) was the rule, and this was to be implemented even if it imposed costs by way of structural adjustment on the part of Community member states. Any exceptions to the principle of free access were to be negotiated on a joint basis. As far as the Community was concerned, however, the principle of free access was tempered by an escape clause that could be invoked unilaterally whenever circumstances warranted it—either because of the damage imposed on domestic interests or because this rule interfered with others designed to construct a Community regime for the production of a particular product.

Data collected by Jacobson et al. provide a fascinating insight into ACP perceptions. ACP negotiators at the first ACP–EEC Council of Ministers meeting, when questioned regarding which measures they regarded as most promising for promoting the economic growth of developing countries in the next decade, most frequently mentioned market access. Not only was this issue nominated more often than others by ACP negotiators, but also it was considered more important by them than by LDC negotiators in other North-South talks.[2] Given the economic weakness of the ACP and their lack of penetration of the Community market, this emphasis at first sight appears perverse. This paradox can be explained, however, by the ACP Group's perceptions of the Community's contractual obligations under Lomé and the gradual realization—already evident one year after the signature of the Convention—that the Community did not share these perceptions.

Similar divergent interpretations were seen with regard to the special protocols on rum, bananas, and sugar. From the ACP perspective, the Convention—marking the success of their strategy of collective clientelism—guaranteed their position in the Community market. For the EEC, however, the contractual obligation amounted to nothing more than attempting to improve the position of the ACP as long as this did not conflict with other Community objectives of higher priority.

Not only did the ACP soon discover that the contract they had negotiated imposed few constraints on Community behavior, they also found that the much-vaunted equality of the partnership was not reflected in its management. Rather than there being a joint institution charged with the surveillance of the Convention's implementation, this task was undertaken unilaterally by the Commission. Ambiguity in many of the Convention's chapters gave the Commission considerable discretionary latitude for interpretation. As ACP frustrations with Commission interpretations of the Convention's provisions increased, considerable time was devoted to bickering over institutions and procedures for implementing the Convention. Lomé did not escape the contentious issues of management of institutions that have bedeviled the North-South dialogue.

Friction in the relationship was exacerbated by the procedures adopted for the negotiations. Ongoing relations between the Community and the ACP Group were the responsibility of the EEC Commission and the ACP Committee of Ambassadors (resident ambassadors of the ACP states to the European Communities). Here the same frustrations arose as in the negotiations conducted under the Group system at UNCTAD. Both the Commission and the Committee of Ambassadors could negotiate only according to the mandate they received from their respective member states. Once a common negotiating platform was established by the respective groups, often with some considerable difficulty, the negotiators were left with almost no latitude for deviation. Accordingly, a good part of the interaction between the two groups during the implementation of the Convention consisted of the Ambassadors' making demands based on ACP interpretations of the general principles of the Convention, e.g., completely free access for all of their exports, to which the Commission repeatedly responded that it lacked the mandate to negotiate on these terms.

Particularly offensive from the ACP perspective was the paternalistic style to which the Community frequently reverted, despite its lip service to the "equality" of the partnership. This was seen in particular over the rules of origin issue, where the Community insisted that it knew best as regards the type of industrialization desirable for the ACP states. At times, negotiators from the EEC made it perfectly clear they preferred dealing with the Francophone states, which "understood the Community" and typically adopted a deferential attitude, rather than with the more assertive Commonwealth states. As had been the case in the Yaoundé Conventions, the ACP Group found itself excluded from many of the important decisions, e.g., over the quantity of aid to be provided, which aid projects would be financed, and the prices for their sugar. Community behavior in these spheres was akin to that of a traditional patron in unilaterally defining the nature of the relationship. ACP representatives revived Nkrumah's analogy in referring to the partnership as one of the European rider on the ACP horse.

These experiences illustrate a number of the paradoxes of the ACP strategy of collective clientelism. In a relationship between parties of obviously unequal resources, they insisted on formal equality. At the same time, they expected the Community as patron to go beyond the contractual obligations of the relationship in protecting their interests but not to use the latitude it enjoyed as the stronger party to redefine the relationship in any way that would damage their position. Since the Community clearly did not share this perception of its obligations under the "spirit" of the agreement and had acted during Lomé I in a manner that undermined the objectives of the strategy of collective clientelism, the ACP Group proposed that the contractual element of the arrangements be strengthened in the second Convention. Their aspiration was to remove the latitude the Community had enjoyed and had used to redefine the relationship; now they sought to tie the Community's hands as far as possible in its choice of foreign economic policies. This was clearly expressed in an ACP memorandum on the renegotiation of the trade provisions: "the 'special relationship' of the ACP (must) be clearly defined and legally stipulated to the point that any preference erosion [*sic*] be matched by an equivalent compensation."[3] Not surprisingly, the ACP failed in this strategy. The outcome of the Lomé II negotiations was a marginal improvement on some items of interest to the ACP but not a redefinition of the Community's contractual obligations. Lomé II brought no significant change in the security of the arrangements from the ACP perspective.[4]

Frustration on the part of the ACP Group with the manner in which the provisions of the Convention had been implemented, coupled with disappointment at their failure to negotiate a significant improvement in its provisions for Lomé II, led to considerable bitterness. Although collective clientelism had brought some marginal improvements over the relationship enjoyed by the former Associates in the Yaoundé Conventions, it had not realized many of the aspirations of the ACP for the Lomé partnership. No longer was the Convention seriously portrayed as a model for a new international economic order. And, writing at the time that the negotiations for Lomé III are taking place, I find it striking how little attention is being paid to them by the international community in comparison to those for the first Convention.

Why did the strategy of collective clientelism fail to produce the expected returns? Why has the most comprehensive agreement reached in the field of North-South relations proved so disappointing? Two general explanations may be offered. The first relates to the failure of the ACP to bargain effectively in the relationship as a result of internal contradictions in the strategy of collective clientelism, the second, to the changing interests of the European Community, which have caused it to perceive the ACP as increasingly irrelevant to its principal commercial interests.

## CONTRADICTIONS IN THE COLLECTIVE CLIENTELIST STRATEGY

Two principal contradictions existed in the ACP strategy of collective clientelism: the first was the contrast between the *collective* nature of the strategy and the failure of ACP states to act effectively as a group; the second was the tension that existed between ACP demands for equality in the relationship and their insistence on a norm of nonreciprocity.

An inherent contradiction resides between the collective nature of the ACP strategy and the typical structure of patron-client relations. In Galtung's phrase, all clientelistic relationships evince a "feudal interaction structure" in which vertical links to the patron are of paramount importance. Clients typically may not be joined together through any horizontal ties; if they are, often the only characteristic the members of the group have in common is their links with their patron.[5] At its negotiation, the Lomé relationship was only a partial exception to this generalization. As chapter 1 suggested, if collective clientelism was to succeed, ACP states would have to institutionalize their grouping so that it would become the focal point for relations between individual states and the Community. The ACP states failed to do this—in large part because the heterogeneity of the states has caused them to question the credibility of the Group. This led to ACP states' not providing adequate support for the Group's Secretariat and to a lack of interest on the part of the stronger ACP states in playing a leadership role in the Group. Efforts at institutionalization were further undermined by the structure of the relationship, which allowed for little role for the ACP as a Group.

As chapter 2 noted, a striking feature of the first Lomé negotiations had been the forging of a joint negotiating position among ACP countries.[6] In comparison with the Yaoundé negotiations, the "weak" came to the bargaining table much better prepared: as one of the senior Commission participants in the Lomé I negotiations noted, "Whereas in the Yaoundé negotiations the Africans mostly posed problems, during the Lomé negotiations they often proposed the working hypotheses."[7] Success in the Lomé negotiations spilled over into cooperation in other spheres such as regional integration in West Africa.[8] Negotiating the agreement, however, was only a first step: as one of the principal ACP negotiators warned, given the lack of specificity of many of the Convention's provisions, the manner in which it was implemented would be crucial, and here the ACP needed strong institutionalized representation.[9] The ACP have yet to achieve this.

A principal problem faced by the ACP Group has been its lack of credibility even among its own members. Beyond its periodical negotiations with the EEC, the Group has no logical *raison d'être*. Its membership is scattered around the globe, with the consequence that for the regional groupings the most salient economic actors are not other members of the ACP Group, and in the case of some Pacific and Caribbean countries, not even the EEC. Consequently, there has not been a great deal of interest among the countries in the further institutionalization of the Group. Although conferences have been held on improving intra-ACP cooperation (Georgetown, 1976), intra-ACP transport links (Suva, 1977, and Bangui, 1978), and on intra-ACP trade (Nairobi, 1979), their outcome has been wordy resolutions favoring greater institutionalization but few examples of substantive progress or the commitment of resources that might bring such progress in the future. No evidence has arisen that the members of the Group have become more salient for each other as a result of cooperation in the Convention; intra-ACP trade actually declined in relative significance for the Group during the first Convention.[10] Some of the difficulties the Group faces are illustrated by a conference on ACP air transport services held in Addis Ababa in December 1982. This was attended by only one representative from the Caribbean and none from the Pacific; technical documents presented to the conference were from the African Civil Aviation Commission and dealt only with the African continent.

Few of its members have perceived the Group as viable in the long term. Nigeria's ambassador to the Community, for instance, declared at the end of the initial Lomé negotiations that the Convention might not be in the best interests of his country after 1985.[11] Uncertainty over the Group's future, compounded by increasing dissatisfaction with the benefits derived from the Convention, have caused ACP states to be reluctant to invest scarce resources in institutionalizing the Group. An ACP Secretariat was established in 1976 following the Georgetown Declaration on intra-ACP cooperation. But the Secretariat has never been given adequate resources to fulfill its role—which itself had been very narrowly defined by ACP governments. According to one of its senior staff, "the ACP Secretariat is considered to be an instrument which has only a coordinating function and to some extent an advisory one."[12] The Secretariat has not been allowed the latitude enjoyed by the EEC Commission to take initiatives on its own account. In meetings of the ACP Council of Ministers and Ambassadors, its staff were not even permitted to voice their opinions unless specifically invited by the representatives of the ACP governments. A number of ACP governments—particularly Francophone African states—have been extremely suspicious of the Secretariat, whose dominant personalities and intellects have come from the Caribbean. Selection of personnel thus became a highly politicized matter—often at the expense of the best qualified candidates. Budgetary contributions went unpaid; the Secretariat's financial problems eventually were eased, somewhat ironically, by a grant from the EDF.

The Secretariat's weaknesses were exposed in the negotiations for the renewal of the Convention in 1979. With a staff of only a dozen experts, the Secretariat was overwhelmed by the mountain of material that emerged during the negotiations. As a consequence it was unable to undertake the detailed work necessary to give essential statistical and technical support to the ACP case. Although a number of reports had been commissioned from outside experts, in some instances financed by the Commonwealth Secretariat, these were hastily drawn up and rather than their providing the required technical information in areas such as the rules of origin or the processing of ACP raw materials, called instead, in the time-honored academic manner, for further studies. There was an almost total dependence on the EEC for statistical information on the implementation of the Convention—but at the time of the renegotiations the Secretariat did not have direct access to EEC data banks. To cope with the extra workload during the talks, the Secretariat even had to "borrow" secretaries from the Commission. While members of the ACP Group have been quick to criticize the Secretariat for its failure to provide necessary background papers, they have not given it a sufficient budget to enable it to play an effective role in the relationship. Inadequate resources have confined the Secretariat to a role that is largely reactive—to European proposals—and have prevented it from seizing the initiative.

Renegotiation of the Convention brought into the open the diversity of interests, perceptions, and situations that characterizes the Group. This diversity undermined the hope that coalition maintenance would be relatively easy among a group of countries with a shared historical experience and greater homogeneity than the Group of 77 as a whole. Most ACP states were formerly colonies of an EEC member state, but it is misleading to place emphasis on a commonality of experience. Clearly, the Francophone group maintains an identity that differentiates its members very markedly from other African countries. Although the negotiations for Lomé I had achieved a historical precedent in bridging the Anglophone-Francophone divide, deep-seated mutual suspicions and hostility soon reemerged, underscoring the principal cleavage in the ACP Group.

In general, the Francophone states were more enthusiastic about the Convention than their partners, apparently not expecting—perhaps with good reason, given their previous experience of the Yaoundé Conventions—more than modest gains from the new partnership. Their attitude was that of the traditional client—trusting that the patron knows best. As some of their critics within the ACP Group remarked, the perception of the Convention held by some Francophone states was not much removed from that of a begging relationship. On the other hand, Commonwealth countries continued to view the Community with a great deal of suspicion. They were more inclined to take seriously the rhetoric that the Convention was an equal partnership and a model for a New International Economic Order and were consequently more disappointed and more vociferous when it became evident that this was far from being the case. Given their larger cadre of skilled technocrats, it was natural that spokesmen from Caribbean countries came to dominate both the ACP Council of Ministers and Secretariat—apparently at times, much to the discomfort of some of the Francophone states.[13]

The more developed Commonwealth states, particularly Jamaica and Nigeria, had provided the leadership in the negotiations for Lomé I. Commonwealth countries continued to provide the intellectual leadership—at least in terms of outspoken criticism of the EEC—in the talks for the Convention's renewal. But by the time of the first round of renegotiations, disillusionment with the Convention had been experienced on a number of scores. Probably most important was the perception the relationship had brought only limited gains in the trade field, regarded as the most significant dimension of the relationship by the more developed ACP states. In all clientelist relationships the enthusiasm of clients wanes if the expected benefits do not materialize. As Lomé was increasingly perceived as being of little importance to their overall development strategies, so the previous ACP leaders—particularly Nigeria and Jamaica—became more reluctant to expend their scarce resources and to risk their credibility in a fight for a significant extension of the relationship. Both Nigeria and Jamaica were preoccupied with other problems at the time of these negotiations: Nigeria with the issue of Zimbabwean independence and Jamaica with domestic economic problems. Nigeria, the largest oil exporter among the ACP states, displayed no inclination to use its oil weapon in support of the ACP cause (whereas at the time of the renegotiations it was threatening its employment if Britain should reach an agreement with the minority regime in Zimbabwe-Rhodesia). Lomé simply was not perceived as a cause worth fighting for.

Efforts to institutionalize the Group were made all the more difficult by the structure of the relationship, which provides no institutionalized role for the ACP *as a group* in the implementation of the Convention. Most of the important day-to-day business occurs on a bilateral basis between the Commission and individual ACP states. This includes, for example, the preparation of projects for consideration for aid funding and the administration of approved projects, negotiation of the amounts of STABEX transfers, and even the negotiation of voluntary export restraints. Although the ACP Secretariat is informed of these activities, neither it nor the ACP Committee of Ambassadors is given an effective management role in the relationship. Whereas the Commission is the hub of the partnership, the ACP Secretariat is decidedly on the periphery (see figure 9.1). In a preparatory memorandum for the renegotiations (whose phrasing—in terms of "relegation" and "elevation"—is rather unfortunate in that it tends to reinforce the notion that the bilateral aspects of the relationship are the most important), the ACP Secretariat deplored "the observed effort on the part of the EEC countries to elevate issues of primary importance to the bilateral level while relegating areas of cooperation of a secondary nature to the multilateral level."[14]

The essentially bilateral nature of the relationship robs the ACP of a

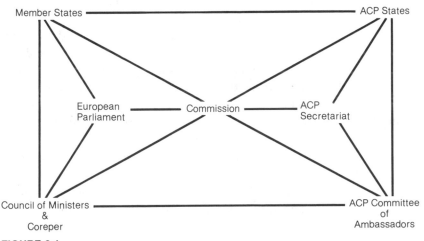

**FIGURE 9.1.**
Relations Between EEC and ACP Instructions

valuable opportunity to socialize and institutionalize their grouping. Yet it is indicative of the perceptions of the ACP states regarding the utility of the Secretariat that they have acquiesced in this bilateral pattern of interaction. One reason for this has been their reluctance to cede any of their decision-making autonomy to an international organization; another has been a perception that individual interests will best be furthered by negotiating on a bilateral basis with the Community, rather than attempt to enlist the weight of the Grouping in support of their cause. For instance, Mauritius negotiated the voluntary export restraint on its textiles on a bilateral basis, rather than politicize the issue by taking it to the ACP Council of Ministers and demand a settlement within the multilateral framework of the Convention. A sign of the lack of importance attached to the Group was seen in December 1982 when only fifteen ministers attended the thirtieth session of the ACP Council of Ministers.

While day-to-day relations are carried out primarily on a bilateral basis, the Convention itself in large part is subject to unilateral management. Again this deprives the ACP of a significant role that might otherwise have been used to strengthen Group cohesion and solidarity. Outside the Centre for Industrial Development, which, as chapter 7 showed, has been starved of resources, and the Technical Centre for Agricultural and Rural Cooperation created by the Second Convention, the ACP Group has no role in the critical decisions taken in implementing the Convention. In the Lomé relationship, the Commission alone decides which requests are eligible for STABEX transfers, which aid projects are suitable for submission to the EDF Committee, etc., functions that in a supposedly equal partnership one would expect to be shared with the ACP. And where questions arise regarding ambiguities in the Convention, the Commission alone is the interpreter. There is no provision for a joint arbitration body in the Convention; the only recourse in the event of a dispute is to the "good offices procedure." However, as chapter 6 noted, on the one occasion on which this was used, the Commission rejected the recommendations. Even in the Yaoundé Conventions there had been a Court of Arbitration (although this had never been used).

Maintenance of the ACP coalition was made more difficult by perceptions by its members of growing competition for the scarce resources provided in the relationship. The ACP perhaps surprised themselves and the world in successfully building a coalition in 1973–75 that achieved many of its principal objectives in the negotiations for the first Convention. But this was a relatively easy victory. Not only was coalition maintenance facilitated by the symbolic importance attached to ACP unity, but many of the Group's importance objectives, while again heavy in symbolic content, entailed little real cost to either party in the negotiations. Once the symbolic objectives, for example, the abolition of reverse preferences, had been achieved, coalition maintenance became more difficult in that many of the issues involved questions of intragroup distribution of benefits. The ACP were aware that the Community, having succeeded in constructing a package that contained something for all ACP states to attract their participation in the first Convention, was unwilling to provide substantial additional resources in support of new initiatives.

As soon as the negotiations for a renewal of the Convention began to focus on specific proposals whose costs and benefits for individual states could easily be assessed, the fragility of the coalition was exposed. Intra-ACP bargaining increasingly assumed the characteristics of a zero-sum game; log-rolling became more difficult. There was a reluctance on the part of many states to support the Group's proposals for new initiatives that would have required a significant volume of funding, since there was a fear that such projects would impinge on existing financial flows. An important example of this was a Nigerian proposal for a special fund for industrial cooperation: representatives of a number of the least developed ACP states argued that the Fund would benefit only the more developed countries within the Group and that its creation would reduce aid flows to the least developed. Similarly, many African states were lukewarm toward the ACP Secretariat's proposals for an ACP Development Bank, fearing that it would detract from the flow of funds to the African Development Bank.

Growing disillusionment with the fruits of collective action, combined with perceptions of the scarcity of resources that the Community was willing to expend on the Convention, led inexorably to a tendency toward a rebilateralization of clientelist ties. Individual ACP states looked to their traditional patrons in the Community to lobby for their particular interests; EEC member states rather than the ACP Group often served as the intermediary between the ACP state and the European Commission.

This naturally facilitated a Community strategy of divide and rule. Similar to the experience of the wider North-South dialogue,[15] the demands of the ACP have tended to take two principal forms: "demands of principle," which have called for sweeping changes in various issue areas, e.g., completely free access to the European market for all ACP exports, abolition of the safeguard clause, indexation of the STABEX system, etc.; and a shopping list of demands relating to the interests of individual ACP states, e.g., access for particular products such as Botswanan beef or Senegalese tomatoes, and the creation of a special category of "semi-landlocked" countries to enable Zaire to benefit from the special concessions in the Convention enjoyed by countries designated as least developed, landlocked, or island. The dual nature of ACP demands has made it easy for the Commission to address the requests of individual states while asserting that the more general principles constitute unreasonable demands.

Transparent attempts were made by the Community during the negotiations for Lomé II to weaken the solidarity of the ACP Group. Most obvious was the behavior of the French government at the Kigali summit of Francophone states held during the final stages of the negotiations, at which Giscard D'Estaing promised a substantial increase in French aid—which many observers believed was an attempt not only to purchase Francophone support for the new Convention but also to bilateralize the relationship once again (since the French Treasury used this increase in bilateral aid expenditure as a justification for its unwillingness to increase the sums available within Lomé).

The Commission also used its considerable local resources in ACP states to attempt to drive a wedge between the domestic governments and their ambassadors in Brussels. The objective was to convince the governments that their ambassadors were behaving irresponsibly in making "excessive" demands during the negotiations. Here the Community was able to exploit the poor communications that existed in many cases between the capitals and their local representatives and with the ACP Secretariat. When the negotiations broke down in May 1979, the Commission dispatched a high-level delegation under Commissioner for Development Cheysson to visit key African and Caribbean capitals and thus bypass the local ambassadors by explaining the Community's position directly to ACP Heads of State.[16] Certainly the Community appeared to believe that participation in the hectic activity of day-to-day negotiations had an important socializing effect on ACP ambassadors, inducing them to take a harder line stance than that desired by their own governments. Some credibility was given to this perspective by the apparent success of Cheysson's tour:

the ACP returned to the bargaining table one month later and accepted a package little different from what had earlier been rejected. ACP ambassadors in fact were radicalized by the experience of negotiating on a daily basis with the Community: besides the regular frustration of the Commission's denying that it had a mandate to bargain on some of the Group's demands, it became obvious that the Community chose to leave all concessions to ministerial meetings when, given the presence of domestically based representatives of ACP governments, they would have a greater political impact.[17]

By virtue of the weakness of horizontal ties among group members in comparison to the vertical ties between them and Community member states, a strategy of collective clientelism faced formidable obstacles. To be successful it would have had to bring immediate payoffs that were perceived as substantial. This was made less likely, however, by the unwillingness of ACP states to invest resources in the institutionalization of the Group. To break out of this vicious circle would have required vision on the part of those states able to provide the necessary resources. Clearly during the first Convention potential leaders of the Group did not perceive the likely payoffs to warrant the investment of scarce resources. Inevitably this has weakened the Group's bargaining power with the Community and led to a rebilateralization of the relationship.

## CONFLICTING NORMS IN THE ACP STRATEGY

Collective clientelism has also been undermined by the conflicting norms sought by the ACP. In essence the ACP demanded many of the advantages of a traditional clientelist relationship without accepting the behavioral norms typical of such relations. While expecting the Community to honor its generalized obligations in the "spirit" of Lomé, they shunned the inequality characteristic of clientelist structures. If it was in the ACP's interest, then the Community was expected to go beyond the Convention, to act arbitrarily to redefine the relationship in the ACP's favor. On the other hand, if the matter at hand was perceived as contrary to ACP interests, the Community was expected to honor the contractual nature of the Convention and to refrain from its redefinition. As the ACP Group became increasingly disillusioned with Community behavior so they attempted to constrain its decision-making latitude by strengthening the contractual element in the Convention.

A fatal flaw in the ACP strategy was that the Group was attempting to impose a relationship on the Community whose asymmetries in obligations were the reverse of the asymmetries in underlying power resources. And, ironically, the ACP's proposed solution to their disappointment with the Convention would have exacerbated this situation. While attempting to strengthen the contractual nature of the Convention, the Group rejected any additional reciprocity on their part. In essence they were attempting to construct a relationship that would have foreclosed independent action on the part of the Community in key areas of economic policy-making but that would have enabled ACP states to obtain the benefits provided by the partnership regardless of the type of policy they pursued.

While attempting to extend the scope of the Community's obligations in the Convention, the ACP appeared to be prepared to offer nothing in return beyond their actual willingness to participate in the arrangement. "Being there" had been an important source of leverage in the negotiations in 1973–75 but was a less potent bargaining resource once the Convention was in operation. Although even the most intransigent of the Community member states had come to accept that strict reciprocity in the commercial field should not be demanded of the ACP, nevertheless Community interest in the Convention was inevitably determined by perceptions of what advantage might be obtained from it. Unfortunately for the ACP, although their spokesmen frequently reminded the Community of the major stake that European commercial interests had in their countries, the Europeans had little reason to believe these would not be sustained in the absence of the Convention.

A critical factor for the evolution of the multilateral partnership was the insufficient attention given to mutual advantages arising from the Convention itself. To bargain effectively for an extension of the relationship the ACP Group needed to be able to barter something in return. They tended, however, to regard with suspicion any EEC proposal that held forth the potential for gains to the Community, as well as to the ACP. Hostile reaction on the part of the ACP to EEC proposals that promised mutual gain can be explained in part by what can be termed the "sovereignty complex" that appeared to dominate the perceptions of many ACP states. As countries that had received their independence relatively recently, they displayed great sensitivity toward any proposal whose implementation might possibly impinge upon domestic decision-making latitude. Inevitably this would have been the case with projects of mutual interest if the EEC was to be assured of the security of potential gains. On the ACP side there appeared to be a widespread perception that "mutual benefit" would inevitably involve unequal exchange, the Community gaining disproportionately. This was apparent in the Group's hostile reaction to Community proposals for guarantees for Community investments in ACP mining industries, joint exploitation of ACP fisheries resources, and the negotiation of long-term supply contracts for certain raw materials.

ACP states found themselves in the paradoxical position of asserting that reciprocity was "based on an assumed equality of obviously unequal parts"[18] while demanding equal status within a contractual relationship. By ignoring the opportunities to pursue projects of mutual benefit at the Group level, they considerably weakened their bargaining position (the Community generally being successful in gaining what it wanted, e.g., fishery agreements, by responding sympathetically to the particular requests of the individual ACP states concerned). Bilateral relations were again strengthened at the expense of multilateral ties and the institutionalization of the ACP Group. Failure to pay sufficient attention to mutual benefits inevitably reinforced Community perceptions of the asymmetry in benefits arising from the Convention and ensured that the ACP came to the negotiating table empty-handed in the role of *demandeurs*. Ironically, the lack of reciprocity served merely to reinforce the tendency of the Community toward the behavior of a traditional patron: paternalism and frequently arbitrary action to redefine the relationship when it perceived this to be in its interests.

## CHANGING COMMUNITY INTERESTS

As chapter 1 noted, the strategy of collective clientelism was constructed on the premise of using affective historical ties from the colonial period as a means of attempting to tie the Community's hands in its future foreign economic policies. Well aware of their declining importance to the Community, the ACP aspired to capitalize on the inertia effects of international regimes to preserve their particularistic advantages in the Community market. Their hope was that the continuing affective ties (or sense of responsibility for their former colonies) would lead the Community to accept obligations derived both from the letter and spirit of the Convention to safeguard ACP interests. This third contradiction of collective clientelism—attempting to use the past to structure the future—proved to be one of its principal weaknesses.

Just as the member states' objectives have been increasingly difficult to obtain within the Community given the growth of complex interdependence, as Haas argues, so too did they find the particularistic relationship with their former colonies to be too constraining.[19] Increasingly the Community has become dependent on its commerce with developing countries to provide a substantial portion of its export markets and thus a major contribution toward its GNP. But it is not the ACP countries that have figured prominently in the Community's growing commercial interdependence with the Third World; rather, the oil-exporting countries of the Middle East, and the Newly Industrializing Countries of Latin America and Asia have become the Community's most important Third World trading partners. Inevitably, the Community's traditional clients have lost out as the Community pursued what it has regarded as more important commercial relations with states in a better position than the ACP to bargain effectively. In those areas where the EEC has some significant dependence on the ACP, e.g., minerals and, to a lesser extent, fishery resources, the unwillingness of the ACP to respond to proposals of mutual interest and their inability to forge a united negotiating front has prevented the Group from effectively mobilizing its principal bargaining resources. Unlike the ACP, the NICs do not come to the negotiating table empty-handed, their primary bargaining resource being their rapidly expanding domestic markets.

The impact of modernization and increasing interdependence on the Lomé relationship is analogous to the inability of traditional landlords to continue to provide a guarantee of social insurance as their position is undermined by the intrusion of the world market.[20] For even if Community member states had wanted to extend the contractual elements of the Convention to guarantee patronage to the ACP (and, perhaps, France alone among the member states would have been enthusiastic about doing so), the Community increasingly found its hands tied by the growing interdependence of the world economy. Increasing interdependence has thus reduced the capacity and will of the Community to play its traditional role of patron toward its former colonies.

For the ACP the problem was that the low-cost concessions available to the EEC had been exhausted in the negotiation of Lomé I. Any extension of the contractual element of the relationship as they desired would have imposed significant costs on the EEC. In the negotiations for the first Convention the Community was willing to make a number of concessions to secure the participation of the ACP. ACP states were successful in their main objective of establishing nonreciprocity as the principle on which commercial cooperation would be based, primarily because this major symbolic advance could be achieved at little expense to the Community. In practice, reverse preferences were less important than traditional commercial links that facilitated continuing Community predominance (while some Francophone states even continued to maintain reverse preferences during the Lomé period). And on this matter, the ACP benefited from the paradox of power within clientelist relations—the Community did not wish to be embarrassed by appearing to exploit its position to demand reciprocity from the weak. Only in the case of sugar did the Community face a hard choice, and even here it was not a matter of taking away existing market shares from European producers but of denying them the right to exclude the ACP Group from its traditional market.

Any major extension of the Lomé relationship beyond the terms of the first Convention, however, as demanded by the ACP, could be achieved only at the expense of European domestic interests or of restricting the Community's freedom of action in its other external economic relations. As Commissioner for Development Claude Cheysson commented: "When a development aid policy ceases to be marginal, when it goes beyond financial aid, it becomes a domestic policy in the industrial countries."[21] The Community was unwilling to countenance this. An extension of the Lomé relationship threatened to impose significant costs on a number of dimensions. Most obvious was the budgetary concern—at a time of financial stringency in Western Europe few of the member states were willing to make any significant addition to the funds already channeled through the Convention, as would have been required if some of the ACP's proposals, e.g., a major improvement of STABEX, were implemented. Second, any substantial modification of the trade provisions would have had consequences for the Community's domestic policies, particularly with regard to industrial restructuring. Again, at a time of high domestic unemployment, this was not a cost that most member states were willing to contemplate. On other dimensions of commercial policy, e.g., the tariff advantages enjoyed by the ACP, an extension of the contractual element in the Convention would have tied the Community's hands in its dealings with other commercial partners. And, finally, a significant improvement of the terms of Lomé, e.g., the indexation of STABEX, threatened to impose costs in terms of setting a precedent that for certain would be cited by the Group of 77 in the wider North-South dialogue in global fora.

As Cox and Jacobson noted in their survey of international organizations, the more salient the subject matter with which the organization was concerned, the more attention it received from national governments.[22] This was certainly true of the Lomé relationship also. Close scrutiny by the Nine of its activities was cited by several senior Commission officials as the major difference between the negotiations for Lomé II and those for the first Convention. As the potential costs arising from the Convention increased, so did the member states' interest in the negotiations. Whereas the Council of Ministers—preoccupied with the threat of British withdrawal from the Community—had allowed the Commission to begin the Lomé I talks without formal approval of the Commission's negotiating memoranda, the Commission was now tightly reigned in. There was no question of the Commission being allowed to commit the Community in advance by publicly proposing new schemes, as had occurred with STABEX. At the time that ACP solidarity was faltering it found itself faced with a far more formidable negotiating partner.

The structure of the relationship prevented the ACP from benefiting from advantages identified as accruing to weaker parties in other unequal relationships. Hirschman has suggested that LDCs might be able to improve their bargaining position within a relationship by taking advantage of the disparity of attention devoted to it: for the weak, it is the central aspect of their economic life and therefore one to whose improvement they will devote their single-minded attention. But for the stronger party, where the relationship is but a very small part of their economic intercourse, less effort will be given to maintaining the relationship in its existing form.[23] In the Lomé partnership, however, this asymmetry is far less obvious. In the first place, the relationship is the most important focus, indeed, the *raison d'être*, for one Directorate-General of the Commission whose staff of more than 350 professionals allows it to perform a monitoring role far beyond the capabilities of the ACP Secretariat or any individual ACP government. Second, since Lomé is a fixed-length agreement, bargaining over its terms and their modification is concentrated in periodic intensive sessions before its expiration. These are immediately "politicized" at the highest level in that they involve ministers from the member states of the Community. Unlike other areas of the Community's activities, the EDF has a budget not derived from the Community's own resources—again the necessity of national governments' voting approval for these funds focuses the attention of Community decision-makers on the relationship. As the Lomé Convention became more costly for the member states, so they were less likely to be caught unawares by a well-prepared adversary, as was the case in 1974–75.

Having enticed the ACP into the relationship in 1974–75 and thereby obtained its principal objective, the Community perceived the price for preserving the arrangement to be low. It displayed a far better appreciation than the ACP of how the balance of bargaining power had shifted since the signature of the initial Convention. In the intervening period, deterioration in the international economic climate had weakened the economies of most ACP states and increased their vulnerability to a curtailment of European assistance. Lack of progress toward the achievement of NIEO goals in global fora meant that a source of negotiating power anticipated by the ACP in 1974 had not materialized. Meanwhile, oil power had rebounded to the disadvantage of most ACP states, their economies being afflicted not only by soaring bills for imported fuels (and Western manufactures) but also by a decline in the prices of many of their primary product exports as a result of recession and reduced demand in the West. Hopes for successful cartels in other primary products proved illusory. And the sugar price, which had been one of the strengths of the ACP negotiating position in 1974–75, had collapsed to one-quarter of the level prevailing during the Lomé I talks. With less uncertainty in the international economic environment in 1978–79, the EEC was less willing to consider proposals that failed to offer mutual benefits. Repeated references were made during the talks to the lack of alternatives facing the ACP, who were also frequently reminded of both the novelty and uniqueness of the Convention. A favorable contrast was drawn between the size of the Community aid effort and that of other DAC countries and of OPEC. Outside the highest level of the Development Directorate within the Commission (and here some believed the motivations were largely the result of personal career and/or bureaucratic interests) there were few references to interdependence with the ACP; rather the most common metaphors employed in relation to the renegotiations were references to power differentials—"our" strength versus "their" weakness.[24]

In most patron-client relations, modernization has tended to improve the bargaining position of clients as new potential patrons emerge, competing to capture client support.[25] In the international system, however, with its more hierarchical structure, there are fewer potential patrons available. For the ACP the problem has been that they do not possess resources regarded as of sufficient short-term value to lead to a competition among potential patrons. Eastern bloc countries do not have the markets or technology or capital to be attractive patrons to the ACP beyond a limited role in supplying armaments. For this reason, Angola and Mozambique—which sought associate status in COMECON and refused to participate in the first two Lomé agreements—are taking part in the negotiations for a third Convention. Another potential patron, Japan, has shown only limited interest in African resources; its consistent balance of trade surplus with Africa has been used to finance imports from Asia.[26] Meanwhile, the United States angered Caribbean countries by refusing to provide them with concessions similar to those introduced by Lomé— and the flawed Caribbean Basin Initiative has not rectified this situation. In the absence of other willing patrons, ACP dependence on the Community has been reinforced.

Like all weaker parties in a clientelist relationship, the ACP were not well placed to threaten the Community. Lacking other sanctions, the only threat available to them was to refuse to sign a new agreement. But even this was less of a weapon than in 1974. As the Community was well aware, the successful conclusion of the initial Convention had changed the balance of the bargaining relationship in that the agreement in operation offered benefits that were difficult for the weak to forego. Accordingly, the ACP were frequently reminded of the possibility that the flow of benefits might be interrupted if delay should occur in reaching a new agreement. This underscores both the importance of the asymmetries in the benefits arising from the Convention for the negotiating strength of the two parties and also the factor of differing time horizons. As Rothstein noted in the context of the global North-South dialogue, the bargaining terms of trade are determined by the ratio of desire and need; whereas the needs and fears of the industrial countries refer primarily to future shortages of materials and may be discounted in the short term with which most negotiations are concerned, the needs of most developing countries are immediate.[27] In the Lomé relationship, the EEC are confronted by some of the world's weakest states; the least developed are least able to gamble.[28]

Community perceptions of its short- and medium-term interests have weighed against any extension of the relationship along the contractual lines to which the ACP have aspired. The diminishing importance of the commercial relationship with the ACP, coupled with the increasing costs of attempting to safeguard the Group's share of the Community market has prompted the Community to reconsider the type of "partnership" it wishes to have with the Group. Acting like a traditional patron, the Community has unilaterally redefined the relationship. Emphasis has increasingly been placed on aid as the cornerstone of Lomé rather than commercial cooperation. In part this is because an extension of aid imposes fewer domestic costs on the Community than the structural adjustment that would be necessary if the trade regime was fully liberalized. Also significant is the evolution that has occurred in Community thinking on North-South issues, particularly within the Development Directorate.

DG VIII has gradually evolved from an organization solely concerned with the Community's ex-colonies in Africa to a body with an increasingly globalist outlook. Expansion of the Community in 1973 and the conclusion of the Lomé Convention marked a significant step in this process. The globalist camp—represented principally by West Germany and the Netherlands—was strengthened by Britain's accession; the domination of DG VIII by French officials was gradually eroded.[29] This was reflected in the Community extending aid to "nonassociates" for the first time in the mid-1970s. Over the remainder of the decade aid provided through the multilateral channel of the Community grew more rapidly than the bilateral aid of the member states; by 1980 it amounted to more than 10 percent of the total disbursed by the Nine. DG VIII has become a major aid agency in its own right with an annual budget of more than $1.5 billion to administer. This is in excess of the aid budgets of both Canada and Sweden; it also exceeds annual Community expenditure on the European Social Fund and the European Regional Development Fund.[30] As Stevens has argued, this gives the Directorate-General for Development an esprit de corps and, one might add, a mission, lacking in those Directorates that have no substantial policy to administer.[31] Administration of its aid program also gives the Commission representation (more than 200 delegates overseas), and not inconsiderable influence, in many developing countries.

DG VIII has apparently tired of its battles with the Directorate-Generals for External Relations and Agriculture in its efforts to preserve the preferential access to the Community market enjoyed by the ACP. Interviews I conducted with senior Community officials during the negotiations for Lomé II brought out the frustrations that many had experienced during the implementation of the Convention. Frequently it was argued that the ACP Group was being unreasonable in its demands that the contractual obligations of the Community under the Convention be fully respected. In short, impatience with the ACP, the bitterness that sometimes characterized the relationship, and the apparent lack of gratitude expressed by their partners for the Directorate's efforts on their behalf, coupled with the difficulties of intra-Community squabbles over ACP preferences, compounded the tendency to perceive the aid dimension as the most fruitful direction in which to steer the Directorate's bureaucratic future.

This tendency was reinforced by the appointment of a new Commissioner for Development Cooperation in 1981. Observers of international organizations have frequently pointed to the importance of the executive head in shaping the task and philosophy of the bodies they direct.[32] In the EEC's Directorate-General for Development, the appointment of a replacement for Claude Cheysson has led to an articulation of new goals for the Directorate. Edgard Pisani appears less willing than his predecessor to be the advocate for the South in the bureaucratic politics of the Community. Rather, his primary interests lie in building up the Directorate as an aid agency, with a particular focus on the least developed countries of the world.[33] Pisani has suggested, for example, that the STABEX scheme be extended to all countries designated as least developed by the United Nations.

This new direction has found support among the member states, reflecting the growing emphasis of national aid agencies on basic human needs strategies. Certainly it answers some of the objections of the more "globalist" member states, which have objected to the lack of clearly defined criteria for distributing Community aid and to the disproportionate share received by some relatively favored (but not necessarily least developed) ACP states. Apparently the Commission intends to implement regionally the basic needs strategy advocated as a possible foundation for future North-South global cooperation.[34] A narrowing and redirection of the principal efforts of DG VIII will also certainly have been welcomed within the Commission since it reduces the chances of the Development Directorate encroaching on the territory claimed by external relations, agriculture, and industry.

For the ACP, however, the new emphasis sounds the death knell of collective clientelism. As Helleiner argued, it is the provisions for commercial cooperation rather than aid that the ACP perceive as the essence of the Lomé arrangements.[35] Disbursements of EDF aid amount to less than 3 percent of the annual value of the ACP exports to the EEC. Commercial cooperation has, however, only a small role in the new Commission orthodoxy. Indeed, one of the justifications made for the new policy is that the experience of implementing the Convention has demonstrated that the ACP in general, and African countries in particular, have been unable to take advantage of the opportunities provided by preferences and market forces. Accordingly, the Development Directorate proposes to concentrate on helping to construct a safety net for these states by providing aid in support of agricultural and rural development.[36] The carrot of increased aid is intended to divert attention away from renewed calls by the ACP on the one hand for managed markets including guaranteed prices for their commodities and on the other for liberalized access to the Community market for ACP exports of agricultural and other "sensitive" products.

Although ACP states in general, but particularly the African countries, may continue to be the principal beneficiaries of the Community's development efforts, the nature of the relationship would be significantly transformed away from the design to which the ACP aspired in their strategy of collective clientelism. A focus on aid would carry the asymmetries in the Lomé partnership to their logical conclusion. Indeed, the lack of reciprocity in the Convention and the ACP Group's unwillingness to consider measures of mutual benefit undoubtedly encouraged an evolution of this nature. An aid relationship in which one side gives and the other receives removes any lingering notions of an "equal partnership." Aid is unilaterally determined by the donor; there is not even the formal constraint on behavior provided by the contractual element of the commercial cooperation provisions. A focus on aid will reinforce the bilateral element of the relationship, the principal talks occurring between the Commission and the national governments of its partners. A focus on basic human needs also inevitably will increase the conditionality of the aid provisions—something the Community member states will welcome given their discontent with their lack of control over the use of STABEX transfers. Such interference conflicts, however, with ACP ideas that respect for their sovereignty should underwrite the equal partnership of the Convention.

Naturally, an evolution of this type will alienate the elites of some of the more developed of the ACP states. This prospect appears to be one the Commission approaches with equanimity—its "think piece" on future development policy notes that "the diversity of the countries covered by the Convention constitutes a *de facto* argument in favour of a regionalized approach under the Convention."[37] To remove the more developed ACP states from the new centerpiece of the relationship would deprive the ACP Group of its intellectual leadership and would, of course, remove those countries with resources, which are best placed to bargain effectively with the Community. A rump of the ACP Group consisting primarily of least developed states would be no better placed to negotiate than the Yaoundé Associates were. A redirection of the Convention toward an aid relationship with an emphasis on basic human needs simultaneously meets a number of Community objectives: to reduce the costs of the Convention in terms of impact on domestic constituencies and the constraints it imposes on other Community foreign economic policies; to increase the conditionality in the relationship, which again serves to satisfy domestic constituencies; to provide a clearer demarcation of the responsibilities of the various directorates of the Commission and to provide DG VIII with a major new bureaucratic task; and, in the process, to fashion an ACP Group that will be more amenable to Community direction. How far this new emphasis in policy will be implemented in Lomé III, if agreement on a new Convention is reached, is unclear at the time of writing.

## LOMÉ: A FINAL ASSESSMENT

Despite the success of OPEC and the remarkable growth of the newly industrializing countries over the last decade, North-South relations remain characterized by considerable asymmetries in resources and capabilities. This is not to assert, however, that the strong will always use their resources to coerce the weak. In many issue areas the powerful have found that it is more efficient to collaborate with weaker states in the system rather than attempt to unilaterally impose their will. Collaboration inevitably involves bargaining, which offers an opportunity for the weak to improve the terms of exchange in their relationships with the strong. Three principal groups of factors can be identified that influence bargaining outcomes: the skill of the negotiating parties, the context in which bargaining takes place, and the relative power resources of the parties.

There is little doubt that the ACP Group failed to capitalize on the few bargaining resources available to them. This was in part due to the contradictions of the strategy of collective clientelism. By failing to institutionalize their grouping and make it the focal point for vertical collaboration in the relationship, they left themselves open to a strategy of divide and rule. By refusing to consider meaningful reciprocity within the relationship, they not only undermined their own claims for equality but also alienated potential allies within Europe; they denied themselves the opportunity of constructing transnational alliances. This was exacerbated by their lack of technical capability, which reduced their ability to bargain effectively on detailed issues.[38] By refusing to consider issues of mutual interest, the ACP condemned themselves to arriving at the bargaining table empty-handed: their principal bargaining resource—their participation in the Convention—had been exhausted in the 1973–75 negotiations. Exit from the Convention was not a credible strategy—instead, in Hirschman's terms, they had to rely on loyalty (the principal strategy of the Francophones) or voice (the tactic favored by the Commonwealth states).

Certainly, the context in which Lomé has been implemented has not been propitious for the realization of the aims of the collective clientelist strategy. From the ACP Group's perspective, it was unfortunate that they were attempting to extend the contractual element in the Convention when the EEC was searching for additional means through which it could circumvent its contractual obligations under GATT. Lomé was in part a victim of the prevailing stagflation. It was also a victim of the Community's difficulties in adjusting to changes in the international division of labor and of a continuing failure to reform the Common Agricultural Policy. As the European Commission acknowledged:

Generally speaking, Europe seems to lag behind the United States and Japan in adapting to competition from the developing countries and appears more vulnerable to an intensification of this competition in the future because of the trend and pattern of the external trade of most Community countries. They tend to export more and import less of the type of products produced by the developing countries (particularly products with a high unskilled labor content) than Japan and the United States, where the process of adjusting the structure of production and foreign trade to competition from these countries has been under way for longer.[39]

Differences in the rates of productive investment and modernization of plant between the member states have complicated the adjustment process and increased strains within the Community. At a time of high domestic unemployment and low rates of growth, the needs of the ACP were given low priority, while the marginal costs they impose on domestic economic interests were magnified out of all proportion in Community calculations. ACP interests, particularly those of sugar producers, also suffered because of the continuing inability of the Community to rationalize its agricultural policies. In a period of crisis in which some member states were seeking to renegotiate their budgetary contributions, ACP interests were again ignored in the desperate search for short-term domestic harmony. Cognitive evolution—the term Haas employs to denote the assimilation of new knowledge leading to cooperation on the basis of perceived mutual interest—is unlikely when the stronger parties are preoccupied with the resolution of short-term domestic crises to which the weaker parties are perceived to have contributed.[40]

Even if the Convention had been implemented in a more favorable economic climate, which might have permitted the Community to offer more concessions to ACP exports, ACP aspirations for collective clientelism would still have been frustrated. Quite simply, the Community did not perceive the ACP as being of sufficient economic importance to warrant the type of relationship the ACP wished to construct. In the absence of consensus on the future nature of the relationship, state power became the key determining variable. European trading and strategic interests have increasingly focused on the Arab world, while European TNCs have concentrated their investment in the newly industrializing countries of Asia and Latin America.[41] A future enlargement of the Community to include Spain and Portugal will lead to a further evolution of its development cooperation policies toward a global perspective given the interests that the new members have in Latin America. Spain has already requested that favorable treatment be given by the enlarged

Community to Latin American exports, especially coffee, tobacco, sugar, and meat, the very products of most concern to the ACP states.[42] Such developments reinforced the perception that the countries of the ACP Group are increasingly irrelevant commercial partners for the EEC, a situation unlikely to be reversed in the foreseeable future unless a major crisis occurs regarding security of supply of raw materials.

That collective clientelism has been a failure undercuts the arguments of some of the more apocalyptic scenarios, which foresee the emergence of neomercantilist regional trading blocs.[43] Loss of interest in the Lomé relationship was a direct response to the continuing diversification of the Community's investment and trading links, which have focused increasingly on the rapidly growing developing countries of Latin America and Asia (which, according to the neomercantilists, are within the sphere of interest of other Northern economic powers). Interdependence does indeed appear to have been globalized sufficiently to cast serious doubt on the potential for regional economic groupings. From the perspective of the universalistic principles of the international trade regime, therefore, Lomé has at worse been a minor irritant. Collective clientelism has had a greater impact, by virtue of its particularism, on the unity of the Group of 77; even here criticism of the Convention has become less strident as the ineffectiveness of the trade advantages enjoyed by the ACP became obvious.

Collective clientelism failed to produce the expected benefits within the context of the Lomé Convention. Is a strategy of collective clientelism always doomed to failure? The Lomé experience certainly points to the difficulties any group of potential clients will face in constructing a relationship of this type. The very essence of clientelism—the predominance of vertical relationships over horizontal—mitigates against the institutionalization of the clients as a collectivity and thus weakens their efforts at bargaining on a joint basis. The larger the number of clients, and the greater the diversity among them in terms of interests, ideologies, size, levels of development, etc., the more difficult it will be to form an effective negotiating coalition. This was made all the more difficult in the Lomé relationship by their being a number of patrons, not all of which had any enthusiasm for acting as a *collective* patron.

A further factor brought out by the Lomé relationship is the unlikelihood of the clients' being able to construct a relationship in which the patron permits constraints to be imposed on its autonomy of action, unless the clients have resources perceived as valuable in the short term by the patron. Here there was a further contradiction in the Lomé relationship: the Community was willing to participate only because of the weakness of the ACP states; more developed former colonies were deliberately excluded from fear that they were well placed to exploit the potential advantages the relationship offered and that this would impose high costs on domestic Community interests. Yet only the more developed members of the Group of 77 have the resources to enable them to provide the reciprocity that will sustain the interest of the patron in the long run. A successful clientelist coalition would need to have resources valued sufficiently by its potential patron to offset the perceived damage the relationship would cause to the patron's domestic constituency.

The unwieldy nature of the ACP Grouping and the absence of reciprocity in the relationship undermined collective clientelism in the Lomé context. A smaller grouping that had managed some degree of institutionalization and, possibly, integration before entering a clientelist relationship might have a greater likelihood of success, particularly if the proposed partnership was less unequal than Lomé. One possibility might be a relationship of this type between ASEAN and Japan. For certain, however, any collective clientelist relationship would be transitory. Like all variants of clientelism, it is an intermediate form that, if successful, will disappear as a result of its own contradictions. Successful clientelism, by promoting the economic development of the clients, eradicates the conditions that give rise to it in the first place. Economic development strengthens the clients so that they no longer need the special protection provided by the patron; they are able to compete effectively on the basis of their own resources.[44] Clientelism would be replaced by a relationship based on the contractual equality of the parties. In Lomé the ACP Group found they had negotiated an arrangement that incorporated the terminology of contract and equality but had a substance more akin to that of a traditional clientelist relationship.

Lomé has, of course, fallen far short of its claims to represent a model for the new international economic order. This has been particularly disappointing to those writers who perceived a regional relationship confined to "functional" issues as offering the best opportunity for an escape from stalemate in the North-South dialogue. A number of commentators have argued that *procedural* factors have been as much a cause of this impasse as substantive issues. Typical of many Northern critics were W.

W. Rostow's comments that the negotiations for a New International Economic Order have been based on "the wrong intellectual conception, the wrong agenda, the wrong negotiating forum, and the wrong cast of negotiators."[45] Initially, Lomé appeared to represent a feasible alternative model; the negotiations brought together a group of developing countries that, in comparison to the wider Group of 77, had a common background, similar levels of development, and therefore, it was presumed, a common interest in solving common problems. Unlike the global North-South dialogue, Lomé focused on "practical" questions—of access for exports, of compensatory finance, of disbursement of aid, and of projects in which it appeared possible to promote mutual interest. And, again in contrast to the NIEO talks, Lomé avoided the troublesome structural questions of attempting to reform international institutions and of changing the locus of managerial control of the international economy. Negotiations between comparatively small groups that focused on functional issues appeared to bring the desired payoff. There was no denying that the Lomé negotiations had ended successfully with the signature of an innovative Convention, in marked contrast to the general lack of progress in other North-South arenas in 1974–75.[46]

While Lomé touches on many of the issues raised in the global dialogue, neither its contents nor the manner in which it has been implemented correspond with the aspirations of the Group of 77. The European Community has consistently resisted ACP requests for the inclusion in the Convention of some of the central terminology of the NIEO demands, e.g., references to ACP sovereignty over their natural resources, the obligation of the Community to pursue policies of structural adjustment, and the need for a code of conduct for transnational enterprises. Implementation of the Conventions has shown that the Community has little respect for the contractual obligations it had claimed to have undertaken; the corresponding security that Lomé was supposed to have provided was consequently conspicuous by its absence. The Lomé experience must cast doubt on the ability to achieve NIEO objectives within a regional relationship, or at least one in which the asymmetries of the parties are as marked as those between the ACP and EEC.

In the New International Economic Disorder, the less vulnerable are best placed to pursue their domestic interests at the expense of those of weaker parties. Here it is important not to mix cause and effect. Lomé is not itself a major cause of the imbalance in vulnerabilities between the EEC and the ACP; if it is to be criticized, it is for a failure to do much to help correct them. Particularly disappointing from the ACP perspective was the unwillingness of the Community to promote the "dynamic complementarity" to which reference is made in the second Convention. As the preceding chapters have demonstrated, the Community has given little support to measures that might have helped diversify ACP economies: STABEX remains confined to raw materials or products that have undergone only minimal processing; the industrial cooperation provisions of the Convention have been starved of resources; manufacturing industry continues to be relatively neglected in EDF and EIB assistance. Meanwhile, the Community resisted ACP measures that might have widened their economic alternatives: export-processing zones, the creation of an ACP Development Bank, etc. Existing dependencies have been perpetuated, if not significantly exacerbated.

Although Lomé contained improvements on the terms of the Yaoundé Conventions, the new agreement represented incremental change rather than a revolutionary new agreement. If, in Gruhn's terminology, Lomé was symbolic of an "inching towards interdependence,"[47] emphasis should be placed on "inching" rather than "interdependence." Given the desire of the ACP Group for rapid transformation of their economies and for respect of their sovereignty, incrementalism was insufficient. Since Lomé had been heralded as more than this and had been perceived as such by the ACP, their disappointment was all the greater. This was compounded by their frustration with the negotiating process and by their misperception of their importance to the EEC. This arose primarily from the apparent ease with which they had been able to achieve their principal objectives in the initial Lomé negotiations. This fostered the illusion that they were of sufficient significance to the Community that the latter would allow its hands to be tied in order to promote ACP interests. In reality the Group found that the provisions of the Convention were not guaranteed: the Community would invoke one or another of the escape clauses where it perceived that the arrangements imposed a cost on domestic constituencies. This ability to opt out of or redefine aspects of the relationship when they threaten Community interests has enabled it to reap the benefits of the partnership at relatively little cost.

On the other hand, although the relationship has fallen far short of ACP expectations, it provides concrete benefits that would be difficult for many of the recipients to forgo. This is in marked contrast to the continuing stalemate in the global dialogue and to the increasing tendency of the industrialized world to (selectively) emphasize market mechanisms that tend to favor the newly industrializing countries but that offer little to the poorest states. Lomé also offers a framework through which the ACP can compel attention to their demands. ACP states also benefit from a "foot in the door" effect—the very fact that a Convention exists and has to be periodically renegotiated inevitably places pressure on the Community to grant additional concessions/benefits (this effect has not been lost on the Community, however—it has proposed that the Third Convention be of unlimited duration). There are few opportunity costs of membership in the relationship; the ACP Group was successful in their aim in the initial negotiations of reaching an agreement that imposed few constraints on their freedom of action. Few distortions are introduced into their international economic relations as a result of it; the impact of the rules of origin and of the exclusion of processed products from STABEX is, at least in the short and medium term, more important in principle than in practice.

Most of the money available under the Convention has no political strings attached—STABEX transfers, for example, essentially represent a source of unconditional foreign exchange. While other EDF aid does depend on EEC approval of projects (and continues to be biased against productive investments), all ACP states have a multitude of infrastructural needs toward which EEC aid can contribute. And, as chapter 8 demonstrated, collective clientelism has apparently paid dividends in that the ACP share of member states' bilateral aid has not fallen as a result of their benefiting from Community multilateral funds. ACP states remain relatively privileged beneficiaries of aid among all LDCs: their gains from the aid provisions of the Convention again stand in contrast to the tendency in the global community toward declining development assistance transfers.

An aid relationship was not, however, what most of the ACP Group were seeking when they entered the negotiations for the first Convention. Lomé has done little to assist the structural transformation of their economies. It is this very marginality of Lomé—to both the EEC and the ACP—that has caused disillusionment. But for many ACP states, principal victims of the new international economic disorder, even the limited benefits provided under the Convention retain significance. A partnership that focuses predominantly on aid will continue to remain attractive *faute de mieux*. That is the true measure of their tragedy.

# Notes

## 1. Introduction

1. Francois-Xavier Ortoli, President of the Commission of the European Communities; *Die Zeit;* Claude Cheysson, Commissioner for Development; and Babacar Ba, Chairman of the ACP Council of Ministers; all quoted in *The Courier* (March 1975), no. 31, pp. 19, 17, 13, and 7, respectively.

2. The original 46 ACP states were: Bahamas, Barbados, Botswana, Burundi, Cameroon, Central African Republic, Chad, Congo, Dahomey (Benin), Equatorial Guinea, Ethiopia, Fiji, Gabon, Gambia, Ghana, Guinea, Guinea-Bissau, Grenada, Guyana, Ivory Coast, Jamaica, Kenya, Lesotho, Liberia, Madagascar, Malawi, Mali, Mauritania, Mauritius, Niger, Nigeria, Rwanda, Senegal, Sierra Leone, Somalia, Sudan, Swaziland, Tanzania, Togo, Tonga, Trinidad and Tobago, Uganda, Upper Volta, Western Samoa, Zaire, and Zambia. During the period of application of the first Convention thirteen additional states acceded: Surinam (16 July 1976), Seychelles (27 August 1976), Comoros (13 September 1976), Djibouti (2 February 1978), Solomon Islands (27 September 1978), Sao Tome and Principe (1 November 1978), Cape Verde (1 November 1978), Papua New Guinea (1 November 1978), Tuvalu (17 January 1979), Dominica (26 February 1979), Saint Lucia (28 June 1979), Kiribati (30 October 1979), Saint Vincent and Grenadines (27 February 1980). During the second Convention, Vanuatu (18 March 1981), Zimbabwe (1 March 1982), Belize (5 March 1982), Antigua and Barbuda, and St. Christopher and Nevis joined the ACP Group; Greece acceded to the Convention as the tenth EEC Member State on 8 October 1981. Parties to the Convention thus number almost half the total membership of the United Nations.

3. Preamble to the first Lomé Convention.

4. Richard Falk, "Foreword" to Ellen Frey-Wouters, *The European Community and the Third World: The Lomé Convention and Its Impact* (New York: Praeger, 1980), p. vii.

5. Writings on Lomé from a dependency perspective include the following: Dan Nabudere, "The Lomé Conventions and the Consolidation of Neo-Colonialism," in *Essays on the Theory and Practice of Imperialism* (Dar es Salaam: Tanzania Publishing House, 1979); Esko Antola, "The European Community and Africa: A Neo-Colonial Model of Development," *Peace and the Sciences* (Dec. 1976), 4:15–32; Ga-Kwame Amoa, "Relations Between Africa and Europe in Historical Perspective," *University of Ghana Law Journal* (1976), 13(1/2); and Johan Galtung, "The Lomé Convention and Neo-Capitalism," *The African Review* (1976), 6(1):33–42. The most comprehensive and persuasive work from this approach is Guy Martin, "The Political Economy of African-European Relations from Yaoundé I to Lomé II, 1963–1980: A Case Study in Neo-Colonialism and Dependency," Ph.D. dissertation, Indiana University, Feb. 1982.

6. Reginald Herbold Green, "The Child of Lomé: Messiah, Monster or Mouse," in Frank

Long, ed., *The Political Economy of EEC Relations with African, Caribbean, and Pacific States* (Oxford, England: Pergamon, 1980), pp. 3–32.

7. Michael Bratton, "Patterns of Development and Underdevelopment," *International Studies Quarterly* (Sept. 1982), 26(3):34. An earlier criticism of dependency approaches to Eur-African relations is found in I. William Zartman, "Europe and Africa: Decolonization or Dependency?" *Foreign Affairs* (Jan. 1976), 54(2):325–343.

## 1. Collective Clientelism

1. Ernst B. Haas defines turbulence as "the confused and clashing perceptions of organizational actors who find themselves in a setting of great social complexity: the number of actors is very large; each actor pursues a variety of objectives which are mutually incompatible, but each is unsure of the trade-offs between the objectives; each actor is tied into a network of interdependencies with other actors who are as confused as he, yet some of the objectives sought by each cannot be obtained without cooperation from others." *The Obsolescence of Regional Integration Theory*, (Berkeley, Calif.: Institute of International Studies, University of California, Berkeley, 1975) p. 18. See also Gerald K. Helleiner, *International Economic Disorder*, (London: MacMillan, 1980) especially ch. 1.

2. Jeff Freiden, "Third World Indebted Industrialization: International Finance and State Capitalism in Mexico, Brazil, Algeria, and South Korea," *International Organization* (Summer, 1981), 35(3):407–32.

3. For instance, Fernando Henrique Cardoso and Enzo Faletto, *Dependency and Development in Latin America* (Berkeley: University of California Press, 1979).

4. See, for example, Anthony Hopkins, *An Economic History of West Africa* (New York: Columbia University Press, 1973); Colin Leys, "Capital Accumulation, Class Formation and Dependency—The Significance of the Kenyan Case," in Ralph Miliband and John Saville, eds., *The Socialist Register 1978* (London: 1978), pp. 241–266; and Gavin Kitching, *Class and Economic Change in Kenya* (New Haven, Conn.: Yale University Press, 1980).

5. Structuralist approaches, e.g., Celso Furtardo, *Development and Underdevelopment* (Berkeley: University of California Press, 1964), and *Economic Development of Latin America* (London: Cambridge University Press, 1970), place much greater emphasis on internal economic characteristics as factors blocking development. Christian Palloix notes that most countries today are in intermediate positions in the international division of labor, being at the same time dependent on other countries for the import of some of their producer goods and exporting other producer goods to other countries. *Travail et production* (Paris: Maspero, 1978).

6. Peter Evans, *Dependent Development* (Princeton, N.J.: Princeton University Press, 1979), p. 292.

7. Charles P. Kindleberger, *Foreign Trade and the National Economy* (New Haven, Conn.: Yale University Press, 1962).

8. On the weakness of the postcolonial state, see John S. Saul, "The State in Post-Colonial Societies," in Ralph Miliband and John Saville, eds., *The Socialist Register 1974* (London: 1974); Saul, "The Unsteady State: Uganda, Obote and General Amin," *Review of African Political Economy* (Jan.-April 1976), no. 5, pp. 12–38; and Colin Leys, "The Overdeveloped Post-Colonial State: A Re-evaluation," in *ibid.*, pp. 39–48.

9. Robert M. Price, *Society and Bureaucracy in Contemporary Ghana* (Berkeley, Calif.: University of California Press, 1975); and Thomas M. Callaghy, *The State-Society Struggle: Zaire in Comparative Perspective* (New York: Columbia University Press, 1984), ch. 1.

10. William G. Demas, *The Economics of Development in Small Countries with Special Refer-*

*ence to the Caribbean* (Montreal: McGill University Press, 1965); see also the special issue of *World Development* on islands (Dec. 1980), 8(12).

11. Rita Cruise O'Brien and G. K. Helleiner, "The Political Economy of Information in a Changing International Economic Order," *International Organization* (Autumn, 1980), 34(4):445–70.

12. Donald Rothchild and Robert L. Curry, Jr., *Scarcity, Choice, and Public Policy in Middle Africa* (Berkeley, Calif.: University of California Press, 1978), especially ch. 4; Gerald K. Helleiner, "World Market Imperfections and Developing Countries," in William R. Cline, ed., *Policy Alternatives for a New International Economic Order* (New York: Praeger, 1979).

13. Wassily Leontief et al., *The Future of the World Economy* (New York: Oxford University Press, 1977), p. 11. A useful discussion of one country's experience with a policy of national self-reliance is Thomas J. Biersteker, "Self-Reliance in Theory and Practice in Tanzanian Trade Relations," *International Organization* (Spring 1980), 34(2):229–64.

14. Ernst B. Haas, "Why Collaborate? Issue-Linkage and International Regimes," *World Politics* (April 1980), 32(3):376.

15. Stephen D. Krasner, "Transforming International Regimes: What the Third World Wants and Why," *International Studies Quarterly* (March 1981), 25(1):120.

16. "Asian-African Conference Communique, Bandung, 24 April 1955," in Alfred George Moss and Harry N. M. Winton (compilers), *A New International Economic Order: Selected Documents 1945–75* (New York: UNITAR/Verlag Dokumentation, 1978), 1:2–3.

17. Measured as a percentage of the GNP of DMEs, overseas development assistance fell consistently so that by 1973 its real value was 30 percent less on a per capita basis than it had been a decade before. Gerald K. Helleiner, "Introduction," in Helleiner, ed., *A World Divided* (Cambridge: Cambridge University Press, 1976), p. 2. Expressed in an alternative way, the real value of ODA supplied by DAC countries declined by 7 percent in a period in which their own real income grew 60 percent. Disillusionment on the part of LDCs was reflected in the focus on a "widening gap" between their incomes and those of the industrialized countries. See Barbara Ward, J. D. Runnalls, and L. d'Anjou, eds., *The Widening Gap* (New York: Columbia University Press, 1971).

18. Robert Gilpin, "Economic Interdependence and National Security in Historical Perspective," in Klaus Knorr and Frank B. Trager, eds., *Economic Issues and National Security* (Lawrence, Kansas: University Press of Kansas, 1977), pp. 19–66; Karl Polanyi, *The Great Transformation* (Boston: Beacon, 1957); Stephen D. Krasner, "State Power and the Structure of International Trade," *World Politics* (April 1976), 28(3):317–47; and Edward Hallett Carr, *The Twenty Years' Crisis 1919–1939* (New York: Harper and Row, 1964).

19. See, for example, the 1972 Georgetown Declaration and Programme of Action, which noted: "The Foreign Ministers deplored the tendency on the part of the greater powers to monopolize decision-making on issues which were the proper concern of all countries. They could not suffer the destiny of the world to rest with a small syndicate of states. Major problems could be neither adequately examined nor satisfactorily solved without the active and equal participation of all." "Georgetown Declaration and Programme of Action, 1972," adopted by the Conference of Ministers of Foreign Affairs of Non-Aligned Countries, Georgetown, 12 Aug. 1972, Resolutions 30 & 37. Text reprinted in Moss and Winton, *A New International Economic Order*, pp. 379–80.

20. T. Baumgartner and T. R. Burns, "The Structuring of International Economic Relations," *International Studies Quarterly* (June 1975), 19:126–59.

21. Branislav Gosovic and John Gerard Ruggie, "On the Creation of a New International Economic Order: Issue Linkage and the Seventh Special Session of the UN General Assembly," *International Organization* (Spring 1976), 30(2):313–19; Catherine H. Gwin, "The

Seventh Special Session: Toward a New Phase of Relations Between the Developed and Developing States?" in Karl P. Sauvant and Hajo Hasenpflug, eds., *The New International Economic Order: Confrontation or Cooperation Between North and South?* (Boulder, Colorado: Westview Press, 1977), pp. 97–117.

22. Krasner, "Transforming International Regimes," especially pp. 137–43.

23. This assumes, of course, that the unity of the Third World coalition is maintained—which is by no means obvious given the increasing divergence of interests between the middle-income countries and the less developed, especially over matters such as automaticity of transfers, generalized systems of preferences, and the management of the international monetary system.

24. A participant at the International Wheat Agreement negotiations in 1978–79 commented that the developing countries "justifiably felt that although they were attending the negotiations, they were being effectively excluded from the decision-making process." Quoted in Theodore Cohn, "The 1978–79 Negotiations for an International Wheat Agreement: an Opportunity Lost?," *International Journal* (Winter, 1979–80), 35(1):140.

25. Tigani E. Ibrahim, "Developing Countries and the Tokyo Round," *Journal of World Trade Law* (Jan./Feb. 1978), 12(1):1–26.

26. Haas, "Why Collaborate?" p. 371.

27. Robert L. Rothstein, *Global Bargaining* (Princeton, N.J.: Princeton University Press, 1979), p. 15.

28. By no means was this exclusively the responsibility of the South. See Daniel P. Moynihan, "The United States in Opposition," *Commentary* (March 1975), pp. 31–44.

29. Rothstein commented: "The two sides cannot agree on what is a fair outcome because the intellectual framework of beliefs, values, and perceptions is itself in dispute; that is, the idea of what is fair and legitimate cannot be resolved when the two sides disagree about the game that they are really playing." *Global Bargaining*, p. 151. See also Gerald K. Helleiner, "The Refsnes Seminar: Economic Theory and North-South Negotiations," *World Development* (June 1981), 9(6):539–56; also Helleiner, *International Economic Disorder*. For a survey of alternative approaches to North-South relations, see Robert W. Cox, "Ideologies and the New International Economic Order: Reflections on Some Recent Literature," *International Organization* (Spring, 1978), 33(2):257–302. For an example of professional intolerance, see Harry G. Johnson, "Commodities: Less Developed Countries' Demands and Developed Countries' Response," in Jagdish N. Bhagwati, ed., *The New International Economic Order: The North-South Debate* (Cambridge, Mass.; MIT Press, 1977), pp. 240–51. For pleas for a search for mutual interests, see Bhagwati, "Introduction," in *ibid.*, pp. 1–24; Richard N. Cooper, "A New International Economic Order for Mutual Gain," *Foreign Policy* (Spring, 1977), 26:66–120; and Reginald Herbold Green and Hans W. Singer, "Toward a Rational and Equitable New International Economic Order: A Case for Negotiated Structural Change," *World Development* (June 1975), 3(6):427–44.

30. Lynn K. Mytelka, "The Salience of Gains in Third World Integrative Systems," *World Politics* (Jan. 1973), 35:236–50. On the African experience, see John Ravenhill, "Regional Integration and Development in Africa: Lessons from the East African Community," *Journal of Commonwealth and Comparative Politics* (Nov. 1979), 17(3):227–46; and Christian P. Potholm and Richard Fredland, eds., *Integration and Disintegration in East Africa* (Washington, D.C.: University Press of America, 1980).

31. On the importance of the presence of a hegemonic state within regional groupings, see Karl Deutsch et al., *Political Community in the North Atlantic Area* (Princeton, N.J.: Princeton University Press, 1968). Cf. Stephen D. Krasner, "Power Structure and Regional Development Banks," *International Organization* (Spring, 1981), 35(2):303–28.

32. On the SADCC, see Michael Clough and John Ravenhill, "Regionalism in Southern Africa: the SADCC," in Michael Clough, ed., *Changing Realities in Southern Africa* (Berkeley, Calif.: Institute of International Studies, University of California, Berkeley, 1982). On CARICOM, see Andrew Axline, *Caribbean Integration* (London: Frances Pinter, 1979).

33. Mahbub ul Haq, "Beyond the Slogan of South-South Co-operation," *World Development* (Oct. 1980), 8(10):743–52; Arturo L. Goetz, "Beyond the Slogan of South-South Co-operation," *World Development* (June 1981), 9(6):583–86.

34. Stephen D. Krasner, "Oil Is the Exception," *Foreign Policy* (Spring 1974), 14:68–83. See also Marian Radetzki, "The Potential for Monopolistic Commodity Pricing by Developing Countries," in G. K. Helleiner, ed., *A World Divided* (Cambridge, England: Cambridge University Press, 1976), pp. 53–76; Philip Connelly and Robert Perlman, *The Politics of Scarcity: Resource Conflicts in International Relations* (New York: Oxford University Press, 1975); Anthony Edwards, *The Potential for New Commodity Cartels* (London: Economist Intelligence Unit, 1975).

35. Albert O. Hirschman, *National Power and the Structure of Foreign Trade* (Berkeley, Calif.: University of California Press, 1980), p. xi. This corresponds with the third strategy available to the state class of LDCs outlined by Robert W. Cox: to manage dependency relations with core formations in order to acquire resources for domestically determined development goals. "Production and Hegemony: Toward a Political Economy of World Order," in Harold K. Jacobson and Dusan Sidjanski, eds., *The Emerging International Economic Order* (Beverly Hills, Calif.: Sage Publications, 1982), p. 55. For the weaker parties, the potential danger of collective clientelism is that they will become so "hooked" on the special advantages in the relationship that these will serve as a deterrent to diversification. In this case, weakness may be perpetuated as continued inefficiencies preclude effective competition in third markets. To be successful, collective clientelism must be accompanied by effective government action that uses the resources made available through the relationship in order to diversify economic structures. As early as 1960 the Economic Commission for Africa had warned of the danger that the Associates might be tempted "to prefer the short-run advantage of tariff concessions to the long-run gains of industrial development." United Nations Economic and Social Council, "The Impact of Western European Integration on African Trade and Development" [E/CN. 14/72] (7 Dec. 1960), p. 95.

36. Carl Lande, "Networks and Groups in Southeast Asia: Some Observations on the Group Theory of Politics," *American Political Science Review* (Jan. 1973), 67(1):114.

37. S. N. Eisenstadt and Louis Roniger, "Patron-Client Relations as a Model of Structuring Social Exchange," *Comparative Studies in Society and History* (Jan. 1980), 22(1):59.

38. Hirschman, *National Power*, p. 108. Compare John Stuart Mill's famous statement: "The West Indies are a place where England finds it convenient to carry on the production of sugar, coffee, and a few other tropical commodities. All the capital employed is English; almost all that industry is carried out for English uses. . . . The trade with the West Indies is, therefore, hardly to be considered as external trade, but resembles the traffic between town and country, and is amenable to the principles of home trade."

39. See also Steve Langdon and Lynn K. Mytelka, "Africa in the Changing World Economy," in Colin Legum et al., *Africa in the 1980s* (New York: McGraw-Hill, 1979), who note that in only 8 of the 35 independent African states has a non-EEC country become the major trading partner (p. 151).

40. For instance, 44 percent of total EEC bilateral aid goes to Africa (the figure for Belgian bilateral aid is 82.4 percent, for French, 58 percent) compared with 34 percent to the more populous LDCs of Asia. Data derived from Commission des Communautés Euro-

péennes, Direction Générale de l'Information, *Dossier Sur L'Interdépendance Europe—Tiers-Monde* (Bruxelles: 28 Août 1978) [481/X/78], p. 303.

41. This is an unweighted mean. If the outliers—Papua New Guinea, Equatorial Guinea, Guyana, Western Samoa, and Guinea—are removed, the mean is close to 50 percent.

42. In 1980, for instance, France gave Senegal an emergency loan of $105m to enable it to avoid default on its debts. *Washington Post*, 29 July 1981, p. A21.

43. James C. Scott, *The Moral Economy of the Peasant* (New Haven: Yale University Press, 1976).

44. Fernando Henrique Cardoso, "Associated Dependent Development: Theoretical and Practical Implications," in Alfred Stepan, ed., *Authoritarian Brazil* (New Haven: Yale University Press, 1973), p. 149.

45. Reginald H. Green, "The Child of Lomé: Messiah, Monster or Mouse?" in Frank Long, ed., *The Political Economy of EEC Relations with African, Caribbean and Pacific States* (Oxford: Pergamon, 1980), p. 14.

46. Giovanni Sartori, "Concept Misformation in Comparative Politics," *American Political Science Review* (1970), 64(4):413–28; Robert R. Kaufman, "The Patron-Client Concept and Macro-Politics: Prospects and Problems," *Comparative Studies in Society and History* (1974), 16:284–308.

47. John Waterbury, "An Attempt To Put Patrons and Clients in Their Place," in Ernest Gellner and John Waterbury, eds., *Patrons and Clients in Mediterranean Societies* (London: Duckworth, 1979), p. 335 (my italics); cf. also Carl H. Lande, "Introduction: The Dyadic Basis of Clientelism," in Steffen W. Schmidt et al., eds., *Friends, Followers, and Factions* (Berkeley: University of California Press, 1977), p. xxxi; and Rene Lemarchand, "Comparative Political Clientelism: Structure, Process and Optic," in S. N. Eisenstadt and R. Lemarchand, eds., *Political Clientelism, Patronage and Development* (Beverly Hills, Calif.: Sage, 1981), p. 14.

I have not discovered any literature wherein the idea of clientelism has been applied to macroaggregates. Berman noted that "Patron-client relationships are strikingly similar to the external imperial linkages of neocolonialism." His use of the concept is confined, however, to the personal relations developed by African elites with representatives of foreign governments and transnational corporations, which he sees as an extension of domestic clientelist networks. Nor does Berman argue that clientelism is a strategy that might allow the weaker parties to accumulate benefits that can then be employed to reduce dependency—rather he sees clientelism as merely another means through which neocolonialism is perpetuated. Bruce J. Berman, "Clientelism and Neocolonialism: Center-Periphery Relations and Political Development in African States," *Studies in Comparative International Development* (Summer 1974), 9(2):3–25.

An application of clientelism to the macro level renders one vulnerable to criticisms that the states and governments involved are treated as unitary actors. This is a valid criticism but probably of less importance in the context of ACP governments than elsewhere given the preponderance of states subject to personal rule. For the African case, see Carl G. Rosberg and Robert H. Jackson, *Personal Rule in Black Africa* (Berkeley: University of California Press, 1982).

48. Rene Lemarchand and Keith Legg, "Political Clientelism and Development: A Preliminary Analysis," *Comparative Politics* (Jan. 1972), 4(2)151–52.

49. The countries are Ghana, Ivory Coast, Nigeria, Cameroon, Ethiopia, Kenya, Sudan, Tanzania, Uganda, and Trinidad and Tobago.

50. S. N. Eisenstadt and Louis Roniger, "Patron-Client Relations as a Model of Structuring Social Exchange," p. 51.

51. Keith R. Legg, *Patrons, Clients, and Politicians* (Berkeley: Institute of International Studies, University of California, Working Papers on Development, no. 3, n.d.), p. 12. On the continuing importance for Africa of cultural ties with former colonial metropoles, and the potential benefits of a strategy of linguistic dissociation, see David D. Laitin, "Linguistic Dissociation: A Strategy for Africa," in John Gerard Ruggie, ed., *The Antinomies of Interdependence* (New York: Columbia University Press, 1983), pp. 317–68.

52. See, for instance, Mario Caciagli and Frank P. Belloni, "The 'New' Clientelism in Southern Italy: The Christian Democratic Party in Catania," in Eisenstadt and Lemarchand, eds., *Political Clientelism*, pp. 35–56; James C. Scott, "Patron-Client Politics and Political Change in Southeast Asia," *American Political Science Review* (March 1972), 66(1):91–113; Guenther Roth, "Personal Rulership, Patrimonialism, and Empire Building in the New States," *World Politics* (Jan. 1968), 20(2):194–206.

53. Quoted in *The Courier* (March 1975), 31:8.

54. Legg, *Patrons, Clients, and Politicians*, pp. 13–14.

55. Waterbury, "An Attempt," p. 331.

56. Ernest Gellner, "Patrons and Clients," in Gellner and Waterbury, eds., *Patrons and Clients in Mediterranean Societies*, p. 3.

57. Legg, *Patrons, Clients, and Politicians*, p. 27.

58. Quoted in Guy Martin, "Africa and the Ideology of Eurafrica: Neo-Colonialism or Pan-Africanism," *Journal of Modern African Studies* (June 1982), 20(2):226.

59. Quoted in David Wall, *The European Community's Lomé Convention: STABEX and the Third World's Aspirations* (London: Trade Policy Research Center, 1976), p. 19. Angola and Mozambique, alone among independent black African States, were not signatories to the first two Conventions but are participating in the negotiations for the third.

60. Claude Cheysson, "Preface," in Commission of the European Communities, *Europe and the Third World: A Study in Interdependence* (Development Series No. 2) (Brussels, Feb. 1979), p. 7.

61. Frank Long, "Transnational Corporations, Technology Transfer and Lomé," in Long, ed., *The Political Economy of EEC Relations with African, Caribbean and Pacific States* (Oxford: Pergamon Press, 1980), p. 131.

62. The countries concerned were Central African Republic, Chad, Congo, Dahomey, Gabon, Ivory Coast, Madagascar, Mauritania, Niger, and Senegal. Edward M. Corbett, *The French Presence in Black Africa* (Washington, D.C.: Black Orpheus Press, 1972), p. 106.

63. Private French firms shared a further 40 percent of the capital. *Ibid.*, p. 108.

64. Commission, *Europe and the Third World*, table 33, p. 66.

65. Kahler cites French government figures showing that French companies won a markedly higher percentage (69 percent) of competitive bids in Francophone Africa in comparison with Latin America (55.6 percent) and the Middle East (36.4 percent). Miles Kahler, "International Response to Economic Crisis: France and the Third World in the 1970s," in Stephen S. Cohen and Peter A. Gourevitch, eds., *France in the Troubled World Economy* (London: Butterworth Scientific, 1982), p. 90.

66. Quoted in Rothchild and Curry, *Scarcity, Choice and Public Policy*, p. 255.

67. Robert W. Cox and Harold K. Jacobson, *The Anatomy of Influence* (New Haven, Conn.: Yale University Press, 1974), p. 7; Stephen D. Krasner, "Regimes and the Limits of Realism: Regimes as Autonomous Variables," *International Organization* (Spring 1982), 36(2):502.

68. E Olu Sanu, *The Lomé Convention and the New International Economic Order* (Lagos: Nigerian Institute of International Affairs, Lecture Series No. 18, n.d.), p. 33.

## 2. From Rome to Lomé

1. United Nations Conference on Trade and Development, "Implications for Trade and Development of Developing Countries of Economic Groupings of Developed Countries and/or Preferential Trading Arrangements" [E/CONF. 46/31], vol. 1, p. 26. The effectiveness of the closed nature of the franc zone was seen in that 75 percent of all trade of Francophone African countries in 1956 took place within the zone. G. Van Benthem Van Den Bergh, "The New Convention of Association with African States," *Common Market Law Review* (1963), 1(2):156. Pierre Moussa shows that although some colonies may have enjoyed a net gain, taken together the colonies incurred a significant loss in the mid-1950s on account of the differences between franc zone and world market prices. *Les Chances Economiques de la Communauté Franco-Africaine* (Paris: Librairie Armand Colin, 1957).

2. Thomas Balogh, "Africa and the Common Market," *Journal of Common Market Studies* (1962), 1(1):86.

3. U. W. Kitzinger, *The Politics and Economics of European Integration* (New York: Praeger, 1963), p. 102.

4. Treaty of Rome, Part IV, Article 131. The eighteen countries designated as Associates [EAMA] were Burundi, Cameroon, Central African Republic, Chad, Congo, Dahomey (Benin), Gabon, Ivory Coast, Madagascar, Mali, Mauritania, Niger, Rwanda, Senegal, Somalia, Togo, Upper Volta, and Zaire.

5. For further details on the removal of quantitative restrictions, see P. N. C. Okigbo, *Africa and the Common Market* (Evanston, Ill.: Northwestern University Press, 1967), pp. 36–37; and Carol Ann Cosgrove and Kenneth J. Twitchett, "The Second Yaoundé Convention in Perspective," *International Relations* (May 1970), 3(9):679–89.

6. Carol Cosgrove Twitchett, *Europe and Africa: From Association to Partnership* (Farnborough, England: Saxon House, 1978), p. 22.

7. R. Lawrence, "Primary Products, Preferences and Economic Welfare: the EEC and Africa," in P. Robson, ed. *International Economic Integration* (Harmondsworth, England: Penguin, 1972), pp. 363–67.

8. Alassane D. Ouattara, "Trade Effects of the Association of African Countries with the European Economic Community," *IMF Staff Papers* (July 1973), 20(2):508–9.

9. On GATT's attitude toward the Association provisions of the Treaty of Rome and the first Yaoundé Convention, see William Gorell Barnes, *Europe and the Developing World* (London: Chatham House/P.E.P. European Series 2, Feb. 1967), pp. 10–12; and Gerald Curzon, *Multilateral Commercial Diplomacy* (London: Michael Joseph, 1966), p. 279. For the British proposals, see United Kingdom, *The United Kingdom and the European Economic Community* (London: H.M.S.O., Nov. 1961), [Cmnd. 1565].

10. Communauté Economique Européenne Commission, *Association des Etats d'Outre Mer à la Communauté: Considerations sur le futur regime d'association* [VIII/COM (61) 110 final], (Bruxelles, 12 Juillet, 1961). Maintenance of French price supports in the absence of a ban on imports of the agricultural products and their processed end-products would have been disastrous for the Associates and for French processing industries. As Lemaignen notes, the French demand for groundnut oil could have been satisfied by Italian or Belgian oil mills, which imported groundnuts from Nigeria at a price 30 percent below that being paid by France. Robert Lemaignen, *L'Europe au berceau* (Paris: Librairie Plon, 1964), p. 143.

11. I. William Zartman, *The Politics of Trade Negotiations Between Africa and the European Economic Community: The Weak Confront the Strong* (Princeton, N.J.: Princeton University Press, 1971), *passim*.

12. Consumption taxes deterred increased imports of tropical products in Community

countries. Taxes on coffee ranged from 40 percent in France to 87 percent in Germany to 140 percent in Italy. Calculation of the price elasticity of demand for coffee in EEC countries suggests that the abolition of consumption taxes would have stimulated a considerable increase in demand. Estimates for Germany and Italy ranged from −0.9 to −1.30; for France from −0.26 to −0.5; and for Belgium −0.5. United Nations Economic and Social Council, "The Impact of Western European Integration on African Trade and Development" [E/CN.14/72] (7 Dec. 1960), p. 42, n. 2. The German levy of 4 DM per kilo of imported coffee was contrasted by Diori Hamani, President of the Associates' Council of Ministers, with the 1.20 DM per kilo received by growers in the Ivory Coast. *Towards an Improved Associationship* (Paris: Eurafor-Press, n.d.), p. 17. Revenue collected by the German government from consumption taxes on coffee amounted to $180 million in 1959 alone, a figure not far short of the total German contribution to the first EDF. Kitzinger, *Politics and Economics*, p. 117. Lemaignen had commented that "this whole question of tariff preferences is trifling . . . if we consider the level of consumer taxes which some countries apply to these products." Quoted in Aaron Segal, "Africa Newly Divided?" *Journal of Modern African Studies* (1964), 2(1):73–90.

13. However, a Community study of trade between the Associates and the EEC concluded that in aggregate the terms of trade of the EAMA improved marginally over the period 1962–67. Their import capacity also increased during the same period but at a rate lower than that of other LDCs. Commission des Communautés Européennes, *Les échanges commerciaux entre la CEE et les Etats africains et malgache associés 1958–1966/7* (Série Aide au Développement 1969–2), pp. 72ff.

14. Diori Hamani, *Towards an Improved Associationship*, p. 12.

15. In July 1967 the Community had agreed, as part of the establishment of a single market for fats and oils, to provide price supports to Associates' oils and oilseeds production. The Agreement was not ratified. Zartman, *Politics of Trade Negotiations*, pp. 184–85.

16. *Convention of Association Between the European Economic Community and the African and Malagasy States Associated with That Community and Annexed Documents, 22 July 1969* (Brussels: Commission of the European Communities, n.d.), Article 20.

17. Zartman, *Politics of Trade Negotiations*, p. 195.

18. Frank Ellis, John Marsh, and Christopher Ritson, *Farmers and Foreigners* (London: Overseas Development Institute, 1973), p. 11.

19. Lemaignen, *L'Europe au berceau*, p. 148.

20. R. Lawrence, "Primary Products, Preferences and Economic Welfare," p. 364.

21. Peter Robson, "Africa and EEC: A Quantitative Note on Trade Benefits," *Bulletin of the Oxford University Institute of Economics and Statistics* (Nov. 1965), 27(4):301–3.

22. Stephen H. Goodman, "EEC: The Economics of Associate Membership," *Journal of Development Studies* (Jan. 1969), 5(2):138–41; Catrinus Jepma, "An Application of the Constant Market Shares Technique on Trade Between the Associated African and Malagasy States and the European Community (1958–1978)," *Journal of Common Market Studies* (Dec. 1981), 20(2):175–92; Joanna Moss, "The Yaoundé Convention, 1964–1975" (Ph.D. dissertation, New School for Social Research, New York, March 1978); John Ravenhill, "Asymmetrical Interdependence: The Lomé Convention and North-South Relations" (Ph.D. dissertation, University of California, Berkeley, Nov. 1981); and Charles Young, "Association with the EEC: Economic Aspects of the Trade Relationship," *Journal of Common Market Studies* (Dec. 1972), 11(2):120–35. Some of the perils of quantitative analysis of the Yaoundé trade data are inadvertently exposed in an article by Norman D. Aitken and Robert S. Obutelewicz; they conclude that "83 percent of total African associated country exports to the EEC was accounted for by the EEC trade preferences." In reality, less than one-third

of the Associates' exports by value enjoyed a preferential tariff margin in the EEC market. Aitken and Obutelewicz, "A Cross-Sectional Study of EEC Trade with the Association of African Countries," *Review of Economics and Statistics* (Nov. 1976), 58(4):425–33; quotation is on p. 432.

23. Ravenhill, "Asymmetrical Interdependence," pp. 100–109; Jepma, "An Application," p. 184.

24. Ravenhill, "Asymmetrical Interdependence."

25. Mordechai E. Kreinen, "EEC Trade Relations—Historical Background," in Kreinen, ed., *Trade Relations of the EEC* (New York: Praeger, 1974), p. 6.

26. Young, "Association with the EEC," p. 132.

27. Kreinen, "Some Economic Consequences of Reverse Preferences," in *Trade Relations of the EEC*, p. 66.

28. Adrian Hewitt, "The European Development Fund as a Development Agent: Some Results of EDF Aid to Cameroon," *ODI Review* (1979), 2:46.

29. *Quatrième Rapport Annuel d'Activité du Conseil d'Association a la Conférence Parlementaire de l'Association*, p. 29.

30. *Troisième Rapport Annuel d'Activité du Conseil d'Association a la Conférence Parlementaire de l'Association*, p. 23.

31. *Septième Rapport Annuel d'Activité du Conseil d'Association a la Conférence Parlementaire de l'Association*, p. 27.

32. *Eighth Annual Report on the Activities of the Association Council to the Parliamentary Conference on the Association*, p. 43. Apparently the Community did indeed "take note" since the subject was not reported in accounts of subsequent activities of the Association Council.

33. Zartman, *Politics of Trade Negotiations*, pp. 169–74.

34. Articles in the Convention relating to the right of Associates to establish customs unions or free trade areas with third parties were extremely vague. Questioned in the GATT working party about their meaning, the Community representative could state only that "the precise significance of these words had not yet been tested and that each concrete case would have to be examined on its merits." GATT, *Basic Instruments and Selected Documents*, 14th Supp. (Geneva: GATT, July 1966), p. 107. In the early 1960s the Community appeared to be opposed to the Associates' entering into agreements with states deemed to be politically undesirable—notably Guinea and Ghana.

35. In a letter of 10 Aug. 1965 to the Presidents of the American Republics, the Inter-American Committee for the Alliance for Progress stated: "although we are opposed to the creation of spheres of influence we commend for urgent consideration, a policy of transitory defensive measures to compensate for such preferences. It is inequitable for the products of some of the developing countries to enjoy preferences outside the hemisphere plus non-discriminatory access to the US market. A policy to compensate for such discrimination against Latin America should be worked out pragmatically, on a commodity-by-commodity basis, with provisions which would facilitate return to non-discriminatory trade as discriminating practices are removed elsewhere." Quoted in *Towards a Global Strategy of Development*, Report by the Secretary General of UNCTAD (New York: United Nations, 1968) [TD/3/rev. 1], p. 52.

36. *New York Times*, 28 Oct. 1967, p. 31.

37. Charles Van der Vaeren, *Evolution of Financial and Technical Cooperation Between the EEC and Associated Developing Countries* (Brussels: Commission of the European Communities, Directorate-General for Development Aid, March 1970) [443/VIII/FED/70-E], p. 3.

38. David Jones reported a weighted annual average receipt per capita for the period

1969–71 of $7.69 for the EAMA and $4.16 for the associables. *Europe's Chosen Few* (London: ODI, 1973), pp. 32–33. Jones provides an excellent overview of the Community's aid policies in the Association period. See also the Community's own review of the first fifteen years of the EDF: Commission des Communautés Européennes, Direction Générale du développement, *Fonds Européen de Développement 1960–1975* [X/444/75-F], 2 vols. (hereafter referred to as FED).

39. Total population of the EAMA (excluding Somalia) grew from 48.958 million in 1957 to 76.542 million in 1972—an increase of 56 percent. Calculated from figures in FED, vol. 1, p. 13.

40. Ravenhill, "Asymmetrical Interdependence," pp. 132–33.

41. The pattern of EDF allocations might be perceived as a continuation of the French colonial practice of favoring the more advanced colonies (many of the early staff of the Commission's Development Directorate had experience in the French colonial civil service). From 1947–57 Gabon received $49.6 million in French aid while Chad, with six times the population but only half the per capita income of Gabon, was granted only $55.8 million. Segal, "Africa Newly Divided?" p. 74.

To be fair to the Community, the change over the last decade in international attitudes to priorities in aid allocation should be noted. There is a danger here of evaluating performance in the 1960s according to criteria that became accepted only in the 1970s. As late as 1969 the Pearson Commission recommended that intercountry allocations be determined primarily on two (domestic performance) criteria: adequate and sustained increases in the ratio of domestic savings to national income and in the ratio of exports to imports. Lester B. Pearson *et al.*, *Partners in Development* (New York: Praeger, 1969), p. 132. See also the contributions by Rosentein-Rodan, Chenery and Bruno, and Eckaus in Jagdish Bhagwati and Richard S Eckhaus, eds., *Foreign Aid* (Harmondsworth, England: Penguin, 1970).

42. The 27 factories consisted of 6 abattoirs, 5 oil mills, 2 sugar refineries, 2 tea factories, 1 cement works, 5 textile plants, 3 hydroelectric plants, 2 flour mills, and 1 ginning plant. FED, 1:148.

43. FED, 1:275.

44. Hewitt, "The European Development Fund," p. 46.

45. Calculated from FED, 1:67–70.

46. *Ibid.*, p. 223.

47. *Ibid.*, pp. 162–63.

48. *Ibid.*, pp. 163–64.

49. *Ibid.*, p. 164.

50. Quoted in Joseph S. Nye, *Pan Africanism and East African Integration* (Cambridge, Mass.: Harvard University Press, 1965), p. 215.

51. Kwame Nkrumah, *Ghana Parliamentary Debates*, 25 Sept. 1962, quoted in Dennis Austin, "Britain, Commonwealth Africa and the EEC," in Pierre Uri, ed., *From Commonwealth to Common Market* (Harmondsworth, England: Penguin, 1968), p. 156. See also Ali A. Mazrui, "African Attitudes to the European Economic Community," in Lawrence B. Krause, ed., *The Common Market: Progress and Controversy* (New York: Praeger, 1964), pp. 121–35. That the Commonwealth's fears of the political connotations of Association were not entirely illusory was suggested by the statements of some of the representatives of the EAMA at this time. For instance, the Minister of Finance of Madagascar asserted in March 1962 that "we are mistaken if we consider association to be an economic act alone. It is a political act of the first order, since it provides our essential economic and cultural orientation towards Europe and since for us economic development is the political imperative." Quoted in Segal, "Africa Newly Divided?" p. 86.

52. United Kingdom, *The United Kingdom and the European Community* (Cmnd. 1565, Nov. 1961).

53. Joseph S. Nye, *Pan Africanism*, pp. 212–13; Zartman, *Politics of Trade Negotiations*, p. 21.

54. The CET after 1964 for cocoa was 5.6 percent, for cocoa paste 25 percent, and for cocoa powder 27 percent. Austin, "Britain, Commonwealth Africa and the EEC," p. 148.

55. Nye, *Pan Africanism*, p. 219.

56. Okigbo, *Africa and the Common Market*, p. 116. Even Ghana, most vociferous of the Commonwealth critics of Association, is reported to have made inquiries about application for associate status in 1965, the year before Nkrumah's downfall. W. Scott Thompson, *Ghana's Foreign Policy 1957–1966* (Princeton, N.J.: Princeton University Press, 1969), p. 363.

57. Okigbo, *Africa and the Common Market*, p. 114.

58. A face-saving arrangement had broken the deadlock of the GATT Working Party that investigated Part IV of the Treaty of Rome: it was agreed to put aside issues of the legality of the provisions and of general principles and to concentrate on any special problems that arose, the Community having agreed to make adjustments where necessary. But Nigeria had not been party to the earlier discussions and made a strong attack on the legality of the Convention. Curzon, *Multilateral Commercial Diplomacy*, p. 283.

59. Zartman, *Politics of Trade Negotiations*, pp. 87–88.

60. *Ibid.*, pp. 93ff.

61. Dharam Ghai estimated that the East African states would lose approximately 200,000 Kenyan pounds each year in customs revenue as a result of the agreement. "The Association Agreement Between the European Economic Community and the Partner States of the East African Community," *Journal of Common Market Studies* (Sept. 1973), 12(1):83–84.

62. This had been the tenor of the Jeanneney Report as early as 1963 and was repeated with more vigor in the Gorse Report submitted to the Chaban-Delmas government in June 1971.

63. Commission Memorandum on a Community Policy for Development Cooperation, E.C. *Bulletin*, Supp. 5/71, Annex to 9/10 (1971); quotes on pp. 3 and 7.

64. Memorandum from the Commission on a Community Policy on Development Co-operation: Programme for Initial Actions (2 Feb. 1972), E.C. *Bulletin*, Supp. 2/72.

65. Peter Tulloch, "Developing Countries and the Enlargement of the EEC," in Bruce Dinwiddy, ed., *Aid Performance and Development Policies of Western Countries* (New York: Praeger, 1973), p. 97.

66. E. Olu Sanu, *The Lomé Convention and the New International Economic Order* (Lagos: the Nigerian Institute of International Affairs, Lecture Series 18, n.d.), p. 7.

67. Details of these maneuvers can be found in contemporary issues of *West Africa*. See also Isebill V. Gruhn, "The Lomé Convention: Inching Towards Interdependence," *International Organization* (Spring 1976), 30(2):249–54; and M. K. Whiteman, "The Lomé Convention," *World Survey* (Oct. 1975), 85:5–12. Although not on the formal agenda at the ECA, informal discussions regarding future relationships with the Community were held, including talks with officials from the Commission of the Communities who had participated in drafting the ECA Report. Corrado Pirzio-Biroli, "Foreign Policy Formation Within the European Community with Special Regard to Developing Countries" (mimeo). France also chose this time to mend fences with Nigeria, a Minister-Delegate in the French Foreign Ministry being dispatched on a goodwill mission to Lagos in February 1973.

68. Quoted in "Africans Stand Firm on EEC Terms," *West Africa* (8 April 1974), No. 2964, p. 37.

69. "Memorandum of the Commission to the Council on the future relations between the Community, the present AASM states, and the countries in Africa, the Caribbean, the Indian and Pacific Oceans referred to in Protocol No. 22 to the act of accession," presented to the Council on 9 April 1973. E.C. *Bulletin*, Supp. 1/73. Quotes on pp. 5 and 6.

70. The Community had yet to reconcile itself with Part IV of GATT on preferential treatment for LDCs: there was no mention of this new section of the GATT Treaty in the Memorandum, which instead continued to refer to the necessity of justifying the Association arrangements under Article XXIV and thus the need to establish the legal fiction of a free trade area. The Memorandum states that "In practice there are only two possible ways of derogating from Article 1 of GATT wich (sic) lays down the general principle, to be observed and applied by all contracting parties, of the most favoured nation clause. One possibility is offered by Article XXIV which permits an exception to be made in the case of customs unions or free trade areas. The other possibility is Article XXV which provides for exceptional waiver arrangements to be introduced subject to strict controls by the Contracting Parties. . . . Quite clearly, Article XXIV offers obvious advantages over Article XXV." *Ibid.*, p. 14. GATT members, however, had already provided for a waiver of the most favored nation principle, albeit for a limited period of 10 years, by voting in June 1971 in favor of the creation of generalized systems of preferences.

71. *Ibid.*, p. 13.

72. *Ibid.*, p. 12.

73. Thirty-four African countries were represented at the meeting. Guinea, the only former French colony not to participate in the Yaoundé Conventions, maintained its hostility toward the Community and did not attend. Equatorial Guinea was also not represented.

74. Quoted in "Africa Meets Europe in Brussels: 2," *West Africa* (August 1973), 6(2930):1062.

75. *Marchés Tropicaux* (3 Août 1973), quoted in Romain Yakemtchouk, *La Convention de Lomé* (Bruxelles: Academie royale des Sciences d'Outre mer, 1977), p. 83. On the significance of ACP unity, see Gruhn, "Inching Towards Interdependence"; and A. K. Russell, "The European Community and Africa: Lomé, UNCTAD, CIEC," in A. G. Kemp, ed., *Africa and the EEC in the Light of Lomé and UNCTAD IV* (Aberdeen: Aberdeen University African Studies Group, 1977).

76. "Africans Stand Firm on EEC Terms," *West Africa* (8 April 1974), 2964:397, quoting Olu Sanu and S. Djim Sylla (executive secretary of the ACP for the Brussels negotiations).

77. This section on sugar draws extensively from the excellent article by Carole Webb, "Mr. Cube versus Monsieur Beet: The Politics of Sugar in the European Communities," in Helen Wallace, William Wallace, and Carole Webb, eds., *Policy-Making in the European Communities* (London: Wiley, 1977), pp. 197–226.

78. Ellis, Marsh, and Ritson, *Farmers and Foreigners*, pp. 26–27, table 5.

79. Surplus production within the Community was the cause of its refusal to accept the export quotas assigned to it in the International Sugar Agreement, thereby removing what slim prospects the Agreement had of bringing some stability to the international sugar market.

80. Webb, "Mr. Cube versus Monsieur Beet," pp. 207–8.

81. As chapter 6 demonstrates, this failure to pay attention to long-run trends in the sugar market rebounded to the disadvantage of the ACP.

82. The choice of Lomé as the location for the signature of the Convention that inevitably bore its name touched on a number of sensitivities. Yaoundé was clearly unacceptable to the Commonwealth, given the connotations with the previous conventions of Association. Yet choice of a Francophone capital appeared essential if Francophone states were not

to feel that they were no longer central to the relationship. Lomé was promoted by Nigeria in part because Togo had enthusiastically supported Nigerian proposals for the creation of a West African Economic Community. In a further gesture toward Commonwealth sensitivities, the words "association" and "associates" were dropped. Henceforth the relationship was to be a "partnership" in which the non-Europeans were to be known simply as the ACP. Forty-six ACP states were original signatories to the Convention. They were: 19 states previously associated under the Yaoundé Conventions: Burundi, Cameroon, Central African Republic, Chad, Congo, Dahomey, Gabon, Ivory Coast, Madagascar, Mali, Mauritania, Mauritius, Niger, Rwanda, Senegal, Somalia, Togo, Upper Volta, and Zaire; 21 Commonwealth states listed in Protocol 22: Botswana, Gambia, Ghana, Kenya, Lesotho, Malawi, Nigeria, Sierra Leone, Swaziland, Tanzania, Uganda, Zambia, Bahamas, Barbados, Guyana, Grenada, Jamaica, Trinidad and Tobago, Fiji, Western Samoa, and Tonga; and six countries of Africa of "comparable economic structure": Ethiopia, Liberia, Sudan, Guinea, Equatorial Guinea, and Guinea-Bissau.

83. See, for instance, Johan Galtung, "The Lomé Convention and Neo-Capitalism," *The African Review* (1976), 6(1):37.

## 3. STABEX and SYSMIN

1. Quoted in "Report Drawn Up on Behalf of the Joint Committee on the Sixth Annual Report of the ACP–EEC Council of Ministers for the Period from 1 April 1981 to 31 December 1981 and an Analysis of the Early Experience of the Second Lomé Convention" (Rome: ACP-EEC Consultative Assembly, Working Document [ACP/CCE/38/82], 3 Nov. 1982), part B, p. 25.

2. Commission of the European Communities, "Renewal and Enlargement of the Association with the AASM and Certain Commonwealth Developing Countries," *Bulletin* of the European Communities, Supp. 1/73, p. 20.

3. Interview with a senior Commission official, July 1980.

4. These figures refer to the system under Lomé II; during the first Convention the dependence thresholds were 7.5 percent (except for sisal, for which the threshold was 5 percent) and 2.5 percent for the LLICs; the fluctuation thresholds were 7.5 percent and 2.5 percent respectively. The same lower dependency threshold for sisal was maintained in Lomé II.

5. Sugar is covered by a separate protocol "of unlimited duration." This provides that ACP producers will receive prices "within the range prevailing in the Community" for specified quantities of their exports to the EEC. This arrangement has the effect of at least partially indexing the price received (since European farmers have been successful in raising the price paid to European producers under the CAP) but offers no guarantee regarding export earnings. The sugar protocol is discussed in chapter 6.

6. Other products have been added to the scheme since its introduction. During the first Convention, vanilla, cloves, sheep's and lamb's wool, mohair, gum arabic, pyrethrum, essential oils of cloves, niaouli, ylang ylang, and sesame seeds were included. The list for the second Convention was amended to extend coverage to cashew nuts, pepper, shrimps and prawns, rubber, squid, cotton seeds, oil cake, peas, beans, and lentils. Of these additional products only rubber is a significant ACP export, accounting for approximately 1 percent of total ACP earnings from the export of STABEX products to the Community. The other eighteen products combined account for only 3 percent of ACP exports of STABEX products and only 1% of the Group's total earnings.

7. Commission of the European Communities, "Comprehensive Report on the Export

Earnings Stabilization System Established by the Lomé Convention for the Years 1975 to 1979" [SEC(81) 1104] (Brussels, 13 July 1981), p. 43.

8. The Community issued a statement asserting it had "agreed to the inclusion of this product (iron ore) only for the sake of securing a general agreement and remains firmly opposed to mineral products being included in the system." *The Courier*, no. 31 (March 1975), p. 25. A scheme (SYSMIN) to assist ACP producers of minerals was included in the second Lomé Convention. This is discussed later in this chapter.

9. Commission, "STABEX in Lomé II," unnumbered document, Nov. 1979.

10. Internal Community document. The Commission estimated that the "risks" that would have to be covered if tobacco was included in STABEX amounted to 15 mua for Malawi and 10 mua for Tanzania. This was substantially more than the estimated total cost of including rubber (7 mua budget for both Liberia and Cameroon) and has increased significantly with the accession of Zimbabwe to the Convention. A second CAP product excluded from the system—beef—is of significant interest to Botswana.

11. Commission Communication to the Council, "Report on the Operation During 1975 of the System set Up by the Lomé Convention for Stabilizing Export Earnings" [COM (76) 656 final] (9 Dec. 1976), p. 13. At the ACP request, the second Lomé Convention allows for the "globalization" of products and subproducts for the purpose of meeting the dependence threshold—which reduces the effect of the scheme as a deterrent against processing for those commodities where processed products, as well as the raw material, are included in STABEX.

12. See, for instance, *Opinion of the Presidents of the Chambers of Commerce of the Ports of the North Sea on the Renegotiation of the ACP-EEC Convention* [r/1922/f/78] (10 July 1978), p. 5. During the Lomé II negotiations, future inclusion of sisal products within STABEX was made dependent on ACP producers' reaching agreement with EUROCORD, the group representing European manufacturers of rope and string.

13. Internal Community document. The following table illustrates how the value of trade in STABEX products for Nigeria for the period 1974–78 varies with different dependence thresholds.

| Dependence Threshold | Total | Yearly Average (in mua) |
|---|---|---|
| 0 | 939.6 | 187.9 |
| 2% | 493.1 | 98.6 |
| 4% | 397.5 | 79.5 |
| 6% | 72.9 | 14.6 |
| 7.5% | 0 | 0 |

14. France—Ministère de la Coopération, "La Stabilisation des Recettes d'Exportation: Conséquences pour la CEE des accords de Lomé et d'une extension à d'autres produits pour les pays en voie de développement," *Etudes et Documents*, no. 21, (Septembre 1975), pp. 12–13.

15. "Compensatory Finance To Stabilize Export Earnings," *ODI Briefing Paper*, no. 1 (March 1979), p. 3.

16. During the negotiation of the Second Lomé Convention there was an interesting example of the sensitivities involved in the classification. Zaire, whose economy in recent years

has regressed rapidly toward subsistence levels, requested to be categorized as a landlocked country, or failing that, for a special category of "semi-landlocked" countries to be established so that it might benefit from concessional treatment. Under Lomé I, Zaire was considered to be neither landlocked nor least developed. The Commission responded by offering to classify Zaire as "least developed," a suggestion that was reported to have been indignantly rejected by the Zaire government. Eventually the Commission agreed to extend to Zaire the treatment given to landlocked countries although it would not be classified under this category.

17. "Compte Rendu de la 3ème Séance de Travail ACP/CEE Sur la Stabilisation des Recettes d'Exportation" (9 Novembre 1978), p. 3.

18. Communication de la Commission au Conseil, "Une action internationale de stabilisation des recettes d'exportation" (n.d.), p. 4. A supplementary Commission Communication to the Council noted three aspects of the IMF Facility "which beneficiaries might regard as irksome: interest charges; the obligation to redeem; and the margin of appreciation." *International Action on Stabilization of Export Earnings* [COM (75) 294 final] (11 June 1975), p. 8.

19. The phrase is that of J. M. Finger and Dean A. Derosa, who describe some of the problems in "The Compensatory Finance Facility and Export Instability," *Journal of World Trade Law* (Jan.–Feb. 1980), 14(1):14–22.

20. Annual Report of the Court of Auditors for the 1978 financial year, *Official Journal of the European Communities*, no. C 326 (31 Dec. 1979), p. 217.

21. African, Caribbean, and Pacific Group of States, *STABEX: A Review* by S. K. Rao (Commonwealth Secretariat) [ACP/1/79], pp. 20–21, 31–32. An analysis of some of the problems involved in indexation is presented in J. D. A. Cuddy, *International Price Indexation* (Lexington, Mass.: Lexington Books, 1976). See also Cuddy, "Indexation: A Missing Link in ACP/EEC Relations?" in Frank Long, ed., *The Political Economy of EEC Relations with African, Caribbean and Pacific States* (Oxford: Pergamon Press, 1980), pp. 53–90.

22. Initially Burundi, Ethiopia, Guinea Bissau, Rwanda, and Swaziland benefited from coverage of their exports to all markets. Cape Verde, Western Samoa, Tonga, Comoros, Lesotho, Seychelles, Solomon Islands, and Tuvalu were later added to the list.

23. Commission [SEC(81) 1104], "Comprehensive Report," p. 40.

24. For the complete list of situations, see [SEC(81) 1104], "Comprehensive Report," pp. 53–56.

25. Since some of the transfers went to countries whose exports to all destinations were covered by the system (in which case the issue of trade diversion did not arise), the actual percentage of transfers subject to negotiation was higher than these figures suggest.

The Community's Court of Auditors noted that a considerable increase in the number of reductions occurred during the last two years of the first Convention (at a time when the funds available were close to being exhausted). The largest reductions were applied to transfers for products which had generated the highest compensation payments, and concentrated on three countries (Liberia, Sudan and Senegal) which received 30 percent of all transfers under Lomé I but suffered 73.4 percent (by value) of all reductions. Court of Auditors, "Annual Report concerning the financial year 1980", *Official Journal of the European Communities* (31 Dec. 1981) p. 165.

26. Annual Report for 1977, *Official Journal of the European Communities*, no. C 313 (30 Dec. 1978), p. 148.

27. *Ibid.* p. 150.

28. *Ibid.*

29. In a subsequent report the Court of Auditors noted that "In the absence of well-

defined rules for arriving at the statistics which should serve as the basis for the calculation of the transfer, the figures finally adopted owe more to negotiations than to mathematical analysis, with the result that in certain cases the actual amount of the transfer exceeds that of the initial request; in other cases, it is equal or lower." Annual Report for 1978, *Official Journal of the European Communities*, no. C 326 (31 Dec. 1979), p. 312.

30. Reginald Herbold Green, "STABEX: What Is To Be Done?" in *The Renegotiation of the Lomé Convention* (London: Catholic Institute of International Relations, 1978), p. 17.

31. Even the Community's own Court of Auditors commented: "The Court found that, in some cases, the negotiations not only took into account the statistical and commerical factors provided for under the Lomé I Convention, but also other elements outside the framework of the Lomé I Convention." *Official Journal of the European Communities* (31 Dec. 1981), C344, 24, p. 163. This did not always work to the disadvantage of the ACP: the Court found that during the negotiations for Lomé II, the Commission had granted a transfer to Liberia to cover losses of export earnings from iron pellets, a product *not covered* by the scheme. At this time the Commission was attempting to convince ACP iron producers that iron be transferred from STABEX to SYSMIN.

32. European Communities, Court of Auditors, "Comments on the Operation of the Export Earnings Stabilization System," attached as appendix to [COM (80) 211 final], p. 1.

33. [COM (80) 211 final], p. 10.

34. *Ibid.*, appendix, p. 2.

35. *Ibid.*, appendix, p. 17.

36. H. W. Singer, "The Distribution of Gains Between Investing and Borrowing Countries," *American Economic Review* (1950), 40:482.

37. [COM (80) 211 final], p. 14.

38. Commission report on the 1977 operation of STABEX [COM (79) 277 final], p. 17. Member states were by no means united in their views regarding provisions in the second Convention on the use of transfers. The Italian government noted the risk of encouraging continued production in obsolete sectors, while the French government reaffirmed the principle that the ACP states had freedom of choice over their use of the transfers. Initially, the Presidency of the Council of Ministers proposed the future text declare that transfers must be employed to "benefit the section which caused the transfer or other sectors important to development, and *notably to measures of diversification.*" Internal Community document (emphasis added).

39. Commission of the European Communities, *Synthesis Report on the Overall Impact of STABEX Operations 1975–79, Based on Ten ACP Case Studies* [SEC (82) 1336] (13 Sept. 1982), p. 40.

40. [COM (80) 211 final], p. 2. The grant element in repayable STABEX transfers varies according to the time that elapses before repayment is required. Herrmann estimated that it ranged from 6.28 percent to 10.22 percent of total repayable transfers during the first Convention. More generous terms for repayment, introduced in Lomé II, will increase the grant element in repayable transfers and thus the extent to which STABEX provides concessional aid to the higher income group of ACP states. Roland Herrmann, "On the Economic Evaluation of the STABEX System," *Intereconomics* (Jan.–Feb. 1982) 17(1):7–12.

41. Although procedures exist for the payment of advance transfers, only seven were made during the first Convention (the Commission noting that it had received "a mere ten or so requests"). [SEC (81) 1104], p. 34. Another EEC study found that ACP states were either unaware of the mechanism through which advance payments could be obtained or were unable to provide the necessary statistics [SEC (82) 1336]. On average a period of five months elapsed during the first Convention between a regular request and the payment of

a transfer. Since the payment occurred almost inevitably during the financial year following that in which the loss of earnings had been experienced, any effect on earnings stabilization would be coincidental.

42. Herrmann, "On Economic Evaluation," pp. 7–12.

43. [COM (79) 277 final]. Similarly, the Court of Auditors concluded that "apart from the ten or so special cases observed during a specific year, the final impact on the economies of the recipient ACP States was probably slight. Sporadic transfers cannot have lasting effect, and the amount of financial resources involved is usually too small. Among the few recipient countries where the volume of aid reached a significant proportion during a financial year, some chose to allocate these funds simply to sustaining the flow of imports rather than promoting economic development." Appendix to [COM (80) 211 final], p. 20.

44. Louis M. Goreux, *Compensatory Financing Facility*, (Washington, D.C.: International Monetary Fund, Pamphlet Series no. 34, 1980), p. 44.

45. The value of the European unit of account expressed in terms of SDRs fluctuated considerably over the five-year period of the first Convention. At the midpoint in 1977, the unit of account was worth 1.15 SDR. Multiplication of the STABEX figures by this value gives an approximation of their relative magnitude in SDRs.

46. Benin, Cape Verde, Gabon, Ghana, Liberia, Madagascar, Niger, Somalia, Swaziland, Tonga, Upper Volta.

47. Mike Faber and Roland Brown, "Changing the Rules of the Game," Commonwealth Secretariat Internal Paper (mimeo, n.d.), p. 1. A much abbreviated version of this document is published as "Changing the Rules of the Game: Political Risk, Instability and Fairplay in Mineral Concession Contracts" in *Third World Quarterly* (January 1980) 2(1):100–119.

48. *Ibid.*, p. 2.

49. Commission of the European Communities, *Instruments of Mining and Energy Cooperation with the ACP Countries* [COM (79) 130 final] (Strasbourg, 14 March 1979), table 6.

50. Commission of the European Communities, "Relations between the European Community and the ACP States in the mining sector." [COM(83) 651 fin]. (8 Nov. 1983) pp. 10–11.

51. "Raw Materials and Political Risk," Submission by 14 European Mining Companies to the President of the Commission of the European Communities (May 1977), attached as appendix A to Faber and Brown, "Changing the Rules"; quotation is on p. 5.

52. *Ibid.*, *loc. cit.*

53. *Ibid.*, pp. 10–12.

54. *Ibid.*, p. 9.

55. Internal Community document, dated 13 Oct. 1978.

56. Claude Cheysson, speech to Comité Paritaire ACP-EEC, Bordeaux, 30 Jan. 1979 (mimeo), pp. 5–6. In an internal document the Commission acknowledged it had interpreted Article 19, 4 of the Convention, which allows for reductions of STABEX transfers if earnings are caused by trade policy measures, in an arbitrary manner in reducing the amount paid to Sierra Leone for a fall in earnings from iron ore exports, by a figure calculated to represent certain expenses that were normally incurred by the company whether or not the mines were in production.

57. Claude Cheysson, quoted in *Agence Europe*, no. 2640 (16 March 1979), p. 8.

58. Commission of the European Communities, *Instruments of Mining and Energy Cooperation with the ACP Countries* [COM (79) 130 final] (14 March 1979), p. 2.

59. *Ibid.*, *passim.*

60. The Commission had responded to the companies' memorandum by sending a com-

munication to the Council in which the companies' principal proposals were endorsed and generalized to form the basis of a European policy toward investments in LDCs. Commission of the European Communities, *Need for Community Action To Encourage European Investment in Developing Countries and Guidelines for Such Action* [COM (78) 23 final] (30 Jan. 1978).

61. This earlier memorandum listed the main problems relating to raw materials supply as the following:

1. insufficient knowledge of the present and future outlook for each raw material
2. the prospect of relative or absolute shortages in the medium and long term
3. insufficient diversification of sources of supply
4. the trend toward processing raw materials in their countries of origin
5. the risk of temporary bottlenecks and price fluctuations

"The Community's Supplies of Raw Materials," pp. 6 ff.

62. A scheme of this type had been suggested as early as 1972. See Commission of the European Communities, *Proposal for a Council Regulation Establishing a System of Community Guarantees for Private Investments in Non-Member Countries* [COM (72) 1461] (20 Nov. 1972).

63. [Neg. EEC/ACP/100/79], 16 May 1979.

64. Article 49 of the second Convention characterizes the system's objectives as follows:

With a view to contributing towards the creation of a more solid basis for the development of the ACP States and in particular towards helping them cope with a decline in their capacity to export mining products to the Community and in their export earnings which correspond to that decline, a system shall be established to assist these states in their efforts to remedy the harmful effects on their income of serious temporary disruptions beyond the control of the ACP States concerned, wherever these disruptions affect those mining sectors on which their economies are largely dependent.

65. Information obtained from interviews with ACP officials, July 1979. The new Convention devotes a new Title to Mineral Products, rather than include SYSMIN with the Sugar Protocol and STABEX in Title II "Export Earnings from Commodities." Nowhere in the Convention is there a reference to the sovereignty of the ACP over their natural resources, although this was one of the points emphasized by the Group during the negotiations.

66. The 15 percent dependence threshold was the classic "split-the-difference" outcome of negotiations where the EEC initially proposed a 20 percent threshold and the ACP responded with a figure of 10 percent.

67. Quoted in J. A. Fralon, *Le Dossier de Lomé II* (Brussels: Agence Européenne d'Informations, 1979), p. 197.

68. Annex XLII, "Declaration of the ACP States on the Scheme for Mineral Products":

1. The ACP States appreciate the introduction of a scheme for the treatment of the ACP/EEC trade in mineral products.
2. The ACP States however regret that the provisions of Title III, by not stabilising the export earnings of the ACP States from those mineral products, do not adequately meet the problems of the ACP countries whose countries are heavily dependent on exports of mineral products.
3. The ACP States request the Community to agree to re-examine the entire scheme early in the implementation period with a view to improving it and widening its provisions to take account of the economic effects on the producing states of instability in the export earnings from mineral products.
5. Furthermore, throughout the negotiations for the new Convention of Lomé, the ACP States submitted a series of requests for the inclusion of a number of mineral products in the system applicable to this category of products.
6. The Community, however, did not accept the inclusion of some of these products.

7. The ACP States stress the importance of these products for economies of certain ACP States and emphasize the need for the Community to continue the examination of these requests with a view to having these products included in the course of the implementation of the second Convention of Lomé.

69. UNCTAD, "Review of STABEX and SYSMIN," Report by the UNCTAD Secretariat with the assistance of Adrian Hewitt [TD/B/C.1/237] (22 Nov. 1982), p. 38.

70. [COM(83) 651 fin] "Relations between" p. 5.

71. See *inter alia* Theodore H. Moran, *Multinational Corporations and the Politics of Dependence* (Princeton, N.J.: Princeton University Press, 1974); and Franklin Tugwell, *The Politics of Oil in Venezuela* (Stanford, Calif.: Stanford University Press, 1975).

72. World Bank, *Accelerated Development in sub-Saharan Africa: An Agenda for Action* (Washington, D.C.: World Bank, 1981); "STABEX", *The Courier* (May–June 1983), 79:72–83.

## 4. Commercial Cooperation

1. As a GATT study commented:

In the developed countries considered, taken together, the trade position of ACP countries in respect of industrial manufactures appears relatively weak even in comparison to that of other developing countries. Unlike some of the latter whose economies are more diversified and whose exports consist increasingly of products at a higher level of processing, most of the ACP countries are still largely exporters of raw materials and primary products that have undergone little or no transformation. This is the case even in the EEC, their principal market.

GATT memorandum (internal ACP document).

2. Exports of agricultural products from LDCs grew by 2.6 percent p.a. over the period 1960–1975, less than half the rate achieved by industrialized countries. LDC exports of nonfuel minerals grew at approximately 5 percent p.a., more rapidly than those of industrialized countries. Hollis B. Chenery and Donald B. Keesing, *The Changing Composition of Developing Country Exports* (Washington, D.C.: World Bank Staff Working Paper No. 314, Jan. 1979), pp. 9–10. But all nonfuel primary products will contribute only 18 percent of the growth of LDC exports in the period 1975–1985 according to World Bank projections. *World Development Report 1978* (Washington, D.C.: World Bank, 1978), p. 28.

3. "The Lomé Convention: Possibilities for Improvement," memorandum submitted by Matthew McQueen, in Second Report from the Select Committee on Overseas Development, Session 1977–78, *Renegotiation of the Lomé Convention* (London: H.M.S.O, 1978), 2:61–62. The seven products concerned were coffee, cocoa beans, cocoa butter, cocoa paste, tea, tobacco, and vegetable oils.

4. Two points should be noted in this context. First, the ACP states' obligation to grant nondiscriminatory MFN treatment to the member states refers to their "trade" and not merely to imports. In the context of concern over security of supplies of raw materials in which the first Convention was signed, the Community insisted that the principle of nondiscrimination be applied also to exports, to preclude the possibility of member states' becoming victims of selective boycotts.

Second, during the negotiations for Lomé II, the ACP argued there was an imbalance in the obligations for the respective parties with regard to MFN treatment. Whereas the ACP were obliged to grant most favored developed country status to the Nine, they were not guaranteed treatment equivalent to that granted by the Community to the most favored preferred developing country. Here, again, the language of the Convention is particularly vague, especially Article 2, which employs such phrases as "to ensure, as a general rule."

Clearly one effect of such terminology has been to give considerable discretionary power to the Community in its interpretation of these articles.

5. Quoted in *The Courier*, no. 47 (Jan.–Feb. 1978), p. 18.

6. David Wall, "Industrial Processing of Natural Resources," *World Development* (April 1980), 8(4):306. See also G. K. Helleiner, "Structural Aspects of Third World Trade: Some Trends and Some Prospects" (mimeo); and Richard N. Cooper, *The Economics of Interdependence* (New York: McGraw-Hill, 1968), especially p. 65.

7. A preparatory study by the GATT Secretariat, intended to assist the ACP Group in the Tokyo Round negotiations, reported that of 37 CCCN headings covering 52 tariff lines of interest to the ACP in the EEC market, only nine tariff lines falling within four product groups were dutiable and not covered by the Community's GSP scheme. Internal ACP document.

8. Internal Community document.

9. ACP Group, "The Community's 1978 Generalized Scheme of Preferences: Its Implications for the ACP's Position in the Community Market" [ACP/508/77] (1977), p. 4.

10. *Ibid.*, p. 2.

11. Internal ACP document.

12. Quoted in [ACP/508/77], p. 2. The *Annual Report of the ACP–EEC Council of Ministers (1 March 1981–31 December 1981)* (Libreville, 13 May, 1982) records (p. 26) that at the Council of Ministers in 1981, the Community made a statement "to the effect that the Community (GSP) scheme offered the possibility of remedying any unfavorable situations which might arise for the ACP States and that, whenever the ACP States requested, the Community was prepared to examine any appropriate specific action with them.

"The ACP States indicated that they took the Community's statement to mean that the Community would withdraw, in whole or in part, any provisions of the scheme which are shown to be prejudiciable [sic] to the interests of the ACP States. The Community said that it did not subscribe to the ACP States' interpretation of the statement."

13. Internal Community document. ACP states have not been consistent in their attempts to defend their tariff advantages—in part, one suspects, because of their embarrassment at being perceived as undermining LDC solidarity. In 1977 the Brazilian government sent a memorandum to the EEC requesting a zero tariff in the 1978 GSP for cocoa products. It noted that the ACP states "declared formally during the meetings of the International Cocoa Organization in London last June to not be opposed to the benefits conceded by the EEC for cocoa being extended to other exporting countries of this product." The Commission underlined to the ACP the inconsistencies in the positions that they had taken on the one hand in ACP-EEC circles, and on the other, in international fora.

14. EEC/ACP first meeting on commercial cooperation, *Rapport Sommaire*, no. 5, (10 Nov. 1978).

15. "Outcome of the Proceedings of the Ministerial Conference on 21 December 1978" (mimeo).

16. Internal Community document. These conclusions are similar to those reached by academic commentators on the GSP, who have argued that the complexities of the national schemes have favored the more advanced among the LDCs whose bureaucracies have been able to cope with these difficulties, and also transnational corporations, which are able to quickly divert their products to markets where quotas are unfilled. See, for example, Tracy Murray, "Tariff Preferences and Multinational Firm Exports from Developing Countries," in William G. Tyler, ed., *Issues and Prospects for the New International Economic Order*, (Lexington, Mass.: Lexington Books, D. C. Heath, 1977), pp. 129–47; and Murray, *Trade Pref-*

*erences for Developing Countries*, (London: MacMillan, 1977). Murray notes that the insecurity connected with the GSP deters foreign investment in beneficiary countries.

17. EEC Spokesman's Group, *Information Memo* no. P-92, (Oct. 1979), p. 1.

18. F. Durieux, Director-General Adjoint, presentation to the Committee on Commercial Cooperation (mimeo, 7 Nov. 1978).

19. *Ibid*. Realizing the largely unnecessary bitterness that its stance has caused, the Commission has subsequently adopted a more conciliatory position. In its proposals to the Council for the Lomé III negotiations, the Commission noted the need to avoid negotiations that "spoil the climate of EEC-ACP relations and the image of the Community even though the economic interests at stake are small." Accordingly, the Commission proposed that any *exceptions* to the principle of free access for agricultural products be listed in a protocol annexed to the new Convention. "Commission Communication to the Council on Guidelines for the forthcoming ACP-EEC Negotiations" [COM(83) 153 fin] p. 59. The Council appears to have ruled out this proposal.

20. Thomas B. Birnberg, "Trade Reform Options: Economic Effects on Developing and Developed Countries," in William R. Cline, ed., *Policy Alternatives for a New International Economic Order* (New York: Praeger, 1979), p. 230. In comparison to the distribution of gains from a liberalization of trade in industrial products, African and Caribbean states would share a sizable benefit from a reduction of tariff and nontariff barriers in agriculture. Birnberg estimates that 13 percent of the benefits derived from a reduction in the agricultural sphere would accrue to African states and 16 percent to those of the Caribbean. *Ibid.*, p. 231.

21. Quoted in Commonwealth Secretariat, *The Lomé Convention and the Common Agricultural Policy* (London: Commonwealth Secretariat, Commonwealth Economic Papers no. 12, Dec. 1978), p. 19.

22. ACP Group, *ACP Foreign Trade* [ACP/6/79], p. 84.

23. Conflicts that have arisen over the three protocols attached to the Convention on trade in specific products—bananas, rum, and sugar—are examined in chapter 6.

24. Other instances where the ACP have accused the EEC of using health regulations as nontariff barriers to their exports include Community directives relating to the aflatoxin content of groundnut oilcake and a proposal (subsequently dropped) for the compulsory incorporation of milk powder in certain types of oilcake.

25. Second Report from the Select Committee on Overseas Development, 1:xxxv.

26. Interviews with Mrs. Mathe, Ambassador of Botswana to the European Community, and with members of the ACP Secretariat, July 1979. Negotiators for the ACP had hoped that greater security for ACP producers would be ensured by attaching a protocol on beef to the new Convention. This was rejected by the Community, and instead the new regime was guaranteed by an exchange of letters between the two parties in which the EEC pledged that the arrangements would not be vulnerable to an invocation of the safeguard clause by the Nine.

Community reluctance to agree to a beef protocol was apparently derived from its concern that the special provisions contradicted the spirit of the CAP. During the first Convention the Commission had been instructed to seek alternatives to the solution eventually negotiated: the minutes of a meeting of the Committee of Permanent Representatives (COREPER) noted that "several delegations have regularly insisted that a solution less prejudicial to the principles of the CAP be researched by the Commission." In the meantime, the delegates, with the exception of the Irish, agreed that the least worst solution was to reintroduce for one more time the previous regime, although only for 12 months and not 18 as the Commission had proposed.

Ireland's position was based on an opposition in principle to any imports of beef by the Community, the belief being that Irish farmers would be able to fill any Community deficits (the Community, of course, was suffering from a beef surplus at this time; the consequence of the high guaranteed prices paid by the CAP was a beef "mountain" roughly ten times the size of the ACP annual quota). From the Irish perspective, the ACP were merely part of a larger problem in which Community producers had been asked to make concessions in order to enable the Nine to meet its external commitments, e.g., to the GATT. (Interview with member of the Irish delegation to the Community, June 1979).

An indication of the value of the beef concessions to Botswana was given by Commissioner Cheysson in a speech to the *Comité Paritaire* in Grenada in 1978. ACP exporters were required to impose an export tax equivalent to the value of the 90 percent reduction in variable levies under the regime. Botswana, it was estimated, gained from this a sum of between 11 mua and 14 mua each year, equivalent to approximately two-thirds of its aid allocation from the EDF for the whole Convention.

27. ACP Group, *Customs Cooperation* (Brussels, Jan. 1979), pp. 17–19. It is probably no coincidence that 92 percent of the products the Community regards as "sensitive" are subject to the "processing" requirements of List A. Matthew McQueen, "Lomé and the Protective Effect of Rules of Origin," *Journal of World Trade Law* (March–April 1982), 16(2):125.

28. *Ibid.*, pp. 36–37. Birnberg, "Trade Reform Options," notes that LDCs may qualify for the United States' GSP if 35 percent of the value of the final product is added locally (p. 235).

29. ACP, *Customs Cooperation*, p. 24.

30. Select Committee, *Renegotiation of the Lomé Convention*, 1:xxxi.

31. Statement by Commission Director-General, Klaus Meyer, to the ACP–EEC Committee on Commercial Cooperation, 28 Nov. 1978.

32. "ECC Response to ACP Memorandum on the Rules of Origin" (mimeo) Feb. 1979, pp. 1–2.

33. Protocol No. 1, Title 1, Article 1, 3 of the first Convention.

34. ACP Group, *ACP Memorandum on the Rules of Origin in a Successor Arrangement to the Lomé Convention* [ACP/724/78], pp. 20–21.

35. Statement by Klaus Meyer to the ACP–EEC Committee. ACP states expressed their displeasure by attaching a unilateral declaration to the second Convention (Annex XLIII), which provided their own definition of an "ACP Fish." Under the Yaoundé Conventions, the ownership requirement had been 75 percent.

36. Michael B. Dolan cites an instance where an ACP country sought permission to use Swedish metal hooks in the manufacture of fishing flies but was instructed to seek an EEC supplier—and eventually used a French source. "The Lomé Convention and Europe's Relationship with the Third World: A Critical Analysis," *Journal of European Integration* (May 1978), 1(3):374. In its response to the ACP memorandum on the rules of origin, the Community stated that by virtue of derogations, "the industries concerned have the time to revise their supply circuits in order to conform to the normal rules" (p. 12). In December 1981 "the Community stated that it was opposed to any further extension of the derogation for artificial fishing flies since Community suppliers could provide the necessary material to enable ACP manufacturers to benefit from the provisions of the convention on cumulative origin." *Annual Report of the ACP–EEC Council of Ministers (1 March 1981–31Dec. 1981)*, p. 32.

37. Cited in *ACP Customs Cooperation*, p. 23.

38. Select Committee, *Renegotiation of the Lomé Convention*, 1:xxxii. The ACP Group have argued that the refusal of the Community to allow the principle of cumulation of value

added to be applied to their relations with other developing countries undermines the trade provisions of the Convention, which permit ACP countries to offer more favorable tariff treatment to other LDCs than they grant to the Community and, consequently, discourages regional economic cooperation.

39. Quoted in *ACP Customs Cooperation*, p. 4.

40. [ACP/724/78], *passim*.

41. "EEC Response," p. 1.

42. Matthew McQueen, "Lomé and Protective Effect," p. 130.

43. [ACP/724/78], pp. 7–9.

44. IMF *Survey*, 4 May 1981.

45. Internal ACP document.

46. David Wall, "Industrial Processing of Natural Resources," *World Development* (April 1980), 8(4):303–16.

47. Eric Tollens, "Fruit and Vegetables," in Commonwealth Secretariat, *The Lomé Convention and the Common Agricultural Policy* (London: Commonwealth Secretariat, Dec. 1978), p. 51.

48. Matthew McQueen, "The Relationship Between the Rules of Origin and Offshore Production," in Select Committee, *Renegotiation of the Lomé Convention*, 2:66.

49. *Ibid.*, 2:67. This reasoning was accepted by the Select Committee. See *ibid.*, 1:xxxii. This argument obviously is heavily indebted to proponents of product-life cycle and obsolescing bargains theories, such as Wells, Vernon, and Moran.

50. *Ibid.*, 1:xxxii. Where EEC inputs are used, there is no requirement for specific processing to gain originating status.

51. See J. M. Finger, "Tariff Provisions for Offshore Assembly and the Exports of Developing Countries," *Economic Journal* (June 1975), 85(338):365–71; Finger, "Trade and Domestic Effects of the Offshore Assembly Provision in the United States Tariff," *American Economic Review* (1976), pp. 598–611; and Birnberg, "Trade Reform Options," pp. 240–45. There are two significant differences between U.S. and European provisions for offshore assembly. The U.S. provision apples to any firm that purchases U.S. components for assembly into products for sale in the United States, whereas the European provisions apply only to EEC firms. Second, the European scheme is limited to the assembly or processing of components abroad, whereas the U.S. provisions do not limit the foreign stage of the production process to processing or assembly. See Finger, "Tariff Provisions for Offshore Assembly," especially pp. 365 & 369.

52. See Commission of the European Communities, *The European Community and the Textile Arrangements* (n.d.). The EEC as a whole maintains a positive balance of trade in textiles; in clothing, the balance is negative, but net imports constitute only a modest share of the EEC market. Nevertheless, imports have had a severe impact on particular sectors of the industry that becomes all the more sensitive for politicians when these sectors are concentrated within (often economically depressed) regions.

The U.S. textile industry used the breathing space afforded by the early effective restrictions imposed under the MFA to undertake a substantial program of restructuring. This has been so effective that its exports are now causing problems on the European market. In 1979, EEC imports of textiles from the United States rose by 65 percent, whereas imports from the ACP rose by only 22 percent (from 16,106 tonnes in 1978 to 19,621 tonnes, in comparison with total textile imports in 1979 from MFA suppliers of 1,697,247 tonnes). Data cited in *Telex Africa*, no. 145 (14 May 1980), p. 3. See also Michael B. Dolan, "European restructuring and import policies for a textile industry in crisis," *International Organization* (Autumn 1983), 37,4:583–615.

53. On the Ivory Coast experience, see Bonnie Campbell, "Neo-colonialism, Economic Dependence and Political Change: Cotton Textile Production in the Ivory Coast," *Review of African Political Economy* (Jan.–April 1975), no. 2, pp. 36–53; Lynn Krieger Mytelka, "Direct Foreign Investment and Technology Transfer in the Ivorian Textile and Wood Industries," *Entwicklungs-landerforschung* (Bonn: Friedrich-Ebert-Stiftung, 1981), pp. 61–80. See also Mytelka, "Crisis and Adjustment in the French Textile Industry," in H. Jacobson and D. Sidjanski, eds., *The Emerging Economic Order* (Beverly Hills, Calif.: Sage, 1982), pp. 129–66; and L. K. Mytelka and M. Dolan, "The Political Economy of EEC–ACP Relations in a Changing International Division of Labour," in C. Vaitsos and D. Seers, eds., *European Integration and Unequal Development* (London: Macmillan, 1980).

54. "Declaration présentée par le porte-parole de la Communauté concernant la politique communautaire dans le domaine des produits textiles" (Commission, mimeo, 10 Nov. 1977), emphasis added.

55. *Ibid.*

56. Quoted in *Agence Europe*, no. 2840 (2 Feb. 1980). Mauritius was not the only ACP country to suffer as a result of the problems of the British textiles industry: In March 1980, U.K. experts expressed concern to other member states at the rapid increase in Tanzanian exports of cotton yarn to the British market. Again, the figures involved were minuscule in comparison with total British imports (Tanzanian sales to Britain in 1979 had amounted to 57 tonnes, whereas 100 tonnes were imported in the first two months of 1980). Nevertheless, Britain asked the Commission to examine the matter thoroughly in consultation with the Tanzanian authorities "in order to avoid a worsening situation." Quoted in *Telex Africa*, no. 142 (26 March 1980), p. 7.

57. Minutes of the 3rd Meeting on Commercial Cooperation, 14 Nov. 1978 (mimeo).

58. In 1976, ACP states purchased textiles of a total value of 150 mua from the EEC and exported 56 mua to the Community. "Minutes of the 3rd Meeting."

59. In 1979 an Ivorian spokesman was quoted as saying that the Ivory Coast now envisages only "a minor development of its textiles exports to Europe over the next several years, far less than was anticipated four years ago." *Bulletin de l'Afrique Noire*, no. 1018 (3 Oct. 1979), p. 19727; cited in Mytelka, "Direct Foreign Investment," n. 52.

60. *Telex Africa*, no. 145 (14 May 1980), p. 7.

61. Lynn K. Mytelka, "The Lomé Convention and a New International Division of Labour," *Journal of European Integration* (Sept. 1977), 11:75.

62. Mytelka clearly overstates the extent to which the first Lomé Convention was intended to promote changes compatible with "the global redeployment of manufacturing activity then underway." In doing so she has to fall back on the argument that the EEC's treatment of African textile exports during Lomé I signaled "its decision to abandon a strategy of African industrialization." Whereas Lomé I manifested "a concern with the changing global locus of manufacturing activities," Lomé II, she asserts, reflects a change in European interests in that it is primarily concerned with the securing of supplies of raw materials; ACP manufactured exports were now to be subjected to safeguard clauses "changed in such a way as to make them easier to apply." To argue that European interests shifted so dramatically—in the short period of three years between the signature of the first Lomé Convention and the opening of negotiations for its successor—from a commitment to a new international division of labor to an abandonment of African industrialization is to severely stretch the facts to fit a (misleading) argument. Similarly, only very selective quotation from the two Conventions could lead to the conclusion that the safeguard clauses in Lomé II are more restrictive than those in Lomé I (see the comments in section 4 of this chapter). In reality, the change in emphasis between the two Conventions can better be explained as a

reflection of the shift in bargaining power in the relationship. Whereas the Community found it expedient to acknowlege ACP aspirations for industrialization in the first Convention when it was concerned to secure their participation, in the renegotiations—and the second Convention which resulted—it was able to place primary emphasis on securing its own interests in the relationship since there was a perception that few concessions were necessary to ensure continuing ACP participation. Quotations are from Mytelka, "The Limits of Export-Led Development: The Ivory Coast's Experience with Manufactures," in John Gerard Ruggie, ed., *The Antinomies of Interdependence*, (New York: Columbia University Press, 1983), on pp. 248, 262, and 267 respectively.

63. Jagdish N. Bhagwati, "Market Disurption, Export Market Disruption. Compensation and GATT Reform," in Bhagwati, ed., *The New International Economic Order* (Cambridge, Mass.: M.I.T. Press, 1977), ch. 6.

64. *ACP–EEC Ministerial Conference*, Freeport, Bahamas (March 1979) [ACP-CEE/CONF/2/2/79 rev. 2], p. 4.

65. *Ibid.*, p. 6. The ACP had proposed:

The contracting parties commit themselves to hold regular consultations within the institutional framework of the Convention in order to examine the necessary structural and commercial adjustments within the Community so that anticipated ACP exports may be sold and thus to avoid, as far as possible, recourse to the safeguard and to limit the damage ACP States risk from its imposition.

66. Internal Community document.

67. Ironically, the member states have been most indignant when ACP countries failed to fulfill their obligations under the trade regime. Complaints were made to Cameroon on the subject of its prohibition of imports of certain tires—import licenses had to be accompanied by attestation from its Bureau for Trade Relations with the Peoples' Republic of China that this body was unable to supply tires of the desired quality and type. Similarly, Britain complained that Ethiopia had imposed a ban on the import of British four-wheel drive vehicles because of obligations undertaken in bilateral trading agreements with third countries. (Minutes of COREPER meetings). This raises the issue of the compatibility of the Convention with the desire of some ACP countries to enter into barter arrangements organized on an interstate bilateral basis with third countries.

## 5. Trade Between EEC and ACP

1. Carol Cosgrove Twitchett, *Europe and Africa: From Association to Partnership* (Farnborough, England: Saxon House, 1978), p. 164.

2. A list of ACP countries and the subgroupings employed in this study is provided in appendix A.

3. This includes intra-ACP trade, which is, however, an extremely small part of total ACP trade. From 1975 to 1978 intra-ACP exports as a percentage of total ACP exports fell from 5.65 percent to 4.66 percent; in the same period intra-ACP imports as a percentage of total ACP imports fell from 6.13 percent to 4.93 percent. A large part of intra-ACP trade consists of Nigerian oil exports to the Caribbean.

4. Eurostat, *EC-ACP Trade : A Statistical Analysis 1970–1981* (Luxembourg : Eurostat, 1983), p. 29.

5. See the special edition of *The Courier*, no. 52, (Nov.–Dec. 1978).

6. The ACP share of U.S. oil imports increased from 10 percent in 1970 to 37 percent in 1981, Eurostat, *EC-ACP Trade*, p. 31.

7. The Hirschman index is calculated by squaring the percentage shares of each country, adding them, and then taking the square root of the total. If the eight member states

(counting Belgium/Luxembourg as a single unit) had shared equally in EEC imports from the ACP, then the Hirschman index would have been the square root of 8 × (12.5 squared), i.e., 35.36. Albert Hirschman, *National Power and the Structure of Foreign Trade* (Berkeley: University of California Press, 1980).

8. Eurostat, *EC-ACP Trade*, p. 108.

9. *Ibid.*, p. 31.

10. Data derived from *Ibid.*, pp. 127–49.

11. Christopher Stevens and Ann Weston, "Trade Diversification: Has Lomé Helped?" in Christopher Stevens, ed. *EEC and the Third World: A Survey 4, Renegotiating Lomé* (London: Hodder and Stoughton, 1984), ch. 2.

## 6. Three Problematic Protocols

1. Ian Smith, "Can the West Indies' Sugar Industry Survive?" *Oxford Bulletin of Economics and Statistics* (May 1976), 38(2):127.

2. Ian Smith, "EEC Sugar Policy in an International Context," *Journal of World Trade Law* (March–April 1981), 15(2):103.

3. The motives leading to the establishment of the CSA were described by its former Director, John Southgate, as follows:

The governments of the exporting countries were determined not to return to the economic and social conditions of the thirties whose consequences had been described in the Moyne Report on the West Indies. The Commonwealth industries wanted to rehabilitate factories and improve agriculture which had suffered not only from the depression of the thirties but from the shortages of capital and supplies during the war. They recognised that this would be impossible if they lost the security of the market and stability of price which during and after the war had been afforded by British bulk purchase of the Commonwealth's exportable surplus. Both governments and industry were therefore anxious for a long-term agreement. The British Government for its part wanted to encourage Commonwealth production partly to lessen expenditure of dollars on imports and partly to get rid of rationing.

Quoted in Simon Harris and G. B. Hagelberg, "Effects of the Lomé Convention on the World's Cane-Sugar Producers," *O.D.I. Review*, (1975) pp. 39–40. See also Vincent A. Mahler, "Britain, the European Community, and the Developing Commonwealth: Dependence, Interdependence, and the Political Economy of Sugar," *International Organization* (Summer 1981), 35(3):467–92.

4. David Jones, "The Commonwealth Sugar Agreement and the European Economic Community," *Bulletin of the Oxford University Institute of Economics and Statistics* (Aug. 1967), 29(3):211–32; Michael Moynagh, "The Negotiation of the Commonwealth Sugar Agreement, 1949–1951," *Journal of Commonwealth and Comparative Politics* (July 1977), 15:170–90.

5. Moynagh, "Negotiation of Commonwealth Sugar Agreement."

6. Jones estimates that Antigua, Mauritius, and St. Kitts would have lost approximately one-third of the value of their visible exports in 1965 if CSA sugar had been sold at world market prices. "Commonwealth Sugar Agreement," table 6, p. 223.

7. *Ibid.*, p. 216.

8. Smith, "Can the West Indies' Sugar Industry Survive?" p. 130.

9. Jones, "Commonwealth Sugar Agreement," quoting the First Annual General Report of the Commission.

10. *Ibid.*, p. 221.

11. The Commission proposed that it should be allocated an export quota of 800,000 tonnes under the ISA, which, given its commitment to import 1.3m tonnes of Commonwealth sugar, would have made it a net importer.

12. Harris and Hagelberg, "Effects of Lomé Convention," p. 49.

13. *Lettre de M. D. F. Williamson, co-President CEE du sous-Comité ACP-EEC du sucre adressée a S.E. M. l'Ambassadeur Chasle, co-President ACP du sous-Comité ACP-EEC du sucre* [ACP-CEE/123/77] (30 Septembre 1977), Annex II. The definition eventually agreed was that circumstances of *force majeure* were those which "were unavoidable and unforeseen, or foreseen but inevitable or irresistible and arose from causes outside the control of the State concerned and were not the result of its own actions in reducing production or withdrawing or diverting its sugar supplies." *Second Annual Report of the ACP-EEC Council of Ministers* (Brussels: 14 March 1978), p. 41.

14. Albert Te Pass, "From the Commonwealth Sugar Agreement to the Lomé Sugar Protocol," *The Courier* (Sept.–Oct. 1982), 75:56.

15. This saving was effected because the Community supply was in surplus; either EEC sugar in the same amount or this quantity of ACP sugar would have had to be exported. New quotas for the four states were as follows (with the original quota in parentheses): Congo 4,957 (10,000); Kenya 93 (5,000); Surinam 2,667 (4,000); and Uganda 409 (5,000). All figures are in tonnes.

16. *Annual Report of the ACP-EEC Council of Ministers (1 March 1981—31 Dec. 1981)* (Libreville: 13 May 1982), p. 40.

17. *Report of the ACP–EEC Council of Ministers (1 April 1976–29 Feb. 1980): ACP–EEC Cooperation Analysis-Application* (Brussels: 25 July 1980), pp. 84–85.

18. *Second Annual Report of the ACP-EEC Council of Ministers*, p. 40. The Council eventually rescinded the proposal and offered the ACP the same price increase as that provided for white sugar.

19. Smith, "EEC Sugar Policy," p. 99.

20. "French Sugar: An Opportunity for EEC," *Financial Times*, June 18, 1979.

21. [L.613/79/ACP].

22. Commission of the European Communities, Spokesman's Group and Directorate-General for Information, "Sugar, the European Community and the Lomé Convention," *Europe Information* (1979) 19/79, p. 6.

23. Smith, "EEC Sugar Policy," p. 101.

24. *Ibid.*, p. 107.

25. *The Economist* (31 Jan. 1981), 278 (7170):17. Four British sugar merchants asked the Commission to take the British Sugar Corporation—the principal beet refiner—to court under Articles 85 and 86 of the Treaty of Rome, alleging "abuse of dominant position." They claim that the price advantages given to beet refiners are enabling the BSC to squeeze out its competition. *The Economist* (13 Dec. 1980), 277 (7163):48.

26. Te Pass, "From the Commonwealth Sugar Agreement," p. 57.

27. Smith, "EEC Sugar Policy," p. 102.

28. Commission of the European Communities, "The Common Agricultural Policy and the EEC's Trade Relations in the Agricultural Sector (Effects on Developing Countries)" [SEC(82) 1223], p. 56.

29. GATT, *European Communities—Refund on Exports of Sugar: Complaint by Australia; Report of the Panel* [L/4833] (Geneva, 1979), quoted in Smith, "EEC Sugar Policy," p. 103. See also Smith, "GATT: EEC Sugar Export Refunds Dispute," *Journal of World Trade Law* (November–December 1981) 15(6)534–43.

30. Commission of the European Communities, Spokesman's Group, "Inconsistencies in the Policies Pursued by the Community and Member States: The Example of Sugar," *Information Memo* P-130 (Nov. 1978), p. 1.

31. *Ibid.*, p. 2.

32. Council of the European Communities General Secretariat, press release no. 5890/81, p. 14.

33. *Annual Report of the ACP-EEC Council of Ministers (1 April 1976–31 March 1977)* (Suva: 14 April 1977), p. 9.

34. *Second Report from the Select Committee on Overseas Development Session 1977–78: The Renegotiation of the Lomé Convention* (London: HMSO, 1978) 1:xxxv. In the second Convention, the rate of growth for quotas for the eight was raised to 18 percent p.a.; that for the U.K. remained at 40 percent p.a.

35. Internal Community document.

36. In discussing earlier negotiations for a common definition of rum, an official from the British Ministry of Agriculture, Fisheries, and Food commented: "I think we gave the French an enormous party, with steel bands, but they still did not agree that it was rum that they were drinking! The curious situation is that the DOMs [French overseas departments] are technically part of the Community, part of France, so this rum is the only rum made in the Community. The French have always tried to get agreed a definition of rum which fits their product—but if you gave it to a man from Barbados, he would say it was hardly rum at all—you have to be French to like it, basically speaking. The former British colonies produce a purer type of rum than the former French colonies do—it is much purer, and nicer, and this is why we are not prepared to agree to any definition of rum which would prevent the sale of proper rum in the Community from the former British territories in the Caribbean." Mr. J. H. V. Davies in testimony to the Select Committee, reported in *Second Report*, 2:127.

37. *Report of the ACP–EEC Council of Ministers (1 April 1976–29 Feb. 1980)*, p. 44.

38. *Réponse des Etats ACP à la lettre du 16 Juin 1977 (ACP-CEE/96/77) par laquelle la Communauté a fait part de sa réponse au memorandum ACP du 15 Mars 1977 relatif au Protocole No. 6 sur les Bananes* [ACP/33/78] (23 Janvier 1978).

39. *Report of the ACP–EEC Council of Ministers (1 April 1976–29 Feb. 1980)*, p. 44.

40. *Compte rendu sommaire de la première réunion du Groupe d'experts gouvernementaux ACP–CEE, institué sous la tutelle du Groupe mixte permanent sur les bananes (Bruxelles: le 13 Juin 1978)*, p. 7.

41. "The German Banana Market," *The Courier* (March–April 1983), 78:91–93.

42. "Réponse de la CEE au Memorandum des Etats ACP sur les bananes transmis a la Communauté le 24 Janvier 1978" (mimeo).

## 7. Industrial Cooperation

1. *Annual Report of the ACP–EEC Council of Ministers (1 April 1976–31 March 1977)* (Suva, 14 April 1977), p. 43.

2. Quoted in African Group for Negotiations with the EEC, "Draft Memorandum Presented by the ACP Countries to the EEC on the Subject of Industrial Cooperation" (mimeo, n.d.), p. 1.

3. *Ibid.*, p. 2.

4. *Ibid.*, pp. 3–4.

5. *Ibid.*, passim.

6. Steven J. Warnecke, "The Lomé Convention and Industrial Cooperation: A New Relationship Between the European Community and the ACP States?" in Karl P. Sauvant and Hajo Hasenpflug, eds., *The New International Economic Order* (Boulder, Colo.: Westview Press, 1977), p. 338.

7. Centre for Industrial Development, *Centre for Industrial Development: A Review of Its Activities and Achievements Under Lomé I* (Brussels: Centre for Industrial Development, 13 March 1980), p. 1.

8. Interviews with staff of the Centre, July 1979 and June 1980; *Annual Report of the ACP–EEC Council of Ministers (1 March 1981–31 Dec. 1981)* (Libreville, 13 May 1982), p. 56.

9. European Parliament, *Report on the Negotiations for a New Lomé Convention* [Document 487/78] (1 Dec. 1978), p. 19.

10. ACP Group of States, *ACP Memorandum on the Role of the CID in a Successor Arrangement to the Lomé Convention* [ACP/401/79 (Secr. INDCOOP) Rev. 2] (3 May 1979), p. 1.

11. Interview, June 1980.

12. CID, *A Review of Its Activities*, p. 6.

13. Centre pour le Développement Industriel, *Rapport D'Activité Annuel 1977–78*, p. 12.

14. ACP Group, "Fund for Industrial Cooperation" (mimeo, 16 April 1979), p. 1.

15. Katharina Focke, *From Lomé 1 towards Lomé 2* (European Parliament, 1980), p. 31.

16. ACP Group, "Fund for Industrial Cooperation", and *Role of the CID*.

17. Internal Community memorandum, 4 May 1979.

18. Annex 10 to the second Convention provided for a joint study to be carried out on "the ways and means of tapping additional financial resources for industrial development of ACP States." This was to be completed within nine months of the new Convention's signature. In March 1981, a group of experts under the chairmanship of the Nigerian, Professor K. Onitiri, submitted a report on complementary financing to the ACP–EEC Committee of Ambassadors. By the end of 1983, no action had been taken on the report.

19. *Commission Report to the ACP/EEC Council of Ministers on the Administration of Financial and Technical Cooperation in 1976 Under the Lomé Convention* [COM(77) 11 fin], p. 6.

20. Internal Community memorandum.

21. Internal Community memorandum.

22. Internal Community memorandum.

23. Commission des Communautés Européennes, *Coopération Industrielle: La Restructuration industrielle dans la Communauté: Déclaration de la Communauté Economique Européenne* (Paris: 27 April 1976), p. 3.

24. ACP–EEC Consultative Assembly, *Draft Report on the Possibilities for Closer Cooperation with Representatives of Economic and Social Groups in the ACP and EEC countries* (mimeo, 11 May 1978).

25. Helen O'Neill, "The Renegotiation of the Lomé Convention—A Question of Adjustment," in TROCAIRE, *The Renegotiation of the Lomé Convention* (Dublin: Trocaire, 1979), pp. 24–31. See also Santosh Mukherjee, *Restructuring of Industrial Economies and Trade with Developing Countries* (Geneva: International Labour Organisation, 1978).

26. Second Report from the Select Committee on Overseas Development Session 1977–78, *Renegotiation of the Lomé Convention* (London: HMSO, 1978), 1:xxix. Similarly, in its recommendations on industrial cooperation in the second Convention, the Broeksz Report to the European Parliament asserted:

It is clear that the Community must do more than simply make available a certain amount of money and technical knowledge. The Community must restructure its own market so as to encourage the manufacture of certain industrial products in the ACP States. The purchasing power which would then be created in the ACP States would also benefit the Community's industry.

European Parliament Document 487/78, p. 19.

27. Commission of the European Communities, *Need for Community Action To Encourage European Investment in Developing Countries and Guidelines for Such Action* [COM(78) 23 final] (Brussels, 30 January 1978), p. 1.

28. *Ibid.*, passim.

29. Council of the European Communities, *Directives de negotiations pour la nouvelle Convention* (28 June 1978), p. 4.

30. Commission of the European Communities, *Articles Promotion des Investissements* [NEG. CEE–ACP/102/79] (16 Mai 1979), p. 1.

31. Quoted in Jose Alain Fralon et al., *The New EEC–ACP Convention: From Lomé I to Lomé II* (Bruxelles: Agence Européenne d'Informations, 1979), p. 208.

32. Interview, June 1980.

33. *Agence Europe* No. 2786 (n.s.) (10 November 1979), pp. 6–7. According to the text of the ACP letter, "retroactivity is not implied." The EEC letter states, however, that "retroactivity is not implied as a general principle." The letters were not incorporated in the first published version of the Convention. They are reproduced in full in the Documentary Appendix to Christopher Stevens, ed., *EEC and the Third World : A Survey 1* (London: Hodder and Stoughton, 1981), pp. 145–47.

34. Cheysson (mimeo document).

35. Interview, June 1980. The Community continues to perceive the role of the Centre to be primarily in assisting import-substituting industrialization. In 1981 it was announced that the Centre would be giving priority to the rehabilitation and expansion of existing industry in ACP states. *Annual Report of the ACP–EEC Council of Ministers (1 March 1981–31 Dec. 1981)*, p. 53.

36. The Community has opposed the creation of an ACP Development Bank, presumably because it fears that it would be obliged to make a substantial financial commitment to it and because the Bank would reduce its present unilateral control of the instruments of financing industrial cooperation.

37. See, for example, Commission of the European Communities, *The European Economic Community and Changes in the International Division of Labor (Report of an Expert Group on the Reciprocal Implications of the Internal and External Policies of the Community)* [VIII/13677/78] (Brussels, Jan. 1979); and Richard Blackhurst, Nicolas Marian, and Jan Tumlir, *Trade Liberalization, Protectionism and Interdependence* (GATT Studies in International Trade No. 5) (Geneva: GATT, Nov. 1977).

Although Article 66 of the second Convention lists as an objective the promotion of "new relations of dynamic complementarity in the industrial field between the Community and the ACP States," the Community continues to resist any reference to an obligation for domestic structural adjustment. In 1981 no agreement was reached on a topic for a major seminar on industrial cooperation: the ACP had proposed "industrial restructuring," the EEC proposed "agro-industries"—itself a nice illustration of the parties' perceived priorities in the field of industrial cooperation. *Annual Report of the ACP–EEC Council of Ministers (1 March 1981–31 Dec. 1981)*, p. 50.

## 8. Financial and Technical Cooperation

1. According to the Deniau Memorandum: "As regards financial and technical cooperation, the enlargement of the Association will necessarily mean that the Community will have to increase its financial aid substantially. Anything else would have the result of penalizing the countries at present associated, or giving differential treatment to future partners; neither is a tenable hypothesis." Commission of the European Communities, *Renewal and Enlargement of the Association with the AASM and Certain Commonwealth Developing Countries* (1973), p. 7. Similarly, Protocol no. 22 to the Treaty of Accession for Britain, Ireland, and Denmark, stated: "The accession of the new Member States to the Community and the possible extension of the policy of association should not be the source of any weak-

ening in the Community's relations with the Associated African and Malagasy States which are parties to the Convention of Association signed on 29 July 1969."

2. David Wall, *The European Community's Lomé Convention* (London: Trade Policy Research Centre, 1976), p. 13. C. H. Kirkpatrick suggests the reduction in per capita values was closer to 40%. "Lomé II," *Journal of World Trade Law* (July/August 1980), 14(4):355.

3. The twenty countries are Bahamas, Barbados, Botswana, Fiji, Gambia, Ghana, Guyana, Jamaica, Kenya, Lesotho, Malawi, Nigeria, Seychelles, Sierra Leone, Swaziland, Tanzania, Trinidad and Tobago, Uganda, Zambia, and Zimbabwe.

4. John Hills, "The European Development Fund: Proposals for the Renegotiation," in Catholic Institute for International Relations, *The Renegotiation of the Lomé Convention* (London: CIIR, 1978), pp. 1–11.

5. John White, "ACP/EEC Financial and Technical Cooperation" (mimeo), paragraphs ix and 39.

6. *Ibid.*, paragraph 38.

7. *Ibid.*, paragraph 40.

8. Commission of the European Communities, *Commission Report to the ACP–EEC Council of Ministers on the Administration of Financial and Technical Cooperation in 1982, Under the Lomé Convention* [COM(83) 486 final], table 11.

9. Internal Community document.

10. ACP Group, *Difficultés auxquelles se heurtent les états ACP pour la mise en oeuvre de la coopération financière et technique dans le cadre de la Convention de Lomé* [ACP/368/79] (Brussels: 6 Mai 1979), p. 8.

11. *Report of the ACP–EEC Council of Ministers (1 April 1976–29 Feb. 1980)*, p. 134. For some countries only a very small proportion of their allocations had been paid by the end of 1980, e.g., Papua New Guinea (4%), Mauritius (6%), Nigeria (9%), Sudan (14%), Surinam (14%), and Zaire (17%). The final payment under the first EDF (1959–64) was made in 1981! Court of Auditors of the European Communities, "Annual Report concerning the financial year 1980", *Official Journal of the European Communities* 31 Dec. 1981) p. 153.

12. Quoted in Adrian Hewitt, *The European Development Fund and Its Function in the EEC's Development Aid Policy* (London: Overseas Development Institute Working Paper no. 11, Aug. 1982), p. 22.

13. White, "ACP/EEC Financial and Technical Cooperation," paragraph 29.

14. *Ibid.*, paragraph 30.

15. Internal Community document.

16. John Carlsen, "Industrial Cooperation in the Lomé Convention: The Case of Kenya and Tanzania" (Copenhagen: Centre for Development Research, mimeo, n.d.), p. 34.

17. *Ibid.*, p. 39.

18. Robin Sharp, *EEC/ACP: One More Time? A Critical Guide to Renegotiation of the Lomé Convention* (Amsterdam: Euro Action Agency for Cooperation and Research in Development, n.d.), p. 26. The Commission itself recorded that aid for agriculture under the Fourth EDF had led to an additional 1.7m hectares' being used for cash crops, compared with 900,000 hectares for food production. *Commission Report to the ACP–EEC Council of Ministers on the Administration of Financial and Technical Cooperation in 1980, Under the Lomé Convention* [X/461/1982-EN], p. 11.

19. Court of Auditors, "Annual Report concerning the financial year 1980" p. 156.

20. *Report of the ACP–EEC Council of Ministers*, p. 126.

21. Carlsen, "Industrial Cooperation in the Lomé Convention," p. 32.

22. White, "ACP/EEC Financial and Technical Cooperation," paragraph 32 (emphasis in original).

23. "Resolution by the ACP–EEC Council of Ministers of 20 May 1983 on Financial and Technical Cooperation," annex to *Commission Report to the ACP–EEC Council of Ministers on the Administration of Financial and Technical Cooperation in 1982*, p. 11. By the end of the second year of Lomé II the Commission had planned to commit on average 38.6 percent of the allocations for the indicative programs. This proportion proved to be only 30.2 percent and for 24 countries, including 10 least developed, it was less than 15 percent. Only 3.2 percent of programmable aid had been disbursed by the end of 1982.

24. Internal Community document.

25. Similarly, the Court of Auditors found that many projects were malfunctioning within months of their completion simply because the ACP states concerned either could not afford to undertake the necessary maintenance or because the expensive European equipment was too sophisticated to maintain and impossible to repair given the poor local facilities. The court concluded that this process was irreversible unless "it is accepted that an increasingly large proportion of future funds is to be devoted to salvaging the achievements of earlier EDF projects, with the disturbing consequence that a 7th or 8th EDF may be anticipated purely to serve as a 'Repairs Fund.'" Court of Auditors of the European Communities, "Annual Report concerning the financial year 1981," *Official Journal of the European Communities* (31 December 1982) p. 119.

## 9. Conclusions

1. As the report of the ACP–EEC Council of Ministers recorded: "the ACP States on several occasions brought to the attention of the Community the unilateral manner in which the Community had interpreted and applied certain provisions of the Convention, in particular the provisions relating to prior information and consultation between the Contracting parties. In this regard, the ACP States expressed concern at the fact that the Community had supplied them with information on the Community's offer at the GATT multilateral trade negotiations, its proposals on the generalized preferences and its draft agreements with third countries, for example, too late for effective consultations to take place. Furthermore, the ACP States expressed serious concern, on those occasions when the Community informed and consulted them, at the limited nature of the action taken by the Community to accommodate their preoccupations. On several occasions, therefore, the ACP States pointed out to the Community that the action taken by the Community was unilateral and against the letter and spirit of the Convention." *Report of the ACP–EEC Council of Ministers (1 April 1976–29 Feb. 1980)* (Brussels: ACP–EEC Council of Ministers, 25 July 1980), p. 14. The ACP Group also complained bitterly at the time of the Greek accession to the Community that they had not been adequately consulted.

2. Harold K. Jacobson et al., "Revolutionaries or Bargainers? Negotiators for a New International Economic Order," *World Politics* (April 1983), 35(3):348–49.

3. ACP Secretariat, "Draft Memorandum on Renegotiations" [ACP/64/78 (Amb. Reneg.) Rev. 4] (Brussels, 1 March 1978), p. 39. ACP dissatisfaction with the implementation of Lomé I was reflected in their statement at the beginning of the negotiations for its successor: "In our view, these negotiations cannot be regarded as a mere holding operation limited to the rearrangement, adaptation or adjustment of the Lomé Convention. The ACP is not interested in a purely cosmetic exercise. We reject any such approach and see grave danger and little real benefit for any of the contracting parties deriving from it. We of the ACP have come to seek to negotiate for the eighties, a new Convention which must represent a significant step forward as did Lomé in 1975." *Statement by the President of the Coun-*

cil of ACP Ministers on the Occasion of the Opening of the Negotiations of the Successor Arrangement to the Lomé Convention [ACP/340/71/Rev.2], pp. 8–9.

4. Negotiations for the second Lomé Convention are examined in greater detail in John Ravenhill, "The Lomé II Negotiations: A Little Is Preferable to Nothing," in I. William Zartman, ed., *North-South Negotiations* (forthcoming).

5. See, for example, James C. Scott, "Patron-Client Politics and Social Change in South-East Asia," in Steffen W. Schmidt et al., eds., *Friends, Followers, and Factions* (Berkeley: University of California Press, 1977), p. 128; Johan Galtung, "A Structural Theory of Imperialism," *The African Review* (April 1972), 1(4):93–138.

6. Isebill V. Gruhn, "The Lomé Convention: Inching Towards Interdependence," *International Organization* (Spring 1976), 30(2):241–62.

7. Corrado Pirzio-Biroli, "Foreign Policy Formation Within the European Community with Special Regard to Developing Countries" (mimeo), p. 233.

8. Rothchild and Curry asserted that "such a dynamic process of social learning through external bargaining encounters [with the EEC] gives every indication of contributing to internal African unity." Donald Rothchild and Robert L. Curry, Jr., *Scarcity, Choice and Public Policy in Middle Africa*, (Berkeley: University of California Press, 1978), p. 265.

9. Ambassador E. Olu Sanu, *The Lomé Convention and the New International Economic Order* (Lagos: The Nigerian Institute of International Affairs, Lecture Series No. 18, n.d.). Sanu quotes the Economic Commission for Africa, which commented that "the strengthening of horizontal relations between developing countries would require an increased measure of self-restraint, mutual confidence and firmness. It will also demand mechanisms for consultation and joint negotiation of priorities and projects, more extensively and more technically oriented than those employed in negotiating the Lomé convention itself. Perhaps more than anything else it will require a degree of generosity of the stronger towards the weaker among ACP states and in general, an unusual degree of economic diplomacy." [E/CN.14/EC/90/Rev.3], p. 14.

10. Intra-ACP exports as a percentage of total ACP exports fell from 5.65 percent in 1975 to 4.66 percent in 1978; intra-ACP imports as a percentage of all ACP imports fell from 6.13 percent to 4.93 percent in the same period. *Report of the ACP–EEC Conference on the Development and Promotion of ACP Trade Held in Nairobi (Kenya) from 7-16 November 1979* [ACP/810/79(Secr. INTRA-ACP)] (Brussels: 31 Dec. 1979), pp. 113–14.

11. Sanu, *The Lomé Convention*, p. 35.

12. Peter Gonzales, "The ACP Secretariat" (mimeo, 30 June 1978), p. 8.

13. These observations are supported by data on the attitudes of participants in North-South discussions collected by Jacobson et al. They found that the former Yaoundé Associates were the most enthusiastic about the Convention. In general they also found that the higher the per capita income of the developing country, the more radical were the views of their delegates. Harold K. Jacobson et al. "Revolutionaries or Bargainers?" pp. 335–67. African states complained that their Caribbean counterparts could afford to take a more critical stance toward the Community in the Lomé II negotiations because they were generally less heavily dependent on the Community in their foreign trade and because the Sugar Protocol was not scheduled for renegotiation. Resentment at Caribbean domination of the ACP Group was reflected in a proposal that the chair of the ACP Council of Ministers, which rotated on the basis of African, then Caribbean, then Pacific country, should be amended to an A.A.C.A.A.P. sequence.

14. ACP Secretariat, "Draft Memorandum on Renegotiations," p. 36.

15. Robert L. Rothstein, *Global Bargaining* (Princeton, N.J.: Princeton University Press, 1979).

16. "Cheysson Returns from Exploratory Talks in Africa," *Agence Europe*, no. 2693 (n.s.), 7 June 1979. On the problem of poor communications in developing countries' foreign policies, see Maurice East, "Foreign Policy-Making in Small States: Some Theoretic Observations Based on a Study of the Ugandan Ministry of Foreign Affairs," *Policy Sciences* (Dec. 1973), 4:491–508.

17. Once again, this points to the lack of institutionalization of the ACP in Brussels. Although the initial negotiations for renewing the Convention take place between the Commission and the ACP Committee of Ambassadors, the most important meetings are at ministerial level. Whereas the European Commission acts in tandem with the Presidency of the EEC Council of Ministers at such meetings, the Brussels-based ACP ambassadors and ACP Secretariat are largely excluded from the ministerial meetings where the ACP are represented by ministers from their national capitals.

Contrasting views are found in the literature regarding the socialization and radicalization effects on delegates from LDCs of participation in group discussions in the North-South dialogue. Spero and Rothstein both assert that participants come to hold views that diverge from those of the ministries in their home capitals; Jacobson et al. suggest that group discussion in intergovernmental organizations is a secondary rather than a primary determinant of viewpoints. Joan Spero, "The 'Global Negotiation': Agenda, Progress, and Problems," in Roger D. Hansen, ed., *The "Global Negotiation" and Beyond* (Austin: Lyndon B. Johnson School of Public Affairs, University of Texas at Austin, 1981), p. 28; Robert L. Rothstein *Global Bargaining*, p. 207; Jacobson et al., "Revolutionaries or Bargainers," p. 340.

18. Sanu, "The Lomé Convention," p. 17.

19. On the constraints imposed on the member states of the EEC by complex interdependence, see Ernst B. Haas, *The Obsolescence of Regional Integration Theory*, (Berkeley: Institute of International Studies, University of California, Berkeley, 1975).

20. See Scott, *The Moral Economy of the Peasant*.

21. Quoted in Corrado Pirzio-Biroli, "Foreign Policy Formation," p. 249.

22. Robert W. Cox and Harold K. Jacobson, *The Anatomy of Influence* (New Haven, Conn.: Yale University Press, 1974), p. 34.

23. Albert O. Hirschman, *National Power and the Structure of Foreign Trade* (Berkeley: University of California Press, 1980), pp. ix–x.

24. Cf. Raymond F. Hopkins, "The International Role of Domestic Bureaucracies," *International Organization* (Summer 1976), 30:3.

25. Mario Caciagli and Frank P. Belloni, "The 'New' Clientelism in Southern Italy: The Christian Democratic Party in Catonia," in S. N. Eisenstadt and Rene Lemarchand, eds., *Political Clientelism, Patronage and Development* (Beverly Hills, Calif.: Sage Publications, 1981), pp. 35–56.

26. In 1980 Japan supplied 12.8 percent of total ACP imports but consumed only 3.9 percent of total ACP exports. *The Courier* (March–April 1983), no. 78, p. 56. On the relationship between Japan and Africa, see Joanna Moss and John Ravenhill, *The Emerging Japanese Economic Influence in Africa: Implications for the United States* (Berkeley: Institute of International Studies, University of California, 1984).

27. Rothstein, *Global Bargaining*, pp. 104–5.

28. As Zartman noted with reference to the Yaoundé negotiations: "Not only were the weak unable to bend the strong significantly by walking out; in addition it was actually the weak that felt the pressure of passing time more painfully than did the strong. Thus, rather than being able to boycott tactically, the weak had to press for procedural speed as well as substantive benefits, adding to the burden of their demands." *The Politics of Trade Negotiations*, p. 227.

Community perceptions of the lack of credibility of any ACP threat to withdraw from the relationship are evident in its proposal that future Conventions should have a framework of unlimited duration. With the present system of renegotiations every five years, "Unnecessary confrontations are caused, when everyone knows from the outset that the Convention will be renewed in one form or another." Commission of the European Communities, "Memorandum on the Community's development policy." *Bulletin of the European Communities* (1982) Supplement 5/82: 20.

29. "Crossed Purse Strings," *The Economist* (28 June 1975), 254(6879):37.

30. Adrian Hewitt, "The European Development Fund and its Function in the EEC's Development Aid Policy," (London: Overseas Development Institute Working Paper no. 11, 1982), p. 5.

31. Christopher Stevens, "Policy-making on North-South Issues: the Importance of Administrative Organisation," *Millennium: Journal of International Studies* (Spring 1982), 11(1):14–26.

32. Robert W. Cox, "The Executive Head: An Essay on Leadership in International Organization," *International Organization* (1969), 23(2):205–30.

33. Christopher Stevens, "New Directions Under Commissioner Pisani," in Stevens, ed., *EEC and The Third World: A Survey 3*, *The Atlantic Rift* (London: Hodder and Stoughton, 1983), p. 184.

34. Roger D. Hansen, *Beyond the North-South Stalemate* (New York: McGraw-Hill, 1979). Cf. also the Brandt Commission's Report, *North-South* (London: Pan, 1980). A basic needs approach would require a substantial reorientation of the emphasis of EDF aid. Whether this will prove practicable, especially given that it will inevitably reduce the share of the member states in EDF contracts, remains to be seen.

35. Gerald K. Helleiner, "Lomé and Market Access," in Long, ed., *The Political Economy of EEC Relations*, p. 184.

36. Proposals for the new strategy are detailed in Commission of the European Communities, "Memorandum on the Community's Development Policy," *Bulletin of the European Communities*, Supp. 5/82. The new strategy would have the advantage of producing task expansion for the Commission—the memorandum envisages its playing a leading role in coordinating the bilateral aid policies of the member states in support of a basic needs strategy.

37. *Ibid.*, p. 21.

38. The ineffectiveness of ACP negotiating strategy stands in marked contrast to that of some of the higher income developing countries. See, for example, John S. Odell, "Latin American Trade Negotiations with the United States," *International Organization* (Spring 1980), 34(2):207–229.

39. Commission of the European Communities, Directorate-General for Economic and Financial Affairs, *Structural Change in the Community: Outlook for the 1980s* (Brussels, 1979).

40. Ernst B. Haas, "Words Can Hurt You; or, Who Said What to Whom About Regimes," *International Organization* (Spring 1982), 36(2):207–44. See also Paul Taylor, *The Limits of European Integration* (New York: Columbia University Press, 1983).

41. Lynn K. Mytelka and Michael B. Dolan, "The Political Economy of EEC–ACP Relations in a Changing International Division of Labour," in Dudley Seers and Constantine Vaitsos, eds., *Integration and Unequal Development* (London: Macmillan, 1980).

42. Camilo Barcia, Chef Adjoint de la Mission d'Espagne auprès des Communautés Européennes, in Loukas Tsoukalis, ed., *The European Community: Past, Present and Future* (Oxford: Basil Blackwell, 1983), p. 222.

43. See, for instance, Michael Hudson, *Global Fracture: The New Economic Order* (New

York: Harper and Row, 1977); and Mary Kaldor, *The Disintegrating West* (Harmondsworth, England: Penguin, 1979).

44. Cf. Rene Lemarchand and Keith Legg, "Political Clientelism and Development: A Preliminary Analysis," *Comparative Politics* (Jan. 1972), 4(2):177.

45. Walt W. Rostow, "Beyond the Official Agenda: Some Crucial Issues," in Hansen, *"Global Negotiation" and Beyond*, p. 31. See also the comments by Spero and Hansen in the same volume, and Rothstein, *Global Bargaining, passim*.

46. See, for instance, Geoffrey Barraclough, "The Struggle for the Third World," *New York Review of Books* (9 Nov. 1978), 25:17.

47. Gruhn, "Inching Towards Interdependence."

# Index

Abidjan, 85

Accession, Treaty of, 80, 83; *see also* Britain

ACP Group, *see* African, Caribbean and Pacific Group

ACP-EEC joint institutions: Committee of Ambassadors, 311-12, 318; Consultative Assembly, 265; Council of Ministers, 139, 182, 230, 272, 301, 302, 310-11, 316-17, 319

Addis Ababa, 85, 315

Adjustment policy, industrial: in EEC, 264-66

Africa: aid to, 278; Development Bank, 320; European relations, 35, 64; freight rates, 173; mining investment in, 133; negotiating position, 86, 253-54; sugar, 89; unity, 28, 73

African, Caribbean and Pacific Group (ACP): aspirations, 3-4, 24-29, 33-34, 85-86, 102, 151, 253-54, 275; Committee of Ambassadors, 178, 318, 321-22; Council of Ministers, 317, 318, 319; demands for Lomé II, 296-97, 312-13; dependence on EEC, 24-27, 338-39; Development Bank, 273, 320, 339; economic characteristics, 9-13, 172, 254; intra-group trade, 315, 366n; membership, 213-14, 341n, 354n; origins, .81–86; Secretariat, 156, 315-16, 317, 318, 320, 321, 327; sovereignty complex, 146, 274, 323-24; trade under Lomé, 185-211; weaknesses, 21-22, 313-22, 328-30, 334

Agricultural Guarantee and Guidance Fund (FEOGA), 223, 235

Agricultural products: Associates', 52, 83; in GSP, 157, 173; Lomé I negotiations, 85, 88; Lomé II negotiations, 161-63; proposals for Lomé III, 332; Treaties of Rome & Yaoundé, 57; in STABEX, 106,

132; tariffs, 154–55; *see also* Common Agricultural Policy; *and under individual product headings*

Aid, *see* European Development Fund

Air Mines Company (SOMAIR), 37

Algeria, 162

Aluminum ore and products, 25, 59; SYS-MIN Coverage, 104, 142; trade with ACP, 39, 203, 204, 206, 207, 208, 209

Andean Pact, 20

Anglophone Africa, 74, 76, 157, 165, 316; *see also* Commonwealth Africa

Angola, 52, 329

Animal products (skins, leather, oils), 38, 39, 59, 172; in STABEX, 104, 105, 107, 126; trade with ACP, 205, 207, 208, 209, 210

Arusha Agreement, 76-78, 80, 95, 186

ASEAN, *see* Association of South East Asia Nations

Asian Commonwealth, 13, 80

Associated African and Malagasy States (EAMA), 47, 55-56, 63, 79, 81, 83-85; aid from EEC, 65-72; trade with EEC, 57-65

Association Council, 62-63

Association of South East Asian Nations (ASEAN), 337

Association Secretariat, 81

Australia, 24, 136, 165; sugar exports, 90, 226, 228, 237, 240

Bahamas: aid, 293; economic structure, 10; STABEX transfers, 111

Bananas, 25, 39; Association Period, 50, 52, 54, 55, 58, 59, 61, 71; Lomé Protocol, 245-51, 311; STABEX coverage, 101, 104, 124, 126, 127; trade in, 203, 204, 207, 247

Bandung Conference of Asian-African States, 15

**THE POLITICAL ECONOMY OF INTERNATIONAL CHANGE**
*John Gerard Ruggie, General Editor*